Justice, Equity, Diversity, and Inclusion in Education

A volume in
Current Perspectives on School/University/Community Research
R. Martin Reardon and Jack Leonard, *Series Editors*

Current Perspectives on School/University/ Community Research

R. Martin Reardon and Jack Leonard, *Series Editors*

School–University–Community Research in a (Post) COVID-19 World (2023)
 R. Martin Reardon and Jack Leonard

School–University–Community Collaboration for Civic Education and Engagement in the Democratic Project (2022)
 R. Martin Reardon and Jack Leonard

Learning to Read the World and the Word: School-University-Community Collaboration to Enrich Immigrant Literacy and Teacher Education (2021)
 R. Martin Reardon and Jack Leonard

A Place Called Home: School-University-Community Collaboration and the Immigrant Educational Experience (2021)
 Jack Leonard and R. Martin Reardon

Alleviating the Educational Impact of Adverse Childhood Experiences: School–University–Community Collaboration (2020)
 R. Martin Reardon and Jack Leonard

Integrating Digital Technology in Education: School–University–Community Collaboration (2019)
 R. Martin Reardon and Jack Leonard

Innovation and Implementation in Rural Places: School–University–Community Collaboration in Education (2018)
 R. Martin Reardon and Jack Leonard

Making a Positive Impact in Rural Places: Change Agency in the Context of School-University-Community Collaboration in Education (2018)
 R. Martin Reardon and Jack Leonard

Exploring the Community Impact of Research–Practice Partnerships in Education (2017)
 R. Martin Reardon and Jack Leonard

Justice, Equity, Diversity, and Inclusion in Education

School–University–Community Research

edited by

R. Martin Reardon
East Carolina University

Jack Leonard
University of Massachusetts, Boston

INFORMATION AGE PUBLISHING, INC.
Charlotte, NC • www.infoagepub.com

Library of Congress Cataloging-in-Publication Data

A CIP record for this book is available from the Library of Congress
http://www.loc.gov

ISBN: 979-8-88730-723-7 (Paperback)
   979-8-88730-724-4 (Hardcover)
   979-8-88730-725-1 (E-Book)

Front cover: "Unity" by Michelle Erickson (2023) President's Collection of Art,
William and Mary. Used with permission.
(Photo courtesy of Robert Hunter)

Ceramicist Michelle Erickson created this piece consisting of three interconnected
cups labeled "humanity," "equality," and "unity." These three qualities sustain us in our
journey towards justice, equity, diversity, and inclusion.

Back cover and Introduction: "KHADINE-a-Londres" by Bruno Catalano.
(Photo courtesy of @edenenterprises.marketing)

Copyright © 2024 Information Age Publishing Inc.

All rights reserved. No part of this publication may be reproduced, stored in a
retrieval system, or transmitted, in any form or by any means, electronic, mechanical,
photocopying, microfilming, recording or otherwise, without written permission
from the publisher.

Printed in the United States of America

CONTENTS

Introduction ix

SECTION I
COLLABORATIVE ACTION

1 Moving From Parent Engagement to Family Collaboration: Reconsidering K–12 Educational Systems for Diversity, Equity, and Inclusion 3
Rachel Renbarger, Liza Rodler, LaMicah Lindsey, and Risa Sackman

2 Coming Together as Classmates: Participatory Heritage as Socially Just and Age-Friendly Praxis Through an Intergenerational School–University–Community Preservation Project 27
Ayana Allen-Handy, Karena Alane Escalante, Isaiah Lassiter, Jahyonna Brown, Ronald Ray, Catherine Nettles, Arania Goldsmith-Carter, Michelle S. Allen, and Bonnie Poole-Linder

SECTION II
FORMAL PARTNERSHIPS

3 The Dynamic and Reciprocal Dimensions of an Equity-Focused: Research Practice Partnership 49
Mary A. Avalos, Wendy Cavendish, Jennifer Murray, LaKesha Wilson-Rochelle, and Jennifer Andreu

v

vi ▪ Contents

4 Practicing Equity in Research–Practice–Policy Partnerships: Case of Illinois 69
Heather E. Price, Malik S. Henfield, Eilene Edejer, and Ken Fujimoto

5 The Promise of District–University–Community Partnerships in Navigating the Tensions of Change 91
Kevin Tan, Nicole Rummel, and Rachel Roegman

SECTION III
DISRUPTIVE ASPECTS

6 Checking the Box or Doing the Work? The Importance of Faculty Perspectives on Service and the Relationship to Power in Higher Education, and the Role of DEIJ Initiatives in Culture Change 119
Kari Havenaar, Dyann Logwood, and Cassandra Barragan

7 Towns and Gowns: A Study in Crisis Leadership 141
S. Gavin Weiser, Linsay DeMartino, and Paige Buschman

SECTION IV
RIGHTFUL PRESENCE

8 Disability as Diversity in Higher Education Spaces 163
Rebecca B. Smith Hill and Chelsea VanHorn Stinnett

9 A Teacher's Successful Efforts to Support Diversity and Equity: Despite Contextual Obstacles 187
Mariana Alvayero Ricklefs

10 Understanding Teacher Perceptions of LGBTQ+ Representation Through Portraiture 211
S. Luke Anderson

Contents · **vii**

SECTION V
SOCIAL EMOTIONAL LEARNING

11 Cultivating Collaboration and Centering Community:
Making Youth Matter: A School–University–Community-
Based Partnership 237
Celeste L. Hawkins

12 Culturally Relevant Social and Emotional Student Support
in Title I Schools Increasing the Opportunity
for Student Growth.. 259
Marie Byrd

About the Editors 277

About the Contributors.. 279

INTRODUCTION

> *The arc of the moral universe is long, but it bends toward justice.*
> —Dr. Martin Luther King, Jr., *Remaining Awake Through a Great Revolution*

As Dr. Martin Luther King, Jr. intimated in his speech in the National Cathedral (March 31, 1968), there is a sense of moving towards—of journeying—rather than arriving in the context of justice (and, I would add, equity, diversity, and inclusion). We who embark on this journey are incomplete—not fully formed, despite our amazing competence in so many ways. We are travelers in the fashion of the figure in Catalano's KHADINE sculpture (https://brunocatalano.com/sculptures_/KHADINE-a-Londres), gazing unfazed on a world of superlative human achievements, clasping our bag firmly in one hand even though there is something missing in our core. In fact, as in KHADINE, our bag holds us together individually but, in relationship to our fellow travelers, our baggage holds us apart.

Justice, Equity, Diversity, and Inclusion in Education, pages ix–xvii
Copyright © 2024 by Information Age Publishing
www.infoagepub.com
All rights of reproduction in any form reserved.

x ▪ Introduction

BENDING SLOWLY

The length of the arc of progress related to educational justice, equity, diversity, and inclusion is frustrating, as is well illustrated in the case of North Carolina. In 1994, five school districts in the low-wealth counties of Hoke, Halifax, Robeson, Vance, and Cumberland filed suit against the state in a case known as *Leandro v. State* (1997), arguing that "their school districts did not have enough money to provide an equal education for their children, despite the fact that they taxed their residents higher than average" (Public School Forum of North Carolina, n.d.-a, para. 1). Some 26 years later, the disparity across North Carolina counties in terms of per-pupil funding was still pronounced: In 2020–2021, Orange County "spent $83 more per student than the seven lowest spending counties combined" (Public School Forum of North Carolina, n.d.-b, para. 3).

The designation of a county as "low-wealth" can be a proxy for its being demographically "low White"[1] and such is the case in *Leandro v. State*: Hoke County 40.4% White (92nd in North Carolina), Halifax County 39.7% White (93rd), Robeson County 25.8% White (100th), Vance County 39.2% White (95th), and Cumberland County 42.4% White (90th) (United States Census Bureau, 2021). The *Leandro v. State* (1997) lawsuit was named after Robb Leandro who was in Grade 8 in Hoke County at the time his mother, Kathy, filed the suit on his behalf on the basis that the inadequate funding of education in the county lessened the quality of the education the children were provided.

The lawsuit was not resolved by the time Robb Leandro graduated either high school or college or law school. Currently, he is an attorney (specializing in health care regulations) working at the same firm as the attorneys who represented him over 20 years ago and *Leandro v. State* remains "the longest running piece of litigation in the history of the state. The case is truly remarkable" (Former North Carolina Supreme Court justice Robert F. Orr, as quoted by Lincicombe, 2020, para. 5; see also McColl, 2020). The North Carolina Supreme Court, after hearing for the fourth time what is the current version of the case—*Hoke County Board of Education v. State* (2022)—Robb Leandro having aged out of the original case many years ago—fulminated on November 2, 2022:

> For twenty-five years, the judiciary has deferred to the executive and legislative branches to implement a comprehensive solution to this ongoing constitutional violation. Today, that deference expires. If this Court is to fulfill its own constitutional obligations, it can no longer patiently wait for the day, year, or decade when the State gets around to acting on its constitutional duty "to guard and maintain" the constitutional rights of North Carolina schoolchildren. (*Hoke County Board of Education v. State*, 2022, para. 4)

The legislature has yet to get around to deciding on the day, year, or decade for action to acting on its constitutional duty and address the educational inequity in North Carolina, but it is quite decided that the Supreme Court cannot allocate funding to do so (Carolina Journal Staff, 2023). In 2019, a comprehensively researched informed estimate of the cost to rectify the situation was $6.86 billion (WestEd et al., 2019, p. 8).

JEANES'S PHILANTHROPY AND THE "NEXT NEEDED THING"

At an earlier point on the bending arc in North Carolina, whereas elected leaders may have been impeded by their baggage, an individual stepped-in to alleviate inequitable educational outcomes. At the age of 72, Anna Thomas Jeanes, a "visionary Quaker philanthropist" (Fitzgerald & Reinhardt, 2020, para. 1) living in Philadelphia determined to give away the fortune the Jeanes family had amassed. Among other projects, a few months before she died in 1907, Jeanes endowed the Negro Rural School Fund (later renamed the Jeanes Fund) to enhance primary education in the South.[2]

The benefits envisioned by Jeanes were soon delivered. In 1908, Jackson Davis, the superintendent of Henrico County Schools in Virginia, successfully sought assistance from the Negro Rural School Fund for employing Virginia Estelle Randolph as a "supervising industrial teacher to travel to each of the [B]lack schools in Henrico County" (Henrico County Virginia, n.d., para 3). Randolph had graduated from Richmond Colored Normal School and began teaching c.1890 at a small rural school where "I enrolled 14 pupils. The school was old, and the grounds were nothing but a red clay hill" (Henrico County Virginia, n.d., para 2). Following Superintendent Davis's receipt of the Jeanes funding, Randolph became the first Jeanes Supervising Industrial Teacher in the south and visited each of the 20 schools in the county on a weekly basis. Her report of her activities during her first year as a Jeanes Supervisor became known as the "Henrico Plan."

The affordances of the Jeanes Fund and the Henrico Plan were swiftly apparent and widespread: by 1909–1910 there were 129 Jeanes teachers in 13 states and, by 1915, there were 36 Jeanes teachers in North Carolina—more than in any other state—looking to do "the next needed thing"—the Jeanes slogan that encapsulated the motivation of those associated with it (Dudley Flood Center for Educational Equity and Opportunity, n.d., para. 5).

The contemporary incarnation of Jeanes program is the Jeanes Fellows Program—a partnership between The Innovation Project (TIP) and the Dudley Flood Center for Educational Equity and Opportunity "designed to provide consistent and intentional infrastructure to support community-school relationships using an equity lens" (Dudley Flood Center for

xii ▪ Introduction

Educational Equity and Opportunity, n.d., para. 1). TIP is a "non-profit collaborative working group of North Carolina public school district leaders" founded in 2015 as a service by two members of a Raleigh firm "to envision the future of education and design equitable, learner-centered strategies to get there" (Innovation Project, 2023a, para. 1). In early October 2023, TIP announced the awarding of a $21.5 million grant through the federal Teacher and School Leadership Incentive Program within the U.S. Department of Education to fund the Reimaging Teaching Talent program—a "partnership which provides 79 schools across eight school districts the opportunity to work together in a networked improvement community" (Innovation Project, 2023a, para. 2). The networked improvement community will engage the 12 historically Black colleges and universities in North Carolina to address a major next needed thing and establish "a direct pipeline of educators, create year-long, multi-stakeholder, and equity-driven recruitment and retention systems, and provide support to new educators who are trying to pass the Praxis Tests" (Innovation Project, 2023b, p. 1). Politicians may be burdened by their baggage and disinclined to act, but, in this instance, community members, universities, and researchers will collaborate to ensure that the moral arc still bends.

ROSENWALD'S PHILANTHROPY

In 1907, Anna Jeanes had insisted that both Booker T. Washington (Tuskegee Institute) and George Frissell (Hampton Institute)—both of whom had approached her for funding for their efforts (African American Schools of Louisa County, Virginia, n.d., para. 2) and whom she had chosen to form the racially integrated board of her foundation—travel to Philadelphia to receive the $1 million check that financed the Negro Rural School Fund (Fitzgerald & Reinhardt, 2020, para. 7). In 1911, on a visit to Chicago, Booker T. Washington met and became friends with Julius Rosenwald—the president of the Sears, Roebuck & Co. department store chain (Lassiter, 2015). Washington convinced Rosenwald of the need to improve elementary education for African Americans in rural areas and Rosenwald helped finance the building of six pilot schoolhouses in rural Alabama.

These schools thrived, so Rosenwald launched a fund to support building more schools across the South on a collaborative model. The Rosenwald fund provided seed money, but the members of the community provided the bulk of the funding. In one instance, out of a total cost of $4,500 for one school, the Rosenwald fund contributed $1,000, the local school board (at that time, controlled by White community members) contributed $3,000, and Black community members contributed $500 (Lassiter, 2015).

Lassiter (2015) cited the National Trust for Historic Preservation estimates that, by 1928, the Rosenwald program had resulted in the construction of 4,977 schools, 217 teachers' homes, and 163 shop buildings serving more than 663,000 students and costing $28.5 million. The success of the collaborative Rosenwald model is impressive. Given that, in the above example, the local school board contributed three times the amount of money the Rosenwald fund provided, one ponders what baggage hampered the school board members from getting around to deciding on the day, year, or decade for action.

Between the start of the Rosenwald program and its abrupt end in 1932 with the death of Julius Rosenwald, 813 buildings had been constructed in 93 of the 100 North Carolina counties (Johnson, 2006). Johnson (2006) attributed the demise of the Rosenwald schools to consolidation and desegregation in the 1960s. The hope of consolidation and desegregation was the improvement in the quality of education for all. Forty-six of the Rosenwald schools in North Carolina (the most in the state) were constructed in Halifax County—which, some 60 years later, was one of the five county school districts that joined with the Leandro family to file suit against the state because of the vast inequality in educational opportunity. One could well join with the majority of the North Carolina Supreme Court justices in decrying the baggage that disinclines the state legislators from getting around to deciding on the day, year, or decade for action.

JUSTICE, EQUITY, DIVERSITY, AND INCLUSION

We have subdivided this volume into five sections. All chapter authors took seriously our charge to foreground the interplay among justice, equity, diversity, and inclusion in their research endeavors, yet we suggest that there are subtle differences among the chapters that constitute bases for grouping them.

Collaborative Action

In Section I, the collaborative nature of the projects the authors discuss is strongly in evidence. In Chapter 1, Renbarger and colleagues focus on how educational leaders in a range of different locations across the United States have facilitated the transition from prioritizing parent engagement to family collaboration. They foreground the interplay among the design of appropriate policy initiatives, the raising of awareness among community members, and the creation of appropriate programming. In their account of their work, revisions of vision and mission statements underpinned the effectiveness and sustainability of the transition. In Chapter 2, Allen-Handy and an impressive

xiv ▪ Introduction

number of co-authors bring to the forefront an issue that is common to many cities in the United States: Long-term residents of what were low-income housing areas in the downtown have been priced-out of their homes after redevelopment projects brought gentrification in their wake. Allen-Handy et al. highlight a project to address an easily overlooked consequence of the displacement of long-term residents—the diminution of the sense of self among those who remain and the loss of the historical record.

Formal Partnerships

In Section II, the perspective shifts slightly to bring formal partnerships among researchers and practitioners in community contexts to our attention. In Chapter 3, Avalos and colleagues showcase the dynamism and reciprocity that is part-and-parcel of an equity-focused research practice partnership—especially in the wake of COVID-19. The context of their work was an urban middle school serving a high number of Latinx students in which their work was oriented to facilitating student and teacher well-being. In Chapter 4, Price and colleagues recount how they harnessed the strength of inter-organizational relationships to enhance equity in collaboration with both practitioners and policymakers to improve the educational prospects of children. They attribute the transformation of an otherwise purely academic study into a project with the potential for impact on practice to the collaboration among the team members from the outset. Rounding out Section II, in Chapter 5, Tan and colleagues paint a fine-grained portrait of the promise— and sometimes the perils—for researchers and district personnel of a district university–community partnership across a tension-filled 5-year time span in the history of the school district, the community, and the United States. Their real-time reflections on their journey with their collaborators in that context and across that time span made it clear to them that transformative social emotional learning engaging both youth and adults offered the best prospects for planting the seeds of lasting change.

Disruptive Aspects

Although implicit across all the chapters, diversity comes to the fore in Section III as does the impact of COVID-19. Havenaar and colleagues remind us in Chapter 6 of our proximity to the trauma of the pandemic. They focus their discussion on the inequity endured by women and BIPOC faculty at a university that their pilot study brought to light in the context of the pandemic. The disproportionate assignment of service responsibilities with scant support for the performance of those responsibilities seemed to

Introduction • **xv**

emanate from a prevailing sense of gender- and race-based privilege and power amounting to "gender and cultural taxation." Weiser and colleagues write in a similar vein in Chapter 7 and recall the massive disruption to the staid ways of the academy spurred by the pandemic. They ponder the lessons that are on offer as our healing from the trauma of those years continues or as our memory of unresolved crises fades. Leveraging the affordances of photovoice and a phenomenological approach, they offer sobering findings regarding the decline of both the democratic endeavor and the level of civic engagement among those in the academy coupled with the increasing adoption of neoliberalist perspectives.

Rightful Presence

Both the chapters in Section IV foreground the concept of rightful presence (Calabrese Barton & Tan, 2020). In Chapter 8, Smith-Hill and Van-Horn Stinnett reframe disability among college students as diversity. Based on their review of the literature and an example of inclusion, they argue persuasively that such inclusion of students with disabilities—particularly those with intellectual disabilities—benefits both the higher education system and the community as well as granting them their rightful presence. In Chapter 9, Ricklefs discusses a single-case study of a teacher who implemented linguistically responsive teaching techniques to successfully support English learners—students who used another language in addition to English—in their classroom. In an otherwise unwelcoming environment, this teacher adroitly leveraged pedagogical practices that built on the students' language proficiency in their additional language to facilitate their learning of English. In Chapter 10, Anderson focuses on teacher perceptions of LGBTQ+ students who sometimes experience their living and learning environment as unwelcoming. In some states, teachers labor under regulations that constrain what they teach and the language they use. In such contexts, teachers may place themselves in jeopardy should they choose to ignore those regulations.

Social Emotional Learning

Hawkins discusses the Making Youth Matter (MYM) mentoring program in Chapter 11. MYM was implemented as a collaborative endeavor between the School of Social Work at Eastern Michigan University and Ypsilanti Community Schools with the aim of promoting positive outcomes among participating youth and supporting students' academic, social, and emotional welfare. Byrd reinforces the importance of social emotional learning

xvi ▪ Introduction

in Chapter 12. In bringing this volume to a close that touches upon each of the themes of justice, equity, diversity, and inclusion, Byrd highlights the crucial role of social and emotional development that is culturally relevant in maximizing the potential for education to enhance outcomes for youth in general and especially for those who attend Title 1 schools.

NOTES

1. In a previous volume in this series, I asked an author to justify their choice of "white" (lower case) as "the dialectical opposite of Black" (Gotanda, 1991, p. 4) instead of following the advice provided in the *Publication Manual of the American Psychological Association* (2020): "Racial and ethnic groups are designated by proper nouns and are capitalized. Therefore, use 'Black' and 'White'" (p. 142). That earlier author did not answer my question, but I respected their choice.

   Bohonos and Sisco (2021) opted to use the lower case "white" in their work and referenced Gotanda (1991) who, in turn, had expressed indebtedness to Kimberlé Crenshaw in formulating their rationale as follows: "To the extent that Black 'summarizes' relations of racial subordination, white 'summarizes' racial domination. As a term describing racial domination, 'white' is better left in lower case, rather than privileged with a capital letter" (p. 4). Perhaps terms that evoke racial distinctions inevitably implicate hierarchy—not just when subordination/domination relationships are the focus of the discussion.

   Perhaps there is a better way to refer to individuals who differ based on their taxonomic categorizations, as Yudell et al. (2016) argued because, despite its convenience, "race is neither a relevant nor accurate way to understand or map human genetic diversity" (para. 3). My default position aligns with the advice of the *Publication Manual* in considering the terms "Black" and "White" as proper nouns (and therefore capitalized) for as long as they remain in currency.

2. I am indebted to Ashley Kazouh (associate director, The Dudley Flood Center for Educational Equity and Opportunity) for enlightening me about the Jeanes Fund and the achievements of those associated with it. I would also to acknowledge the work of Ann McCall who has played a key role in the Jeanes Fellowship and the Innovation Project.

REFERENCES

African American Schools of Louisa County, Virginia. (n.d.) *The Jeanes Fund* http://louisaheritage.org/enlg/JeanesFund.htm

American Psychological Association. (2020). *Publication manual of the American Psychological Association* (7th ed.).

Bohonos, J. W., & Sisco, S. (2021). Advocating for social justice, equity, and inclusion in the workplace: An agenda for anti-racist learning organizations. *New Directions*

for Adult & Continuing Education, 170, 89–98. https://doi.org/10.1002/ace
.20428

Calabrese Barton, A., & Tan, E. (2020). Beyond equity as inclusion: A framework
of "rightful presence" for guiding justice-oriented studies in teaching and
learning. *Educational Researcher, 49*(6), 433–440. https://doi.org/10.3102/
0013189X20927363

Carolina Journal Staff. (2023, October 3). Leandro plaintiffs ask state's highest court
to steer clear of latest dispute. *The Carolina Journal.* https://www.carolinajournal.
com/leandro-plaintiffs-ask-states-highest-court-to-steer-clear-of-latest-dispute/

Dudley Flood Center for Educational Equity and Opportunity. (n.d.). *The Jeanes Fellowship Program.* https://floodcenter.org/jeanes-fellowship-program/

Fitzgerald, K. S., & Reinhardt, E. (2020). The legacy and philanthropy of Anna Thomas Jeanes. *Friends Journal.* https://www.friendsjournal.org/the-legacy-and
-philanthropy-of-anna-thomas-jeanes/

Gotanda, N. (1991). A critique of "Our constitution is color-blind." *Stanford Law
Review, 44*(1), 1–68. https://doi.org/10.2307/1228940

Henrico County Virginia. (n.d.). *Virginia E. Randolph.* https://henrico.us/history/
historical-figures/virginia-e-randolph/

Hoke County Board of Education v. State, 2022-NCSC-108 (2022). https://www.ncforum
.org/wp-content/uploads/2022/11/November-2022-Supreme-Court-Ruling
.pdf

Innovation Project. (2023a). https://tipnc.org/

Innovation Project. (2023b, October 3). *The innovation project awarded educator effectiveness grant from U.S. department of education* [Press release]. https://tipnc
.org/wp-content/uploads/2023/10/TIP-TSL-Grant-Press-Release_10223.pdf

Johnson, K. T. (2006). *Rosenwald fund.* NCPedia. https://www.ncpedia.org/
rosenwald-fund

Lassiter, T. (2015). *The Rosenwald schools of North Carolina.* EdNC. https://www.ednc.
org/the-rosenwald-schools-of-north-carolina/

Leandro v. State, 346 N.C. 336, 488 S.E.2d 249 (1997).

Lincicome, E. (2020, June 24). Landmark NC education decision marks 25 years.
North State Journal. https://nsjonline.com/article/2020/06/landmark-nc
-education-decision-marks-25-years/

McColl, A. (2020). Everything you need to know about the Leandro litigation.
EdNC. https://www.ednc.org/leandro-litigation/

Public School Forum of North Carolina. (n.d.-a). *Leandro v. State of NC: Background
& resources.* https://www.ncforum.org/leandro/

Public School Forum of North Carolina. (n.d.-b). *Local school finance study.* https://
www.ncforum.org/lsfs/

United States Census Bureau. (2021) *North Carolina 2020 census.* https://www.census
.gov/library/stories/state-by-state/north-carolina-population-change-between
-census-decade.html

WestEd, Learning Policy Institute, & Friday Institute for Educational Innovation
at North Carolina State University. (2019). *Sound basic education for all: An
action plan for North Carolina: Executive summary.* WestEd. https://wested.box
.com/s/vuh2qfg6n4xchjniyexwc10jgdhmdksa

Yudell, M., Roberts, D., & Tishkoff, S. (2016). Taking race out of human genetics.
Science, 351(6273), 564–565. https://doi.org/10.1126/science.aac4951

SECTION I

COLLABORATIVE ACTION

CHAPTER 1

MOVING FROM PARENT ENGAGEMENT TO FAMILY COLLABORATION

Reconsidering K–12 Educational Systems for Diversity, Equity, and Inclusion

Rachel Renbarger
FHI 360

Liza Rodler
VPD Government Solutions

LaMicah Lindsey
FHI 360

Risa Sackman
FHI 360

Justice, Equity, Diversity, and Inclusion in Education, pages 3–26
Copyright © 2024 by Information Age Publishing
www.infoagepub.com
All rights of reproduction in any form reserved.

ABSTRACT

School districts must engage in family and community collaboration (FCC) to provide more diverse, equitable, and inclusive K–12 education. In this chapter, we investigate how school districts create systemic change to improve their collaborative efforts with families and local organizations. Through a multiphase research approach, we interviewed family members, educators, administrators, researchers, and community organization leaders to uncover how districts have designed policy, improved public awareness, and created programming to strengthen collaboration. Policy changes included creating dedicated staff positions around collaboration, establishing decision-making bodies that reflected community diversity, and building formal partnerships with community organizations to meet the needs of students and families. Public awareness approaches included developing new vision and mission statements that reflected district commitments to equitable collaboration and using those statements as tools to further FCC initiatives. District programming efforts included providing professional development to address deficit mindsets and embracing opportunities to build relationships with families. We conclude the chapter with recommendations for practice and research.

A child's healthy development in the United States is intrinsically tied to both their education experience and their family support, yet school districts do not always value or actively seek family partnership in the formal education process. This is especially true for families from marginalized[1] groups. Prior to the COVID-19 pandemic, many districts relied on traditional one-way parent involvement strategies that emphasized physical attendance over equitable engagement (Jensen & Minke, 2017; Mapp & Kuttner, 2013) but researchers have increasingly argued for the importance of going beyond traditional, one-off events (Henderson et al., 2007) to create systems for more authentic collaboration with families and communities as a means to improve student academic outcomes (Henderson & Mapp, 2002; Henderson et al., 2007). However, traditional norms and deficit-based mindsets persist, such as assuming parents who do not attend school events are not interested in engaging with their child's learning—an assumption which has hindered many district efforts to strengthen partnerships with families and community groups (Mapp & Bergman, 2021).

Yet all of this changed in Spring 2020 when the COVID-19 pandemic forced schools to rely on caregivers to support learning at home. The abrupt transition to remote learning was difficult for many families. As a result, districts had to think creatively about how to meet family needs, particularly families in under-resourced communities that often suffered from limited access to computer devices and connectivity, limited support for children from caregivers who worked full time, and unmet basic needs (Soltero-González & Gillanders, 2021).

As memories of COVID-19-related school disruptions begin to fade, it is important to assess and recalibrate the state of family engagement in our schools. School districts and families established new types of partnerships out of necessity to get through the pandemic, but close collaboration has not been sustained (Bergman, 2022). One reason is that the pandemic exacerbated preexisting teacher shortages, as increasingly stressful environments and low salaries caused qualified teachers to leave the profession (Renbarger & Rodler, 2023b). Staff are stretched thin, making it more challenging to find the time and space to connect with families.

The pandemic also posed challenges for including another long-standing resource for supporting student success: community organizations. Local businesses, philanthropic groups, and religious institutions provided needed resources and built connections among families and districts (Jacques & Villegas, 2018; Renbarger & Rodler, 2023a). When schools and districts create systems and structures that support collaboration with both families and communities, schools and districts become places where all feel welcome and where children have what they need to thrive. Systemic change is necessary to embed family and community collaboration (FCC) into the DNA of a district. We believe it is exactly the kind of investment our schools most need to become the equitable and supportive environments our children and families deserve.

BACKGROUND

Researchers have shown that when district staff and teachers involve families in their child's education, those children have better outcomes in academics, attendance, social-emotional well-being, and college and career readiness (Grant & Ray, 2019). This is especially true when education systems approach family engagement in the spirit of partnership with the broader district community, which we describe as family and community collaboration (FCC). FCC goes beyond transactional, unidirectional communication, whereby staff tell families and local organizations about student performance and behavior, to bidirectional communication and shared decision-making, whereby the perspectives and contributions of all groups, particularly marginalized groups, are valued. For districts to implement FCC successfully, they must create systems that build capacity, nurture trust and respect, and sustain authentic partnerships.

Despite all that is known about the importance of engaging families, structural racism[2] within the American educational system makes FCC harder to achieve (Merolla & Jackson, 2019). Schools located in neighborhoods with high percentages of communities of color are more chronically underfunded (Baker et al., 2023) and students of color are disproportionately

6 ▪ R. RENBARGER et al.

disciplined (United States Government Accountability Office, 2018), which send families the message that schools are not supporting their children's needs. Eurocentric, middle-class perspectives may lead educators to assume all families have adequate financial resources, transportation, and childcare to prioritize FCC (Auerbach, 2010). Thus, although Parent Teacher Associations (PTAs) and other parent organizations provide a great venue for parent[3] involvement and shared decision-making, biased perspectives may cause parents who are racially marginalized and have low incomes to feel less welcomed (Posey-Maddox et al., 2014), or seen as helpers rather than leaders (Griffin, 2012; Williams & Sanchez, 2012). African American parents report feel alienated (Bartz et al., 2017; Brandon et al., 2010), or stereotyped as angry Black individuals when they voice a concern (Doucet, 2008). Consequently, the district environment explicitly and implicitly demonstrates that only certain students and families—particularly White, middle-class ones—are viewed as worthy of engaging (e.g., Ishimaru, 2019). This chapter will provide concrete examples of how a set of school districts overcame common challenges to fully collaborate with all families (Renbarger et al., 2022) in systemic ways for the purposes of supporting racial equity.

THEORETICAL FRAMEWORKS

Three theoretical frameworks guide our work. In the Dual Capacity-Building Framework for Family–School Partnerships (Dual Capacity-Building Framework) developed for the U.S. Department of Education, Mapp and Kuttner (2013) described the capacities needed for creating partnerships; the organizational conditions needed to sustain partnership opportunities; the goals for FCC at local, state, and federal levels; and the ultimate outcomes for staff and families when these partnerships are developed. Mapp and Kuttner (2013) described this framework as a "compass" (p. 6) to create a path that considers the district context.

More recently, Ishimaru et al. (2019) proposed a conceptual framework on Equitable Community–School Collaborations (ECSC) that criticized FCC for viewing caregivers and families through a deficit lens and instead challenged schools to prioritize family assets. Rather than detail how families should fit the model of traditional, one-way parent engagement, educators must implement (a) systemic change goals, (b) concrete methods to build capacity and relationships for all groups, (c) strategies to ensure marginalized families are co-leaders in this work, and (d) plans to create context-specific change. While many of these framework components are analogous to the Dual Capacity-Building Framework, the ECSC highlights a distinct role for marginalized families within collaboration. We use both

FCC frameworks as a foundation for our work and align our team's focus on equity for all families.

Our team also uses a systems change framework (Badgett, 2022) to detail specific ways systemic change could and should happen at the district level. Scholars have encouraged the use of systems change frameworks to address injustice at multiple levels to support transformational change (Badgett, 2022). Adapting the systems change framework for FCC, we define this transformational change as occurring through:

- *Policy changes* that codify district priorities into plans and actions that ensure the necessary funding, infrastructure, staffing, and permanent programs to support FCC.
- *Public awareness* strategies that reflect educators' commitment to equity and asset-based FCC and intentionally align the goals of the community and the district.
- *Programmatic change* that leads to systemic outcomes rather than individual responsibility (e.g., overcoming biases) or filling an equity gap (e.g., tutoring).

Addressing social injustice through these three systemic change levers not only supports individual transformation but also addresses racism at state, federal, and global levels. In our work, we consider how systemic racism[4] can be redressed through each lever to transform FCC and make it more equitable for all families, community members, and school stakeholders. We frame this chapter around the three systemic change levers but acknowledge that both the Dual Capacity-Building (Mapp & Kuttner, 2013) and ECSC (Ishimaru et al., 2019) frameworks provide additional context for FCC-specific changes.

PURPOSE

We outline ways school district administrators, families, community organizations, and researchers have made programmatic, policy, and public awareness changes to improve FCC and redress structural racism in K–12 education. We also explore how those committed to improving FCC can sustain commitment beyond a few dedicated leaders and offer a vision for how others can improve FCC in their own communities.

ABOUT OUR STUDY

The Connected & Engaged: Family and Community Collaboration (C&E) project aimed to understand current practices around FCC; explore

8 ▪ R. RENBARGER et al.

practitioner, family, and community members' perspectives on those best practices; and create actionable resources to support better FCC writ large. Funded by the Bill and Melinda Gates Foundation over 18 months, C&E team members conducted a landscape analysis of existing research, held focus groups and interviews, and highlighted strategies in action to create a website and resources for districts and educational leaders to use. C&E focused this study on the experiences of marginalized communities and sought participation from members of many groups within the FCC space, with the goal of supporting school district staff to adopt more equitable and inclusive FCC approaches.

Our C&E team is part of the U.S. Education Department of FHI 360, a global nonprofit organization. We recognize the importance of bringing together researchers, education practitioners, policy and advocacy specialists, content strategists, and outreach and dissemination experts. The core C&E team continually seeks to center the work on the voices, experiences, and perspectives of members of diverse populations. To this end, we consulted with an advisory group of content experts, caregivers, researchers, national nonprofit leaders, and community-based organizations (CBOs) to provide consistent field voice throughout the study phases.

Positionality

We are committed to recognizing the positionality of the members of our team, while ensuring that our research centers on the populations of focus and stays true to our equity goals. We have a range of lived experiences related to FCC—former K–12 teachers (Lindsey, Renbarger, & Sackman), administrators (Sackman), policy practitioners (Rodler), caregivers (Lindsey, & Sackman), and trained educational researchers (Lindsey, Renbarger, & Rodler). The writing team includes three White women (Renbarger, Rodler, & Sackman) and one Black woman (Lindsey), with two of the White women (Renbarger & Rodler) completing all in-person data collection. C&E's initial qualitative research team also included a Latinx man, two Black women, an Asian American woman, and two White women. We acknowledge the privilege and power associated with having the resources to enable us to dedicate time to this work.

Our backgrounds shaped how we related to the work. Our identities likely benefited the data collection in some ways (e.g., understanding educators' perspectives) while limiting it in others (e.g., racial and gender differences in FCC). Thus, we intentionally recruited other researchers, practitioners, and families who identified as racially and ethnically marginalized throughout the study process to provide a fuller understanding of what equity in FCC could and should look like. For this chapter, we needed to intentionally uncover and reflect how race and racism related to the findings and broader literature.

Study Process

This case study was part of and informed by a larger C&E project that involved a critical interpretive synthesis of the FCC literature (Renbarger & Rodler, 2023a) and a phenomenological study of FCC challenges encountered by district personnel (Renbarger et al., 2022). We utilized a multiple case study approach to investigate district-level systems and structures in their real-world contexts because case studies provide insight into a phenomenon at multiple sites of interest, rely on multiple sources of evidence, and help explain complex topics through multiple in-depth illustrations (Creswell, 2013; Yin, 2018). We purposively sampled cases that demonstrated systemic change for racial equity that differed in context including size of the school district, student population demographics (race, number of multilingual students, Title I eligibility), and geography (urbanicity and region in the United States).

To identify district cases, we issued a national call for recommendations via professional networks, the C&E study advisory board, social media, and the Community Insights Network (an online network of caregivers and K–12 practitioners). We collected information from districts via an online survey about the four key opportunities for change we identified for quality FCC (e.g., fostering collaborative decision-making; Renbarger et al., 2022). The research team reviewed all recommended school districts and conducted additional online research to determine the size of the school district, student population demographics, and geographical region. We conducted semi-structured focus groups with administrators in 11 school districts that appeared to demonstrate multiple strengths in FCC, served racially and economically diverse populations, and provided contact information. We selected three school district cases to visit and profile from among those we interviewed—districts that had different sizes, regions, student population demographics, and FCC strategies—a California district (Western, large, predominantly Latinx); an Alabama district (Southern, medium, predominantly Black); and an Ohio district (Midwestern, small, predominantly Black).

At each site, we worked with district staff prior to our site visits to recruit participants who were active in FCC activities. We visited each site for approximately 4 days in spring 2023 to observe collaborative events (e.g., PTA meetings, "multicultural night") and conduct semi-structured interviews with site participants. As shown in Table 1.1, in total, across all three site visits, we interviewed a mix of participants: five students, six caregivers, 11 educators (teachers, principals, school-based specialists), 16 district support

TABLE 1.1 Details of Study Participants

School District	Key Initiatives and Goals	Participants
Alabama District	• Key goal in the district's strategic plan is improving stakeholder engagement. • Initiatives and local partnerships foster opportunities for collaborative decision-making by teachers, families, and community organizations.	• 5 district staff (superintendent; federal programs administrator; 21st century program coordinator; social worker; and ELL specialist) • 1 CBO partner (higher education) • 1 caregiver • 2 students • 2 principals • 2 teacher
California District	• Committed to building staff capacity to strengthen relationships with families. • Focus on strategic two-way communication, meeting families' basic needs, and strengthening partnerships with community groups to make families and students feel valued and supported.	• 10 district staff (superintendent; director of communications and community engagement; director of access and equity; director of wellness, mental health, and community outreach; director of English language learners (ELL) programs; director of student services; wellness center coordinator; wellness center administrative assistant; wellness center consultant; and chief academic officer) • 2 CBO (local business and faith-based partner) • 2 caregivers • 2 students • 2 principals • 2 teachers
Ohio District	• Strives to foster strong partnerships with community resources. • Family and community collaboration (FCC) goals guided by task forces prioritizing equity and offering leadership opportunities for families and community members.	• 3 district staff (superintendent; family engagement specialist; and supervisor of community and school partnerships) • 4 CBO (two health partners; public libraries director; and community organization) • 3 caregivers • 1 student • 1 principal

staff (superintendents, family engagement specialists, coordinators), and seven community partners.

In alignment with case study methodologies (Yin, 2018), we collected additional multiple forms of data beyond the screening survey and initial focus groups including interview transcripts, event observation notes, research memos based on our experiences, archival records (i.e., federally reported census and district demographic data), and documents (e.g., district website, strategic plan, caregiver communication platforms, news stories) to understand district FCC structures and practices.

We analyzed each case separately before conducting cross-case analysis. Two of the team members (Renbarger & Rodler) who had conducted the site visits initiated the within-case analysis by holistically coding (Saldaña, 2016) the multiple data sources to understand broadly how districts approached systemic change for racial equity. During second-cycle coding, three team members (Lindsey, Renbarger, & Rodler) pattern coded (Yin, 2018) the sources to identify the strategies districts used in each of the systemic change categories to address racial inequities. We then conducted pattern matching (Yin, 2018) that focused on the "how" of creating systemic change to create an overall case description of their processes (Yin, 2018). Another team member (Lindsey) conducted descriptive coding (Saldaña, 2016) of interview transcripts to ensure no systemic change levers were missed and verified the case descriptions. Upon completion of all within-case analyses, we conducted cross-case syntheses by comparing sites and identifying similarities and differences in their systemic change approaches. During coding check-ins between coders (Lindsey, Renbarger, & Rodler), differences arose in how districts spoke of race, ethnicity, and other demographic characteristics, which led to an additional round of coding of interview transcripts to illustrate the language shifts via participant examples.

We adhered to Tracy's (2010) quality indicators of qualitative research (e.g., worthy topic, rich rigor, sincerity, credibility, resonance, significant contribution, ethical, and meaningful coherence) through working with multiple communities to create the topic, uncover solutions, analyze results, and disseminate findings. Team members also increased trustworthiness by participating in individual and team positionality conversations to uncover and address biases (Creswell, 2013). During data collection, the team used prolonged engagement (Lincoln & Guba, 1985) to build trust and rapport with participants by holding multiple planning calls and staying multiple days in the field. During analysis, we triangulated the data sources by including interviews, observations, and archival data and used investigator triangulation by including multiple team members in the data analysis process to support the credibility of the findings (Patton, 2015). An audit of synthesized analyzed data was conducted by the C&E study advisory board to ensure the trustworthiness of the findings and collaborate on additional findings, and we also showed case descriptions to the three sites for feedback before finalizing them (Birt et al., 2016).

FINDINGS: SYSTEMIC CHANGE STRATEGIES FOR EQUITABLE FCC

Below, we highlight the events and collaborative processes we observed during our site visits to the three school districts on which our study focused (in

12 ▪ R. RENBARGER et al.

Alabama, California, and Ohio), alongside illustrative quotes from study participants who were working to improve FCC. We also demonstrate how personnel in the same three school districts engaged in race evasion or avoided discussions about race. Together, these findings provide hope for transforming FCC within K–12 schools while highlighting how much more must be done to firmly acknowledge race and racism and engender true transformation.

Policy (Institutional)

District policy decisions are a critical lever for transformational change, as they codify district priorities into concrete plans for FCC infrastructure, funding, and staffing. District policymaking happens within the context of federal, state, and local policies, which can be both supportive and limiting. For example, Title I of the Every Student Succeeds Act (ESSA, 2015) requires educational leaders to develop family engagement plans and allocate ESSA funding to support programming. At the same time, decades of funding formulas based on property taxes and recent bans on discussing race and sexuality within classrooms deplete the resources of districts on the one hand and constrain the ability of educators to collaborate with families on the other. Still, we found instances that showed districts could create their own policies to mitigate these structural challenges and ensure commitment to FCC was not tied to a single leader.

To support systemic FCC, all three districts created policies outlining new FCC initiatives and provided the resources (e.g., funding, staffing) needed to execute them. District staff and interview respondents at all three sites described the impact of promising school-level policies and progressive district leadership. One California district staff member declared,

> We're really lucky that our superintendent and Board of Education were forward thinking in establishing the [wellness] center.... They already had this structure in place and when I came in, it was really just a matter of accelerating that growth.

To facilitate opportunities, each district designed policies that supported permanent FCC infrastructure and created regular opportunities for connection among all demographic groups, though solutions varied across the districts, depending on their size and financial situation. For example, the California and Ohio districts funded multiple staff positions to focus on family engagement and community relationships and invested in physical spaces that supported FCC (e.g., wellness centers), while the Alabama and California districts allocated time and resources for professional development (PD) to strengthen staff capacity to engage in FCC. In Ohio, creating FCC staff positions elevated its importance and ensured that at least two people could focus solely on FCC. One Ohio principal, in discussing the hiring of a family engagement specialist, said, "I felt it was really a hinge point when she joined, like the district is putting their money where their mouth is and they're committing to this work." With equity in mind, the California and Ohio districts strategically employed staff who shared experiences and identities with marginalized populations and encouraged them to focus on improving services for families with the greatest needs. By creating positions and physical spaces to serve families, each of the three districts laid the foundation for greater engagement and success for FCC.

While there were advantages to designating FCC positions, the California and Alabama districts chose to spread FCC responsibilities across departments to prevent siloed services. In California, district policymakers wrote FCC into the job descriptions of most cabinet-level staff (e.g., director of academic services, director of equity and access, director of communications), requiring them to engage with families and community groups weekly. While this policy strategy was used by a larger district, it also appeared feasible for smaller districts or districts with limited funding. By holding multiple leaders accountable for various aspects of FCC and tying those responsibilities to strategic goals, all three districts ensured that FCC would remain a priority.

As another policy priority, all three districts discussed the critical connection between students' success and families' health and wellness. District superintendents and other central office staff in each district said investing funds and time district-wide efforts that support student and family wellness was important for meeting students' needs. A founding member of the California district's family wellness center stated,

> our whole goal is to eliminate barriers to learning, whatever that is... [such as] basic needs to students, or extending services to connect them with needed [housing] or medical services. We know that without those services, those are barriers in students' lives.

To build a culture of care and respect for students' needs, all three districts strived to meet needs directly (e.g., providing free transportation) or through building partnerships with community service providers and referring students to their services. All three districts had policies for meeting all students' basic needs (e.g., transportation, food, clothing, housing, health care) and recognized these supports were most critical for marginalized groups (e.g., unhoused families, families with low incomes). These strategies all involved creating a physical space at a school site to house caseworkers and materials. In one case, the California district repurposed a trailer

14 ▪ R. RENBARGER et al.

at a centrally located school to house a food pantry, a free clothing "store," laundry and shower facilities, and meeting space for mental health counselors and staff employed under the McKinney-Vento Homeless Assistance Act (Title IX, Part A of ESSA, 2015), who work with children and youth who are experiencing homelessness. The Alabama district co-located district social workers and nonprofit staff in an old school building, allowing for warm handoffs between district staff and local agencies. The Ohio district leveraged state funding to create a school-based health center, run entirely by a local hospital system, that serves as a full-service doctor's office. Importantly, each district took steps to make these spaces welcoming. As one California district social worker mentioned, "I want them to know that there is no shame to where they're at, because I've been there before, too...I share my story with them and I share that we're all in this together." The three districts varied in their capacity, local service landscape, and families' needs, yet they all found ways to mitigate some systemic inequities in local health, housing, and social service systems.

In addition to formal programs, district staff and educators across all three sites recognized actions they could take as individuals to support FCC. For example, several Alabama and Ohio principals stood at the car drop-off line every morning to greet families; the California superintendent left weekly voicemails for all caregivers; the Alabama superintendent hosted monthly coffee chats in different communities to meet with families in small groups; and an Alabama language specialist attended non-academic events (e.g., theater performances, sporting events) to support students and share information with families. Demonstrating care and persistence strengthened community members' trust in district leaders, particularly for communities that had been marginalized in the district in the past.

Public Awareness (Cultural)

Public awareness is integral to the ethos of FCC: the educators, leaders, families, students, and community organizations that collaborate to support young people in the district. To achieve systemic FCC, all collaborators must align their goals, plans, and actions and promote public awareness of the importance of equity and asset-based mindsets.

To advance equitable FCC, the three districts we visited used mission and vision statements, language change, and partnerships with CBOs to reflect and further the cultural shift to prioritizing FCC and equity in their district community. As one Ohio district administrator noted, "our district no longer has equity as a separate goal in our strategic plan. It's embedded in all of our goals." These districts understood that without having FCC in their guiding documents, the district community would continue to see FCC as

Moving From Parent Engagement to Family Collaboration • **15**

something "extra" rather than an integral part of everyone's job. While all three districts wrote and approved equity policies, California and Ohio took further action, using them as tools to reinforce mindset changes. By integrating mission and vision into strategic planning conversations, district leaders reinforced the cultural shifts to prioritize equity and acknowledge the assets of families and community groups.

Aligning language is another important component of public awareness. Leaders in the Ohio and California districts added inclusive language on families' specific needs and assets to the FCC plans in their districts rather than preserving traditional ideas about who should be involved and how. All three districts conducted surveys and two (California and Ohio) encouraged home visits to understand what families wanted and needed regarding FCC. Using this information, the three districts implemented differentiated accommodations (e.g., providing transportation, meals, and childcare at FCC events), which demonstrated their recognition that caregivers and members of community groups often faced structural barriers to collaboration such as lack of time, inflexible work schedules, and negative encounters with district personnel. FCC work in these three districts thus included families from every background, including those with barriers to education, housing or financial insecurity, and varying family structures. A district resource coordinator in California said, "We believe in meeting our families where they're at [and] understanding where they've been." The Ohio and California districts exemplified their cultural shift by changing their terminology. Staff began using "family" or "caregiver" instead of "parent" to reflect their inclusion of diverse family structures involving grandparents, other extended family members, and non-biological caregivers.

Public awareness is required for CBOs (e.g., local businesses, faith-based groups, youth-based services, and volunteer groups) to collaborate authentically with districts to support students. Leaders in all three districts worked to ensure community partners were aligned in their goals for students and aware of district FCC goals. Without this alignment, CBOs might interact with the schools in ways that did not advance FCC goals. Leaders in all three districts recognized that outside organizations needed to be included to help respond to families' needs. As the Alabama district superintendent said regarding the district partners, "These are all partners doing great things. But often we do things in isolation. When we're able to pull together and unify that focus and align in that focus, we're able to do a whole lot more." By embracing this more inclusive perspective of FCC, these districts showed they valued what community members could bring and worked with them to create a sustainable partnership. With better public awareness in the three communities we visited, district staff, teachers, family members, and community partners sat at the same table to discuss what areas needed improvement and what resources members could bring

Programming (Individual)

Programmatic changes support systemic change in FCC by ensuring all individuals in a district community have the knowledge, mindset, and tools they need to collaborate. Respondents across the C&E study phases described individual-level actions that were critical to supporting FCC, including adopting asset-based mindsets, learning about evidence-based FCC practices, and participating in FCC activities. These actions can be taught and encouraged through programs for district staff, educators, caregivers, and CBO staff. It is important that all members of a school community believe that all caregivers, students, and community members have wisdom and power to share. For example, the Ohio district superintendent stated, "I truly believe that students that are thoughtful and empowered within their school spaces make the spaces better, but also hold all the adults accountable." In the California district, two CBOs offered paid fellowships for caregivers (specifically, caregivers of color) to learn best practices in advocacy, organizing, and engagement. Using PD funding, the Alabama district partnered with a local university to create a leadership academy where teams of teachers and family members learned best practices and designed school-based projects. These year-long trainings built individual capacity to engage in systemic transformation through providing educators and families with the time, space, and resources needed to create change.

The three districts also created learning structures to sustain the building of caregivers' and community members' capacity over time. Leaders in the Ohio and California districts created ongoing citizen-led task forces to serve specific populations (e.g., African American caregivers, multilingual caregivers) or district priorities (e.g., equity, discipline, early childhood). They often included the superintendents or set up structures to meet with superintendents regularly to ensure that administrative and citizen groups worked together collaboratively. In a related strategy, leaders in the California district hired and trained caregivers to serve as parent ambassadors who served as bridges between caregiver communities and school-based staff, with a direct line of communication to the superintendents. One parent ambassador said of the experience, "We all matter. No matter your culture, no matter your race, there is a little bit of something for everyone. You know, it's noticed, and it's not watered down." By investing leadership time

Moving From Parent Engagement to Family Collaboration ▪ **17**

in these mechanisms, supporting participants' development, and highlighting the contributions of specific groups, leaders in these districts ensured that families had long-lasting opportunities for engagement that were designed to outlast any individual district leader.

Administrators and educators in all three districts acknowledged the importance of student voice in decision-making. One exemplary type of task force revolved around an oft-forgotten group in FCC: students. The California district created a student advisory group that included district-led trainings in strategic planning. Students met with district and school staff to learn how the planning process works and provide feedback. By investing in students' capacity building, including time for listening and relationship building, the district leaders reinforced their commitment to empowering students. Table 1.2 summarizes the strategies we discerned.

TABLE 1.2 Summary of Strategies by Lever of Change	
Lever of Change	**Strategies**
Policy	1. Strengthen FCC infrastructure by funding staff members to work on FCC efforts, invest in physical spaces that support FCC, and allocate existing time and resources for FCC PD. 2. Establish external partnerships with community services and create a one-stop shop that serves families' basic needs. 3. Create opportunities that promote permanent decision-making structures to support ongoing opportunities for power-sharing with marginalized families (e.g., community task forces and parent ambassadors).
Public Awareness	1. Create shared mission and vision statements that incorporate inclusive language, so all school, community, and family members are valued. 2. Be specific and use terms such as "shared power" and "shared decision-making" when referring to FCC in mission and vision statements. 3. Use the term "family" or "caregiver" instead of "parent" to include more types of family structures. 4. Provide numerous opportunities to engage CBO and community partners in decision-making conversations.
Programming	1. Provide training to district staff, educators, caregivers, and CBO staff aimed to change mindsets and build capacity (adopting asset-based mindsets, learning about evidence-based FCC practices, and participating in FCC activities). 2. Ensure district leadership engages in these trainings to demonstrate their commitment and model best practices. 3. Be accessible and visible to parents (e.g., greet families at car drop-off, leave weekly voicemails for families, attend non-academic events). 4. Prioritize student, family, and CBO perspectives by creating task forces and advisory groups that facilitate long-term learning opportunities for specific groups.

Limited Systemic Change Regarding Racial Equity

The purpose of FCC is to engage families of all racial and ethnic groups by building trust and prioritizing students' and families' needs and concerns. Our conversations with personnel in three districts showed that many strategies focused on culture and equity. Unexpectedly, we found that despite a deep commitment to equity, personnel in each district struggled in some way with conversations related to race and how to engage members of marginalized groups in FCC efforts. Based on respondents' language—or lack of equity-focused language—two themes surfaced: race evasion and hyperfocus on specific marginalized groups.

Race Evasion

Respondents in one district avoided mentioning racism, similar to the "anything but racism" phenomena documented by sociologists (Bonilla-Silva & Baiocchi, 2001) and in education (Harper, 2012; McNair et al., 2020). While some participants in the other two districts acknowledged race and its connection to FCC (e.g., through creating African American caregiver councils to address African American students' needs), respondents in one district instead used language that described families' finances, caregivers' work schedules, and where families lived to paint a picture of race without naming race. For example, one principal said their school had students who are "from very different family backgrounds" and diverse in terms of national origin, where they live, and family structure (e.g., grandparents as caregivers), without explicitly mentioning race or racism. They spoke to symptoms of racism, such as immigration issues, housing segregation, and economic instability, without naming how these issues relate to race or racism in their district. Similarly, when asked about students' demographics, another principal explained,

> I have stay-at-home moms, and then I have moms and dads who have PhDs, who are medical doctors, who are engineers, military.... I have working-class people who work as garbage truck guys or as RNs [registered nurses].... We have kids in million-dollar homes, we have kids in community housing.... It's like a big melting pot.

Noting this wide variety of backgrounds without naming any racial or ethnic groups—implicitly suggesting these issues affect all racial groups equally—avoided addressing core issues of structural racism and its impacts on school success and FCC. Intentionally addressing challenges caused by race and racism is critical to achieving FCC and improving racial equity (Banaji et al., 2021).

Prioritization of Specific Marginalized Groups

It was evident through our discussions that, amid political turmoil, leaders in some districts wanted to focus FCC resources on supporting students most impacted by COVID-19, nationwide policies, and bullying. These districts leaders strived to focus on specific racial and ethnic groups in response to identified needs. However, in some cases, focus on only a few specific populations created division among families over how FCC resources were allocated. In their own ways, leaders in each of the three districts sometimes set out to remediate or fix caregivers' attitudes about schools, as opposed to letting families take control and voice their experiences, expectations, and interests in FCC (Ishimaru et al., 2019). When a district prioritizes student scores instead of student and family needs, certain marginalized groups fall through the cracks. For example, personnel in one district aligned many of their FCC initiatives to meet the needs of African American students and families. One administrator noted, in focusing on African American student achievement, "The district has really boosted that level. I think we have some of the highest African American graduation rates in this area [state]." Yet, while the district's African American community achieved the desired goals, other groups were not prioritized (even though Hispanic students made up the majority of the population) and their barriers to achievement were not addressed. To achieve true racial equity, district staff must apply systemic change levers for all racial and ethnic groups.

CONCLUSION

Many researchers and members of organizations in the FCC field believe policy change is the first step to creating quality FCC (Constantino, 2021). Adaptation of job descriptions, use of local resources, and creation of decision-making bodies aligned with many of the policy recommendations from the literature (e.g., Constantino, 2021)—particularly as these policy changes combine with programmatic and cultural changes—create the larger, more effective social movement needed for educational change (Leonard & Woodland, 2022). However, district leaders must ensure that these policies are implemented authentically and effectively. For example, all three districts had some form of student advisory groups, but to date only one district has used the opportunity for youth capacity building and authentic two-way discussion. All policies must be monitored for authentic engagement and collaboration to avoid cursory, less effective methods for change.

Our study found that districts understood that their leadership and educators needed FCC training to engage all families and that they needed to include family and community members in similar programming to ensure district decisions responded to all needs. Professional development supports systemic change, but best practices with bias training—such as managing attendees' discomfort and evaluating the effectiveness of professional development (Carter et al., 2020)—were not the norm. Professional development providers and district leaders must adhere to best practices to meaningfully facilitate changes in mindsets. We learned from leadership in all three districts the importance of having leaders and educators spend time in the community as part of their regular learning to build relationships, listen to needs, and connect with the broader population—particularly members of those communities that have been marginalized or who have lost trust in the education system. But we also learned that asking district leaders and educators to engage with the community on top of their other responsibilities may exacerbate the ongoing educator recruitment and retention problems that already affect students, particularly students of color (Carter Andrews et al., 2019).

To create public awareness, leaders in the three districts we studied wrote new mission and vision statements that honored FCC and equity, created specific FCC staff positions, used more inclusive family descriptors, and/or prioritized partnerships with outside organizations. In recent years, leaders in many organizations began focusing on including diversity, equity, and inclusion in the mission and vision statements of their organizations (e.g., Fontanarosa et al., 2021), and research suggests that this practice benefits students (Dooley, 2019). Participants in our C&E study knew about their district leaders' new commitment to equity and could point to specific aspects of their mission and vision statements as a rationale for committing to the equity work. These findings suggest a shift from previous research that found that district staff did not know these types of statements and did not believe the statements impacted their daily practice (Gurley et al., 2015). Similarly, leaders of larger organizations have created guidelines around using more inclusive language (e.g., American Psychological Association, 2021) that align with the efforts of leaders in school districts to engage all families and partner organizations respectfully. These guidelines help to embrace "communication that acknowledges the power differentials and dynamics of our society and their deleterious effects" (Andoh, 2022, para. 2).

Importantly, leaders in the three districts we studied emphasized the need to work with local organizations as part of public awareness. Partnering highlighted not only the assets the community members could bring to the educational setting, but also how authentic collaboration with external organizations could improve community members' perceptions about schools. To do this, the district leader needed to create a common vision of success with partners, share data to identify needs and possibilities for collaboration, and regularly commit to the partnership. Sharing power with community groups in these ways means students and families receive more services than under traditional, hierarchical, or informal partnerships (Warner & Zhang, 2022).

Decades of research have found that educational systems reflect the larger issues in America, with systemic racism being no exception (e.g., Banaji et al., 2021). While this study highlighted many hopeful strategies for dismantling racist structures in FCC, educators trying to strengthen equity still struggled with evading conversations around race and might be hyperfocused on a subset of their students. When district personnel are silent about race, they legitimize Whiteness, which can trickle down to impact students and families (Castagno, 2008). Equity-minded educational practitioners must be ready to talk about race without resorting to euphemisms and coded language (McNair et al., 2020). Understanding and discussing racism are the first steps in preventing it. Finally, district leaders must critically examine data for all subgroups and identify action steps to ensure FCC efforts do not ignore any marginalized groups (McNair et al., 2020).

Implications for Research

Systemic change theory states that all levers (programmatic, cultural, and policy) need support from one another to work cohesively toward transformational change. However, future researchers should help inform which lever (policy, program, or public awareness) might lead to more impactful FCC for districts, based on their characteristics. Such input can help district leaders make the most efficient choices with their limited capacity. In our study, leaders in all three districts faced many barriers to equitable FCC that were beyond their control, such as legislation that threatened to silence vital societal discourse on racism and sexism, and uncertain educational funding. Researchers should inform discussions about how to support state and federal systemic change to strengthen the work occurring in schools. District leaders must identify which FCC levers can simultaneously support racial equity change so that accountability for such change extends beyond them. We encourage future research to integrate the existing frameworks— such as those we described here—to effect change more quickly, rather than creating yet another framework for FCC.

Implications for Practice

Although the leaders in three districts in our study are part of a growing cadre of educators who have created innovative programs and initiatives to support and collaborate with families from marginalized groups, other district leaders have fallen short of promoting racial justice within their schools and communities. We respectfully suggest that district leaders adopt the systems change framework that was the foundation for our work and learn from the examples we presented here to dismantle district-wide systems that perpetuate Whiteness in FCC and disrupt the remnants of White supremacy in education. Engaging in these critical practices can support not only student success, but also an educational environment in which mutual trust and respect among students, families, staff, and the community is the norm (e.g., Flamboyan Foundation, 2021; Ishimaru et al., 2019; Kim & Gentle-Genitty, 2020). In times of political turbulence, educational leaders likely need to start with changing hearts (McNair et al., 2020). For hearts to change, district leaders should prioritize known methods for creating change, such as identifying how individual roles relate to racial structures and understanding individual power and influence to enlighten colleagues who do not see racism in education (Edirmanasinghe et al., 2022). Raising consciousness is an important first step to ensure that FCC programmatic and policy changes work toward the intended goals. Once enough (not necessarily all) hearts understand racial equity and its role in the system, we recommend that all district leaders, teachers, and school staff engage in professional development sessions that align with best practices for bias training (Carter et al., 2020) to explain different forms of racism (i.e., personal/internalized racism, interpersonal racism, institutional racism, and structural racism), show how those different forms impede effective FCC. District leaders must simultaneously work to co-create vision and mission statements with families and community members that integrate FCC and guide district activities and the daily practice of educators. As Özdem (2011) described regarding higher education institutions in Turkey, "Mission and vision statements should not be treated as cool sentences to adorn the websites and brochures of the universities, they should be put into action" (p. 1893). School district leaders should use mission and vision statements as guideposts, if such are not already in practice, to create a welcoming environment for marginalized family members as they serve collaboratively as decision-makers, leaders, and key members of the FCC partnership.

Limitations

Throughout the rounds of data collection, we attempted to recruit participants who were demographically representative of their district contexts. We included students when possible, but future researchers should include more students, particularly those familiar with collaborative processes and equity issues, and work intentionally with community members to recruit youth who can speak to equity and FCC. In addition, we faced district-specific challenges that limited our ability to understand the dimensions of race and racism as fully as we wished across all contexts.

NOTES

1. We use the term "marginalized" to denote groups historically and currently oppressed within society, such as people of color, individuals with low incomes, and people with disabilities. However, when other research or participants use another term, we retain their preferred term.
2. We use Merolla and Jackson's (2019) definition of structural racism: "A social system in which racial categorization serves as a primary organizing feature bestowing privilege on some groups and disadvantage on others, serves as the fundamental cause of racial disparities in educational outcomes" (p. 2).
3. Throughout this chapter, we use the term "caregiver" to encompass a wider definition than "parent" to include grandparents, aunts and uncles, adoptive parents, and other individuals who support a student's growth.
4. Throughout this chapter, we use a definition from Banaji et al. (2021) for systemic racism: "the processes and outcomes of racial inequality and inequity in life opportunities and treatment" perpetuated through institutional structures, social structures, individual mental structures, and daily interactions (p. 2).

REFERENCES

American Psychological Association. (2021). *Equity, diversity, and inclusion: Inclusive language guidelines.* https://www.apa.org/about/apa/equity-diversity-inclusion/language-guidelines.pdf

Andoh, E. (2022, September). *Why inclusive language matters.* American Psychological Association. https://www.apa.org/ed/precollege/psn/2022/09/inclusive-language

Auerbach, S. (2010). Beyond coffee with the principal: Toward leadership for authentic school–family partnerships. *Journal of School Leadership, 20*(6), 728–757. https://doi.org/10.1177/105268461002000603

Badgett, A. (2022, September 19). Systems change: Making the aspirational actionable. *Stanford Social Innovation Review.* https://doi.org/10.48558/84HA-E065

Baker, B. D., Di Carlo, M., & Weber, M. (2023). *The adequacy and fairness of state school finance systems* (5th ed.). Albert Shanker Institute; University of Miami School of Education & Human Development; Rutgers Graduate School of Education. https://www.schoolfinancedata.org/wp-content/uploads/2022/12/SFID 2023_annualreport.pdf

Banaji, M. R., Fiske, S. T., & Massey, D. S. (2021). Systemic racism: Individuals and interactions, institutions and society. *Cognitive Research: Principles and Implications, 6*(82), 1–21. https://doi.org/10.1186/s41235-021-00349-3

Bartz, D., Collins-Ayanllaja, C., & Rice, P. (2017). African-American parents and effective parent involvement programs. *Schooling, 8*(1), 1–9.

Bergman, E. (2022). *Unlocking the "how": Designing family engagement strategies that lead to school success.* Learning Heroes. https://bealearninghero.org/wp-content/uploads/2022/03/Unlocking-The-How-Report.pdf

Birt, L., Scott, S., Cavers, D., Campbell, C., & Walter, F. (2016). Member checking: A tool to enhance trustworthiness or merely a nod to validation? *Qualitative Health Research, 26*(13), 1802–1811. https://doi.org/10.1177/1049732316654870

Bonilla-Silva, E., & Baiocchi, G. (2001). Anything but racism: How sociologists limit the significance of racism. *Race & Society, 4*(2), 117–131. https://doi.org/10.1016/S1090-9524(03)00004-4

Brandon, R. R., Higgins, K., Pierce, T., Tandy, R., & Sileo, N. (2010). An exploration of the alienation experienced by African American parents from their children's educational environment. *Remedial and Special Education, 31*(3), 208–222. https://doi.org/10.1177/0741932509338350

Carter Andrews, D. J., Castro, E., Cho, C. L., Petchauer, E., Richmond, G., & Floden, R. (2019). Changing the narrative on diversifying the teaching workforce: A look at historical and contemporary factors that inform recruitment and retention of teachers of color. *Journal of Teacher Education, 70*(1), 6–12. https://doi.org/10.1177/0022487118812418

Carter, E. R., Onyeador, I. N., & Lewis, N. A., Jr. (2020). Developing & delivering effective anti-bias training: Challenges & recommendations. *Behavioral Science & Policy, 6*(1), 57–70. https://doi.org/10.1353/bsp.2020.0005

Castagno, A. (2008). "I don't want to hear that!" Legitimating Whiteness through silence in schools. *Anthropology & Education Quarterly, 39*(3), 314–333. https://doi.org/10.1111/j.1548-1492.2008.00024.x

Constantino, S. M. (2021). *Engage every family: Five simple principles.* Corwin Press.

Creswell, J. W. (2013). *Qualitative inquiry & research design: Choosing among five approaches* (3rd ed.). SAGE.

Dooley, T. P. (2019). Searching for social equity among public administration mission statements. *Teaching Public Administration, 38*(2), 113–125. https://doi.org/10.1177/0144739419867121

Doucet, F. (2008). How African American parents understand their and teachers' roles in children's schooling and what this means for preparing preservice teachers. *Journal of Early Childhood Teacher Education, 29*(2), 108–139. https://doi.org/10.1080/10901020802059441

Edirmanasinghe, N., Goodman-Scott, E., Smith-Durkin, S., & Tarver, S. Z. (2022). Supporting all students: Multitiered systems of support from an antiracist and critical race theory lens. *Professional School Counseling, 26*(1), 1–12. https://doi.org/10.1177/2156759X221109154

Every Student Succeeds Act. (2015). *20 U.S.C. § 6301.* https://www.congress.gov/114/plaws/publ95/PLAW-114publ95.pdf

Flamboyan Foundation. (2021). *Family engagement matters.* https://flamboyanfoundation.org/resource/family-engagement-matters/

Fontanarosa, P. B., Flanagin, A., Ayanian, J. Z., Bonow, R. O., Bressler, N. M., Christakis, D., Disis, M. L., Josephson, S. A., Kibbe, M. R., Öngur, D., Piccirillo, J. F., Redberg, R. F., Rivara, F. P., Shinkai, K., & Yancy, C. W. (2021). Equity and the JAMA Network. *JAMA Oncology, 7*(8), 1119–1121. https://doi.org/10.1001/jamaoncol.2021.2927

Grant, K. B., & Ray, J. A. (2019). *Home, school, and community collaboration: Culturally responsive family engagement* (4th ed.). SAGE.

Griffin, D. (2012, May 1). The need for advocacy with African American parents. *Counseling Today.* https://ct.counseling.org/2012/05/the-need-for-advocacy -with-african-american-parents/

Gurley, D. K., Peters, G. B., Collins, L., & Fifolt, M. (2015). Mission, vision, values, and goals: An exploration of key organizational statements and daily practice in schools. *Journal of Educational Change, 16,* 217–242. https://doi.org/ 10.1007/s10833-014-9229-x

Harper, S. R. (2012). Race without racism: How higher education researchers minimize racist institutional norms. *Review of Higher Education, 36*(1), 9–29. https://doi.org/10.1353/rhe.2012.0047

Henderson, A. T., Mapp, K. L. (2002). *A new wave of evidence: The impact of school, family, and community connections on student achievement.* Southwest Educational Development Laboratory.

Henderson, A. T., Mapp, K. L., Johnson, V. R., & Davies, D. (2007). *Beyond the bake sale: The essential guide to family-school partnerships.* The New Press.

Ishimaru, A. M. (2019). From family engagement to equitable collaboration. *Educational Policy, 33*(2), 350–385. https://doi.org/10.1177/0895904817691841

Ishimaru, A. M., Lott, J. L., II., Torres, K. E., & O'Reilly-Diaz, K. (2019). Families in the driver's seat: Catalyzing familial transformative agency for equitable collaboration. *Teachers College Record: The Voices of Scholarship in Education, 121*(11), 1–39. https://doi.org/10.1177/016146811912101108

Jacques, C., & Villegas, A. (2018). *Strategies for equitable family engagement.* State Support Network. https://shorturl.at/sDIQU

Jensen, K. L., & Minke, K. M. (2017). Engaging families at the secondary level: An underused resource for student success. *The School Community Journal, 27*(2), 167–191.

Kim, J., & Gentle-Genitty, C. (2020). Transformative school–community collaboration as a positive school climate to prevent school absenteeism. *Journal of Community Psychology, 48*(8), 2678–2691. https://doi.org/10.1002/jcop.22444

Leonard, A. M., & Woodland, R. H. (2022). Anti-racism is not an initiative: How professional learning communities may advance equity and social-emotional learning in schools. *Theory Into Practice, 61*(2), 212–223. https://doi.org/10 .1080/00405841.2022.2036058

Lincoln, Y. S., & Guba, E. G. (1985). *Naturalistic inquiry.* SAGE.

Mapp, K. L., & Bergman, E. (2021). *Embracing a new normal: Toward a more liberatory approach to family engagement.* Carnegie Corporation of New York. https://doi .org/10.15868/socialsector.38504

Mapp, K. L., & Kuttner, P. J. (2013). *Partners in education: A dual capacity-building framework for family–school partnerships.* U.S. Department of Education, Southwest Educational Development Library. https://www2.ed.gov/documents/ family-community/partners-education.pdf

McNair, T. B., Bensimon, E. M., & Malcom-Pequeux, L. (2020). *From equity talk to equity walk: Expanding practitioner knowledge for racial justice in higher education.* Wiley. https://doi.org/10.1002/9781119428725

Merolla, D. M., & Jackson, O. (2019). Structural racism as the fundamental cause of the academic achievement gap. *Sociology Compass, 13*(6). https://doi.org/ 10.1111/soc4.12696

Özdem, G. (2011). An analysis of the mission and vision statements on the strategic plans of higher education institutions. *Educational Sciences: Theory and Practice, 11*(4), 1887–1894. https://shorturl.at/eivQR

Patton, M. (2015). *Qualitative research and evaluation methods: Integrating theory and practice* (4th ed.). SAGE.

Posey-Maddox, L., Kimelberg, S. M., & Cucchiara, M. (2014). Seeking a 'critical mass': Middle-class parents' collective engagement in city public schooling. *British Journal of Sociology of Education. 37*(7), 905–927. https://doi.org/10.10 80/01425692.2014.986564

Renbarger, R., & Rodler, L. (2023a, April 13–16). *Challenges, solutions, and gaps: A critical interpretive synthesis of family and community collaboration literature* [Paper presentation]. American Educational Research Association Annual Meeting, Chicago, IL, United States.

Renbarger, R., & Rodler, L. (2023b). *Systemic supports for family and community collaboration: Strengthening the educator workforce.* FHI 360. https://connected andengaged.fhi360.org/collaboration-policy-solutions/systemic-supports-for -family-and-community-collaboration-educator-workforce/

Renbarger, R., Rodler, L., Espina, G., Thompson, A., Detgen, A., Sobers, M., Fernandez, F., Sackman, R., Williams, P., & Newsome, E. (2022). *Roadblocks to effective district, family, and community collaboration: A phenomenological study of potential challenges and solutions.* [Manuscript submitted for publication]. FHI 360.

Saldaña, J. (2016). *The coding manual for qualitative researchers* (3rd ed.). SAGE.

Soltero-González, L., & Gillanders, C. (2021). Rethinking home-school partnerships: Lessons learned from Latinx parents of young children during the COVID-19 era. *Early Childhood Education Journal, 49*(5), 965–976. https://doi .org/10.1007/s10643-021-01210-4

Tracy, S. J. (2010). Qualitative quality: Eight "big-tent" criteria for excellent qualitative research. *Qualitative Inquiry, 16*(10), 837–851. https://doi.org/10.1177/ 1077800410383121

United States Government Accountability Office. (2018). *K–12 education: Discipline disparities for Black students, boys, and students with disabilities* (GAO-18-258). https://www.gao.gov/products/gao-18-258

Warner, M. E., & Zhang, X. (2022). Joint use between communities and schools: Unpacking dimensions of power. *Community Development, 54*(4), 496–511. https://doi.org/10.1080/15575330.2022.2124529

Williams, T. T., & Sánchez, B. (2012). Parental involvement (and uninvolvement) at an inner-city high school. *Urban Education, 47*(3), 625–652. https://doi .org/10.1177/0042085912437794

Yin, R. K. (2018). *Case study research and applications: Design and methods* (6th ed.). SAGE.

CHAPTER 2

COMING TOGETHER AS CLASSMATES

Participatory Heritage as Socially Just and Age-Friendly Praxis Through an Intergenerational School–University–Community Preservation Project

Ayana Allen-Handy
Drexel University

Karena Alane Escalante
Drexel University

Isaiah Lassiter
Drexel University

Jahyonna Brown
Drexel University

Ronald Ray
West Philadelphia Alumni Association

Catherine Nettles
West Philadelphia Alumni Association

Arania Goldsmith-Carter
West Philadelphia Alumni Association

Michelle S. Allen
West Philadelphia Alumni Association

Bonnie Poole-Linder
West Philadelphia Alumni Association

Justice, Equity, Diversity, and Inclusion in Education, pages 27–45
Copyright © 2024 by Information Age Publishing
www.infoagepub.com
All rights of reproduction in any form reserved.

ABSTRACT

Many urban communities are experiencing gentrification and the associated residential displacement. These changes in one prominent Black community in Philadelphia have made preserving the history and legacy of the local high school an urgent endeavor. This intergenerational participatory heritage project highlights a partnership between a public high school and a private university and employs an educational design led by community brokers. In this paper, we discuss participatory heritage as a cultural process that our multigenerational team engages in to inspire generations of leaders dedicated to preserving Black culture and social justice in urban communities. Grounded in critical race theory (CRT) and intergenerational responsible leadership theoretical frameworks, we highlight the positive impacts of a mutually beneficial collaboration, and the strengths we brought and the challenges we confronted in sustaining a cohesive university–school–community partnership.

As members of many urban communities in the United States contend with the impacts of gentrification (Tuck et al., 2014) and displacement of residents, it is imperative that marginalized communities deploy their agency to ensure the preservation of their historical archives and their past, present, and future narratives (Allen-Handy et al., 2021). Given that many Black communities, specifically, are still recovering from the ravages of the COVID-19 global pandemic and the reckoning for justice across the intersections of race, ethnicity, gender, age, and class, the power of preserving stories is an urgent undertaking. As a form of preservation, participatory heritage involves multiple stakeholders in a common project that bridges between past and future legacies. Participatory heritage is a dynamic means for democratizing research in pursuit of truth, particularly in education (Caswell et al., 2016). As an inclusive, co-constructed process of archival collection building and memory making, participatory heritage often takes place outside of formal cultural heritage institutions, and it is reflective of grassroots movements of preservation (Roued-Cunliffe & Copeland, 2017).

Authors of extant literature affirm the positive impacts of participatory cultural heritage and the benefits of marshaling partnerships and resources among communities, academic institutions, businesses, nonprofits, and governmental sectors to preserve public histories (Liew et al., 2022; Ziegler, 1974). However, there are few programs that engage marginalized communities through authentic partnerships that center intergenerational, justice-oriented, equity-based, and community-driven approaches which position communities as leaders of their own participatory heritage projects ([PHP], Allen-Handy & Thomas-EL, 2018; Goldenberg, 2016). Cultural heritage preservation and community memory projects provide a powerful platform for empowered communities, particularly Black communities as the tenets of cultural heritage preservation draw upon many of the culturally sustaining pedagogies centered throughout the African Diaspora (Paris, 2012). Working in partnership with community members is often positioned from a deficit perspective of "empower*ing*" communities rather than moving from a space that wholeheartedly recognizes that communities are already empowered through the process of their lived experience. This is the stance we adopted for this project, and it guides our collective pursuit of preserving meaningful histories through participatory heritage.

Participatory heritage is a cultural process that involves communities in identifying and defining their heritage (Phillips & Stein, 2013; Shilton & Srinivasan, 2007; Uricchio, 2009). PHP can foster positive community-university relationships (Li, 2016), create intergenerational connections (Allen-Handy et al., 2021), and result in increased social- and self-empowerment for marginalized communities (Shilton & Srinivasan, 2007). Existing research attests to the key role of cultural affirmations (Allen et al., 2013) and heritage in illuminating educational spaces, but few researchers engage older adults and youth together in Black communities to contend with the effects of rapid gentrification.

SCHOOL, UNIVERSITY, AND COMMUNITY COLLABORATION

Our PHP is a partnership between the Justice-Oriented Youth (JoY) Education Lab in the School of Education at Drexel University (https://drexel .edu/soe/research/labs/joy-lab/) and students at a local high school (West Philadelphia High School, WPHS), and demonstrates how university faculty and students, WPHS students, and older adult alumni co-constructed an ongoing intergenerational participatory-heritage research project. The purpose was and continues to be to preserve and share the history and long-standing legacy of WPHS through preserving its archives and artifacts—dating back to 1911—and to preserve oral histories collected from alumni. WPHS is a treasure for the historically Black community it serves and is the first high school located west of the Schuylkill River in an urban northeast community. In recent years, the leadership of the school district sold the original 1911 school building to developers who gutted it and converted the building into high-end apartments—leading to the effective pricing out of many long standing Black residents. With the escalation of neighborhood development projects financed by anchor institutions magnifying the impact of other gentrifying forces, the demographics of the WPHS attendance zone are rapidly shifting and inevitably impacting local educational institutions in addition to engendering broader sociopolitical and economic changes (McCullough et al., 2022).

Over the course of the last 5 years, our university–public high school partnership has co-constructed a project that is supported by a staff consisting of 12 youth archivists, five older adult archivists ("the elders"), a WPHS teacher, a university professor, four graduate students, and one undergraduate student. In accordance with our social justice orientation, we aspire to combat ageism and maintain an age-friendly communal space. According to Schniedewind and Davidson (2014), "Ageism is any attitude, action, or institutional structure that subordinates a person or group because of age, or any assignment of roles in society based on age" (p. 17). Ageism impacts people of all ages, including youth and older adults. Jarrott et al. (2021) called on educational authorities to address outdated, ageist stereotypes that are often both implicit and subconscious. In American society, young people and older adults are often disadvantaged based on their acceptance by others in their environment and by their restricted access to goods and power. We advocate for inclusivity to help create new ways to increase intergenerational and multicultural engagement. Working with older alumni of a now-closed local high school, we have created a learning environment that is oriented to reinforcing cultural and historic preservation using an equity-based lens and exemplifies a grassroots model of how to empower marginalized communities (Allen-Handy et al., 2021). Historically, older adults' social engagement and contribution are valued among Black, Indigenous, and people of color (BIPOC) cultures (Martinson & Minkler, 2006). High school students and older alums in BIPOC communities can unite to enhance creativity through interactive educational opportunities (McBride, 2007; UN Women, 2023). Through our intergenerational justice-oriented preservation project, university and community members devised radical solutions to preserve the longstanding history of WPHS and to recognize and value historical records.

Our overall objective in this chapter is to share our project and our lived experiences in engaging in this work across our diverse identities in the hope that our work will inspire others to recount their stories and preserve their own histories. We describe the history of our project, the context of gentrification, and the preservation of participatory cultural heritage through our intergenerational partnership. Ultimately, we aspire to redefine the role of historical archivists and disrupt ageism by highlighting diversity, equity, inclusion, and belonging (DEIB) at the intersection of race, ethnicity, age, and other identities, by embracing community members of all ages, and by inspiring reciprocal relationships at the intersection of schools, universities, and communities.

Theoretical Grounding

While there are different paradigms within educational research, we operate under an advocacy/participatory lens, which Creswell (2015) described as a philosophical worldview concerned with historically disempowered and marginalized communities (Baldwin, 1963/2013). By focusing on oppression and the lack of voice, we center critical approaches that Lather (2003) also described as emancipatory in nature. Critical theory has its own research agenda and methodology, and critical theory sets the epistemological basis of our participatory heritage project. Participatory research, an instance of critical theory, "breaks with conventional ways of construing research, as it concerns doing research *with* people and communities rather than doing research *to* or *for* people and communities" (Cohen et al., 2018, p. 56). As this work is situated within the complex histories of gentrification and racism (Drexel University sits upon the land of the indigenous Native American northeastern Lenape people; Marsh, 2014)—we employ a critical lens as an important centering discourse informing our theoretical framework and methodology. Critical qualitative research "embodies the emancipatory, empowering values of critical pedagogy" because, like critical race theory, critical qualitative research "represents inquiry done for explicit political, utopian purposes, a politics of liberation, a reflexive discourse constantly in search of an open-ended, subversive, multivoiced epistemology" (Denzin et al., 2008, p. 7). We recognize the importance of indigenous critics by addressing how indigenous cultures are sites of resistance, since research is inextricably linked to European imperialism (Smith, 2021). Through participatory action research, we connect CRT principles of emancipatory practices, intergenerational responsible leadership theory, and action to advance new discourse about what education looks like in diverse contexts (DeCuir-Gunby et al., 2018). These interdisciplinary theoretical foundations are central to understanding the complexities of the experiences of people living in U.S. urban communities.

Critical Race Theory

We employ a critical race theory ([CRT]; Crenshaw, 1994) perspective in tandem with an intergenerational responsible leadership theoretical framework (Puaschunder, 2017). CRT stems from critical theories and allows researchers to analyze qualitative data at the micro level and connect it to broader social systems (Winkle-Wagner et al., 2019). CRT encourages scholars to be considerate of racial histories in their positionality and work to dismantle racial oppression (Winkle-Wagner et al., 2019).

Over the last two decades, CRT has evolved to become an "increasingly permanent fixture in the toolkit of educational researchers seeking to critically examine educational opportunities, school climate, representation, and pedagogy" (Ledesma & Calderón, 2015, p. 206). As a theoretical lens, CRT is employed in research to examine how data relative to racism and race relations unfold and progress over time (Sulé et al., 2017). For example, CRT has been used in education to explore topics including racism in pedagogy along the P–20 educational continuum (DeCuir & Dixson, 2004). Many applications focus on five tenets: counter-storytelling, the permanence of racism, Whiteness as property, interest conversion, and the critique of liberalism (DeCuir & Dixson, 2004; Ladson-Billings, 1998).

Intergenerational Responsible Leadership Theory

In alignment with CRT, we employ intergenerational responsible leadership theory (Puaschunder, 2017) which draws attention to the impact across multiple generations of various social issues. Intergenerational perspectives are rooted in critical theory and are most often employed to enlighten advocacy/participatory research endeavors (Sirdenis et al., 2019). According to Puaschunder (2017), developing networks through "intergenerational connectedness and social interaction" can lead to social change (p. 94). Intergenerational responsible leadership theory can also underpin multidisciplinary research approaches, including both quantitative and qualitative studies, as well as research in education (Puaschunder, 2017).

Intergenerational responsible leadership theory was developed in the corporate field and was built on the idea that leaders have a responsibility to consider the needs of their successors, including future generations. Just as corporate executives consider the long-term impact of their decision-making on their constituents, so do community members, educators, and other community leaders consider the long-term impact of the legacy they leave for their local communities. The sense of accountability to future generations transfers effectively from business to education and finds voice in shared activism at the intersection of universities, communities, and schools in alignment with the consideration of racial histories and positionality in CRT (Crenshaw, 1994). Brooks and Lopez (2018) share a useful model of a community justice-oriented partnership that further emphasizes the value of relational skills and communication across groups to have a positive impact on education.

For our purpose in this chapter, the blending of intergenerational responsible leadership theory and CRT captures the essence of the multilayered experiences of local residents with long and complex histories of interaction with the local universities and schools. The use of intergenerational frameworks has allowed researchers to focus on the diverse experiences across age groups and the social constructions of ageism which are commonly underemphasized in K–12 education contexts but are pertinent to capturing generational nuances in perspectives (Allen, 2016; Cohen et al., 2018; Sirdenis et al., 2019). Jarrott and colleagues (2022) demonstrated that intergenerational programming cannot only connect students with older adults, but offer mutual benefits grounded in values of collectivism and reciprocity. Along the same lines, Wan and Antonucci (2016) point out that intergenerational programming allows people to learn about perspectives different from their own—a critical skill to address issues of social justice. Given that historic preservation is intricately situated within education and policy (Matero, 2021), a critical stance is appropriate to investigate the impact of intergenerational programs to redefine preservationists of American history and disrupt the ageism and gentrification observed in today's urban educational contexts. Exploring university, school, and community partnerships through the lens of CRT and intergenerational leadership provides a basis for encapsulating the tangible material and intangible artifacts that attest to the impact of racism as, over time, a community has endured its multigenerational consequences. Both CRT and intergenerational responsible leadership invoke an anti-racist research approach to foreground the indigenous knowledge embedded within local communities. Anti-racism refers to the practice of actively identifying and opposing racism, and committed stakeholders believe they have an ethical responsibility to advance equity and social justice (García-Vázquez et al., 2020; Kendi, 2019).

We focus on the combined tenets of CRT (Bell, 1980; Crenshaw, 1994) and the intergenerational responsible leadership lens, to capture the intersection of race and age in gentrifying educational contexts. Intergenerational frameworks, more broadly, have emerged in the legal and business fields and are commensurable with the social sciences, including education (Puaschunder, 2017), although, to the best of our knowledge, no previous study has integrated an intergenerational framework in education with a focus on institutional racism.

UNIVERSITY–SCHOOL–COMMUNITY PARTNERSHIPS

University–community engagement is the collaboration and mutually beneficial exchange of knowledge and resources between a university and its immediate community (Kimiecik et al., 2023). The relationship between a university and a community is complex and interdependent (Clifford & Petrescu,

2012). A university's impact on its surrounding community can drive socio-economic transformation, cultural development, and mutual learning opportunities. (Clifford & Petrescu, 2012; Kimiecik et al., 2023). For example, Onyx (2008) analyzed a social capital research program in Australia over 10 years to assess university–community engagement as a catalyst for eliciting knowledge through storytelling. Within university–community engagement, university faculty can be mediators, collaborators, and render independent critical analysis by offering their research expertise, knowledge of literature, and leveraging institutional infrastructure to support broader research within and for the community (Onyx, 2008). However, university administrators tend to view "community" simplistically and often use terms like "volunteer" to describe community members involved in community-based research efforts, devaluing those community members' contributions to research and overlooking the reality that the research would not be possible without community involvement (Beaulieu et al., 2018; Renwick et al., 2020). Given the critical roles that community members have within the university–community relationship, "volunteer" is not a term that adequately describes the extent of their influence (Renwick et al., 2020).

There are many forms of university–community engagement, such as internships, academic service projects, work-based learning, industry placement programs, applied research, organization, community capacity building, student volunteer projects, and collaborations through grants (Clifford & Petrescu, 2012; Onyx, 2008). As university administrators expand the footprint of their institutions, it is imperative that they acknowledge the complex interrelationships between their institutions and the communities in which they are located (Beaulieu et al., 2018) and how the extent to which the land new buildings occupy and the extent to which their faculty and staff play a role in the transformation of a community impact outcomes for better or for worse (Addie & Fraser, 2019; Onyx, 2008).

Participatory Research

Participatory research emphasizes public participation in producing academic knowledge by actively including community members in the research (Barker, 2004). Weerts and Sandmann (2008) conducted a multi-case study that compared patterns of engagement across six research-oriented institutions (three land-grant and three urban institutions) to understand challenges in developing reciprocal university–community relationships. Using the knowledge-flow theory framework, the directionality of knowledge within the partnership was classified as either "one-way" or "two-way." In a one-way flow model, university collaborators perceived communities as commodities and community stakeholders as knowledge consumers, whereas in a two-way model, they viewed the community stakeholders as learning partners (Weerts & Sandmann, 2008).

The findings of Weerts and Sandmann (2008) were complemented by the findings of Clifford and Petrescu (2012), who identified challenges within partnerships on an institutional and interpersonal level. Clifford and Petrescu (2012) identified similar one-way and two-way collaborations but included external factors as a third level of complexity. Both studies found that politics and bureaucracy, power (im)balance, and identity development to be the most common challenges faced when implementing engagement and sustaining university-community partnerships. For example, community members often viewed institutional collaborators as untrustworthy and were skeptical regarding the sincerity of their engagement, especially when they perceived that their engagement was based on self-interest (Weerts & Sandmann, 2008).

Schools at the Convergence

Kimiecik et al. (2023) expanded on the research focused on university–community partnerships to include schools as the convergence of the other two organizations in a case study involving Purdue University, three high schools, and community organizations. According to Kimiecik et al. (2023), university–school–community partnerships differed from traditional university–community partnerships because they provided opportunities for schools to draw on resources from both other two organizations to foster engagement, enrich student learning, and increase collaborative leadership efforts to support youth. In this sense, universities have the potential to contribute to the transformation or revitalization of the communities in which they reside.

Social Justice

Social justice is both a process and a goal involving fighting for equality, equity, and civil democracy across social groups, especially populations often marginalized, underrepresented, and undervalued (Adams et al., 2018; Beaulieu et al., 2018). Beaulieu et al. (2018) construed social justice to be a moral obligation oriented to developing complementary university–school–community relationships. From their perspective, citizenship requires university leadership to merge the roles of scholarly institutions and members of the local community (see also Barker, 2004). If the merging is seamless, the outcomes include mutual enrichment, maximum impact,

36 • A. ALLEN-HANDY et al.

and alignment of the faculty members' research agendas to the community members' needs (see also Weerts & Sandmann, 2008).

Project Team

Our current team of 12 is an intergenerationally diverse community comprising youth, young adults, middle-aged adults, and elders (age range: 18–70 years; see Table 2.1). In 2018, we began our project with seven high school juniors and seniors. In 2021, we received university support through an age-friendly initiative to advocate for generational diversity and intergenerational connectivity through the intersectionality of aging, race, ethnicity, and health disparities. Five older adult alumni of WPHS—one each from the classes of 1969, 1971, and 1986, and two from 1973—officially joined our research team. We recruited participants through our already-established partnership with the WPHS Alumni Association. Our youth and older adult participants have received professional development in participatory heritage archival skills and qualitative research methods. Our project includes scanning and storing artifacts, including collecting yearbooks starting from 1911 for preservation.

We meet weekly to enact our project goals and to engage in meaningful discussions about how we can redefine the identity of traditional preservationists. We address the following critical questions regarding the relationship between archives across generations and power:

TABLE 2.1 Project Participants

Pseudonyms	Age	Race	Gender	Project Role
Jemah	21	Black/AA	female	School Youth and Alumni
Haydee	29	Hispanic/Latina	female	University Graduate Assistant
Isaac	33	Black/AA	male	University Graduate Assistant
Ariana	43	Black/AA	female	University Faculty
Amara	53	Black/AA	female	School Alumni
Brittany	66	Black/AA	male	School Alumni
Richard	67	Black/AA	female	School Alumni
Elizabeth	68	Black/AA	female	School Alumni
Raquel	70	Black/AA	female	School Alumni
Jennifer	18	Black/AA	female	High School Student
Ivan	18	Black/AA	male	High School Student
Samuel	18	Black/AA	male	High School Student

1. What does it mean to redefine the identity of traditional preservationists?
2. What does it mean for the WPHS legacy to persist?
3. What does it mean to disrupt ageism and the traumatic effects of gentrification?

These questions inform our critical participatory action research (cPAR) approach, which posits social change as the outcome of the interaction among broader historical, economic, and sociopolitical contexts (MacDonald, 2012).

THE LESSONS WE LEARNED TOGETHER

Breaking Down Ageist Barriers

When multiple generations participate in cultural preservation efforts, participants can gain increased motivation to participate in preservation activism (Held, 2019; Mammadova, 2017). However, this project has not been without its limitations and challenges. We include reflections from the intergenerational team to capture narratives of our experiences in harnessing school, university, and community energy for collective action. These reflections were drawn from a recorded focus group conducted among the multigenerational project team members. Affording communities myriad opportunities to engage their own agency can support positive interactions among institutions and the community, leading to the building of relationships rooted in mutual respect and ethical care. As trust develops, participants' affection for each other deepens. For example, participants often shared that they enjoyed the intergenerational interactions. One participant shared that they were both impressed and inspired by the team dynamics and many of the team members shared that they saw potential and longevity in the project:

> I'm impressed with the team, looking at this and [the] ages of you . . . and that you are accomplished and achieving so much so early in your lives. You are an inspiration to me, and I would think that the youth that become involved with the project will also be inspired.

Wrestling With Bureaucracy

Challenges related to navigating the bureaucracy of the university and communicating effectively across age differences arose as a recurrent theme in our project. Financially reimbursing our youth and elder team members for the time they committed to the project was an important tenet of reciprocity. Alumni and students were hired through the university as per diem employees; however, to be hired, they needed to apply through the institution, which required a background check, FBI fingerprinting, resume, work permits for the high school students, and references in addition to the online application. Since many of the older adults were retired, and the youth were under the age of 18 in 2018, numerous onboarding requirements were seen as barriers to our intergenerational cultural heritage project. University per diem employees were expected to know how to navigate various online platforms, which was a significant barrier to age-friendly collaborations. Many of our alumni and students had difficulty navigating enterprise software that was not designed to welcome individuals of all technological skill levels. The time reporting systems to submit timesheets for compensation were also so tedious that formal mentorship opportunities were needed during onboarding. To get financially reimbursed for their time, alumni and students had to complete their timesheets online every other Friday, but they found that the system was not designed to welcome users of all levels of technological expertise. As we question what radical solutions can inform a school, university, and community partnership, we continue to examine and criticize the structural systems in place at universities that prevent the effective inclusion of intergenerational school and community partnerships. Despite these barriers, our team members persevered and remained engaged.

Reciprocal Learning: Virtual Literacy and Verbal Communication

Another theme that arose in this university–school–community partnership was the shifting multigenerational team dynamics around verbal and online communication. Interestingly, what the youth modeled technologically for the older adults through digital literacy, the older adults modeled in terms of effective verbal communication through dialogue. As Jarrott et al. (2022) highlighted, the intergenerational programming offers mutual benefits across generations—older adults can learn about technological expertise and younger participants engage in collaborative professional development. As educators, it is critical to understand how communication norms may vary across intersections of age and race as well as across contexts as distinct as education and local communities. In this light, reciprocity across our diverse identities emerged in the form of both hard and soft skills as members learned to navigate different communication and technological literacy norms. At times, the older adults stated that face-to-face communication appeared to be an "arduous task" for our younger

Coming Together as Classmates • **39**

members due to their high dependence on technology, which they contrasted to their ability to form multiple personal connections with classmates. For example, one participant shared:

> What we [older adults] have as a group that I think that y'all [youth] have most of all is...we lack technology, we lack that [virtual] communication—but what we [older adults] have is a personal connection to each other, which allows us to still just like, [Ariana] was saying and me and [Richard] fifty plus years, and in our I mean [Richard] and her classmates makes more than fifty-five going on fifty-five years. (Amara)

Over time, the dynamics between young adults and older adults naturally shifted. Another alumnus commented on the growth he observed in Jemah—one of the younger women in the project:

> Before, we barely got anything out of her. She would be there all the time, but she never really communicated. Now she smiles and talks, and I know she still think I'm crazy. But I like the idea. I see her growing and blossoming and becoming more confident in herself. (Richard)

Jemah began as a high school student involved in the project, graduated in 2020, and began to work while staying involved in the project as a per diem employee. She recently applied and will enroll as an undergraduate student at Drexel in the upcoming school year, pursuing a double major in French and Economics. The transition from her role as high school youth to young adult leader of the project to undergraduate student at the university serves as a prime example of her involvement in the local community, her alma mater, and the university. Her experience and cultural knowledge of the community make her an exceptional leader in bridging university and community members together.

Community Histories and Archivists

Local community members are resilient and skillful in preserving their cultural heritage by regularly exchanging information and collecting obituaries. Despite the barriers to accessing external funding and federal support for the historic preservation of their communities, many residents are proactive in leveraging their community cultural wealth as nontraditional archivists. One older adult shared:

> I have every obituary that my mother ever saved, along with all the funerals and stuff that I've been going to as well, and as I'm looking through it...I'm like, this is a family tree right here. It's like all you know, all my parents, I

40 ▪ A. ALLEN-HANDY et al.

mean like my mother, my grandmother, her mother, and just to show people and my daughter how to keep it kind of going. (Ariana)

Ariana's preservation effort at the family level was grounded in her commitment to include her family legacy as a community strength. She organized obituaries as historical artifacts that were not only of interest to her mother who first collected them, but for the subsequent generations. As an example, she described wanting her daughter to join her in continuing the archival practices. During that exchange, another older adult member realized that long before the creation of this project, she, too, was gathering and documenting history as a community archivist:

I just realized that I have history in my drawer upstairs. Like you say, about people who passed away, I got maybe a hundred obituaries, the funerals I've been to, and I never thought. I'll put that in the drawer, but I can look back and see into my life and the people I knew. (Amara)

Participants continued to highlight stories of one another in the community to highlight the cultural wealth they share with one another. As collaborators from universities and institutions and residents, and community members come together as classmates and neighbors, diverse stakeholders can emulate the value and respect for the local knowledge exchange, just as Elizabeth shared:

Some guy came up to me and said, "Hey I seen your hat!" It's just amazing. As soon as you see the [school] colors, you know right away and it makes me smile. It makes me so happy because, you know, this project has really got people thinking about the West Philly community and school... The people I graduated with in 1971, I mean, they still get together once a month since the pandemic. We meet with different classmates, share information, and have fun. That's how we're trying to preserve the history. (Elizabeth)

In this instance, Elizabeth described people in the community as enthusiastic about preserving their cultural heritage. She leveraged the social capital of her school and community to advocate on behalf of broader efforts to advance social justice and historical preservation efforts.

CONCLUSION

We have highlighted a university–school–community partnership among the members of an educational research lab at a private university and a public high school. As many urban communities are experiencing rapid gentrification and residential displacement, the intergenerational project we described in this paper focused on preserving and restoring the historical artifacts of a school and community. Extant literature highlights the root of university–community partnerships and the benefits and challenges to sustaining a cohesive university–school–community relationship. The energy generated by socially just partnerships can drive educational transformation within communities and schools in which individuals may battle against inequalities. However, when there is an imbalance of power and conflicting objectives within a partnership, challenges may arise that negatively impact the members of the community and affect the members of the most vulnerable populations, including school-aged youth and older adults.

The benefits of our intergenerational heritage project included the ability to employ youth and older adults as university members, provide academic opportunities to co-publish and disseminate research, and build agency by expanding access to skills typically acquired by students at the university level. The most significant challenges we encountered in implementing our project were regarding the bureaucracy of the university. Bureaucratic procedures impacted our ability to compensate our community partners for the time they committed to our project. By contrast, the management of intergenerational differences in perspective among youth and older adults led to participants' developing impressive insights.

Our project serves as a model of a socially just and age-friendly university–school–community partnership based on our blending of CRT and intergenerational responsible leadership theory. Our project fostered intergenerational connectivity as an act of social resistance to the marginalization of histories by means of counter-storytelling that re-centered African American experiences through the effective inclusion of multicultural histories at the intersection of school, community, and university.

We contend that similar partnerships can develop collaborative projects that integrate younger and older adults' perspectives and foster cultural sustainability by preserving the historical documents and archives of the community members. Our multi-year, multigenerational project revealed the existence of strong creative preservationist customs among the members of this African American community. Cultural heritage projects provide an opportunity for university personnel to come together with school and community members to redress social inequities in education through the preservation of counter-stories of the African American experience, as well as helping to (re)define American history based on their collective preservation efforts.

REFERENCES

Adams, M., Blumenfeld, W. J., Catalano, D. C. J., Dejong, K., Hackman, H. W., Hopkins, L. E., Love, B., Peters, M. L., Shlasko, D., & Zuniga, X. (Eds.). (2018). *Readings for diversity and social justice* (4th ed.). Routledge.

Addie, J.-P. D., & Fraser, J. C. (2019). After gentrification: Social mix, settler colonialism, and cruel optimism in the transformation of neighbourhood space. *Antipode, 51*(5), 1369–1394. https://doi.org/10.1111/anti.12572

Allen A., Scott L. M., & Lewis C. W. (2013). Racial microaggressions and African American and Hispanic students in urban schools: A call for culturally affirming education. *Interdisciplinary Journal of Teaching and Learning, 3*, 117–129. https://files.eric.ed.gov/fulltext/EJ1063228.pdf

Allen, J. O. (2016). Ageism as a risk factor for chronic disease. *The Gerontologist, 56*(4), 610–614. https://doi.org/10.1093/geront/gnu158

Allen-Handy, A., Meloche, A., Brown, J., Frazier, A., Escalante, K., Walker, M., Burns, I., Edwards-Chapman, N., Ervin, Q., Thomas, A., Thomas, M., Wortham, I., Bugg, D., Dia, J. (2021). Preserving history for the persistent legacy of our school: A youth-led participatory heritage project. *Preservation, Digital Technology & Culture, 50*(1), 15–29. https://doi.org/10.1515/pdtc-2021-0003

Allen-Handy, A., & Thomas-EL, S. L. (2018). Be(com)ing critical scholars: The emergence of urban youth scholar identities through research and critical civic praxis. *Urban Education, 57*(8), 1450–1481. https://doi.org/10.1177/0042085918814589

Baldwin, J. (2013). *The fire next time* (1st vintage international ed.). Vintage International. (Original work published 1963)

Barker, D. W. M. (2004). The scholarship of engagement: A taxonomy of five emerging practices. *Journal of Higher Education Outreach and Engagement, 9*(2), 123–137.

Beaulieu, M., Breton, M., & Brousselle, A. (2018). Conceptualizing 20 years of engaged scholarship: A scoping review. *PloS one, 13*(2), 1–17. https://doi.org/10.1371/journal.pone.0193201

Bell, D. A. (1980). Brown v. Board of Education and the interest-convergence dilemma. *Harvard Law Review, 93*(3), 518–533. https://doi.org/10.2307/1340546

Brooks, S. L., & Lopez, R. E. (2018). Designing a clinic model for a restorative community justice partnership. *Washington University Journal of Law & Policy, 48*, 139–177.

Caswell, M., Cifor, M., & Ramirez, M. H. (2016). "To suddenly discover yourself existing": Uncovering the impact of community archives. *The American Archivist, 79*(1), 56–81. https://doi.org/10.17723/0360-9081.79.1.56

Clifford, D., & Petrescu, C. (2012). The keys to university–community engagement sustainability. *Nonprofit Management and Leadership, 23*(1), 77–91. https://doi.org/10.1002/nml.21051

Cohen, L., Manion, L., & Morrison, K. (2018). *Research methods in education* (8th ed.). Routledge.

Crenshaw, K. (1994). Demarginalizing the intersection of race and sex: A Black feminist critique of antidiscrimination doctrine, feminist theory, and antiracist politics. In A. M. Jaggar, *Living with contradictions: Controversies in feminist social ethics* (1st ed., pp. 57–80). Routledge.

Creswell, J. W. (2015). *Educational research: Planning, conducting, and evaluating quantitative and qualitative research* (5th ed.). Pearson.

DeCuir, J. T., & Dixson, A. D. (2004). "So, when it comes out, they aren't that surprised that it is there": Using critical race theory as a tool of analysis of race and racism in education. *Educational Researcher, 33*(5), 26–31. https://doi.org/10.3102/0013189X033005026

DeCuir-Gunby, J. T., Chapman, T. K., & Schutz, P. A. (Eds.). (2018). *Understanding critical race research methods and methodologies: Lessons from the field.* Routledge.

Denzin, N. K., Lincoln, Y. S., & Smith, L. T. (2008). *Handbook of critical and indigenous methodologies.* SAGE. https://doi.org/10.4135/9781483385686

García-Vázquez, E., Reddy, L., Arora, P., Crepeau-Hobson, F., Fenning, P., Hatt, C., Hughes, T., Jimerson, S., Malone, C., Minke, K., Radliff, K., Raines, T., Song, S., & Vaillancourt Strobach, K. (2020). School psychology unified antiracism statement and call to action. *School Psychology Review, 49*(3), 209–211. https://doi.org/10.1080/2372966X.2020.1809941

Goldenberg, B. M. (2016). Youth historians in Harlem: An after-school blueprint for history engagement through the historical process. *The Social Studies, 107*(2), 47–67. https://doi.org/10.1080/00377996.2015.1119667

Held, M. B. E. (2019). Decolonizing research paradigms in the context of settler colonialism: An unsettling, mutual, and collaborative effort. *International Journal of Qualitative Methods, 18*, 1–16. https://doi.org/10.1177/1609406918821574

Jarrott, S. E., Leedahl, S. N., Shovali, T. E., De Fries, C., DelPo, A., Estus, E., Gangji, C., Hasche, L., Juris, J., MacInnes, R., Schilz, M., Scrivano, R. M., Steward, A., Taylor, C., & Walker, A. (2022). Intergenerational programming during the pandemic: Transformation during (constantly) changing times. *Journal of Social Issues, 78*(4), 1038–1065. https://doi.org/10.1111/josi.12530

Kendi, I. X. (2019). *How to be an antiracist.* One World.

Kimiecik, C., Gonzalvo, J. D., Cash, S., Goodin, D., & Pastakia, S. (2023). Building a university–school–community partnership to improve adolescent well-being. *Children & Schools, 45*(1), 27–34. https://doi.org/10.1093/cs/cdac029

Ladson-Billings, G. (1998). Just what is critical race theory and what's it doing in a nice field like education? *International Journal of Qualitative Studies in Education, 11*(1), 7–24. https://doi.org/10.1080/095183998236863

Lather, P. (2003). Critical inquiry in qualitative research: Feminist and poststructural perspectives: Science "after truth." In K. B. deMarrais & S. D. Lapan (Eds.), *Foundations for research: Methods of inquiry in education and the social sciences* (pp. 203–216). Taylor & Francis Group. https://doi.org/10.4324/9781410609373

Ledesma, M. C., & Calderón, D. (2015). Critical race theory in education: A review of past literature and a look to the future. *Qualitative inquiry, 21*(3), 206–222. https://doi.org/10.1177/1077800414557825

Li, N. (2016). Whose history, whose memory? A culturally sensitive narrative approach. In M. Page & M. R. Miller (Eds.), *Bending the future: Fifty ideas for the next fifty years of historic preservation in the United States* (pp. 136–139). University of Massachusetts Press. http://www.jstor.org/stable/j.ctt1hd19hg.25

Liew, C. L., Goulding, A., & Nichol, M. (2022). From shoeboxes to shared spaces: Participatory cultural heritage via digital platforms. *Information, Communication & Society, 25*(9), 1293–1310. https://doi.org/10.1080/136911 8X.2020.1851391

MacDonald, C. (2012). Understanding participatory action research: A qualitative research methodology option. *Canadian Journal of Action Research, 13*(2), 34–50. https://doi.org/10.33524/cjar.v13i2.37

Mammadova, A. (2017). Development of fieldwork activities to educate the youth for the biological and cultural preservation in rural communities of Ishikawa Prefecture, Japan. *International Journal of Environmental & Science Education, 12*(3), 441–449.

Marsh, D. G. (2014). *A Lenape among the Quakers: The life of Hannah Freeman.* University of Nebraska Press. https://doi.org/10.2307/j.ctt1d9njd0

Martinson, M., & Minkler, M. (2006). Civic engagement and older adults: A critical perspective. *The Gerontologist, 46*(3), 318–324. https://doi.org/10.1093/geront/46.3.318

Matero, F. (2021). Historic preservation: An American perspective on a professional discipline. *Change Over Time, 10*(1), 2–7. https://doi.org/10.1353/cot.2021.0004

McBride, A. M. (2007). Civic engagement, older adults, and inclusion. *Generations Journal, 30*(4), 66–71. https://www.proquest.com/scholarly-journals/civic-engagement-older-adults-inclusion/docview/212262996/se-2

McCullough, C. R., Datts, K., Allen-Handy, A., Sterin, K., & Escalante, K. (2022). Zip code colonization: Counter-narratives of gentrification's traumatic impact on Philadelphia's Black educational communities. *Journal of Trauma Studies in Education, 1*(3), 23–44.

Onyx, J. (2008). University-Community engagement: What does it mean? *Gateways: International Journal of Community Research and Engagement, 1*(2008), 90–106. https://doi.org/10.5130/ijcre.v1i0.512

Paris, D. (2012). Culturally sustaining pedagogy: A needed change in stance, terminology, and practice. *Educational Researcher, 41*(3), 93–97. https://doi.org/10.3102/0013189X12441244

Phillips, R. G., & Stein, J. M. (2013). An indicator framework for linking historic preservation and community economic development. *Social Indicators Research, 113*(1), 1–15. http://www.jstor.org/stable/24719399

Puaschunder, J. M. (2017). *Global responsible intergenerational leadership: A conceptual framework and implementation guidance for intergenerational fairness.* Vernon Press.

Renwick, K., Selkrig, M., Manathunga, C., & Keamy, R. 'Kim.' (2020). Community engagement is . . . : Revisiting Boyer's model of scholarship. *Higher Education Research & Development, 39*(6), 1232–1246. https://doi.org/10.1080/072943 60.2020.1712680

Roued-Cunliffe, H., & Copeland, A. (Eds.). (2017). *Participatory heritage.* Facet. https://doi.org/10.29085/9781783301256

Schniedewind, N., & Davidson, E. (2014). *Open minds to equality: A sourcebook of learning activities to affirm diversity and promote equity.* Rethinking Schools.

Shilton, K., & Srinivasan, R. (2007). Participatory appraisal and arrangement for multicultural archival collections. *Archivaria, 63*, 87–101. https://archivaria.ca/index.php/archivaria/article/view/13129/14371

Sirdenis, T. K., Harper, G. W., Carrillo, M. D., Jadwin-Cakmak, L., Loveluck, J., Pingel, E. S., Benton, A., Peterson, A., Pollard, R., & Bauermeister, J. A. (2019). Toward sexual health equity for gay, bisexual, and transgender youth: An intergenerational, collaborative, multisector partnerships approach to structural change. *Health Education & Behavior, 46*(1), 88S–99S. https://doi.org/10.1177/1090198119853607

Smith, L. T. (2021). *Decolonizing methodologies: Research and indigenous peoples* (3rd ed.). Zed.

Sulé, V. T., Winkle-Wagner, R., & Maramba, D. C. (2017). Who deserves a seat? Colorblind public opinion of college admissions policy. *Equity & Excellence in Education, 50*(2), 196–208. https://doi.org/10.1080/10665684.2017.1301836

Tuck, E., McKenzie, M., & McCoy, K. (2014). Land education: Indigenous, post-colonial, and decolonizing perspectives on place and environmental education research. *Environmental Education Research, 20*(1), 1–23. https://doi.org/10.1080/13504622.2013.877708

UN Women. (2023, March 1). WeRise app promoting gender equality through gaming. *Africa Renewal.* https://shorturl.at/zFKY9

Uricchio, W. (2009). Moving beyond the artefact: Lessons from participatory culture. In M. van den Boomen, S. Lammes, A.-S. Lehmann, J. Raessens, & M. Tobias Schäfer (Eds.), *Digital material: Tracing new media in everyday life and technology* (pp. 135–146). Amsterdam University Press. https://www.jstor.org/stable/j.ctt46mxjv.12

Wan, W. H., & Antonucci, T. C. (2016). Social exchange theory and aging. In *Encyclopedia of Geropsychology* (pp. 2182–2190). Springer Singapore. https://doi.org/10.1007/978-981-287-082-7_285

Weerts, D. J., & Sandmann, L. R. (2008). Building a two-way street: Challenges and opportunities for community engagement at research universities. *The Review of Higher Education, 32*(1), 73–106. https://doi.org/10.1353/rhe.0.0027

Winkle-Wagner, R., Lee-Johnson, J., & Gaskew, A. (2019). *Critical race theory and qualitative data analysis in education.* Routledge.

Ziegler, A. P. (1974). *Historic preservation in inner city areas: A manual of practice* (1st revised ed.). Ober Park Associates.

SECTION II

FORMAL PARTNERSHIPS

CHAPTER 3

THE DYNAMIC AND RECIPROCAL DIMENSIONS OF AN EQUITY-FOCUSED

Research Practice Partnership

Mary A. Avalos
University of Miami

Wendy Cavendish
University of Miami

Jennifer Murray
Miami-Dade County Public Schools

LaKesha Wilson-Rochelle
Miami-Dade County Public Schools

Jennifer Andreu
Miami-Dade County Public Schools

Justice, Equity, Diversity, and Inclusion in Education, pages 49–68
Copyright © 2024 by Information Age Publishing
www.infoagepub.com
All rights of reproduction in any form reserved.

ABSTRACT

This chapter describes the journey of an emerging RPP as partners set out to explore post-COVID-19 impacts with an explicit focus on advancing equity in a focal middle school. The initial phase of our research collaboration centered the lived experiences of teachers in an urban middle school serving high numbers of Latinx students to identify factors that were and continue to be important for facilitating student and teacher well-being during and post-COVID-19 (American Institutes for Research, 2023). Along with the challenges experienced during the launch of the partnership, navigational strategies that addressed them and led to affordances for the RPP are discussed, with implications from lessons learned concluding the chapter.

Research practice partnerships (RPPs) are long-term, collaborative relationships between researchers and practitioners who share an interest in solutions to problems of practice for improving educational outcomes (Coburn et al., 2014). Many RPPs seek to advance equity for historically marginalized students, which can be challenging in rigidly structured institutions (Donovan, 2013) and today's politicized context (Finnigan, 2023). Although RPPs vary based on goals, composition, research approaches, and funding sources (Farrell et al., 2021, p. iv), RPPs can improve outcomes for persistent problems of practice (e.g., Coburn et al., 2021). Moreover, RPPs focused on equity have the potential to "move entire school systems toward greater equity, reducing disparities related to race and ethnicity, social class, gender and sexual identity, disability status, and other dimensions of inequality" (Farrell et al., 2021, p. 7). One example of an equity focused RPP is the Chicago Alliance for Equity in Computer Science, which seeks equity in computer science education for every student in Chicago Public Schools. In partnership with faculty from local universities, the Chicago Public School's Office of Computer Science personnel meet weekly to discuss priorities and problems related to the project's instructional coaching, professional learning communities, curricula, student demographics, and advanced computer science courses to promote equitable systems at the partnership and district levels (Henrick et al., 2019). These meetings impact decision-making processes by collaboratively identifying issues that can be addressed by the RPP team and discussing study findings. Addressing equity at every stage of the RPP planning and implementation process is critical to support the equitable development and outcomes of partnerships (Henrick et al., 2019).

Our equity focused RPP in Miami Florida, part of the American Institutes for Research COVID-19 Equity in Education (AIR-CEE) project, started in 2019 with funding from the Gates Foundation (which was seeking to support RPPs with a focus on in-depth understandings around COVID-19 impacts on schools and/or youth-centered organizations). This chapter describes the development of our[1] emerging RPP focused on increasing school engagement to foster equitable learning opportunities during the aftermath of COVID-19.[2] Two research questions guided the work of the RPP: (a) "What are urban middle school teachers' perceptions of teaching experiences during and after COVID-19?" and (b) "Moving forward, what suggestions can be gleaned from their experience to (re)build a healthy school environment?" Typically, publications describing the work of RPPs focus on the challenges experienced, leaving many questions around how to come up with strategies and approaches that work well (Coburn & Penuel, 2016; Farrell et al., 2019). Thus, to fill this gap in the literature, along with the challenges, we describe navigational strategies that led to affordances for our RPP with an explicit focus on advancing equity in K–12 schools. The district context situates the emerging RPP's journey, and thereafter we describe what was learned during the first two years utilizing Farrell and colleagues' (2021) four RPP dimensions to frame our work: equity focused goals, the dynamic composition of the RPP team, the navigation of the approach to research, and working within (and around) funding structures. These dimensions have been identified as "essential for the field to address its continued commitment to RPPs" (Farrell et al., 2021, p. 10). We conclude with the extent to which the RPP: (a) met project goals and the conditions that supported or hindered progress; (b) cultivated the development of a range of skills, knowledge, dispositions, and orientations needed to engage in partnership efforts; (c) facilitated learning to inform what institutional transformations are needed to work towards more just futures; and (d) informed operational capacity for RPPs through pursuit of dedicated funding (Farrell et al., 2021). We also provide implications for the field that can move RPPs forward to realize greater levels of equity and systems change and build sustaining partnerships for the long-term relationships needed for future work (Doucet, 2019; Kirkland, 2019).

RPP SETTING AND CONTEXT

Miami-Dade County Public Schools (M-DCPS) is the third largest U.S. school district, with the county's diverse population reflecting the future demographics of many U.S. cities (Krogstad, 2019). With only 6% of students identifying as white (non-Hispanic), an ethnically diverse population makes up the county's public school student demographics. Approximately 73% of children enrolled in M-DCPS benefit from the federally funded Free/Reduced Lunch program (Assessment, Research, and Data Analysis, 2022). About 17% of the student population receives English for speakers of other languages services and 25% receive Exceptional Student Education services (Assessment, Research, and Data Analysis, 2022).

52 ▪ M. A. AVALOS et al.

Before the RPP began, the University of Miami partners, Mary and Wendy, had years of experience teaching in public schools and leading research projects with multiple district partners (although not with the RPP partners). The university partners had worked on numerous projects to foster equity in schools and other youth settings in the areas of language and literacy (Avalos et al., 2022; Avalos & Jones, 2019; Avalos & Secada, 2019; Carlo et al., 2023), responsive professional development for teachers (Avalos & Cavendish, 2023; Cavendish, Barrenechea et al., 2020), facilitating student engagement in special education (Cavendish, Connor, & Perez, 2020; Cavendish et al., 2017; Connor & Cavendish, 2020), and equity focused education policy (Artiles et al., in press; Cavendish et al., 2019; Cavendish & Samson, 2021).

The school district partners, Jennifer M., LaKesha, and Jennifer A., had years of experience working in the district as teachers, school and district administrators. The partnership was initiated through a virtual meeting with multiple district offices and university faculty during the summer of 2021, which provided an introduction between district partners and university partners. This summer introduction was key as university partners reached out in November to request a meeting with Jennifer A., the assistant superintendent of the Office of Educational Equity, Access, and Diversity (OEEAD) about the AIR-CEE RPP opportunity. During this time, the M-DCPS Office of Economic Opportunity had launched OEEAD and district RPP partners (Jen M., & LaKesha) had been hired into their leadership roles to support the work of the OEEAD, which monitors, evaluates, validates, and supports M-DCPS programs and initiatives that provide greater avenues for educational opportunities. In collaboration with Florida's Office of Equal Educational Opportunity, the OEEAD also provides advisory services and information to the school district, schools, parents, students, and community groups on a wide range of topics impacting educational equity on the basis of race, gender, ethnicity, national origin, disability, age, and marital status. The OEEAD assists in monitoring the school district's compliance responsibilities pertaining to educational equity according to Florida legislation (Florida Educational Equity Act, 2011) and other federal legislation relating to equity, access, and diversity in education.

SELECTING A FOCAL SCHOOL SITE

In 2020–2021, the M-DCPS partners had initiated an Equity Walk and Talk project with middle and high school administrators who volunteered to participate; the goal of the Equity Walk and Talk was to augment efforts toward equity during the 2021–2022 school year and beyond. During school site visits, M-DCPS in conjunction with the Intercultural Development

The Dynamic and Reciprocal Dimensions of an Equity-Focused • **53**

Research Association (https://www.idra.org/) visited select schools across the district. The purpose of these visits was to assess school culture and climate from a classroom to campus level to ascertain how the school looks, feels, and sounds while also examining established routines and protocols. The second part of the initiative was an equity training where participants learned how to foster a culture and climate that is reflective and culturally responsive while they examined disproportionality in school discipline at their respective school sites. Administrators engaged in meaningful conversations and learned about the significance of building relationships and a culture of culturally responsive practices. Additionally, the university partners recently led and completed a grant-funded project with over 100 district secondary teachers that included a professional development focus on culturally responsive teaching. Sebastian Middle School (SMS), one of the schools participating in the district Equity Walks, had four teachers who also participated in this university grant project, and we agreed that building on the work with participating grant teachers in culturally responsive instruction would be ideal. The school's administrator who participated in the Equity Walk agreed to have the RPP carry out an exploratory COVID-19 project at her school.

A member of the Magnet Schools of America, winner of the School of Excellence Merit Award, and a Title I school, SMS enrolled approximately 649 students during 2020–2021. According to school-based data released by our M-DCPS partners, the students attending SMS that year identified as Hispanic (95.9%), Black Non-Hispanic (1.5%), and White (2.4%; other less than 1%), with 15.3% receiving services for English language learners and 18% eligible for Exceptional Student Education. The school's established academic goals to ensure academic improvement for all students during the 2021–2022 school year included an increase in achievement in English language arts, mathematics, science, end-of-course assessments, and school-wide acceleration in advanced course work.

COVID-19 PROTOCOLS

When students and teachers left school in March 2020 for spring break, COVID-19 was spreading quickly across the globe; however, not many fathomed the societal impact and more specifically the impact on teaching and learning that was about to occur. Students did not return to in-person learning after spring break and, for the remainder of the 2019–2020 academic year, teachers navigated different ways to teach, learn, and engage students within the reality of COVID-19. Over the 2020 summer months, students recovered course credits during summer school and received extra assistance in high-stakes assessment accountability areas for English and Math. As the

2020–2021 school year approached, the M-DCPS School Board met with health experts and established a plan to "Reopen Smart, Reopen Safe." As part of this initiative all schools would open virtually with remote instruction, referred to as My School Online. M-DCPS was originally scheduled to open on August 19, 2020; however, with a new K–12 learning management platform, the district delayed the opening of schools for one week to give teachers time to acclimate to the system and plan lessons. The extra week was also a time for students and parents to learn the new system and get ready for remote instruction. On August 31, 2020, M-DCPS officially opened for the 2020–2021 school year with remote instruction. During the first two weeks of school, M-DCPS was inundated with infrastructure challenges, including a cyber-attack that prevented any access to the K–12 platform. During the September 9th school board meeting, the board voted to eliminate the use of the K–12 platform. This decision forced teachers and students to scramble to connect using a different virtual meeting platform to continue their online teaching from September 10th until further notice.

Over the next few weeks, district officials engaged in continued communication with local health experts who reevaluated local conditions. While this constant re-evaluation was in the best interest of school personnel, students, and families, it contributed to the uncertainty of day-to-day school operations and made consistent instructional routines difficult to maintain. Political and ideological pressures also exacerbated the situation. During an emergency school board meeting on September 22, the board announced that students would have the option to return to traditional brick and mortar schooling beginning on October 14; however, after this decision, the Florida Department of Education (FLDOE) sent a letter to M-DCPS stating that students must return by October 5th as part of the state-approved reopening plan. The school board met once again and ultimately decided to open schools on October 5th per the FLDOE plan. As not all students returned to school physically on October 5, teachers were required to teach using multiple modes (e.g., face-to-face, online, or dual modality with some students in a physical classroom and others online simultaneously). Only teachers who had district-approved Americans With Disabilities Act (ADA) accommodations were given priority for online instruction when both types of modalities were offered. By the following school year (August 2021), all teachers and staff were expected to return exclusively to brick-and-mortar schools and classrooms to offer students in-person or online instruction. The choice for students' in-person versus online school attendance rested with parents. Teachers who were caregivers for vulnerable family members or who had health conditions were given priority to work remotely; however, ongoing COVID-19 contagion and subsequent required quarantining continued to pose a significant challenge for teaching and learning in schools.

INITIATING AN RPP WITH AN EQUITY FOCUS

Our RPP story begins as the United States was coming out of the COVID-19 pandemic in late Fall 2021. Even though the end of the pandemic was in sight, teachers, administrators, and school personnel continued to pivot and adapt, while school districts continued to make operational decisions with limited infrastructure and resources needed to navigate the changes occurring daily. The varying levels of guidance and lack of resources experienced by school personnel in this district aligns with other urban districts at that time where almost 80% of districts wanted more guidance from the government on how to manage the instructional changes (Vegas, 2020). Notably, the pandemic had profound effects on the well-being of school personnel, which translated to multiple effects on academic outcomes and student well-being (Steiner et al., 2022). The well-being of school personnel reflected an increase in job-related stress, which has been negatively linked with teachers' and principals' physical and mental health (Wolfram et al., 2013), resulting in high levels of absenteeism, turnover, and ultimately, attrition resulting from decisions to leave the teaching profession (Diliberti et al., 2021; Steiner & Woo, 2021). For example, in Florida there were 4,961 teacher vacancies in August 2021 and, by August 2022, that number jumped to 6,006. Understanding the reasons for educator attrition are essential for improving the working conditions in schools (Steiner et al., 2022). Thus, the initial phase of our RPP collaboration centered the lived experiences of teachers in an urban middle school to identify factors that were and continue to be important for facilitating student and teacher well-being during a time of crisis, such as this pandemic (Miami-Dade County Public Schools & University of Miami, 2022).

DEVELOPING EQUITY FOCUSED GOALS

Although the overall effects of COVID-19 were just coming to light at the time our RPP work started, the project's definition of equity related to disproportionate COVID-19 impacts on school personnel, students, and families. Disproportionate impact from disruptions to other social systems, including health care and employment, also compounded challenges in the education arena. Tai et al. (2022) pointed out how the pandemic disproportionately impacted Black, Latinx, and Indigenous Americans with higher rates of hospitalizations and deaths than that experienced by White Americans from the beginning of COVID-19 through 2021. Additionally, beyond the health and mortality impacts, fallout from the pandemic dramatically widened wealth, employment, and housing gaps (OECD, 2022).

Within the context of COVID-19 and the multiple tragic events that led to the Black Lives Matter movement, there was heightened awareness of inequities and a need to work for greater equity and opportunities for all students in the district, particularly Black and Brown students. The timing was right to initiate an RPP with an equity focus and, as RPP team members, our shared mission to seek equity for all students was key in leading us to work together. The RPP partners shared the vision and mission of working toward greater equity for all students in schools and communities disproportionately impacted by COVID-19 as part of their organizations' goals, but more importantly, their personal commitments drove the RPP team's efforts to explore how the pandemic's effect on social systems specifically affected school enrollments and engagement. The disproportionate rate of student absenteeism because of COVID-19 was a matter of equity. M-DCPS had *re-engaged* (i.e., re-enrolled) 98% of returning K–12 students, either in-person or through distance-learning; however, at the time our partners were discussing potential directions for the RPP project, over 2,000 students district-wide were still considered *disengaged* or absent from school on a consistent basis. Per M-DCPS data, the disengaged students were almost exclusively low-income (99.9% free/reduced-price lunch) and nearly half received additional services (e.g., 19% had Exceptional Student Education status, 22% were English Language Learners, and 4% were from migrant, homeless, or foster care families). Apart from academics, many schools offer other supports for students from historically minoritized communities, including meals, consistent structures, and access to peer groups and caring adults (Maier et al., 2017). Since schools provide more than academic learning, our RPP chose to focus on understanding the current levels of student and teacher engagement at SMS with a goal to work towards increasing equity through school enrollment and engagement, while acknowledging the impact of intersecting systems on student access to and engagement in school. As common with many RPPs (Penuel & Gallagher, 2017), we experienced challenges in getting started and carrying out our initial plan. Getting started, what worked well, and how our RPP approached challenges when launching the RPP are described in the next sections.

COMPOSING A DYNAMIC RPP TEAM

Conversations between the university and district partners about the possibility of becoming an AIR-CEE RPP began in November 2021. The goals of the AIR-CEE project are to establish a network of RPPs across the country to learn from COVID-19 and to work toward addressing systemic inequities in schools and communities (American Institutes for Research, 2023). During the initial meeting, the AIR-CEE goals were introduced by Mary and

Wendy, with an invitation to consider forming an equity-focused RPP that could be based on mutual interests across the team. A couple of weeks later, a follow-up meeting confirmed the OEEAD partners' interest in working on the AIR-CEE RPP, and exploratory ideas for possible research foci were presented and discussed.

NAVIGATING THE APPROACH TO RESEARCH

As RPP partners, we agreed to focus on research that would be important for, and if possible, build on work that had been started by the district partners (Farrell et al., 2018). Additionally, it was agreed that the work should inform the district's overall pandemic recovery efforts and contribute to the equity-in-education knowledge base more broadly (Henrick et al., 2017). Beginning with and using a district's perspective to drive the research focus of a new RPP can be seen as a challenge (Booker et al., 2019). However, this approach afforded a collaborative connection to validate all team members' diverse forms of expertise (Henrick et al., 2017), while providing a head start on a focus for the AIR-CEE project that built on previous work by both district and university partners (described above).

Due to COVID-19 protocols, the RPP team met virtually with the school administrator periodically, and in February 2022 the plan for the study was finalized. This was a scaled-back plan for the study due to changes in funding expectations, as described below. The scaled back research plan was to begin with the RPP partners attending a school staff meeting in early April to commence teacher recruitment for interviews that the university partners would carry out and oversee. This timeline would also suffice for the university institutional review board and district office research review processes and approvals. Thus, within the context of existing COVID-19 protocols, it was a combination of the M-DCPS Equity Walks and a previous university grant-related project that the RPP partners used as a springboard to explore engagement in SMS, the focal school.

RPP RESEARCH METHODS

The RPP's research plan was guided by two key research questions: (a) "What are urban middle school teachers' perceptions of teaching experiences during and post-COVID-19?" and (b) "Moving forward, what suggestions can be gleaned from their experience to (re)build a healthy school environment?" An interview guide was developed and after teacher recruitment, a schedule for teacher focus groups was set. The interview guide included open-ended questions related to the broad domains of (a) experiences of events during the initial school proceedings during COVID, (b) perceptions of experiences and engagement returning to school, and (c) personal and/or school efforts to address perceived challenges and strengths. Sample questions included:

- Please tell us about the policies and procedures at your school during COVID and the first year of school shutdowns?
- How were things different this past year?
- What were the major challenges for you?
- What worked well?
- How does your school facilitate/support school engagement?
- What are your priority recommendations for supports/resources/ practices to improve engagement at your school?

After the interviews, the teacher interview/focus group audio files were transcribed verbatim. Qualitative analysis of the transcripts was completed through three levels of coding. This process resulted in 492 open codes. Focused codes were then assigned to identify related concepts across participant responses. A total of 13 focused codes categorized participant response patterns. And finally, four conceptual categories were identified from the focused codes: student well-being; teacher well-being, school environment, and home-school involvement. The teacher perspectives converged around challenges to and recommendations for improving the school environment and home-school involvement in ways that could increase student and teacher well-being.

(Re)Navigating the Approach to Research

Although the research plan was in place and protocols were developed and agreed upon by the RPP team and school, some unexpected challenges and potential hinderances to the project occurred, which is not unusual (Booker et al., 2019). Our research plan required a last-minute change as the SMS administrator decided to accept a new administrative position at a different school in the district. This delayed the proposed April virtual teacher recruitment meeting, which did not take place until early June, during the final faculty meeting of the year, adding to the complexities around teacher recruitment for the project. Understandably, after a difficult year between COVID-19 protocols and regular routines, most teachers were not interested in participating in focus groups and just six of over 30 possible teachers consented to be interviewed. We attempted to involve the new school administrator in planning meetings throughout the year, and the administrator did join our initial meetings; however, after February's meeting, when the study plan was finalized, we noticed the administrator's declining interest in joining our online meetings and her responses to emails were not as timely as they had been initially. In retrospect, this should have signaled a potential issue since two-way communication (Nelson et al., 2015) and key stakeholder participation can prevent problems for partnerships (Klar et al., 2018; Pollock, 2013). Although we were initially disappointed with the study participation rate, the interviews provided a snapshot of the challenges faced by teachers during the year along with their suggestions to improve school culture (Miami-Dade County Public Schools & University of Miami, 2022).

WORKING WITHIN AND AROUND FUNDING STRUCTURES

As noted, in the initial stages of building the RPP, our funding expectations were not met, which required creative thinking and flexibility from both sets of partners and ultimately compelled us to modify the research plan. Commonly cited as a challenge for RPPs, funding (Penuel & Gallagher, 2017) or limited resources (Coburn et al., 2021; Coburn et al., 2014) also became an issue for us. The AIR-CEE provided some initial funding ($5,000) but it was only one-fifth of the amount expected by RPP partners for the project, and we hoped to receive additional funds. Our initial RPP research plan, created with input from all RPP partners, was a two-phase research plan focused on the use of participatory research methods (Cornwall & Jewkes, 1995) in order to (a) better understand pre- and post-COVID-19 changes in specific metrics available through the AIR-CEE asset maps (see https://cee-asset-maps-air-esri.hub.arcgis.com/) to identify areas for local improvement and action, and (b) relay the lived experiences of local families, students, and school personnel. We wanted to explore COVID-19 impacts among a sample population of SMS administrators, teachers, counselors, aides, and staff with a specific focus on sixth grade dis-engaged students and families. As noted in Figure 3.1, this initial plan included a long-term partnership with community-engaged research methods to guide systems change (Fullan, 2020) at the focal school with problem-solving by school personnel (phase two of the project) based on the input gathered from students and families in phase one. When the funding did not materialize, all RPP partners brainstormed and revised the proposal to scale back the plan to instead focus on data collection from school personnel, students, and families (revised phase one), but that scaled back funding did not come through either. To complete the study by the end of the academic year, we decided we should initiate some part of the plan and so we agreed to focus solely on teacher perspectives of student engagement using the $5,000 AIR-CEE funds (revised, final plan two). This would potentially provide insights into the surfacing concerns about the condition of post-pandemic teacher and student engagement and well-being

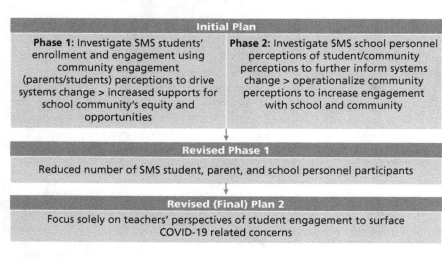

Figure 3.1 Evolving RPP plan.

that M-DCPS schools and districts across the country were experiencing (Irwin et al., 2023; Steiner & Woo, 2021).

The decision to move forward with a focus on teachers allowed the RPP team to create and then share a summary of teacher perspectives with the new school administrator. This positioned the RPP for a follow-up study as an additional $5,000 was received from the AIR-CEE RPP Network in December 2022. The follow-up study (currently in-progress at the time of writing this chapter) will report the new administrator's and additional teachers' perceptions of what worked during 2022–2023 to create shifts, if any, to the SMS culture, teacher and student well-being, and student engagement one year later, post-pandemic. Consequently, the RPP team learned that working with limited resources may require difficult decisions, but we remained hopeful that our continuing partnership may lead to more resources for future RPP work.

DISCUSSION AND IMPLICATIONS

Emerging RPPs face numerous challenges that can make or break the partnership (Booker et al., 2019; Farrell et al., 2019). The previous section provided an overview of our RPP's journey to report what worked well and how challenges were addressed. Here, we offer some future implications based on the extent to which our RPP (a) met project goals, with a consideration of the conditions that supported or hindered progress; (b) cultivated the development of a range of skills, knowledge, dispositions, and orientations needed to engage in partnership efforts; (c) facilitated learning to inform what institutional transformations are needed to work towards more just

The Dynamic and Reciprocal Dimensions of an Equity-Focused • **61**

futures; and d) informed operational capacity for RPPs through pursuit of dedicated funding (Farrell et al., 2021).

Adapting Project Goals

The administrative changes and unmet funding expectations were difficult hurdles faced at the RPP implementation stage; however, these issues served to bring the RPP team closer as we collaborated "alongside" one another to "jointly reflect" and problem-solve for "timely and relevant research findings" (Farrell et al., 2021, pp. 6, 7). As noted, additional funding was needed to carry out the initial two-phase plan for the RPP research study. Even though the RPP carried out a smaller project than originally proposed, we were able to overcome the limited resources by continually returning to the drawing board to discuss new versions of the plan. The collaborative decision-making also guarded against power imbalances and further built trust among partners (Henrick et al., 2017). Further, initially building on a common interest and previous equity work that was important for all the RPP partners and the district, we met the project 's objective of informing the school, district, and broader knowledge base of teachers' perspectives and suggestions for improving school-level engagement and well-being post-COVID-19.

(Re)Engaging in Partnership Efforts

Although differing dispositions and unequal power dynamics can be problematic within and across RPPs (Penuel et al., 2015), we did not experience this as the team valued and respected each other's contributions to planning for implementing the RPP. Moreover, the partners' ability to work closely—building on their respective strengths initially and eventually working across traditional roles (e.g., as researchers and practitioners)—facilitated the development of a range of skills and knowledge for all partners. The dynamic composition of the RPP team, as well as the willingness to work within (and around) funding structures, allowed for cultivating the development of a range of skills, knowledge, dispositions, and orientations for the team members. Further, by crossing traditional researcher and practitioner boundaries and working closely to solve problems, the emerging RPP benefitted from different perspectives to inform next steps (Henrick et al., 2017; Schenke et al., 2017) and move the work forward.

Learning for More Just Futures

The varied knowledge and lived experiences, skills, dispositions, and orientations across team members were helpful to begin the partnership;

however, the team's aligned mission for the project's equity focus was key. Meeting the project objectives for the third iteration of our study plan was achieved by flexibly navigating the research design and approach while working with the limited resources available. By scaling down the proposed study, the team was still able to disseminate potential institutional transformations to work towards school engagement and teacher well-being, which ultimately may lead to greater student well-being (Steiner et al., 2022). The teams' depth of experience working with other partners in various settings, as well as an aligned vision for equity, contributed to collegial dispositions conducive for building capacity across partnership roles to be "good partners" (Penuel & Gallagher, 2017, p. 13). Working within the project's changing funding structures informed operational capacity but also served to build trust among RPP partners and supported interactions that leveled up the RPP's relationships as we worked collaboratively to problem-solve our funding challenges.

Informing Operational Capacity

The Equity Walk and Talk project started by the district and the university's equity focused grant-funded project provided a common equity goal for the RPP, increasing cultural responsivity and student engagement in schools. This common equity focus was key because it promoted buy-in as the RPP built on and expanded previous work that team members already deemed important. As explained above, the crossing of role boundaries to problem-solve fulfilled the needs of the RPP to keep the work moving forward; however, the team members' distinct roles as district administrators and researchers were needed, as well, to complete the study and report findings, which afforded a deeper understanding COVID-19's impacts at the school level. This deeper understanding would not have been possible without the district partners facilitating access to the school and participating teachers for the study or the university partners using confidential and anonymous research methods. To be exemplary partners, we found it important to move in and out of the traditional practitioner and researcher roles (Penuel et al., 2015) for building capacity among team members and meet project goals and objectives.

CONCLUSION

To conclude, this chapter describes dynamic and reciprocal dimensions while launching an equity focused RPP and, specifically, what worked well and how we overcame challenges. The top half of Figure 3.2 shows Farrell and colleagues' (2021) four dimensions and important outcomes that were used to frame our journey. The bottom half of Figure 3.2 includes primary

The Dynamic and Reciprocal Dimensions of an Equity-Focused • 63

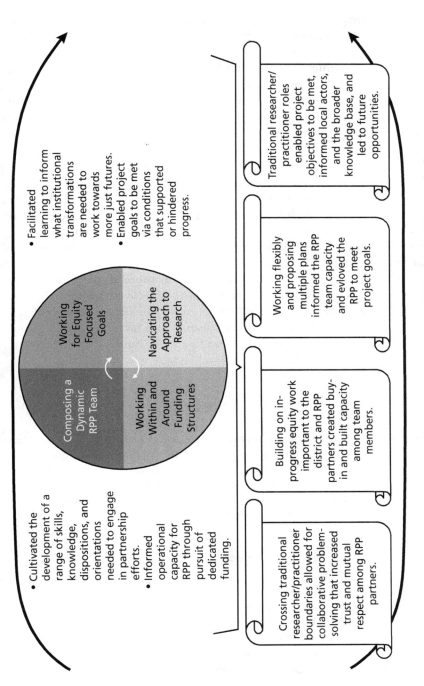

Figure 3.2 Key implications from launching and carrying out an emerging RPP project with an equity focus.

learning points or implications from our work that resulted from reflecting on Farrell and colleagues' (2021) framework. Two encompassing arrows surround the figure since the framework and outcomes worked in concert with the implications to successfully launch the RPP. Primarily, we learned about the importance of crossing traditional role boundaries to build trust and mutual respect among partners in an emerging RPP (Farrell et al., 2018; Henrick et al., 2017). Also, the shared interest for the common equity research focus that built on previous work enabled RPP team members' buy-in, while informing school actors, the district, and broader knowledge base concerning pandemic recovery efforts. Working flexibly and meeting often through the challenges related to changes in funding and school administration necessitated multiple versions of the research plan. Although we found ourselves role-crossing to solve project roadblocks, we relied on and utilized our traditional RPP roles to effectively carry out the project. Our initial study's findings provided suggestions that could improve and inform school culture practices and well-being for greater teacher and student engagement in schools, locally as well as more broadly. By working together to meet the RPP 's (scaled down) objectives, additional (albeit limited) resources were awarded to continue this project a second year, which will further inform the school, district, and broader audience about school engagement and hopefully lead to greater funding to continue our overarching goal of seeking systems-level change.

NOTES

1. Two university Teaching and Learning department faculty (Wendy and Mary) and three district administrators from the Office of Educational Equity, Access, and Diversity (Jennifer M., Jennifer A., and LaKesha) make up the RPP team.
2. RPP supported by the American Institutes for Research, COVID-19 Equity in Education: Longitudinal Deep Dive Project (https://www.air.org/covid-19-and-equity-education-longitudinal-deep-dive)

REFERENCES

American Institutes for Research. (2023). *The COVID-19 and equity in education research-practice partnership network.*

Artiles, A., Cavendish, W., Gamboa-Zapatel, D., & Cabelleros, M. Z. (in press). Disrupting the cultural historical geographies of inclusive education: Notes for (re)framing policy research on disability intersections with "other" identities. In P. Young (Ed.), *Handbook of education policy research.* American Educational Research Association and Routledge.

The Dynamic and Reciprocal Dimensions of an Equity-Focused • **65**

Assessment, Research, and Data Analysis. (2022). *Statistical highlights 2021–2022.* Miami-Dade County Public Schools. https://arda.dadeschools.net/#!/right Column/2102

Avalos, M. A., Brown, M., Schreiner, N., Ghulman, S., Radjocic, S., Deroo, M., Perez, D., & Kibler, K. (2022, November 29–December 3). *Highlighted presentation: Exploring access and opportunity to critical STEM literacies for underrepresented and historically marginalized adolescents* [Conference session]. Literacy Research Association Annual Meeting, Phoenix, AZ.

Avalos, M. A., & Cavendish, W. (2023, April 13–16). *Fostering classroom-level engagement for culturally and linguistically diverse students* [Paper presentation]. Annual meeting of the American Educational Research Association, Chicago, IL.

Avalos, M. A., & Jones, L. D. (2019). Facilitating diverse students' discourse during mathematics discussions: What does teacher talk have to do with it? In P. Spycher & E. Haynes (Eds.), *Culturally and linguistically diverse learners and STEAM: Teachers and researchers working in partnership to build a better tomorrow* (pp. 291–312). Information Age Publishing.

Avalos, M. A., & Secada, W. G. (2019). Linguistically responsive mathematics teaching to foster ELL engagement, reasoning, and discourse. In L. C. de Oliveira, K. Obenchain, R. Kenney, & A. Oliveira (Eds.), *Approaches to teaching the content areas to English language learners in secondary schools* (pp. 165–179). Springer.

Booker, L., Conaway, C., & Schwartz, N. (2019). *Five ways RPPs can fail and how to avoid them: Applying conceptual frameworks to improve RPPs.* William T. Grant Foundation. https://wtgrantfoundation.org/five-ways-rpps-can-fail-and-how -to-avoid-them-applying-conceptual-frameworks-to-improve-rpps

Carlo, M. S., Avalos, M. A., Williams, J., Anthony, J., & Pham, T. (2023, March 23–25). *Effects of Spanish and English definition supports on a word-knowledge application task among 4th grade Spanish-English bilinguals* [Poster presentation]. Biennual meeting of the Society for Research in Child Development, Salt Lake City, UT.

Cavendish, W., Barrenechea, I., Young, A., Díaz, E., & Avalos, M. A. (2020). Urban teachers' perspectives of strengths and needs: The promise of teacher responsive professional development. *The Urban Review.* Advance online publication. https://doi.org/10.1007/s11256-020-00569-9

Cavendish, W., Connor, D., Gonzalez, T., Jean-Pierre, P., & Card, K. (2019). Troubling "the problem" of racial overrepresentation in special education: A commentary and call to rethink research. *Educational Review, 72*(5), 567–582. https://doi.org/10.1080/00131911.2018.1550055

Cavendish, W., Connor, D., & Perez, D. (2020). Choice, support, opportunity: Profiles of self-determination in high school students with learning disabilities. *Learning Disabilities: A Multidisciplinary Journal, 25*(2).

Cavendish, W., Marquez, A., Roberts, M., Suarez, K., & Lima, W. (2017). Student engagement in high-stakes accountability urban schools. *Perspectives on Urban Education, 14,* 1–4.

Cavendish, W., & Samson, J. (Eds.). (2021). *Intersectionality in education: Toward more equitable policy, research, and practice.* Teachers College Press.

Coburn, C. E., & Penuel, W. R. (2016). Research-practice partnerships in education: Outcomes, dynamics, and open questions. *Educational Researcher, 45*(1), 48–54. https://doi.org/10.3102/0013189x16631750

Coburn, C. E., Penuel, W. R., & Farrell, C. C. (2021). Fostering educational improvement with research-practice partnerships. *Phi Delta Kappan, 102*(7), 14–19. https://doi.org/10.1177/00317217211007332

Coburn, C. E., Penuel, W. R., & Geil, K. (2014, February). *Research-practice partnerships at the district level: A new strategy for leveraging research for educational improvement.* William T. Grant Foundation. https://wtgrantfoundation.org/resource/research-practice-partnerships-at-the-district-level-a-new-strategy-for-leveraging-research-for-educational-improvement

Connor, D., & Cavendish, W. (2020). "Sit in my seat": Perspectives of students with learning disabilities about teacher effectiveness in high school inclusive classrooms. *International Journal of Inclusive Education, 24*(3), 288–309. https://doi.org/10.1080/13603116.2018.1459888

Cornwall, A., & Jewkes, R. (1995). What is participatory research? *Social Science & Medicine, 41*(12), 1667–1676. https://doi.org/10.1016/0277-9536(95)00127-S

Diliberti, M. K., Schwartz, H. L., & Grant, D. (2021). *Stress topped the reasons why public school teachers quit, even before COVID-19* (Document no. RR-A1121-2). RAND Corporation. https://www.rand.org/pubs/research_reports/RRA1121-2.html

Donovan, M. S. (2013). Generating improvement through research and development in educational systems. *Science, 340*(6130), 317–319. https://doi.org/10.1126/science.1236180

Doucet, F. (2019). *Centering the margins: (Re)defining useful research evidence through critical perspectives.* William T. Grant Foundation. https://eric.ed.gov/?id=ED609713

Farrell, C. C., Coburn, C. E., & Chong, S. (2019). Under what conditions do school districts learn from external partners? The role of absorptive capacity. *American Educational Research Journal, 56*(3), 955–994. https://doi.org/10.3102/0002831218808219

Farrell, C. C., Davidson, K. L., Repko-Erwin, M., Penuel, W. R., Quantz, M., Wong, H., Riedy, R., & Brink, Z. (2018, July). *A descriptive study of the IES researcher-practitioner partnerships in education research program: Final report* (Technical Report No. 3). National Center for Research in Policy and Practice. https://eric.ed.gov/?id=ED599980

Farrell, C. C., Penuel, W. R., Coburn, C., Daniel, J., & Steup, L. (2021). *Research-practice partnerships in education: The state of the field.* William T. Grant Foundation. https://wtgrantfoundation.org/research-practice-partnerships-in-education-the-state-of-the-field

Finnigan, K. S. (2023). The political and social contexts of research evidence use in partnerships. *Educational Policy, 37*(1), 147–169. https://doi.org/10.1177/08959048221138454

Florida Educational Equity Act, Fla. Stat. § 1000.05 (2011). https://www.flsenate.gov/Laws/Statutes/2011/1000.05

Fullan, M. (2020). Systems change in education. *American Journal of Education, 126*(4), 653–663. https://doi.org/10.1086/709975

Henrick, E. C., Cobb, P., Penuel, W. R., Jackson, K., & Clark, T. (2017). *Assessing research practice partnerships: Five dimensions of effectiveness.* William T. Grant Foundation. https://wtgrantfoundation.org/new-report-assessing-research-practice-partnerships-five-dimensions-effectiveness

The Dynamic and Reciprocal Dimensions of an Equity-Focused • **67**

Henrick, E., McGee, S., & Penuel, W. (2019). Attending to issues of equity in evaluating research-practice partnership outcomes. *NNERPP/EXTRA, 1*(3), 8–13. http://nnerppextra.rice.edu/attending-to-issues-of-equity-in-evaluating-rpps/

Irwin, V., Wang, K., Tezil, T., Zhang, J., Filbey, A., Jung, J., Bullock Mann, F., Dilig, R., & Parker, S. (2023, May). *Report on the condition of education 2023* (NCES 2023-144). U.S. Department of Education, Institute of Education Sciences, National Center for Education Statistics. https://nces.ed.gov/pubsearch/pubsinfo.asp?pubid=2023144rev

Kirkland, D. (2019). No small matters: Reimagining the use of research evidence from a racial justice perspective. *The Digest, 2019*(5). https://wtgrantfoundation.org/digest/no-small-matters-reimagining-the-use-of-research-evidence-from-a-racial-justice-perspective

Klar, H., Huggins, K. S., Buskey, F. C., Desmangles, J. K., & Phelps-Ward, R. J. (2018). Developing social capital for collaboration in a research-practice partnership. *Journal of Professional Capital and Community, 3*(4), 287–305. https://doi.org/10.1108/jpcc-01-2018-0005

Krogstad, J. M. (2019, July 31). *A view of the nation's future through kindergarten demographics.* Pew Research Center. https://pewrsr.ch/2MuOI6D

Maier, A., Daniel, J., Oakes, J., & Lam, L. (2017). *Community schools as an effective school improvement strategy: A review of the evidence.* Learning Policy Institute. https://learningpolicyinstitute.org/product/community-schools-effective-school-improvement-report

Miami-Dade County Public Schools & University of Miami. (2022). *Teachers' perceptions of how to (re)build school community well-being in the aftermath of COVID-19.* American Institutes for Research, The COVID-19 and Equity in Education Research-Practice Partnership Network. https://www.air.org/sites/default/files/2023-10/CEE-RPP-Miami%20Dade-University-of-Miami-Teacher-Perceptions-Handout-3pg-Oct-2023.pdf

Nelson, I. A., London, R. A., & Strobel, K. R. (2015). Reinventing the role of the university researcher. *Educational Researcher, 44*(1), 17–26. https://doi.org/10.3102/0013189X15570387

OECD. (2022, March 17). *The unequal impact of COVID-19: A spotlight on frontline workers, migrants and racial/ethnic minorities.* OECD Policy Responses to Coronavirus (COVID-19). https://www.oecd.org/coronavirus/policy-responses/the-unequal-impact-of-covid-19-a-spotlight-on-frontline-workers-migrants-and-racial-ethnic-minorities-f36e931e/#contact-d4e1852

Penuel, W. R., Allen, A. R., Coburn, C. E., & Farrell, C. (2015). Conceptualizing research-practice partnerships as joint work at boundaries. *Journal of Education for Students Placed at Risk, 20*(1/2), 182–197. https://doi.org/10.1080/10824669.2014.988334

Penuel, W. R., & Gallagher, D. J. (2017). *Creating research practice partnerships in education.* Harvard Education Press.

Pollock., M. (2013). It takes a network to raise a child: Improving the communication infrastructure of public education to enable community cooperation in young people's success. *Teachers College Record, 115*(7), 1–28. https://doi.org/10.1177/016146811311500704

68 ▪ M. A. AVALOS et al.

Schenke, W., Van Driel, J., Geijsel, F. P., & Volman, M. L. L. (2017). Boundary crossing in R&D projects in schools: Learning through cross-professional collaboration. *Teachers College Record, 119*(4), 1–42. https://doi.org/10.1177/016146811711900402

Steiner, E. D., Doan, S., Woo, A., Gittens, A. D., Lawrence, R. A., Berdie, L., Wolfe, R. L., Greer, L., & Schwartz, H. L. (2022). *Restoring teacher and principal well-being is an essential step for rebuilding schools: Findings from the state of the American teacher and state of the American principal surveys* (Document no. RR-A1108-4). RAND Corporation. https://www.rand.org/pubs/research_reports/RRA1108-4.html

Steiner, E. D., & Woo, A. (2021). *Job-related stress threatens the teacher supply: Key findings from the 2021 state of the U.S. teacher survey* (https://doi.org/10.3109/10253890.2012.683465; Document no. RR-A1108-1). RAND Corporation. https://www.rand.org/pubs/research_reports/RRA1108-1.html

Tai, D. B. G., Sia, I. G., Doubeni, C. A., & Wieland, M. L. (2022). Disproportionate impact of COVID-19 on racial and ethnic minority groups in the United States: A 2021 update. *Journal of racial and ethnic health disparities, 9*(6), 2334–2339. https://doi.org/10.1007/s40615-021-01170-w

Vegas, E. (2020). *School closures, government responses, and learning inequality around the world during COVID-19*. Brookings. https://www.brookings.edu/research/school-closures-government-responses-and-learning-inequality-around-the-world-during-covid-19/

Wolfram, M., Bellingrath, S., Feurhahn, N., & Kudielka, B. M. (2013). Emotional exhaustion and overcommitment to work are differently associated with hypothalamus-pituitary adrenal (HPA) axis responses to low-dose $ACTH_{1-24}$ 0(Synacthen) and dexametasone–CRH test in healthy school teachers. *Stress, 16*(1), 54–64. https://doi.org/10.3109/10253890.2012.683465

CHAPTER 4

PRACTICING EQUITY IN RESEARCH–PRACTICE–POLICY PARTNERSHIPS

Case of Illinois

Heather E. Price
Loyola University Chicago

Malik S. Henfield
Loyola University Chicago

Eilene Edejer
Loyola University Chicago

Ken Fujimoto
Loyola University Chicago

ABSTRACT

If we want our education research to work toward just outcomes, it is essential
to work with practitioners and policymakers throughout the research process

Justice, Equity, Diversity, and Inclusion in Education, pages 69–90
Copyright © 2024 by Information Age Publishing
www.infoagepub.com
All rights of reproduction in any form reserved.

as partners in the research (Price, 2021). Working as a collaborative team early and involving partners often during the research process may revise the scope a purely academic study (Price, 2021), but the result will be quality research integrated into policy and practice from the outset (Coburn & Penuel, 2016; Coburn et al., 2013; Snow, 2015) that has the potential to improve opportunities for children. This collaborative process maximizes the chance that educational research will be heard by the policymaking community because they are invested stakeholders in the projects, not just receivers of the information. Genuinely involving practitioners in the process also enhances the likelihood of the uptake of policy into practice. We discuss a descriptive case study using repeated participant observation analysis to illustrate how the principles of diversity, equity, and inclusion (DEI) integrated with the structure of a research–practice–policy partnerships (RPPP) to establish strong inter-organizational relationships that harnessed change systems to advance educational equity.

While there exists a corpus of publication on the *prospects* of research–practice partnerships (RPPs), few authors have published on the relational growth that occurs during the building of a relationship among researchers, practitioners, and policymakers as well as the establishment of trust that is critical for any RPP to develop into a fully functional relationship. Moreover, most RPPs focus on the practitioner–researcher relationship and the policymakers are left aside (Cooper et al., 2021). However, in education, policymakers are essential as system implementers—from local policymakers who are school principals and superintendents to policymakers who sit in the state education departments. In this case study, we discuss a partnership formed to pilot statewide equity metrics using the tenets of diversity, equity, and inclusion (DEI) as three cornerstones of research–practice–policy partnerships (RPPP). We refine our focus further by highlighting the parts played by (a) democratizing research–practice–*policymaker* partnerships, (b) practicing DEI principles to build and improve RPPP work, and (c) stressing open and frequent communication for alignment and effectiveness.

Important relational growth among the participants both within and beyond the boundaries of the three sectors of practice, policymaking, and research occurs when the partners work together. In our case study, we discuss the overall design and structure of an RPPP, how it collaboratively developed, how it embraced and modeled DEI principles, and how communication was central to its success.

CORNERSTONES OF DEI

Cornerstones mark the parameters of a building and establish the foundation upon which to build. Approaching RPPPs with the cornerstones of diversity, equity, and inclusion establishes a strong foundation that balances power and positionality, and facilitates the building of trusted, reliable partnerships.

Principles of DEI

Diversity, equity, and inclusion are essential principles that foster a culture of acceptance, respect, and fairness in various social contexts. Diversity emphasizes, recognizes, and celebrates individual differences, including but not limited to race, ethnicity, gender, age, sexual orientation, and ability. By embracing diversity, individuals and organizations can gain access to a range of perspectives and experiences as well as foster creativity, innovation, and better decision-making (Nishii, 2013).

Equity is another crucial principle of DEI that focuses on addressing and eliminating systemic barriers and biases that lead to unequal opportunities and outcomes for individuals. It emphasizes the fair distribution of resources, rights, and privileges. It aims to ensure that everyone has access to the same opportunities and treatment, regardless of their background or identity, as well as providing supports to rectify historical and societal disadvantages incurred by groups who were marginalized (Thomas & Plaut, 2008). Organizations can promote equity by implementing inclusive policies, ensuring fair compensation and benefits, and offering wide access to opportunities for career advancement (Rynes et al., 2012).

Inclusion is the third principle of DEI, emphasizing the creation of environments where all individuals feel welcomed, respected, and valued. It goes beyond mere representation and actively involves individuals from diverse backgrounds in decision-making processes to ensure their voices are heard and considered. Inclusive environments foster a sense of belonging and psychological safety, enabling individuals to contribute fully their unique perspectives and talents (Kalev et al., 2006). By enacting inclusive practices, organizations can enhance employee engagement, satisfaction, and productivity, leading to positive outcomes for individuals and the organization (McLeod et al., 1996).

DEI in Schooling

Educators play a crucial role in implementing DEI through instructional practices, curriculum design, and classroom environments. Educators can implement DEI by incorporating culturally responsive teaching strategies into their instructional practices. Culturally responsive teaching emphasizes the integration of students' cultural backgrounds, experiences, and perspectives into the curriculum, instructional materials, and classroom discussions (Ladson-Billings, 1994). This approach helps students see themselves reflected in the curriculum and creates opportunities for meaningful connections between their lives and what they are learning (Gay, 2010). Educators can also implement DEI by critically examining and revising the curriculum to ensure it includes diverse voices, experiences, and histories (Banks, 2013). By incorporating diverse perspectives, educators promote a more inclusive and comprehensive understanding of various cultures, identities, and social issues, fostering an appreciation for all students' backgrounds and experiences.

Educators also implement DEI by creating inclusive classroom environments that promote equity and respect for all students. This includes establishing classroom norms that encourage open dialogue, active listening, and mutual respect among students (Cohen et al., 2009). Educators can also implement restorative justice practices to address conflicts and discipline issues in a way that promotes understanding, healing, and growth, rather than implementing punitive measures (Gregory et al., 2016). Furthermore, educators can collaborate with families, community members, and other stakeholders to create a sense of belonging and ensure that diverse perspectives and voices are valued and included in decision-making processes (Gorski & Zenkov, 2011). By fostering inclusive classroom environments and engaging in collaborative efforts, educators contribute to the overall culture of equity, inclusion, and respect in schools and districts.

Educators often learn DEI practices through various professional development opportunities and resources. To build their knowledge, skills, and awareness, formal professional development (PD) workshops, seminars, and training sessions are used to enhance educators' understanding of DEI issues and strategies for promoting inclusion in educational settings (Banks & McGee Banks, 2019). These PDs may cover topics such as implicit bias, culturally responsive teaching, inclusive curriculum design, and creating welcoming, safe learning environments (Cochran-Smith et al., 2015). Additionally, educators can access a wide range of resources, including books, articles, online courses, and webinars that offer insights and best practices related to DEI in education.

Educators also learn informally about DEI through collaboration and dialogue with colleagues, students, families, community members, and others (see Figure 4.1). Engaging in conversations about DEI allows educators to gain multiple perspectives and insights, challenging their assumptions and broadening their understanding (Ladson-Billings, 2014).

Collaborative initiatives, such as professional learning communities and diversity committees, provide spaces for educators to engage in critical discussions, share resources, and develop strategies to enhance equity and inclusion in their classrooms and schools. Educators can also learn from their students by actively listening to their experiences, perspectives, and

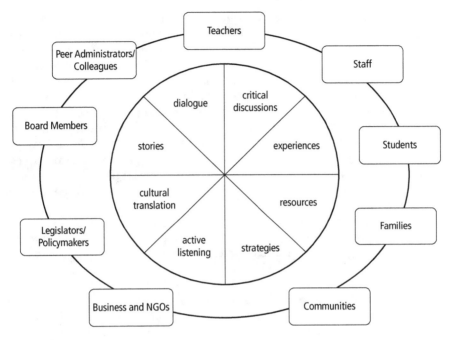

Figure 4.1 DEI multi-voice learning.

cultural backgrounds. Creating opportunities for students to share their stories and engage in meaningful dialogue can deepen educators' understanding of diversity and help them tailor their instructional practices to meet students' unique needs (Villegas & Lucas, 2002). By actively seeking out these learning opportunities and engaging in reflective practices, educators can grow continually in their understanding and application of DEI principles in their teaching practice. Less studied is how DEI is practiced between educators in their non-teaching professional work. As such, we pull from research on organizations to discuss the potential impact of DEI among professionals.

DEI in Work Teams

Ensuring that diversity, equity, and inclusion are taken into account in the composition of work teams can enhance their effectiveness and outcomes. When teams are diverse in terms of race, ethnicity, gender, age, ability, and other dimensions, they bring a wealth of perspectives, experiences, and knowledge to the table (Milliken & Martins, 1996). This diversity of viewpoints fosters creativity, innovation, and problem-solving, as team members can draw upon their unique backgrounds and insights to generate new ideas and approaches (Homan et al., 2008). Diverse teams also consider a wider range of alternatives, resulting in less erroneous decision-making and stronger problem-solving outcomes (Homan et al., 2008).

Equity plays a crucial role in facilitating teamwork by ensuring that all team members can contribute and participate. When equity exists on a team, members sense fairness and trust which enhances their contributions (Canning et al., 2020). The existence of equity increases engagement and commitment to the goals of the team and fosters collaboration and cooperation among team members (Harrison et al., 2002). Equitable practices also mitigate power imbalances and reduce superficial participation since team members perceive their efforts as valued, recognized, and genuinely considered (Canning et al., 2020).

Inclusion is a critical factor in team dynamics because it creates an environment where all team members feel respected, welcomed, and heard in decision-making processes. Inclusive teams provide a psychologically safe space for individuals to express their opinions, ask questions, and challenge the status quo (Edmondson, 1999). This leads to open communication, trust, and a sense of belonging among team members (Nembhard & Edmondson, 2006). Inclusive teams also benefit from increased information sharing and knowledge exchange since team members are more likely to contribute their unique perspectives and expertise (Martins et al., 2004). Consequently, inclusive teams are better equipped to solve complex problems, adapt to change, and achieve high-performance outcomes (Edmondson, 2012).

Practicing DEI enhances interactions, cooperation, and effectiveness among representatives from organizational partners. When organizational leaders prioritize diversity among the representatives in their partnership activities, they create opportunities to bring together a wealth of ideas, expertise, and resources, and facilitate innovation and creativity in problem-solving. By engaging with diverse partners, organizational representatives can develop more comprehensive and inclusive solutions that address the needs of many more constituents (Acharya et al., 2009). Equitable treatment ensures that resources, responsibilities, and benefits are distributed fairly among partner organizations thus fostering a sense of ownership and commitment among the personnel to the goals of the partnership. When organizational partners are treated equitably, it creates an atmosphere of fairness and trust, and establishes a solid foundation for collaboration and cooperation. Inclusive partnerships value and respect the perspectives shared by the representatives of the partner organizations. Creating a safe space for open dialogue among representatives so that differences are acknowledged and leveraged to drive joint decision-making and problem-solving (Canning et al., 2020) gives rise to enhanced outcomes. By embracing

DEI, leaders of organizations can build strong, collaborative partnerships that leverage the strengths and contributions of all involved parties, leading to increased innovation, shared learning, and overall partnership success.

RESEARCH–PRACTICE–POLICY PARTNERSHIP PRACTICES

Research–practice–policy partnerships (RPPPs) are one form of inter-organizational partnership common to education sector work. RPPPs are not sequential where the researcher is the source of knowledge who sends information to the practitioner as a receiver and implementer (Bryk et al., 2015). RPPPs are also not transactional as is common in technical assistance projects where a leader of a policy or practitioner organization contracts a research firm to produce an internal report or analysis for a specific internal task. RPPPs work from the assumption that all the parties involved in the project bring individuals with expert knowledge to the table that complements the others' knowledge (Snow, 2015). The diversity of expertise and experiences representatives bring to the partnership builds strong and effective outcomes because the unintended consequences are lessened through being better imagined and planned for during the development stage. It is the wide range of experiences from those around the table that mitigates these unintended consequences. Moreover, effective RPPPs offer opportunities for all parties to learn more and expand professionally (Snow, 2015).

Designing RPPPs

In keeping with the framework proposed by Farrell and colleagues (2022) as a way of understanding research–practice partnerships, RPPPs similarly engage a wide range of researchers, practitioners, and policymakers from different partner organizations. The members of partner organizations bring with them their accumulated knowledge, access to communication pathways, and ability to mobilize resources. They coalesce and form a boundary infrastructure characterized by boundary spanning—"enacting transitions and interactions across different sites of practice" (p. 198)—boundary practices—"hybrid spaces that serve as a forum where ideas from research and practices can interact" (p. 199)—and boundary objects—"material and conceptual tools... that are critical for joint activity" (p. 199). The boundary infrastructure enables the attainment of intermediary outcomes which have the potential to engender long-term outcomes as the partner organizations collate their knowledge, experience, leadership, and resources to build infrastructure solutions that span boundaries and defy norms. Changes occur

76 ▪ H. E. PRICE et al.

in knowledge, policies, and routines across the research, practitioner, and policy spheres that transform and improve systems.

The typical RPPP framework, such as the one described by Farrell et al. (2022), embeds the assumption that the diversity of viewpoints across spheres of interest induces equity mindsets and practices among participants. While this assumption seems to hold in some circumstances, this design fails to directly account for power and positionality of organizations and individuals involved in the partnership (Tanksley & Estrada, 2022). Without explicit intentions and interventions to mitigate the heavy hand of power and positionality, those engaged in the RPPP who are positionally subordinate likely will feel restrained from fully engaging in the boundary spanning and practices. Such restraint would hinder the development of trust necessary to build and maintain the RPPP relationships among representatives of involved organizations (Tanksley & Estrada, 2022). Embedding DEI practices in RPPPs may mitigate this threat of power and positionality by building trust and engagement to enhance the effectiveness of the partnership.

Central to the RPPPs that we discuss here were educational leaders as fully engaged practitioner-policymakers who also acknowledged and worked to build relational cohesion within positionality and power under the tenets of DEI. As the relationship progressed, the variation in practicing DEI narrowed, shared understandings were built, and expectations improved (see Figure 4.2).

CASE STUDY: IMPLEMENTING DEI IN AN RPPP TO ADVANCE EQUITY PRACTICES IN ILLINOIS SCHOOL DISTRICTS

Rather than devising a state-mandated accountability policy and handing it down to local policymakers and practitioners, the Illinois State Board of Education (ISBE) reached out to collaborate with researchers, staff in regional education offices, and district superintendents during the field trial rollout of the initiative. Together, all parties collaborated on (a) refining metrics before they were fully adopted by the ISBE leaders and (b) putting in place professional development and resources before full deployment. We offer this collaboration as an illustration of the implementation of an RPPP that embodied DEI principles and practices.

Policy Leader: Illinois State Board of Education (ISBE)

Under the strategic plan, ISBE developed equity metrics. As part of this initiative, the agency leaders also embraced DEI principles and practices

Practicing Equity in Research–Practice–Policy Partnerships • 77

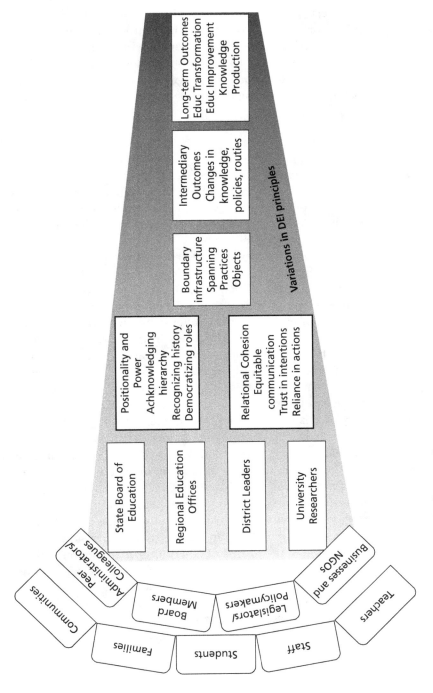

Figure 4.2 A DEI-centered RPPP framework.

78 ▪ H. E. PRICE et al.

as cornerstone tenets. As such, the ISBE leaders decided to (a) focus resources on equity goals, (b) integrate researchers into their design and implementation phases, (c) respond to their constituents' (superintendents, principals, teachers, parents, and community members) concerns, and (d) work with their constituents to continue moving forward their equity goals for the good of children's learning experiences.

Forming the RPPP

To form the RPPP, the ISBE leaders called upon practitioners and researchers who were already practicing DEI in their regular work. From district superintendents to staff in regional offices of education directors to university researchers and among staff working internally at the ISBE headquarters, they formed a large RPPP team.

They created an equity committee comprised wholly of volunteer employees from among the staff at the ISBE headquarters. There was neither any compensation awarded to participants, nor any persuasion exerted on those who volunteered to be a part of the equity committee. Over the years, there was little attrition of the 15–20-member committee who came from multiple offices within the ISBE headquarters from the superintendents' office to the research department to the communications office to the family and community engagement office, among others. Under the leadership of the state superintendent, this enthusiastic group joined the effort to develop and adapt equity metrics and the associated PD supports.

The members of this equity committee initiated the work and invited the practitioners from districts and regional offices of education as well as the university researchers to join the equity effort as an RPPP team. They invited the practitioners and researchers based on the equity work that they knew the invitees were conducting, based on their informal networks, and initiated contact through those networks. The membership of the university researcher teams from two Chicago-area universities was consistent and the practitioner membership waxed and waned based on individuals' availability and the evolution of the project needs. At the end of the pilot phase, more than a dozen district leaders presented to others. In virtual meetings open to all public-school leaders, these district leaders shared about their experiences on developing equity priorities in their districts, collaborating with teachers to develop strategies to attain equity goals, working with parents to improve family integration into equity decisions, and reaching out to community members to build equity expectations.

Bridging Multiple Roles in the RPPP

For an educational professional, the policymaker role and the practitioner role can coexist in the person's responsibilities (Ogawa & Bossert, 1995). Figure 4.3 illustrates the alternating role that superintendents and principals played in their roles as practitioners who implemented the policies handed down to them from their superiors as well as how they complied with those mandates and transferred them to their colleagues. This transmission of policies "down the chain of command" morphs the intention of the policy from the original. In the education sector, this morphing from the transmission is not necessarily a problem; the morphing allows for context considerations to be taken into account, thereby improving implementation and uptake in various educational settings. Practicing DEI facilitates the operation of the Goldilocks Principle (e.g., https://www.interact123.com/post/the-goldilocks-principle-education) in contrast to a "one size fits all" policy approach that can inflict harm on subgroups of learners.

Although superintendents and principals can be both policymakers and practitioners, the two roles have different expectations and goals. Educational policymakers are system designers—from local policymaking by superintendents and regional administrators to policymakers sitting in a state education department bureau. Policymakers also evaluate whether the implemented policies, procedures, and programs work effectively, efficiently, and fairly across different spaces and contexts. Practitioners implement the stipulations of the policies into daily practices. Superintendents put state policies into practice in their districts, principals put superintendents' district policies into practice in their schools, and teachers put principals' school policies into practice in their classrooms.

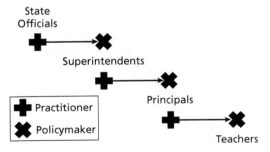

Figure 4.3 Alternating policymaker and practitioner roles.

Developing the Scope of Work

Once the representatives of the various organizations convened for the RPPP, members who worked at the ISBE coordinated the multidimensional scope of work to ensure a comprehensive rollout. These members ensured the cadence of subgroups within the RPPP to concentrate on different aspects of the project. While everyone was not in every subgroup, everyone knew of the whole scope of work and was kept abreast of progress. Communication was critical to avoid duplication of effort as well as to maintain alignment among aspects and ideas of key projects.

RPPP in Action

In this partnership, our (Price, Henfield, Edejer, & Fujimoto) main role as researchers was to conduct a needs assessment of the gaps in equity knowledge among local educational leader practitioners so that policymakers could tailor professional learning activities needed by practitioners for successful implementation of the initiative. We collected these needs assessment data through several means: interactive webinars, help-desk inquiry content, and critical reflection dialogue on the issues and questions that arose during our internal RPPP working meetings. We discuss these next, highlighting the communications aspects of these processes and our efforts to advance DEI practices for the RPPP work.

As with most partnership projects, the RPPP team members initiated and then continued the work with regular weekly meetings. These project management meetings served to (a) share progress on subgroup work, (b) align ideas based on project updates, and (c) give space for the multitude of diverse perspectives to be voiced, heard, and integrated into revisions. In initial meetings, the RPPP team established norms and expectations and designed short- and long-term goals and timelines. The outlines we developed served to document partners' internal processes and procedures which, in turn, allowed all parties to understand the turnaround and lag times they needed to build into any deliverable. These documents also served to demonstrate who—and from which organizations—were working on which dimensions of the initiative. The outlines also allowed all involved to see how some timelines needed to be staggered due to human resource capacity limits.

Designing the PD Webinars

The subgroup developing PD webinars had three goals:

1. Outreach to districts about the initiative.
2. Grow shared meanings around the equity metrics and their purpose.
3. Assess outstanding professional development needs of districts.

Practicing Equity in Research–Practice–Policy Partnerships • 81

The webinar subgroup consisted of three researchers (Price & Edejer plus a post-doctoral scholar), between four and six agency specialist policymakers, and two or three practitioners. It included agency specialists in learning, reporting, family and community relations, and communications. The subgroup met from one to three times a week over 4 months in preparation for each of the six webinars.

A planning meeting gave those of us who were members of the webinar group (Price & Edejer plus the practitioners and policymakers) space to develop an outline of PD topics and propose delivery dates. The webinar group brought the draft outline back to the ISBE leaders and cross-checked with other ISBE program planners as well as practitioners in relation to their district calendars before we finalized the outline. Initial meetings established the technological limited capacity of the ISBE to host interactive virtual workshops with audiences in excess of 100 people. Thus, we used plug-in options to an ISBE virtual platform that allowed audience participation. Mentimeter (https://www.mentimeter.com/) proved invaluable as a tool to gather real-time data from participants. Each webinar the webinar group developed went through several iterations of revisions and a week or more of wordsmithing.

As Figure 4.4 illustrates, the development time in an RPPP that grounds itself in DEI practices and principles will undergo a longer initial development time than if a researcher or single organization developed an analogous project in isolation. Developing a project without consultation can be quick, as the bottom gray line shows, however we contend that the project will be subject to far more iterations and revisions than a project developed by an RPPP. Frustrations among participants will mount across repeated revisions and relational trust and commitment will wane as each goal is missed for the delivery of the next version.

A collaborative DEI-centered RPPP takes more time to develop because the frequent work group sessions reveal differences in expectations, goals,

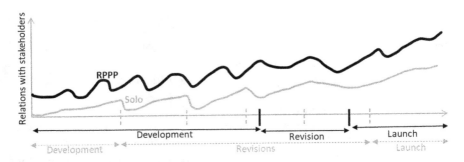

Figure 4.4 Conceptual model of quality and time-on-task for deliverables (Solo vs. RPPP Design).

82 ▪ H. E. PRICE et al.

and even terminology meanings. As the group members meet and openly discuss the plans, the wrinkles get ironed out and, eventually, a solid draft is produced. It certainly takes longer to get an initial draft completed, but practicing DEI means that the many blind spots and biases of a single person or organization will be identified and adjusted. The revision time is, therefore, much shorter and the design process is more efficient under a DEI-based RPPP, as illustrated in the upper line in Figure 4.4.

Deploying the PD Webinars

The RPPP team had truly exercised the practices and principles of DEI, and, arguably as an outcome, deploying the webinars garnered a well-received response from the participants. The use of the Mentimeter plug-in enabled the members of the webinar group (Price & Edejer plus the practitioners and policymakers) to gather real-time feedback from participants on their (a) expectations for the PD session, (b) outstanding needs related to the PD topic, (c) logistical issues with the PD session, and (d) other relevant characteristics of themselves and their districts.

Recordings of the webinars were also made available online by the webinar group members for anyone to access at any time. Recording the webinars raised concerns about confidentiality among the participants. This concern had been voiced by one of the practitioner partners during the development phase and was addressed by the webinar group members by adopting a recording option that kept participants' names hidden.

The webinar group members also incorporated analysis from participants from each prior webinar into the slides of the subsequent webinar. This process demonstrated to participants that their input was heard and integrated, and that they were a part of the development of this equity initiative. After only the first session, for example, participants suggested that the webinar group members should take more time to "hear from the field" about how to "do equity." As a team, the webinar group members recruited practitioners from around Illinois to speak during subsequent webinars as "spotlight districts" to share the progress of their journey within their districts toward equity. This addition to the sessions effectively built trust among the practitioner participants on the webinars and dampened the power and positionality divide between the ISBE, the practitioner participants, and us because the spotlight districts bridged the divide.

Analyzing the PD Webinar Data

Data from the Mentimeter app provided real-time feedback on the effectiveness of each webinar session and the variation in participants' uptake. We (Price & Edejer) assessed the effectiveness of each session by analyzing participants' responses to the informational material and by assessing the complexity of the questions they asked. We also used basic timing data to understand the logistics of each session. For example, after two sessions, we noted a pattern of drop-off from the webinar after 60 minutes—but not 60 minutes after the start time. Instead, there was drop-off 60-minutes after a participant joined, whether they joined on-time or late. When we took this information back to the RPPP weekly meetings, the practitioners suggested that the drop-off likely corresponded with a bell schedule for the end of the school day. When we cross-analyzed the drop-offs with the demographic data of the districts, we found the drop-offs occurred in smaller districts in which the superintendents were often also the high school principals. In response, the webinar team staggered the webinar times to accommodate these participants by ending the webinars before 2:30 p.m.

The webinar group members' bringing the data back to the members of the RPPP group after each webinar session proved invaluable for improving the next session. It also served as a form of member-checking: Different people who were part of the RPPP were able to interpret patterns in the data. Moreover, the frequent meetings of the RPPP members allowed them to bring the results back to their respective team members, member-check with them, and report back their groups members' sentiments. This process enhanced the validity of the data analysis and quickened the pace at which the RPPP members could revise the process, as shown in Figure 4.4.

The successes of the webinars grew quickly and became more pronounced across the short 2-month duration because we integrated frequent, regular, open feedback times into our RPPP meetings. Practicing the principles of DEI among the members of our RPPP and during the webinars with our participants demonstrated that the leaders of the ISBE truly wanted their input, heard their experiences, and valued what they shared as genuine contributions to improving the initiative to enhance educational equity.

Virtual Help Desk

In addition to the statewide webinar sessions, we (under the guidance of Henfield) established a virtual help desk. This communication line allowed participants from individual districts to follow up with us after webinars or contact us with other questions. From our perspective, we understood the importance of confidentiality in encouraging the participants in the districts to ask questions openly, sharing what they learned with participants in other districts, and building reliance and trust. The RPPP members decided on the levels of progression for the help desk (see Figure 4.5). The help desk emails were monitored by one project manager who would first attempt to answer the question by directing the questioner to any of the online materials. If that did not satisfy the questioner, their inquiry would be forwarded to one of us (Price, Edejer, or Fujimoto) to address in an e-mail reply. If the questioner required further information, we organized a brief virtual consultation. We also held two open help desk office hours per week

84 ▪ H. E. PRICE et al.

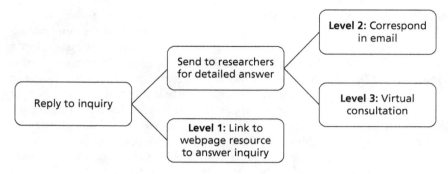

Figure 4.5 Help desk progression.

for the first 2 months, but these proved unnecessary. After discussing with our partners, our suspicion was that the lack of privacy in open office hours discouraged participants from utilizing them. After each help desk inquiry, we added to the frequently asked questions (FAQ) webpage (https://www.isbe.net/Documents/Equity-Journey-Continuum-FAQ.pdf). The FAQ webpage was a repository for the resource materials as we iterated, improved, and reflected on the real-time concerns of the participants in the districts and showed those participants that their inputs were building shared resources for their colleagues.

Critical Reflection

In addition to the regular RPPP meetings as members to share out, debrief, and revise together, the later months of the life of the partnership provided the opportunity for all RPPP members to critically reflect on our accumulated experiences and data on our process, its uptake, and the next steps. The level of trust we had developed and our reliance on each other for feedback and support, together with our openness to genuine listening and integrating of our diverse perspectives and contributions, solidified our relationships so we could honestly and critically reflect together. These solid relationships, grounded in DEI principles, lightened the atmosphere of power and positionality of the ISBE and everyone contributed to the critical reflections. To be sure, structural power and positionality were not absent. Throughout the process, various ISBE members repeatedly emphasized that the project was housed in the ISBE and that the practitioners and us as researchers were valued key informants but not decisionmakers. Final decisions went through a hierarchy of approvals within the ISBE. The RPPP members from the ISBE participated in the collaborative discussions. Some final decisions were made during the RPPP meetings by the two ISBE directors who participated whereas they sent other decisions to the state superintendent for their feedback and final decision. But over the course of the RPPP, the discussion and conversations among partners became more open, less guarded, and more equitable.

Planning Future PD Support

After 6 months of intense work, we (Price, Henfield, Edejer, & Fujimoto) synthesized the learning from the outreach to districts via webinars and help desk interactions. We grouped our learning into themes and cross-referenced the themes with district characteristics to recommend future PD needs as the initiative progressed from pilot year to full implementation.

In the same spirit of practicing DEI, we first shared the outline of the report with the members of the RPPP to garner feedback and input. After reaching consensus for the outline revisions, we drafted the report and shared it with the members of the RPPP for member-checking and general feedback. We incorporated revisions into the final report that then shared it with the members of the RPPP team and the ISBE equity group. Those who were planning the next PDs were well-positioned to meet the needs of the personnel in the districts as they moved forward.

CONCLUSIONS

Individuals developing initiatives and projects in isolation from stakeholders can quickly produce deliverables, but they will be filled with blind spots and errors (Price, 2021). Genuine partnerships that bring together researchers, practitioners, and policymakers around the same table provide the structure to build a solid deliverable, with fewer blind spots, less error, and higher quality. Stakeholders developing deliverables together takes more time on the front end but results in shorter revision times and higher success because the people around the table can front-load the quality checks since they mirror the intended users of those deliverables.

Working together and inviting feedback puts individual stakeholders in a vulnerable position. People in positions of power and leadership need to shoulder this vulnerability first so that the others in the room can observe their level of integrity and experience safety in the group. It is only through repeated acceptance of vulnerabilities, engagement with frequent exchanges, and frequent demonstrations of integrating others' feedback that strong and trusted relationships will be built among those in an RPPP (Brockner et al., 1997; Jones & George, 1998; Mayer et al., 1995). Invoking the principles of DEI can provide cornerstone norms to build upon when initiating an RPPP.

As the members of an RPPP progress through their project, the relationships between individuals in the group can grow or decay. Decay comes from individuals' breaking trust, failing communication, and lacking consideration of others' multidimensional roles and responsibilities. Growth comes from individuals' listening to others, integrating their feedback, sharing out together, and showing reliability as partners who can have tough conversations while keeping the core goals in the forefront (Bryk et al., 2015; Coburn & Penuel, 2016; Coburn et al., 2013; Fishman et al., 2013).

A key conclusion we have reached, based on the success of the process of this RPPP, is the critical importance of collaborative communication. Communication among the partners in this RPPP project: among the ISBE administrators, district leaders, and ourselves as researchers. Communication spanned several domains, including communication about the:

- initiative itself,
- understanding DEI principles,
- goals for messaging to the participants, and
- positionality and power dynamics.

Policymakers who choose to engage practitioners and researchers in partnership increase the face validity of the policy and strengthen the potential impact of their initiative. When a policy possesses face validity, it is more likely to be perceived as credible and fair by those it impacts, which increases their acceptance and willingness to comply with it. Face validity is crucial in ensuring that a policy aligns with the values, beliefs, and expectations of the organizational members, promoting a sense of legitimacy and trust in the policy implementation process (Eisenberger et al., 2010). Additionally, policies with high face validity are more likely to be seen as relevant and meaningful to the day-to-day work of those the policies impact, increasing their motivation to embrace and internalize the objectives of the policies (Truxillo et al., 2015). Therefore, when introducing a new policy, it is essential for policymakers to consider and prioritize face validity to foster positive attitudes, engagement, and successful implementation outcomes. There is no need to focus on increasing "buy-in" by practitioners if they participated in the creation of the policy. Transforming practitioners into decision makers means they are creating the deliverable rather than consuming it (Warren et al., 2018).

FINAL THOUGHTS

In the U.S., education policy is often handed down from a top–down hierarchy that has accumulated a history of one-size-fits-all ideas that trickle down from legislators into classrooms (Ravitch, 2010). This pattern has created a knee-jerk reaction among practitioners to assume policies are ill-informed, temporary, and/or not likely to work in their context (Penuel & Gallagher, 2017; Tseng et al., 2017). It will therefore take repeated interactions among practitioners and policymakers before practitioners trust that their contributions will truly be integrated into policies. Based on our case study, adding researchers into the policy–practitioner interactions as third-party participants can assist in keeping the goals and expectations of the interactions aimed at the goals of the shared project. Together, when all members of the three parties share goals and expectations, a climate of diplomatic discussions can commence. When we additionally practice DEI in our professional interactions, reduce the heavy hand of power and positionality, and create policies that are responsive to the needs of practitioners, we can begin to achieve the intermediate outcomes of organizational learning and change and facilitate the emergence of long-term outcomes including educational improvement, transformational change, and new knowledge production focused on equity in education.

REFERENCES

Acharya, V. V., Baghai, R. P., & Subramanian, K. V. (2009). Labor laws and innovation. *Journal of Law and Economics, 56*(4), 997–1037. https://doi.org/10.1086/674106

Banks, J. A. (2013). *An introduction to multicultural education* (5th ed.). Pearson.

Banks, J. A., & McGee Banks, C. A. (2019). *Multicultural education: Issues and perspectives* (10th ed.). Wiley & Sons.

Brockner, J., Siegel, P. A., Daly, J. P., Tyler, T., & Martin, C. (1997). When trust matters: The moderating effect of outcome favorability. *Administrative Science Quarterly, 42*(3), 558–583. https://doi.org/10.2307/2393738

Bryk, A. S., Gomez, L. M., Grunow, A., & LeMahieu, P. G. (2015). *Learning to improve: How America's schools can get better at getting better.* Harvard Education Press.

Canning, E. A., Murphy, M. C., Emerson, K. T. U., Chatman, J. A., Dweck, C. S., & Kray, L. J. (2020). Cultures of genius at work: Organizational mindsets predict cultural norms, trust, and commitment. *Personality and Social Psychology Bulletin, 46*(4), 626–642. https://doi.org/10.1177/0146167219872473

Coburn, C. E., & Penuel, W. R. (2016). Research–practice partnerships in education: Outcomes, dynamics, and open questions. *Educational Researcher, 45*(1), 48–54. https://doi.org/10.3102/0013189X16631750

Coburn, C. E., Penuel, W. R., & Geil, K. E. (2013). *Practice partnerships: A strategy for leveraging research for educational improvement in school districts.* William T. Grant Foundation. https://shorturl.at/lrOSV

Cochran-Smith, M., Villegas, A. M., Abrams, L., Chavez-Moreno, L., Mills, T., & Stern, R. (2015). Critiquing teacher preparation research: An overview of the field, part II. *Journal of Teacher Education, 66*(2), 109–121. https://doi .org/10.1177/0022487114558268

Cohen, J., McCabe, E. M., Michelli, N. M., & Pickeral, T. (2009). School climate: Research, policy, practice, and teacher education. *Teachers College Record, 111*(1), 180–213. https://doi.org/10.1177/016146810911100108

Cooper, A., MacGregor, S., & Shewchuk, S. (2021). A research model to study research-practice partnerships in education. *Journal of Professional Capital and Community, 6*(1), 44–63. https://doi.org/10.1108/JPCC-11-2019-0031

Edmondson, A. C. (1999). Psychological safety and learning behavior in work teams. *Administrative Science Quarterly, 44*(2), 350–383. https://doi.org/10.2307/ 2666999

Edmondson, A. C. (2012). *Teaming: How organizations learn, innovate, and compete in the knowledge economy.* Wiley.

Eisenberger, R., Karagonlar, G., Stinglhamber, F., Neves, P., Becker, T. E., Gonzalez-Morales, M. G., & Steiger-Mueller, M. (2010). Leader–member exchange and affective organizational commitment: The contribution of supervisor's organizational embodiment. *Journal of Applied psychology, 95*(6), 1085–1103. https://psycnet.apa.org/doi/10.1037/a0020858

Farrell, C. C., Penuel, W. R., Allen, A., Anderson, E. R., Bohannon, A. X., Coburn, C. E., & Brown, S. L. (2022). Learning at the boundaries of research and practice: A framework for understanding research–practice partnerships. *Educational Researcher, 51*(3), 197–208. https://doi.org/10.3102/0013189X211069073

Fishman, B. J., Penuel, W. R., Allen, A.-R., Cheng, B. H., & Sabelli, N. (2013). Design-based implementation research: An emerging model for transforming the relationship of research and practice. *Yearbook of the National Society for the Study of Education, 112*(2), 136–156. https://eric.ed.gov/?id=EJ1018453

Gay, G. (2010). *Culturally responsive teaching: Theory, research, and practice* (2nd ed.). Teachers College Press.

Gorski, P. C., & Zenkov, K. (2011). Countering the conspiracy of silence: Critical race theory and critical whiteness studies in education. In C. E. Sleeter & C. Combleth (Eds.), *Teaching with vision: Culturally responsive teaching in standards-based classrooms* (pp. 11–33). Teachers College Press.

Gregory, A., Clawson, K., Davis, A., & Gerewitz, J. (2016). The promise of restorative practices to transform teacher-student relationships and achieve equity in school discipline. *Journal of Educational and Psychological Consultation, 26*(4), 325–353. https://psycnet.apa.org/doi/10.1080/10474412.2014.929950

Harrison, D. A., Price, K. H., Gavin, J. H., & Florey, A. T. (2002). Time, teams, and task performance: Changing effects of surface- and deep-level diversity on group functioning. *Academy of Management Journal, 45*(5), 1029–1045. https:// psycnet.apa.org/doi/10.2307/3069328

Homan, A. C., Hollenbeck, J. R., Humphrey, S. E., van Knippenberg, D., Ilgen, D. R., & Van Kleef, G. A. (2008). Facing differences with an open mind: Openness to experience, salience of intragroup differences, and performance of diverse work groups. *Academy of Management Journal, 51*(6), 1204–1222. https://doi .org/10.5465/amj.2008.35732995

Jones, G. R., & George, J. M. (1998). The experience and evolution of trust: Implications for cooperation and teamwork. *Academy of Management Review, 23*(3), 531–546. https://doi.org/10.5465/amr.1998.926625

Kalev, A., Dobbin, F., & Kelly, E. (2006). Best practices or best guesses? Assessing the efficacy of corporate affirmative action and diversity policies. *American Sociological Review, 71*(4), 589–617. https://psycnet.apa.org/doi/10.1177/000312240607100404

Ladson-Billings, G. (1994). *The dreamkeepers: Successful teachers of African American children.* Jossey-Bass.

Ladson-Billings, G. (2014). Culturally relevant pedagogy 2.0: A. K. A. the remix. *Harvard Educational Review, 84*(1), 74–84. https://psycnet.apa.org/doi/10.17763/haer.84.1.p2rj131485484751

Martins, L. L., Gilson, L. L., & Maynard, M. T. (2004). Virtual teams: What do we know and where do we go from here? *Journal of Management, 30*(6), 805–835. https://doi.org/10.1016/j.jm.2004.05.002

Mayer, R. C., Davis, J. H., & Schoorman, F. D. (1995). An integrative model of organizational trust. *Academy of Management Review, 20*(3), 709–734. https://doi.org/10.2307/258792

McLeod, P. L., Lobel, S. A., & Cox, T. H. (1996). Ethnic diversity and creativity in small groups. *Small Group Research, 27*(2), 248–264. https://psycnet.apa.org/doi/10.1177/1046496496272003

Milliken, F. J., & Martins, L. L. (1996). Searching for common threads: Understanding the multiple effects of diversity in organizational groups. *Academy of Management Review, 21*(2), 402–433. https://doi.org/10.5465/amr.1996.9605060217

Nembhard, I. M., & Edmondson, A. C. (2006). Making it safe: The effects of leader inclusiveness and professional status on psychological safety and improvement efforts in health care teams. *Journal of Organizational Behavior, 27*(7), 941–966. https://doi.org/10.1002/job.413

Nishii, L. H. (2013). The benefits of climate for inclusion for gender-diverse groups. *Academy of Management Journal, 56*(6), 1754–1774. https://psycnet.apa.org/doi/10.5465/amj.2009.0823

Ogawa, R. T., & Bossert, S. T. (1995). Leadership as an organizational quality. *Educational Administration Quarterly, 31*(2), 224–243. https://doi.org/10.1177/0013161X95031002004

Penuel, W. R., & Gallagher, D. J. (2017). *Creating research practice partnerships in education.* Harvard Education Press.

Price, H. (2021). Communicating with policymakers. In A. Urick, D. E. DeMatthews, & T. G. Ford (Eds.), *Maximizing the policy-relevance of research for school improvement,* pp. 285–314. Information Age Publishing.

Ravitch, D. (2010). *The death and life of the great American school system: How testing and choice are undermining education.* Basic Books.

Rynes, S. L., Bartunek, J. M., Dutton, J. E., & Margolis, J. D. (2012). Care and compassion through an organizational lens: Opening up new possibilities. *Academy of Management Review, 37*(4), 503–523.

Snow, C. E. (2015). 2014 Wallace Foundation distinguished lecture: Rigor and realism: Doing educational science in the real world. *Educational Researcher, 44*(9), 460–466.

Tanksley, T., & Estrada, C. (2022). Toward a critical race RPP: How race, power and positionality inform research practice partnerships. *International Journal of Research & Method in Education, 45*(4), 397–409.

Thomas, K. M., & Plaut, V. C. (2008). The many faces of diversity resistance in the workplace. In K. M. Thomas (Ed.), *Diversity resistance in organizations* (pp. 1–22). Lawrence Erlbaum.

Truxillo, D. M., Bauer, T. N., & Erdogan, B. (2015). *Psychology and work: Perspectives on industrial and organizational psychology.* Routledge.

Tseng, V., Easton, J. Q., & Supplee, L. H. (2017). Research–practice partnerships: Building two-way streets of engagement. *Social Policy Report, 30*(4), 1–17. https://doi.org/10.1002/j.2379-3988.2017.tb00089.x

Villegas, A. M., & Lucas, T. (2002). *Educating culturally responsive teachers: A coherent approach.* State University of New York Press.

Warren, M. R., Calderón, J., Kupscznk, L. A., Squires, G., & Su, C. (2018). Is collaborative, community-engaged scholarship more rigorous than traditional scholarship? On advocacy, bias, and social science research. *Urban Education, 53*(4), 445–472. https://doi.org/10.1177/0042085918763511

CHAPTER 5

THE PROMISE OF DISTRICT–UNIVERSITY–COMMUNITY PARTNERSHIPS IN NAVIGATING THE TENSIONS OF CHANGE

Kevin Tan
University of Illinois, Urbana–Champaign

Nicole Rummel
Bloomington Public School District 87

Rachel Roegman
University of Illinois, Urbana–Champaign

ABSTRACT

In this chapter, we discuss the development of a 5-year district–university–community partnership addressing injustices and diversity, equity, and inclusion (DEI). We highlight our experiences in navigating the tensions of promoting

Justice, Equity, Diversity, and Inclusion in Education, pages 91–116
Copyright © 2024 by Information Age Publishing
www.infoagepub.com
All rights of reproduction in any form reserved.

systemic change, both within the district and broader community. Prior to the COVID-19 pandemic, our partnership focused on promoting the principles of traditional social emotional learning (SEL). Following the murder of George Floyd during the COVID-19 crisis, we pivoted to emphasize issues of race, class, and power in DEI work. Transformative social emotional learning (TSEL) involves young people and adults collaboratively co-examining, co-developing, and co-implementing solutions to address today's injustices. Over the course of our partnership, we worked towards advancing the ideals of TSEL in fostering empathy and action towards the needs of underserved populations.

Overall, we illustrate how dedicated district–university–community partnerships can serve as catalysts for transformative change. Despite encountering the challenges of power relationalities, structural constraints, and political backlash, frontline school personnel and university faculty continued to work collaboratively towards systemic change. We reflect on the tensions of change and discuss our experiences navigating the complexities of social justice and DEI work. Our experience suggests that sustained commitment to equity and inclusivity can serve as the driving force towards meaningful progress towards a more just and equitable educational landscape. In our discussion, we highlight the opportunities for growth and innovation that district–university–community partnerships offer, showcasing how such collaborations can spark transformative change, alleviate injustices, and advance the cause of DEI.

In a rural midwestern district, educators and university faculty were engaged in work on social emotional learning (SEL), and then 2020 hit: The COVID-19 global pandemic and the murder of George Floyd brought to the forefront issues of polarization, race, and class that had always existed, but had been hidden to many. What had been a focus on SEL would become a focus on transformative social emotional learning (TSEL), a process in which young people and adults collaboratively examine, develop, and implement solutions to address today's injustices (Jagers et al., 2019). Like all SEL, TSEL is designed to foster the knowledge, skills, and attitudes associated with developing healthy identities, relationship skills, and empathy; however, TSEL has a special focus on facilitating connection among those of different ethno-racial identities and heritage backgrounds (Jagers et al., 2019). Whereas many SEL programs are implemented in relatively color-neutral ways, TSEL requires educators to attend to issues of race, class, and power.

One of the core principles of TSEL is the centering of the voices and experiences of historically marginalized and minoritized communities and to shape educational practices and policies in ways that alleviate injustices (Jagers et al., 2019). While nothing about traditional SEL approaches suggests that attention to race, culture, or class be omitted, much traditional SEL work offers strategies and curriculum for students as a whole, ignoring the different realities that students of color and low-income students, in particular, face. As such, TSEL has the potential to drive diversity, equity, and inclusion (DEI) action towards enhancing the collective efficacy of districts and communities in effecting social change versus simply encouraging individual students to develop specific skills. Although developing individual skills such as persistence or collaboration are important, understanding how they are developed within systems, including systems of racism and classism[1] that marginalize specific groups of students, is necessary to create change.

In this chapter, we illustrate how one district-university-community partnership worked to shift the district focus from SEL to TSEL to create systemic change before, during, and after the impact of COVID-19 and the racial reckoning following Floyd's murder. District-university partnerships are intended to harness the expertise and resources of both entities. Effectively implementing the goals of TSEL in schools and community requires the collaboration of dedicated school personnel and university faculty to foster the principles of reciprocity and trust, which enabled them to collaboratively address the daily tensions inherent in this important work.

The partnership described here began in 2017. As one central office administrator, Rummel, and two university faculty, Tan and Roegman, we reflect in this chapter on how this partnership transitioned from a focus on general SEL to TSEL work before, during, and after the COVID-19 pandemic. We first present the literature on navigating tensions related to social justice work in schools, followed by concepts that aid in the understanding of our experiences with tensions and resistance. Next, we introduce the community at the center of the partnership and discuss the acclimatization process that occurred before the pandemic, establishing the foundation of the partnership. As the chapter unfolds, we demonstrate how, through continuous engagement through the challenges of the pandemic and the community's demands for racial equity, the members of the partnership gained confidence and developed the resilience to overcome even greater tensions and challenges, weathering the resistance against district-wide systems change towards the vision of TSEL. The post-pandemic period marked a transformative phase of rebuilding, with a central focus on fostering the growth, well-being, and development of students and adults, honoring the principles and ideals of TSEL.

TENSIONS AND RESISTANCE RELATED TO SOCIAL JUSTICE WORK IN SCHOOLS

Public school systems function in many ways like microcosms of society, in which the prevailing sociopolitical events within a community and nation shape the overall atmosphere and culture (Herrera et al., 2020). School district leaders face the challenge of effectively managing tensions and resistance within school systems to foster transformative change. Faase et al. (2022) provided a valuable framework for understanding and navigating the complex landscape of advancing social justice within educational settings. They suggested that the initial encounter with tensions and resistance in fostering social change may be uncomfortable, but that continuous engagement with these tensions builds participants' collective capacity to navigate and overcome them, an experience they compare to working out with exercise resistance bands. Our partnership encountered all the seven areas of tensions and resistance Faase et al. (2022) identified as common in schools seeking to address DEI—system, colleagues, workload, students, parents, expectations, and communication. Addressing tensions and resistance has been our central point of focus as we work towards the vision of an inclusive and equitable learning environment for all. Not all tensions and resistance are inherently negative and disruptive. Instead, tensions and resistance can serve as catalysts for growth, transformation, and positive outcomes; taking advantage of them requires a deliberate reframing of perspective (Faase et al., 2022).

The tensions and resistance we experienced are and have been typical in confronting racism in the American school systems (Donnor, 2016). Bell (1980) shed light on the enduring nature of racism and the persistent inequalities it perpetuates, particularly noting how members of the White middle- and upper-class prioritize safeguarding their own societal advantages. Bell astutely observed that despite efforts to racially integrate public schools, divisions still persisted, indicating the Eurocentric nature of society in which decisions remain rooted in Whiteness. Bell's concept of interest convergence further asserted that White individuals were reluctant to support racial justice initiatives unless they perceived that doing so as advanced their personal interests.

Subsequently, Bell (1992) introduced the concept of racial realism, highlighting that systemic racial inequalities and power imbalances that favor Whiteness have existed and continue to exist. Racial realism refers to the belief that race is a biologically or inherently real category that fundamentally shapes human abilities, behaviors, and social outcomes and urges that

> We must...move on to adopt policies based on what I call: "Racial Realism." This mind-set or philosophy requires us to acknowledge the permanence of our subordinate status. That acknowledgement enables us to avoid despair and frees us to imagine and implement racial strategies that can bring fulfillment and even triumph. (Bell, 1992, pp. 373–374)

Bell (1995) further argued that advancing counternarratives is essential, providing alternative perspectives and challenging prevailing norms, thus empowering marginalized communities to voice their experiences and challenge existing power structures. Our partnership grappled with the challenges of interest convergence and racial realism, as well as the need to develop counternarratives to the ways dominant constituents had been framing issues.

By acknowledging the parallels and drawing lessons from the past, we navigated tensions and resistance with a renewed sense of purpose, resilience, and commitment towards DEI ideals. In addition to those concepts drawn from Bell (1980, 1992, 1995), Harris's (1993) notion of Whiteness as property also articulated a persistent and challenging struggle throughout our work. Whiteness as property encompasses the privileges, advantages, and systemic benefits afforded to certain individuals based on their racial identity (Harris, 1993). This concept compelled us to confront and grapple with the deeply entrenched structures of power and privilege within our society. Our partnership encountered obstacles stemming from these entrenched dynamics that threatened to derail the trajectory of our work.

Through continuous experience engaging with tensions, our partnership honed valuable skills and cultivated the necessary confidence to confront larger challenges ahead. We learned to navigate the delicate balance between pushing boundaries for social justice and ensuring our capacities remained intact. In this process, we discovered that promoting transformative change required partnerships to be dynamic entities, constantly evolving, adapting, and fortifying their collaborative efforts. We argue that it is through similar continuous growth and development of resilience that partnerships can effectively drive lasting and meaningful progress towards the ideals of TSEL: equity and social justice.

Community School District

The Community School District (a pseudonym) is a rural district located close to the University of Illinois, Urbana-Champaign, a public state land-grant institution with a strong commitment to public engagement. The four schools in the district—a high school, a junior high, and two elementary schools (PK–2 & 3–5)—serve a student body that is 87% White. It is one of the few districts experiencing growth in the state; state school enrollment has decreased 7.5% over the past 4 years while the student body of Community School District has grown by 6%. This expansion has consisted disproportionately of non-White students, as shown by the fact that the percentage of Black, Indigenous, people of color (BIPOC) students increased by only 2% between 2017 and 2023. The number of multilingual learners has doubled, necessitating the hiring of the first two English language learner teachers in the district.

Tensions between people of varying socioeconomic statuses characterize the community. The average home value in this rural district is $63,000 above the state average, yet district boundaries include one of the largest trailer parks in the state. Twenty-two percent of students in the district qualify for free/reduced lunches. With these stark contrasts, place of residence becomes shorthand for social status.

The predominantly White, upper middle class, politically and religiously conservative majority exerted a strong influence on community and district policy and practice. The beliefs of the White majority often preponderate in the discussions in the school board room of the district. When introducing themselves during public comments at school board meetings, constituents often state how long they have lived in the community, suggesting that longevity in the community gives them authority over its welfare. In a place where many BIPOC have lived for a short time, this is alienating. The string of monthly microaggressions[2] at the school board meetings tends to disparage anyone not in the majority—White, middle- to upper-class, conservative, cisgendered, and heterosexual demographic.

The board of the only social service agency in the community, a youth club, as well as its major donors, reflect similar patterns as the district board of education, although many youth served by the club qualify for free-reduced lunch. The club was founded in 1994 as a satellite location for a Boys and Girls Club (https://www.bgca.org/about-us/our-mission-story) in a neighboring town. When it faced closure in 2003, the community and the school district worked to keep the club opened as a separate 501(c)(3)—a tax-exempt nonprofit organization—and the district continues to partner with the club to meet the needs of the youth in the community. Currently, the youth club provides free after-school opportunities to junior high students (Grades 6–8) and paid non-attendance school day and summer programming for elementary and junior high school students. The staff of the youth club often find themselves at a crossroads when they wish to advance equity work in the community that might challenge the status quo. For example, there have been threats to withhold funding to the club should it offer programs for LGBTQI+ students.

As the demographics of the community and district have shifted, some White community members have struggled with the implications of new neighbors and new students. SEL has been among the controversial topics, as some community members argue it addresses issues that should be taught at home. Some community members and district employees have been resistant to widening access to educational opportunity, such as de-tracking, that might create more heterogenous and equitable learning environments.

PRE-PANDEMIC: THE PROMISE OF THE PARTNERSHIP

The partnership between the district and the university started in 2017 as a strategy for understanding and addressing the social and emotional health of students, teachers, and families in this overall affluent community. Recognizing the university's wealth of knowledge and expertise in traditional SEL, Rummel, who was then in her second year as assistant superintendent with Community School District, approached the university's community partnership office for support to develop a comprehensive 3- to 5-year plan to enhance student learning and SEL. She was introduced to a social work faculty member (Tan) who was already active in SEL research and who had been very successful in obtaining grant funding with multiple school districts. At this time, Tan's work also drew on a traditional SEL lens, though this was soon to change.

Fostering Collaborative Efforts for Positive Change

Rummel had been prompted to act by growing reports from teachers and principals in the district regarding mental health and anxiety among high-income, high-performing students who felt social pressure to excel academically by taking many advanced placement courses and achieving the highest of grades. Teachers reported incidents of high-achieving students feeling stressed and anxious. There was concern that the strong academic performance and relative absence of behavioral problems led educators to overlook these students' social and emotional needs and focus only on students whose dysregulation was impacting classroom instruction. Teachers and administrators were also concerned that white-collar parents focused on academic performance and achievements to the exclusion of addressing their children's social and emotional well-being. The need for SEL was clear from the start of the partnership; however, the lack of reflection on how students' backgrounds or systemic oppressions might intersect with their socio-emotional well-being was evidence of a traditional SEL approach.

Early conversations between the district and the university personnel centered on creating spaces in schools for students to de-stress and better manage their concerns about postsecondary plans and supporting parents' role in promoting youth socioemotional development. Tan saw these conversations as evidence that the district was committed to laying the groundwork for collaborative efforts aimed at fostering positive change.

A Focus on Traditional SEL

The district administrators were prepared to invest heavily in professional development and support to create a cultural shift within the schools to promote SEL. There was a strong desire to measure the efficacy of these efforts. Within a year of their initial meeting, Rummel and Tan partnered with the district high school administrators to conduct SEL screenings of its ninth-grade students mindful that the transition to high school presents a critical opportunity to address any existing challenges and provide necessary support to ensure students' successful academic and SEL development (Phillips, 2019). Focusing on ninth grade also presented an opportunity to inform interventions that could be implemented in earlier grades.

Ninth-grade students were offered the option in Fall 2018 to complete a self-assessment of their socioemotional needs in areas such as communication, cooperation, assertion, and internalizing concerns. They repeated the same assessment during the last month of ninth grade in Spring 2019. Tan subsequently linked these data with student demographics (e.g., gender, race/ethnicity, free-reduced lunch status, disability status) and grades. The goal was to initiate the gathering of longitudinal screening data of student SEL to track and assess their social and emotional well-being over time. At the same time, this shows the beginnings of a shift from traditional SEL to TSEL as gender, race, class, and disability became central to the data analysis.

The data showed that students who reported more SEL concerns also had lower academic performance; there was a stark disparity in SEL scores between the wealthier student population and the low-income students (see Figure 5.1). These findings contrasted with teachers' initial concerns about the SEL of high-achieving students. The data presented empirical evidence related to SEL[3] and equity the district administrators had to address in their commitment to fostering holistic student development and well-being.

In response to Tan's findings, Rummel implemented proactive measures to address the identified disparities and prioritize SEL supports for

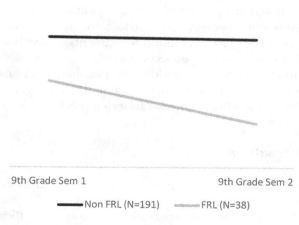

Figure 5.1 Comparison of SEL scores (FRL vs Non FRL Students).

students. Rummel and Tan co-facilitated a discussion involving the high school principal and school social workers to review the SEL data. The school-based team members acknowledged that the data revealed meaningful insights regarding SEL which aligned with their day-to-day observations in the school. Examining data gathered at their own schools heightened their sense of urgency for a system for early identification of ninth graders who struggled socially and emotionally so as to provide the necessary SEL supports to promote student achievement. However, the faculty had not yet embraced TSEL.

Rummel and Tan recognized that the results had been meaningful, but they were keen to bring about systemic and sustainable change that went beyond the consideration of individual student-level SEL data. They recognized the danger of placing the responsibility for poor achievement on individual students or their parents, neglecting the need for systemic reforms to the underlying factors and structural issues that contribute to and perpetuate poor outcomes. They therefore sought to enhance the capacity of the district staff to understand and act upon data in ways that avoided adopting a deficit-oriented perspective and instead adopted TSEL.

To support these efforts, Tan connected Rummel with Roegman, his colleague in the College of Education, who studied how schools use data to advance equity. Roegman conducted a series of interviews with high school personnel to about how they were making sense of and using the SEL data (Roegman et al., 2022). Roegman identified several organizational routines that supported the work of district personnel around traditional SEL and highlighted a need to strengthen educators' skills and use of data, both academic and SEL-related. In addition, Roegman discerned norms related to race and the different ways that students were minoritized within the district that prevented a strong equity focus in both SEL and data use, thus preventing a TSEL approach. Roegman shared these findings with Tan and Rummel and the three discussed what they meant and how to move forward. This analysis had immediate impact because it fostered a data-driven approach within the district, deepening its staff's overall understanding of data and equity.

Building Capacity for TSEL

To bring attention to issues of equity within the data related to students' demographics and academic performance, based on both their own experiences, Roegman's analysis, and a TSEL lens, Rummel, Tan and the high school principal organized a half-day professional development session in January 2020. The teachers, grouped by content area, and the student support team comprising of personnel such as the school counselors and social workers met in person to analyze and discuss the implications of Tan's data collected since 2018. Data were presented in a disaggregated fashion, so that educators could more clearly see disparities related to class, race, achievement, and SEL.

In analyzing the data related to students' free and reduced lunch status, the conversations revealed that some educators held deficit views of students living in poverty. Data showed that students from low-income households had higher feelings of exclusion and disengagement than their wealthier peers, and these conversations made apparent the need to address SEL concerns while helping teachers to view low-income students as capable and college-going.

Strengthening the Partnership

Momentum towards systemic change, based on TSEL and the data-driven process, continued to gain traction and foster transformative progress within the district. It built upon the work Rummel initiated in the 2018–2019 academic year, focusing on the implementation of an SEL-oriented *Responsive Classroom* approach to teaching and discipline (Responsive Classroom, 2023) for Grades K–8, along with *Restorative Practices* (International Institute for Restorative Practices, 2023) for high school students. Through Responsive Classroom and Restorative Practices, the district administrators aimed to address students' SEL needs through:

- teaching and establishing clear expectations and school/classroom norms,
- fostering positive social- and self-awareness,
- building a school/classroom community inclusive of student voice and differences, and
- focusing on repairing and restoring relationships instead of punishment.

District staff responded positively to these initiatives, and the district administrators sponsored certification for some personnel, empowering them to become leaders in traditional SEL programming within their buildings. However, the COVID-19 pandemic would impede the work of the social work faculty in delivering and analyzing the SEL screenings. Resistance to the move toward racial justice would also impact the district administrators' focus on TSEL.

Two critical but previously neglected DEI issues in the district came to the forefront for the partnership just before the pandemic began. First, as the partnership members prepared to facilitate compliance with a state law requiring public schools to educate students about the contributions of the gay, lesbian, and queer community, which was scheduled to come into effect on July 1, 2020. The growing number of incidents of intolerance targeting LGBTQI+ students reinforced the urgency of this change. Secondly, a growing number of Jewish and Islamic families had moved into the community, and these parents raised concerns about classroom Christo-normative practices. Tan connected Rummel with additional university faculty who possessed the expertise necessary to support and empower teachers in their efforts to create a more inclusive and supportive environment. A series of district-wide professional development sessions to provide educators with the tools and strategies to create a more inclusive and supportive environment for LGBTQI+ students were planned for April 2020. The district administrators also began within-house conversations about addressing religious diversity. The COVID-19 pandemic interfered.

PANDEMIC: THE PIVOT TOWARDS TRANSFORMATIVE SEL AND RACIAL EQUITY

The members of both the Community School District and the university felt the rapid and unprecedented disruption caused by the COVID-19 pandemic as keenly as did members of schools and educational systems worldwide. The sudden closure of schools and the rapid shift towards remote learning highlighted stark disparities in students' ability to access technology and other basic needs. Far too many low-income students were not engaging in online learning, and the district personnel had no way to connect with and check on them. The employment of a social worker in the first year of the pandemic and, a year later, a family engagement specialist to support students and families offered some hope.

The racial protests of Summer 2020 brought tensions as well as focusing attention on the needs of BIPOC students. A community rally was held to show support for the BIPOC community in Summer 2020, while some in the community put up blue ribbons in some parts of town to show allegiance to the police. School administrators had already expressed concern that certain students in the district appeared incapable of accepting diversity among their peers, including diversity related to sexual orientation, gender identity, and religion, and the protests and rally highlighted race as another source of division within the student body.

Rummel recognized that fostering positive social awareness and acceptance required work at all levels with school principals, teachers, parents, students, and the broader community. It was clear this would require activities beyond the expertise and bandwidth of district personnel.

Escalating District–Community Tensions Around Racial Justice

In the lead-up to the 2020–2021 school year, a group of vocal community members began to call on the district administrators and the school board to address racial equity and justice. The national public outcry against racial injustice and police brutality in the wake of George Floyd's murder (May 25, 2020) had resonated with segments of the community, and individuals from diverse backgrounds had joined together to demand change. The superintendent and school board president both released public statements acknowledging the sorrow and anger around George Floyd's killing and reiterating their commitment to an inclusive school climate. BIPOC students and former students as well as families and other allies further highlighted the need for anti-racist interventions by sharing their lived experience at school board meetings and demanding the school board members recognize the Black Lives Matter movement and address racism within the school board building. These events manifested a powerful and collective expression of frustration and grief and constituted a call for social reform by highlighting the significance and urgency of addressing systemic racism and promoting racial equity. However, some individuals in the community pushed for a return to the pre-pandemic status quo.

As the demands and urgency of the racial justice movement intensified, the partnership members recognized the need to shift the focus to addressing systemic inequities. Over 600 alumni signed a petition calling on the school board to adopt an anti-racism resolution and urging the superintendent to develop a comprehensive curricular plan that would educate students at every level about race, power, and privilege. The petition demanded professional development and continuing education opportunities for teachers, focusing on cultural competency, implicit bias, and the development of culturally responsive lesson plans. It also demanded the board members share the curricular and professional development plans with the community once they were developed to foster transparency and encourage the community to promote a more inclusive and equitable educational environment.

The Promise of Community Town Hall Conversations and Pivot Towards TSEL

In response to the mounting pressure for increased DEI action, the partnership members recognized the need for collective dialogue with the broader community. An opportunity arose to promote racial healing, unity, and equity through a state grant initiative of $4.5 million. This grant funded

Navigating the Tensions of Change • **103**

grassroots projects and initiatives that fostered dialogue, understanding, and reconciliation among diverse communities. Its objective was to facilitate healing, build trust, and provide avenues for individuals and communities to engage in honest conversations about race, systemic racism, and social justice. The partnership received a grant of $45,000 to facilitate community engagement through town halls, parenting workshops, in-district professional development sessions, and the acquisition of resources for the district.

The town halls served as a pivotal solution designed by the partnership members to address community engagement around DEI. Facilitated by Tan, three in-person sessions were conducted along with a virtual session. These sessions provided a space where constituents shared their perspectives, concerns, and ideas related to DEI within the district, serving as a powerful vehicle for TSEL. Tan highlighted the state mandate to teach about the contributions of the LGBTQI+ community and the district plans to meet this policy. Tan elicited a diverse range of viewpoints to stimulate thought-provoking discussions, encouraging attendees to examine critically their beliefs, broaden their perspectives, and act towards creating a more inclusive, equitable, and socially just society for the young. Tan achieved this through an interplay of storytelling of observations in the community and the dissemination of data based on his research in the district. One example of such research was the study Tan conducted at the onset of the pandemic which initiated a comprehensive survey of teachers, signifying a whole-school, system-wide commitment to supporting both students and educators alike.

The data shared with the community revealed how the pandemic had profoundly affected both students and teachers, necessitating the need for the district leaders to develop tailored supports for each group. For instance, a majority of students (58%) indicated the pandemic had affected their mental and emotional health, and 26% of students reported moderate to extreme impact on their physical health. The cancellation of end-of-school year events, such as prom[4] and graduation, affected 72% of students to a moderate to extreme degree. Students, especially those from low-income families, reported various barriers to learning, including juggling other responsibilities, uncertainty about schoolwork, and a lack of quiet study environments at home. In highlighting these findings, and in emphasizing a TSEL approach, Tan called for a comprehensive understanding and the provision of supports based on students' diverse experiences and circumstances in the light of the varied impacts of the pandemic on their socioemotional, mental, and physical well-being.

Tan referenced the impacts on teachers and discussed worry and anxiety related to COVID-19 including financial stress, concerns about vulnerability to COVID-19 among elderly family members and those with underlying health conditions and worries about the mental and emotional well-being of their families. He highlighted the need to address their well-being and ensure continuity of learning. Years of teaching experience predicted teachers' mental health well-being: Teachers with fewer years of experience ($M = 7.11$ years) reported poorer mental health than those with more experience ($M = 13.52$ years). The need to promote the well-being and success of the teaching workforce was clear.

Community members responded by sharing their own personal experiences, insights, and recommendations on addressing systemic inequities and promoting inclusivity within the district. During the town hall sessions, Tan spoke of the necessity of fostering collective youth and adult action towards co-constructing equitable learning environments, advancing the vision and foundation towards TSEL (Jagers et al., 2019). The town halls created awareness of adults' responsibility in supporting and empowering young people and building their capacity to do so, which necessitates attention to their own socio-emotional needs. Tan shared with the community how the district leaders had already acted on the data by, for example, providing district wide professional development sessions.

The town halls reaffirmed the urgent need for transformative change as attendees called for an educational environment that honors diversity, challenges biases, and empowers all students to thrive academically, socially, and emotionally. They also generated ideas and action steps that could shape the district policies, practices, and curriculum to meet the needs of all students more effectively. The town hall sessions demonstrated the resilience and determination of the university and district personnel. The integration of storytelling and the process of imagining the experiences, perspectives, and feelings of the marginalized with the sharing of research data by the social work faculty were crucial for perspective-taking to occur (Muradova, 2021). Perspective-taking, rooted in the theory of racial ignorance, challenged limited understanding of racial justice dynamics by encouraging individuals to seek out and empathize with the experiences of others (Mueller, 2020). This inclusive and empathetic approach fosters genuine and sustainable systemic change by addressing underlying power dynamics and promoting collective responsibility in combating interest convergence. By embracing perspective-taking, the partnership members seized the opportunity to engage portions of the broader community interested in promoting healing, dialogue, and reconciliation. This active engagement in perspective-taking enabled participants to transcend self-interest and gain a deeper appreciation for the dynamics of DEI and TSEL.

Undesirable Fallout From Town Halls in Promoting Change

The town halls, while successful in fostering dialogue and engagement, also brought about unintended consequences as they became a catalyst

Navigating the Tensions of Change • **105**

for exposing deep-seated divisions and resistance within the community, posing challenges for the partnership members in navigating conflicting perspectives and maintaining a cohesive approach towards DEI. Journalism surrounding the announcement of the awarding of the grant proved destabilizing. For example, a reporter commissioned by the funder presented a draft report announcing the award of the grant to the district to Tan and Rummel. Much to our dismay, the report portrayed the district in a negative light, resurfaced past grievances and reopened old wounds by misrepresenting information gathered from secondary sources. Responding swiftly, the social work faculty sought guidance from the public relations professionals at the university and received support in contacting the grant program officer to provide clarification. Ultimately, this report was not published, but the incident showed that even well-intended media efforts have the potential to harm individuals and groups through re-traumatization of minority groups and negatively impact district leader's earnest pursuit of positive impact (Jackson, 2020).

Unfortunately, fallout from a second, less well-intentioned such incident was not averted. A far-right media platform profiled Tan in a report that distorted and misrepresented his work. The report prompted online harassment, trolling, and threats (Kamola, 2019). Tan promptly informed the relevant university campus officers and sought guidance on moving forward with the planned activities, but their efforts could not entirely alleviate the stress associated with his being targeted by extremist media.

Challenges to the partnership member's commitment to TSEL ensued and included challenges to traditional SEL work as well. The school board members implemented a policy requiring their approval for all research conducted in the district, specifically targeting Tan's research and voicing thinly veiled concern about indoctrination and the teaching of Critical Race Theory. This change to the school district research policy was directly influenced by the town halls, which some school board members found to be threatening. For example, one school board member expressed skepticism about the town hall events and emphasized that the district should focus on academic subjects. Tan has experienced challenges in obtaining research approval subsequently due to misunderstandings and differing perspectives on the nature and importance of both traditional SEL and TSEL.

Interest Convergence and Whiteness as Property as Tensions and Resistance

The aftermath of the town halls highlighted tensons and resistance that can be viewed through the concepts of interest convergence and Whiteness as property. Interest convergence, as Bell (1980) wrote, and the concept of Whiteness as property, as Harris (1993) explored, provide valuable insights into the power dynamics, privilege, and challenges related to racial justice within the partnership. Throughout the partnership's work, it became evident that White individuals and other members of dominant groups were more inclined to support initiatives for racial justice when it directly aligned with their personal interests or yielded personal benefits. For example, there was greater support for a traditional SEL initiative focused on addressing student anxiety but less support for the purchasing of instructional materials more reflective of a diverse student body. Despite the district leadership's sincere efforts to communicate the comprehensive initiatives they had in place to address DEI, some individuals perceived any actions that did not align with their specific wishes as insignificant. This selective engagement and self-focused approach indicated a reluctance to support broader DEI initiatives and constituted a form of resistance to the broader change efforts.

The entrenched nature of Whiteness as property became evident to the members of the partnership through various actions that aimed to control and restrict the faculty's research on SEL within the district. Some community members demanded a narrow focus on academic subjects and decried the partnership member's efforts to address systemic inequities. The school board member's attempts to hinder Tan's traditional SEL work and his TSEL work all reflected how structural racism can uphold and reinforce disparities in society. Individuals from dominant groups felt they had ownership of the resources and opportunities offered by the partnership members due to their social status and privilege. This perception of power reinforced racial hierarchies and perpetuated systemic inequities. Overcoming these obstacles required a collective effort to educate the board members and community members about the importance of SEL and, in doing so, challenge the structures and perspectives that upheld beliefs centered around Whiteness as property.

Tensions and Resistance Within the District

While Tan led the town hall conversations with marginalized community members, tensions and resistance were also emerging among members of the school district. Expectations and communications are common sources of conflicts in driving transformative change within school systems (Faase et al., 2022). Such conflicts often encompass both internal expectations, which teachers and administrators placed on themselves, and external expectations imposed by outside sources, including curriculum-related pressures. Communication challenges further arise from unclear guidelines, misalignment of mission and vision, and differing leadership philosophies (Faase et al.,

2022). Tensions associated with communication included timing of information dissemination and the associated impact on teachers' workload. Such internal tensions added complexity to the process of driving transformative change and required careful navigation and resolution to ensure progress towards the goals of fostering DEI and the principles of TSEL.

The first set of internal tensions emerged during consultative sessions that took place with the school administrators and a consultant from an external national traditional SEL agency hired through the state grant. Although the consultant delivered two well-received parenting workshops, the sessions with the district administrators encountered resistance and discomfort that arose from issues of expectations, communication, and goal misalignment. One of the reasons for this misalignment was the differing approaches to addressing traditional SEL among the consultant, a retired principal, and the school building administrators. The consultant's perspective and ideas did not align with the administrators' expectations and needs. The administrators were hoping to receive concrete guidance on how to implement traditional SEL in their buildings but the consultant's criticism of their implementation without providing solutions or addressing their day-to-day challenges created discomfort. Recognizing this disconnect, the partnership members canceled subsequent sessions with the traditional SEL agency and refocused their work on improving dynamics and furthering TSEL and DEI.

A second set of internal tensions was related to a series of district professional development sessions that the partnership members offered through the state grant in Fall 2020. Some participants perceived a session on history and racism as dry and unengaging; the presenters did not capture the attention or interest of attendees. Another session on working with LGBTQI+ students, intended to prepare teachers to fulfill the state requirement to educate students about the contributions of the gay, lesbian, and queer community, was even more contentious. A presenter made a statement that, to some participants, implied that the Bible was incorrect. Some staff members who held conservative beliefs were extremely offended, and this created a sense of unease and discord among teachers. The presenter's delivery of ideas and the disagreement over religious beliefs seemed to strain the relationship between the presenter and the teachers. In response, Rummel acknowledged the concerns staff raised while gently encouraging them to consider the points the presenter had raised and recognized that teachers were grappling with reconciling their religious beliefs with the state requirement. Further, some teachers struggled to comply with state legal requirements regarding the use of students' preferred names and pronouns. Addressing this tension required the district and building administrators to foster a culture of open dialogue, empathy, and mutual respect, creating a safe space for meaningful conversations.

A third set of internal tensions was related to the implementation of a Black History Month curriculum. Rummel took the initiative to develop content that teachers could deliver in daily 3-minute segments on introducing various aspects of Black history. The segments aimed to educate students and get them interested in the rich cultural heritage and significant contributions of the Black community. To ensure inclusivity and accuracy, Rummel sought feedback from one of Tan's colleagues who specialized in DEI and a group of graduate Black social work students who were actively involved in campus DEI initiatives. Unfortunately, teachers in one of the schools in the district resisted the program. Some said they were uncomfortable delivering the material and that they lacked proper training and expertise. Another group of teachers criticized the program's content, contending that it perpetuated racism. In response to this pushback, Rummel spent time at the school, engaging with teachers to hear their concerns. While this school did not implement the program that had been proposed, Rummel persisted in advancing the agenda of promoting DEI by engaging with teachers and exploring alternative ways of achieving the desired outcome. As a result of Rummel's willingness to allow this school to forge its own path, the teachers took ownership of DEI within their building. The teachers created a leadership group dedicated to listening to student voice. This group of teachers and students found ways not only to celebrate Black History Month and other holidays, but also to focus on addressing difficult topics such as microaggressions and representation.

Racial Realism and Resistance to Counternarratives as Tensions and Resistance

The string of internal tensions and resistance compounded and cascaded, creating a domino effect within the district. These conflicts reflected aspects of racial realism and resistance. Racial realism, which refers to the recognition and acknowledgement of the need for social action to address and counteract the enduring presence of racism in society and the persistent nature of racial inequalities (Bell, 1992), became evident through the internal conflicts and pushback encountered when addressing SEL, TSEL, and DEI issues.

In the case of the professional development session on working with LGBTQI+ students, we interpreted the discomfort and pushback from certain teachers, particularly those holding conservative beliefs, as rooted in a fear of confronting and potentially dismantling their deeply ingrained biases and perspectives. If so, it perhaps reflected a form of coming to terms with a counternarrative, whereby individuals wrestled with their tendency to cling to existing structures and beliefs that upheld systems of privilege and inequality. Rummel recognized the importance of the counternarratives that promoted inclusivity, respect, and a deeper understanding of diversity. Rummel encouraged teachers to engage in open dialogue with empathy and mutual respect, fostering meaningful conversations and an understanding of different perspectives. Rather than giving in to resistance or abandoning DEI plans, Rummel actively sought alternative ways to foster inclusivity and equity within the partnership.

POST-PANDEMIC: THE MOVEMENT TOWARDS SYSTEM-WIDE CHANGE

The post-pandemic period presented an opportunity for a movement towards system-wide change, focusing on DEI and TSEL. The disruptions caused by the pandemic, along with the insights we gained from the town hall discussions, shed light on the glaring disparities in access to resources, educational opportunities, and support systems faced by marginalized students in the community. As the school district and community members continued to embark on the journey of rebuilding and recovering from the pandemic, there was a growing recognition by the partnership members of the urgent need to continue addressing the deeply entrenched inequities and systemic barriers that had been amplified by the COVID-19 crisis. The school district leaders aimed to create a post-pandemic educational landscape that ensured equal opportunities for all students, regardless of their background or circumstances, enabling every learner to thrive and reach their full potential.

Despite encountering conflicts within the school district and the wider community throughout the pandemic, the partnership held to their commitment to equity and inclusivity. As suggested by Faase et al. (2022), tensions and resistance can act as catalysts for growth when addressed with diplomacy and tact. Although the series of challenges were often disheartening and appeared formidable, they spurred the partnership into action, prompted strategic reassessment, and inspired innovative approaches. By embracing adaptability and attentiveness to tensions, the partnership continued to foster a culture that promoted transformative change. These challenges further solidified the partnership's collective determination to challenge oppressive structures and dismantle barriers that perpetuated inequality.

The transformative journey towards system-wide change necessitates ongoing efforts, such as providing professional development for teachers, integrating culturally responsive pedagogy into curricula, allocating resources to support underserved communities within the district, maintaining active community engagement, and establishing mechanisms for monitoring progress and ensuring accountability. The movement towards system-wide change consistently reaffirmed the partnership member's commitment to centering the voices and experiences of historically marginalized groups in the community, including BIPOC individuals, LGBTQI+ individuals, students with disabilities, and those from low-income backgrounds. The objective was not merely to address surface-level DEI, but to foster a profound cultural shift that would permeate all facets of the district. The partnership members acknowledged that creating genuinely inclusive and equitable learning environments necessitated a fundamental change in their own mindsets and practices when it came to understanding conflict and resistance.

Moving Past Obstacles Together

The period following the pandemic presented an opportunity to envision a new direction for the partnership. Recognizing the challenges and constraints inherent in the pursuit of advancing TSEL work within the district, both Rummel and Tan engaged in a process of regrouping and reassessment, with Roegman serving as a regular thought partner and critical friend. They spent time discussing and reflecting on the struggles they encountered over the course of their work during the pandemic. Evidently, working towards system-wide change in this district was going to necessitate navigating restrictions on traditional SEL and TSEL research within the school district, while being mindful of school district teacher's responses and reactions to district DEI initiatives. We decided to adopt a strategic approach—one that would not only acknowledge and celebrate the progress already achieved but also provide a clear roadmap for future endeavors. It became clear to us that it would be imperative to ensure that teachers, administrators, and community members continued to have a comprehensive understanding of and discernible input into our efforts to lead and support TSEL initiatives. To expand the scope of our project to respond to students' socio-emotional needs following the pandemic, the university–district partnership had to grow.

New Partnerships

Post-pandemic, the state-level educational leaders strongly emphasized the need to support SEL and the mental health of students and families. Accordingly, a funding opportunity for Community–Partnership grants worth $635,000 over the course of two years through the American Rescue Plan Elementary and Secondary School Emergency Relief Fund was announced. The objective of this grant was to address the gaps that had emerged in

Navigating the Tensions of Change • **111**

students' social, emotional, behavioral, and mental health needs as a direct result of the pandemic.

Recognizing the significance of this funding opportunity, the partnership members invited the local youth club leadership and leaders of a mental health provider to collaborate in submitting a grant application. Following the success of the grant, an additional social worker was hired to provide services to both the school district and the youth club and support staff and students in addressing their social-emotional needs. In collaboration with the mental health provider, the school district and youth club employees were now able to refer students and families, particularly those from low-income communities, for counseling and family therapy services. The grant funding fully covered these services that constituted a crucial resource unavailable prior to the pandemic but made indispensable by the social and emotional challenges the pandemic had created. The grant also financed the hiring of social work students to deliver afterschool and summer social and emotional programs at the youth club. Community-based parenting workshops were also financed by the grant through the mental health provider. The funds made available by the grant proved to be an invaluable resource for the partnership, enabling us to extend our reach and provide critical socio-emotional support to members of low-income communities for whom such resources were previously inaccessible. The collaborative and expanded network of supports involving the university, school district, the youth club, and the local mental health provider that the grant funding had facilitated enhanced the well-being of students and families and addressed a range of disparities and concerns.

During this time, Roegman invited Rummel, as a representative of the school district, to serve as a community partner for the principal preparation program at the university. Rummel brought valuable insights to the monthly meeting of the program by reflecting on the knowledge, skills, and dispositions that future administrators needed to effectively lead in the sometimes contentious environment.

Creating New Opportunities for Research

The Community–Partnership grant presented an exciting opportunity for Tan to expand his research and extend it to include members of the broader community. Capitalizing on the local annual festival, Tan set up a booth where he distributed mental health awareness stickers and engaged in dialogue with community members while university social work students invited attendees to respond to a survey. Tan's outreach allowed for personal connections that had lain dormant since the town hall sessions to be reestablished. The interactions between university faculty and the community facilitated a deeper understanding of the community needs. Seven hundred individuals participated in the survey, including 300 youth.

The goal of the survey was to gain insight into the mental health and SEL needs of the community. An intriguing finding regarding the perception of mental health support in the community was the discrepancy between adults and youth. Young people felt that mental health resources available for their age group were more available than for adults, whereas adults thought such resources for young people were scarce in both schools and the community. White male participants, whose average age was 40.5 years, reported significantly lower perceptions of mental health resources for young people than adults as a group. This finding suggests that, within this demographic, there may be an awareness gap regarding the availability of mental health support for young individuals. Other findings highlight the importance of addressing and bridging the perception gap when it comes to mental health resources. Tan shared the findings with the school district administration, and the leadership of the youth club and the mental health provider. Follow up conversations based on these data underscored the importance of enhancing awareness and accessibility of mental health services, with a particular focus on young males given our finding that white middle-aged males reported lower perceptions of mental health resources. The findings raised valuable insights, but further investigation is needed to fully understand the implications and meaning of the observed differences based on gender.

District Refocus

After the return to in-person schooling following the pandemic, the school district leadership placed renewed emphasis on supporting students by implementing best practices in teaching and learning. This period of district re-focus was informed by Hattie and Zierer's (2017) research, which emphasized the importance of explicitly teaching of expectations and Sprenger's (2020) research, which focused on strategies that facilitated executive functioning skills.[5] Meeting with a group of teacher leaders, Rummel listened to teachers describe student deficits and found that most of the identified deficits included areas of executive functioning. Teachers spent a year in professional learning communities learning to address academic deficits and SEL, defined as executive functioning, within their specific content area.

As the state educational leaders continued to fund initiatives to address learning loss, the school district and youth club leaders were able to secure a $97,000 joint after-school grant to address learning loss and socio-emotional well-being post-pandemic through a focus on college and career

Navigating the Tensions of Change • **113**

readiness, youth activism, and media literacy. This grant allowed for paid mentors for junior high and high school students who struggled in school academically and/or socially and emotionally. The grant funds also supported the hiring of peer tutors. The result was a decrease in the number of missing assignments and D/F grades, especially at the junior high level.

The staff at each of the grant partner's buildings worked to incorporate TSEL principles into their DEI initiatives and created a DEI committee with an individualized focus on the specific needs of the youth at each site. The high school DEI committee included students and created a safe space for addressing issues among students within the building using the already established Restorative Practices[6] as a framework. The members addressed previously contentious topics such as Black History Month and microaggressions. The member of the junior high DEI committee established a Gay Straight Alliance student group. The members of the DEI committees in the elementary buildings focused on increasing student representation in choosing books and classroom materials and creating more inclusive school celebrations.

Following a lengthy contract negotiation that went well into the school year, the members of a joint administration-union committee focused on supporting teachers' efforts to nurture appropriate student behavior inside their classrooms. Counterproductive behaviors to be discouraged inside the classroom included noncompliance with directions, disengagement from learning, and lack of self-control. District data showed students who were low-income, had an individualized learning plan, or are BIPOC were more likely than their wealthy, White, and/or general education age peers to be removed from the classroom environment. Rummel took the opportunity to alleviate the demographic disparity and began putting district-wide systems in place so that teachers could be supported and, in turn, better support students' SEL needs within the classroom. With the support of Tan and grant funding, the district leaders hired a third party that specialized in implementing positive behavioral intervention systems (PBIS). That third party led a new district leadership group comprised of teachers and administrators through training on how to build and support PBIS in the district.

CONCLUSION

COVID-19 coincided with the racial unrest in 2020 to set the backdrop for one of the most disruptive time periods in recent history. Many school administrators were overwhelmed by the amount of information coming in daily related to COVID-19 and were exhausted by this new work. This was compounded by the polarized beliefs among community members regarding mitigation approaches and issues of racial justice. District administrators across the country focused on reopening schools with new safety protocols in place, as did Community School District administrators who recognized that students were going to need extensive socio-emotional support when returning to school. Additionally, students were going to need support to address issues related to race, gender identity, ethnicity, among others that had afflicted them prior, during, and after the pandemic.

Advancing transformative work within the Community School District was challenging and demanded collaboration. Many district leaders lacked the expertise and knowledge necessary to move the needle and make lasting changes for students and members of the school community. However, tapping into the expertise of university experts, Community School District seized the opportunity to foster growth and support lasting change. As a result of the joint efforts, there is now a DEI committee focused on students and policies and practices in each of the school buildings. The district now has a district team examining systems and reviewing data, allowing for greater emphasis on alleviating actual needs. Representatives from community service organizations are at the table engaging in conversations and bringing expertise and different viewpoints to the discussions and providing direct services to students and families.

NOTES

1. Systems of racism and classism are intertwined societal constructs indicating the perpetuation of discrimination and inequality based on race and social class, respectively. It involves one group wielding power to enact widespread discrimination through institutional policies and practices and differential treatment based on race, ethnicity, and social class (Racial Equity Tools, 2023).
2. Microaggression refers to the routine occurrences of verbal and nonverbal actions, whether deliberate or inadvertent, that convey hostile, derogatory, or unfavorable messages to individuals based on their membership of a marginalized group (Racial Equity Tools, 2023).
3. SEL is measured using the Social Skills Improvement System (Gresham & Elliott, 2008). The composite score of the measure is plotted. We observed that the SEL scores for non-free and reduced (non FRL) lunch students are higher than students who receive free and reduced lunch (FRL) at both ninth grade semester 1 and 2.
4. A formal dance hosted at a high school at the end of the academic year, typically for students in their junior or senior year.
5. Executive functioning refers to a set of cognitive processes, such as working memory, flexible thinking, and self-control, that allow an individual to plan, organize, monitor, and adapt their behavior to accomplish goals (Harvard University Center on the Developing Child, n.d.).
6. Restorative Practices refers to a set of strategies used to repair relationships and resolve conflict after harm to an individual or community. The practices

are rooted in dialogue, empathy, accountability, and community (International Institute for Restorative Practices, 2023).

REFERENCES

Bell, D. A., Jr. (1980). *Brown v. Board of Education* and the interest-convergence dilemma. *Harvard Law Review, 93*(3), 518–533. https://doi.org/10.2307/1340546

Bell, D. (1992). Racial realism. *Connecticut Law Review, 24*(2), 363–379.

Bell, D. A. (1995). Who's afraid of critical race theory. *University of Illinois Law Review, 4*, 893–910.

Donnor, J. K. (2016). Derrick Bell, *Brown,* and the continuing significance of the interest-convergence principle. In G. Ladson-Billings & W. F. Tate (Eds.), *"Covenant keeper": Derrick Bell's enduring education legacy* (pp. 81–90). Peter Lang.

Faase, C., Kohl, S., & Lau, J. (2022). *Coping with tensions: A catalyst for transformative change for teachers and administrators.* Rowman & Littlefield.

Gresham, F., & Elliott, S. N. (2008). *Social skills improvement system: SSIS rating scales.* Pearson.

Harris, C. I. (1993). Whiteness as property. *Harvard Law Review, 106*(8), 1707–1791.

Harvard University Center on the Developing Child. (n.d.). *Executive function & self-regulation.* https://developingchild.harvard.edu/science/key-concepts/executive-function

Hattie, J., & Zierer, K. (2017). *10 mindframes for visible learning and the science of how we learn.* Routledge.

Herrera, S. G., Porter, L., & Barko-Alva, K. (2020). *Equity in school–parent partnerships: Cultivating community and family trust in culturally diverse classrooms.* Teachers College Press.

International Institute for Restorative Practices. (2023). https://www.iirp.edu/

Jackson, S. J. (2020). On #BlackLivesMatter and journalism. *Sociologica, 14*(2), 101–108. https://doi.org/10.6092/issn.1971-8853/11425

Jagers, R. J., Rivas-Drake, D., & Williams, B. (2019). Transformative social and emotional learning (SEL): Toward SEL in service of educational equity and excellence. *Educational Psychologist, 54*(3), 162–184. https://doi.org/10.1080/00461520.2019.1623032

Kamola, I. (2019). Dear administrators: To protect your faculty from right-wing attacks, follow the money. *AAUP Journal of Academic Freedom, 10*, 1–24. https://shorturl.at/hox13

Mueller, J. C. (2020). Racial ideology or racial ignorance? An alternative theory of racial cognition. *Sociological Theory, 38*(2), 142–169. https://doi.org/10.1177/0735275120926197

Muradova, L. (2021). Seeing the other side? Perspective-taking and reflective political judgements in interpersonal deliberation. *Political Studies, 69*(3), 644–664. https://doi.org/10.1177/0032321720916605

Phillips, E. K. (2019). *The make-or-break year: Solving the dropout crisis one ninth grader at a time.* The New Press.

Racial Equity Tools. (2023, September 17). *Racial equity tools glossary.* https://www.racialequitytools.org/glossary

Responsive Classroom. (2023, June 6). *Responsive classroom.* https://www.responsive-classroom.org/

Roegman, R., Tan, K., Tanner, N., & Yore, C. (2022). Following the data: An analysis of two schools' use of social emotional data. *Journal of Educational Administration, 60*(6), 561–578. https://doi.org/10.1108/JEA-10-2021-0198

Sprenger, M. (2020). *Social emotional learning and the brain: Strategies to help your students thrive.* ASCD.

SECTION III

DISRUPTIVE ASPECTS

CHAPTER 6

CHECKING THE BOX
OR DOING THE WORK?

The Importance of Faculty Perspectives on Service and the Relationship to Power in Higher Education, and the Role of DEIJ Initiatives in Culture Change

Kari Havenaar
Eastern Michigan University

Dyann Logwood
Eastern Michigan University

Cassandra Barragan
Eastern Michigan University

ABSTRACT

Faculty continue to struggle to understand the inequities embedded in university structures and the overarching need for DEIJ (diversity, equity, inclu-

Justice, Equity, Diversity, and Inclusion in Education, pages 119–140
Copyright © 2024 by Information Age Publishing
www.infoagepub.com
All rights of reproduction in any form reserved.

sion, and justice) work (Wilson & Tugas, 2022). The COVID-19 pandemic brought to light pre-existing inequities of the distribution of service labor in academia (Docka-Filipek et al., 2023), which included the unacknowledged labor of women and faculty of color (Hogan, 2012). This additional service is most often levied on women and BIPOC faculty, which plays a role in creating barriers to career advancement (Domingo et al., 2022). This pilot-study explored the service engagement of faculty leadership ($N = 21$) at a university in the Midwest United States to provide an understanding of the service responsibilities of non-majority faculty and to compare these obligations across gender and race/ethnicity. Leaders in faculty senate, unions, and DEIJ committees responded to a 2021 survey about service obligations, perceptions of service, and types of service. The results indicated women faculty are more engaged in caregiving types of service than their men counterparts, even with fewer supports for service work. Faculty of color feel less supported and held to a different standard than their White colleagues. The results were explored through a lens of privilege and power with consideration to gender and cultural taxation. In order for faculty to move into higher levels of leadership, it is crucial for institutions to address power dynamics and service inequities that act as obstacles (Morin, 2018). Universities should prioritize service by making it a critical factor for promotion and tenure. However, achieving this requires making systemic changes within the institution where females and faculty of color are actively part of the discussion and are encouraged to share their personal narratives to better inform the institution (Patitu & Hinton, 2003).

Despite ongoing efforts to bring equity into predominantly White institutions (PWI), faculty continue to struggle to understand the inequities that are embedded in university structures and the overarching reasons for the current increase in DEIJ (diversity, equity, inclusion, and justice) work (Wilson & Tugas, 2022). COVID-19 and increased stress from the pandemic have brought to light the inequities in the distribution of labor in academia, especially in service (Docka-Filipek et al., 2023) and the unacknowledged and invisible labor performed by women and faculty of color (Hogan, 2012), which is essential to the functioning of the university. This additional burden of unseen service is most levied on women and BIPOC faculty, which plays a role in creating barriers to career advancement (Domingo et al., 2022). This pilot-research study explores aspects of the service engagement of faculty leadership from a 2021 survey ($N = 21$). The results have been considered through a lens of privilege and power in higher education with focus on gender, race/ethnicity, and the phenomenon of cultural taxation. This study aims to provide a clear understanding of the service responsibilities of non-majority faculty and to compare these obligations across gender and race/ethnicity to gain a comprehensive perspective.

LITERATURE REVIEW

Historically, institutes of higher learning in the United States were established to educate only White men (Wilder, 2013), resulting in environments lacking diversity. The practice of controlling knowledge in the past has resulted in leadership positions being held by those who benefit from White privilege (Moore et al., 2018; Patton, 2016). These systems of oppression are persistent and are allowed to thrive (Ladson-Billings, 2009) through embedded policies and practices designed to maintain the status quo. Typically, DEIJ efforts on university campuses intend to promote a culture of belonging, create spaces and opportunities for acknowledgment and support, and identify and remove barriers while moving toward justice-oriented initiatives (Agresar et al., 2022). But in reality, higher education is subject to the same external influences as any other area of society, as BIPOC faculty are often props in DEIJ efforts rather than the priority (Cooke & Sánchez, 2019).

Emerging political systems in the United States aim to figuratively and literally outlaw DEIJ practices in higher education (Craig et al., 2023). While there is great concern within the higher education community about these oppressive efforts, it is important to remember Whiteness is still the norm in higher education (Rainer, 2015). DEIJ is a direct challenge to power and control in higher education, and external efforts to suppress DEIJ efforts could be interpreted as ongoing ways to keep the perspectives of White men at the center of educational content and the institutions themselves (King-Jordan & Gil, 2021). Areas of study interconnected with DEIJ programs, such as gender and cultural studies curriculums, are also on the verge of being eliminated (Frey Knepp, 2012). Furthermore, programs that highlight diversity are at risk of being, at best, minimized and, at worst, eliminated, putting overwhelmingly female and/or BIPOC faculty of these programs in the position to defend their life's scholarly work against forces that question their validity and worth. Moves to dismantle programs that highlight diversity, equity, and inclusion of cultures other than the historically centered White male experience further emphasize the systemic denial of the White power structure in higher education (Haynes, 2023).

Furthermore, entrenched internal forces are structured to stratify power, even amongst the faculty, as there is a power structure among the instructional staff at universities. Assistant professors are referred to as "junior faculty," and part-time faculty or lecturers are not included as part of a department or instructional staff other than to teach classes when needed. Untenured faculty may encounter difficulties in declining requests from more experienced colleagues without fear of damaging their professional relationships (Martinez et al., 2017). Inequities also exist regarding access to those who are considered to be at the lower end of the power structure, as their labor is often exploited with the veiled threat that a lack of compliance will result in losing their class assignments, committee positions, or other earned or awarded current statuses.

Privilege in Higher Education

Privilege, at its core, refers to receiving benefits and having access to resources based on membership in a group. The concept of privilege in higher education must be considered in the context of the academy itself. From the outside, faculty and students are perceived as belonging to very privileged groups based on socioeconomic status, education, employment, and even having the ability to work at home during the 2020 pandemic lockdowns (Cetrulo et al., 2020). However, inequities of gender and race are omnipresent in society and extend into the academy, despite the outward appearance that privilege is omnipresent. Dominant privilege is not isolated to just the majority population (Rainer, 2015), and while women may outnumber men in higher education, the normative structures still center the White male experience and expectations. Institutionalized White privilege provides an unearned advantage and benefit for White faculty because expectations within the university are based on their White experiences (Sue, 2003). Moreover, the refusal of the dominant culture to acknowledge the unique experiences of women and BIPOC faculty only serves to maintain the systemic structures that have been created and reinforced by the experiences of White men in academia (Owen, 2009).

Privilege in Leadership

Access is the byproduct of privilege because having access to systems of power leads to opportunities for leadership, tenure, promotion, and recognition (Rainer, 2015). Those who are in leadership therefore have the ability to minimize the impact of inequality in their institutions (Geiger & Jordan, 2014), especially if they do not belong to the dominant group. When privilege is not recognized or acknowledged, the work that others do to maintain the institution may not be recognized or acknowledged by leadership, leading to hidden service requirements most often taken on by women and faculty of color (Docka-Filipek et al., 2023; Domingo et al., 2022). The true privilege in leadership is to be able to ignore the advantages and opportunities that leadership provides and the ways it normalizes oppressive structures in higher education (Geiger & Jordan, 2014).

Privilege and Service Obligations

Service is an essential component of faculty work in higher education, but hidden service requirements that are necessary or required of faculty to meet the needs of the institution are met with little to no reward. This necessary, yet under-appreciated, service also may not be formally recognized in the tenure and promotion process (Hirshfield & Joseph, 2012; O'Meara et al., 2017; Padilla, 1994). Women and faculty of color are often those who engage in hidden service, often at the request or expectation of the institution (Hogan, 2012). Furthermore, service that relates to identity or providing support to students may not be explicitly captured on CVs or recognized in tenure and promotion requirements (Domingo et al., 2022).

Service and Gender. Guarino and Borden (2017) posit the differences in service performed by men and women may be a gendered response to acts of service, with reasons ranging from women being more likely to volunteer to being less likely to turn down requests. These gendered responses contribute to women being asked more than men to take on additional service. Additionally, the lack of women reaching positions of power or receiving the same opportunities to advance in their careers as their male counterparts is due, in part, to this unspoken practice of providing service without recognition (Settles et al., 2019). This unrecognized service is often in response to service related to "academic housekeeping" (Docka-Filipek & Stone, 2021), or the care of students and the university. These services of caregiving, which also include academic advising, mentoring, and emotional support (King-Jordan & Gil, 2021), are considered invisible work and can play a role in creating barriers to career advancement (Domingo et al., 2022; Gewin, 2020).

Institutions and departments that place less value on service for the caregiving of the university (Green, 2008) create inequity in promotion, tenure, and overall visibility (Schneider & Radhakrishnan, 2018). This is evident through gendered expectations, including that women negotiate their service obligations less frequently than their male counterparts (Laschever & Babcock, 2021), especially if the authority is male (Bowles et al., 2022). Because male faculty do not have this expectation to care for the university, they are able to pursue service based on their interests and skills and further their research agenda more quickly than their female counterparts (Babcock et al., 2017; Hanasono et al., 2019; Misra et al., 2011). For example, women STEM associate professors spend more time on service and student mentoring than their male counterparts (Misra et al., 2011), with male faculty spending more time on research and less time on service compared to their women counterparts (Babcock et al., 2017; Hanasono et al., 2019; Misra et al., 2011). Gender expectations of society extend into academia and are validated in the reproduction of systemic societal structures (Owen, 2009) wherein White males in positions of power perceive female faculty as choosing additional service and are, therefore, voluntarily impacting their own tenure trajectory. This "epistemology of ignorance" minimizes the privilege of centering on the White male normative experience (Mills, 1997) by ignoring that what may be choice for them is obligation for others.

Service and Race/Ethnicity.   BIPOC faculty are often met with an institutional expectation to represent or speak for other BIPOC faculty and students in the university community (Tippeconnic Fox, 2005) and to engage in uncompensated and often unrelated service related to their BIPOC identity (Domingo et al., 2022; Stein, 1996). It is not uncommon for BIPOC faculty to be specifically asked or expected to lead DEIJ-related efforts (Leider & Dobb, 2022), mentor BIPOC students, serve on DEIJ committees, and address other service activities in which their White colleagues are not expected to participate (Trejo, 2020).

BIPOC faculty, in particular, face intense pressure and expectations to represent diversity in their departments and the university (Cleveland et al., 2018; Hirschfield & Joseph, 2012; Smith, 2010). They are also expected to tend to the needs of BIPOC students (Harper, 2013) in ways their White colleagues are not. Griffin (2013) and Reddick (2004) have noted that Black faculty members often establish a unique connection with BIPOC students who share similar cultural backgrounds, motivating them to provide mentorship, advice, and support. These relationships may be emphasized for faculty and students who work and study at PWIs due to the isolation of having smaller numbers of BIPOC students *and* faculty at these institutions.

While the privilege of education is endemic to academia, the experiences of faculty members of color are "no different from . . . everyday experiences of being Black in America" (King-Jordan & Gil, 2021, p. 383). The experiences of BIPOC faculty in the academy related to their identity can leave them feeling disempowered and obligated to take on extra service that is often invisible (Buchanan & Settles, 2019; Settles et al., 2021). In this way, when only some work by BIPOC faculty is highlighted in very visible ways, such as how DEIJ work often is, it puts these faculty at risk of increased stereotyping and discrimination within the academy (Settles et al., 2019; Seyranian et al., 2008; Turner et al., 1999; Yoder, 2002), while simultaneously experiencing negative reactions from their White colleagues (Cooke & Sánchez, 2019). Faculty members of color are finding themselves teaching colleagues about race/racism (Rideau, 2021), acting as "cultural translators" in their workplace" (Mohamed & Beagen, 2019, p. 344), and feeling pressured to give their perspectives on certain issues or explain certain practices in their culture (Rideau, 2021). BIPOC faculty members may also be perceived as having privilege due to their high visibility in serving their duties. However, this perception does not always result in actual power or privilege and tends to favor those who already possess privilege (Settles et al., 2021). In fact, it could be argued that calling on individuals of color to speak for all people of color is exploitative and oppressive and specifically upholds the structures of inequality in higher education (Rainer, 2015).

Cultural Taxation

Cultural taxation was first described by Padilla (1994) as the tax paid by the non-dominant culture to the dominant culture to remain in the dominant system. In higher education, this tax may take the form of being expected to perform work through service that holds less value to the dominant culture but is then claimed by the dominant culture. Non-prestigious work, such as managing administrative tasks in a department, often falls to women and BIPOC faculty specifically (Docka-Filipek et al., 2023; Hanasono et al., 2019). Other more laborious efforts, such as designing, implementing, and executing DEIJ-related projects at the university level, are often left to BIPOC faculty in addition to their expected service (Leider & Dobb, 2022) without additional compensation, reward, or recognition.

As members of a minoritized faculty population, women and BIPOC faculty members are disproportionately tasked with more services than their White or male colleagues (Docka-Filipek et al., 2023). This is due to their identities not being aligned with the cultural norms of academia (Padilla, 1994). This additional burden is thought to be a profound contributor to the difficulty faculty in historically marginalized groups have had in gaining promotion and tenure (Guillaume & Apodaca, 2022). By being kept out of tenured or leadership positions, BIPOC faculty remain discouraged from challenging the power structures in higher education without risking their professional and personal well-being. Non-marginalized faculty, generally considered White cisgender males, are able to spend up to four times the amount of time on research, which carries more weight towards tenure and promotion (Social Sciences Feminist Network Research Interest Group, 2017). Furthermore, being part of the university community means more than being a token or spokesperson for an entire cultural group. This research specifically addresses the gap in understanding perceptions of the service obligations of women and faculty of color who are also in faculty leadership roles, with consideration of what inequities may exist and what these inequities may mean for future DEIJ efforts.

METHODS

The remainder of this chapter includes findings from a 2022 pilot survey of 21 faculty in leadership positions at a midsized PWI in the Midwest conducted by the authors. The survey asked questions about service and service-related activities, including the impact of COVID-19, and was developed in conjunction

126 • K. HAVENAAR, D. LOGWOOD, and C. BARRAGAN

with the university-level DEI committee and advised by a university survey consultant. Given this was a pilot study, it was imperative to include an open-ended question to gather feedback on both the survey and overall study. The results from this qualitative inquiry will be thoroughly discussed in the findings and limitations sections of this manuscript. A total of 21 responses were received, representing an estimated 20% response rate. The sample had an even distribution of female ($n = 10$) and male ($n = 10$) respondents, with one who preferred not to answer ($n = 1$). See Table 6.1 for the demographics of the respondents. For this survey, we compared the mean scores and standard deviations across gender and race/ethnicity and further analysis was not possible due to the small sample size and to protect the sensitivity of responses. Sample size and responses are provided where appropriate.

Measures

Service Obligations
We measured subjective service obligations by asking how strongly respondents disagreed or agreed, using 6-point Likert-type scale questions

TABLE 6.1 Demographic Frequencies ($N = 21$)		
	n	%
Gender		
Female	10	47.6%
Male	10	47.6%
Prefer not to answer	1	4.8%
Race/Ethnicity		
Non-White	4	19%
White	16	80%
Role		
Tenure-track faculty	3	14.3%
Tenured faculty	14	76.2%
Part-time lecturer	1	4.8%
Full-time lecturer	1	4.8%
Discipline		
Arts and Sciences	7	33.3%
Business	1	4.8%
Education	3	14.3%
Engineering and Technology	5	23.8%
Health and Human Services	4	19.0%

(1 = *strongly disagree*, 6 = *strongly agree*). The four possible responses to the questions about service obligations were as follows: (a) In the past 2 years, I have made an intentional effort to support students or colleagues in unofficial ways (e.g., donating to campus services; having food, supplies, or personal hygiene supplies in your office; providing emotional support; (b) I create service initiatives because I see a need no one else is filling; (c) I have been on committees that have generated outputs that were ignored or not acted on; and (d) I am invited to join committees because of my expertise in a certain academic or administrative area.

Perceptions of Service

We measured subjective perceptions of issues related to service by asking how strongly respondents disagreed or agreed using 6-point Likert-type scale questions (1 = *strongly disagree*, 6 = *strongly agree*). Two questions asking about perceptions of issues related to perceptions of service in the previous 2 years were as follows: (a) I feel there are supports at (this institution) that enable me to successfully complete my service obligations; and (b) I feel students hold me to a different standard than my colleagues.

Types of Service

We measured subjective measures of frequency of participation in committees by asking how often respondents participated (1 = *never*, 2 = *yes, maybe once*, 3 = *yes, a few times*, 4 = *yes, several times*, 5 = *yes, on a regular schedule*) in the following types of service work: (a) ad hoc committees that are formed to complete a task (e.g., prepare for accreditation, create a mission statement, short-term planning, etc.); (b) standing committees (does not include faculty meetings; curriculum related committees, DEI committees, Gen Ed committees, etc.); (c) governance (e.g., union representative, faculty senate, faculty advisory committee, etc.); (d) research, professional journal, or conference reviews—served on a board or committee for a professional organization; and (e) administrative work (e.g., director, chairing committees, social media, website maintenance, etc.).

Data Preparation

Our examination of the data revealed no outliers, leaving the final sample size at 21. We created two variables for this analysis. The first variable addressed the race/ethnicity of the faculty (non-White = 1; White = 2) by including all White, non-hispanic respondents as White (n = 16), and faculty who identified as Black, Asian, or Middle Eastern as non-White (n = 4). The second created variable collapsed responses to the questions related to type of service (*never or rarely* = 1; *sometimes* = 2; *regularly* = 3). Three categories were created: Never or rarely (using response never, N/A, and yes, maybe once); Sometimes (using responses yes, a few times and yes, several times); and Regularly (using response yes, on a regular basis).

Analysis

Because this was a small sample size from a pilot survey, we compared mean scores and standard deviations across gender and race/ethnicity. Additional analysis was inappropriate for this sample size as well as the possibility that confidentiality could be compromised.

FINDINGS AND DISCUSSION

Service work, such as mentoring, committee membership, and teaching, is essential for faculty growth and career advancement. However, many universities do not recognize the importance of service work and the time commitment it requires, leading to disparities in promotions. While the norms of higher education center on the experiences of White men, the expectations and workload burden, especially for service, of non-White and female faculty are significantly higher. Tasks of caregiving for the university, such as administrative tasks and tending to the needs of students, historically fall on women and BIPOC faculty. They are expected to perform these caregiving tasks as well as take on additional service related to their group membership (Docka-Filipek & Stone, 2021) such as DEIJ efforts (Leider & Dobb, 2022). Understanding how faculty perform service is essential to understanding where changes in the academy can remedy this inequity in expectations and service obligations. While these groups are spending more time and energy tending to the needs of their students and university, their White male colleagues are able to spend time on recognized actions, such as research and visible service in leadership roles, reinforcing the normative expectation that what White men do is the overarching standard by which all faculty are measured. This leaves little room to meaningfully acknowledge the invisible work and ever-expanding roles of faculty in caring for their students, their departments, and the institution.

While not formally analyzed, some faculty comments from the survey are worth mentioning to frame the importance of discussions around privilege and service that illustrate the perpetuation of antiquated privilege in higher education such as this. One participant stated:

> Doing or not doing service may not relate to a sense of belonging, depending on the person, the reason they're doing the service, or the support the col-

Checking the Box or Doing the Work? • **129**

> lege gives them for doing service. For example, if the college considers service as an obligation for tenure/promotion, then it is more of a "check the box" action rather than anything used to draw people together.

This demonstration of privilege serves as a reminder that faculty colleagues and particularly those in faculty leadership positions, do not recognize or acknowledge service as anything other than something to do to make tenure, as stated above, a "box to check." The reality is that this is also a demonstration of a lack of understanding of the different meanings service has to women and faculty of color, and thus, it perpetuates the White normative expectations. This supports the work of Geiger and Jordan (2014) and the idea that "societal privilege is the freedom to ignore that privilege" (p. 266).

Service and Gender

Because this work centered on faculty leadership, it was not unexpected that even with this small sample size, male faculty were more engaged in ad hoc committees, standing committees, and governance—those activities that often result in decisions—than female faculty. However, 100% of women in this study were serving on boards and acting as reviewers for research entities in their disciplines, and 90% were engaging in administrative work. When specifically asked about creating a service to fulfill a need, male faculty ($M = 5.0$) more often felt they created this type of service than female faculty ($M = 3.8$; see Table 6.2). This could suggest that the service created by male faculty was likely related to visible administrative or leadership needs, rather than the caregiving needs that are typically fulfilled by women who do not perceive these needs as unfulfilled, but rather as things that just need to be done. Another explanation supports the work of Guarino and Borden (2017) who found that service adopted by women is disproportionately "taking care of the academic family" (p. 19) and points

TABLE 6.2   Means and Standard Deviations of Questions Related to Service by Gender (Female/Male)

	Female		Male	
	M	*SD*	*M*	*SD*
Unofficial service	5.50	0.85	5.70	0.48
Create service	3.80	1.75	5.00	1.05
Outputs	4.60	1.71	4.80	1.48
Expertise	3.44	1.74	3.80	1.87
Supports	2.78	0.83	3.90	1.73
Different standard	4.11	2.15	3.78	2.64

130 • K. HAVENAAR, D. LOGWOOD, and C. BARRAGAN

TABLE 6.3 Frequencies of Response to Questions Sometimes or Regular Participation by Type of Service by Gender (Female/Male)

	Female		Male	
	n	%	*n*	%
Ad Hoc	9	90%	9	90%
Standing	7	70%	10	100%
Governance	7	70%	9	90%
Research	10	100%	8	80%
Administrative	9	90%	8	80%

to the gendered perceptions between creating service to fill a need and fulfilling needs so they are met. Their findings demonstrated similar trends in service allocation and burden among large faculty groups in a Midwest University (Guarino & Borden, 2017) compared to our survey with a small sample size.

Even women in leadership positions are more engaged in the support and care of the institution and discipline than their male colleagues. This could suggest the service provided by male faculty is more related to visible administrative or leadership needs, rather than the caregiving needs that are typically fulfilled by women (See Table 6.3). This suggests that the perception of need is different based on gender. This also demonstrates the care that must be taken in interpreting the mean scores as a metric of who is "doing more work." Both male and female faculty provide service to the university but service work performed by female faculty should not be perceived as voluntary, optional, or equitable, but rather as an omnipresent symptom of gender bias in higher education (Pyke, 2015).

Service and Race/Ethnicity

This research explored specific differences in service between non-White and White faculty leaders, but not by race/ethnicity *and* gender. These findings demonstrate how service differs from the non-dominant population, in the case of this research, between non-White and White faculty. Faculty were asked about their intentional efforts to support students or colleagues in unofficial ways. Non-White faculty ($n = 4$, 100%) strongly agreed they have engaged in unofficial service within the past 2 years ($M = 6.00$), while their White colleagues agreed to a lesser extent ($M = 5.56$; see Table 6.4). These responses are not extremely different, but when examining those who create service because of a perceived need, non-White faculty ($M = 5.50$) were creating necessary service more often than their White colleagues ($M = 4.44$). This finding supports previous research that found not

Checking the Box or Doing the Work? ▪ 131

TABLE 6.4 Means and Standard Deviations of Questions Related to Service by Race (non-White/White)

	Non-White		White	
	M	SD	M	SD
Unofficial service	6.00	0.00	5.56	0.63
Create service	5.50	1.00	4.44	1.59
Outputs	6.00	0.00	4.50	1.55
Expertise	3.00	2.45	3.88	1.59
Supports	2.50	1.73	3.56	1.32
Different standard	4.67	2.31	3.69	2.36

only are students drawn to faculty who share similar racial and/or national identities (Hanasono et al., 2019), but all students, including White and non-White, intentionally seek out BIPOC faculty (Harper, 2013).

This phenomenon of students seeking out BIPOC faculty creates an additional service burden in the form of informal mentoring, advising, and problem-solving at much higher rates than their White colleagues. Because of this, faculty of color are more involved with student-centered service, such as formal and informal advising of students, than their White counterparts. For some individuals, service work is a way to foster a culture of belonging within students; but also, faculty of color are often put into places where they serve as mentors to those around them to create a culture of belonging within a particular department or group, while White faculty are rarely asked and rarely choose to do this type of unofficial service because they have the privilege to make that choice. These relationships may be emphasized for faculty and students who work and study at PWIs due to the isolation of having smaller numbers of BIPOC at these institutions. When faculty are vulnerable, "voluntary" is not an option. BIPOC faculty do not feel empowered, and those in privileged positions often question the experiences of BIPOC faculty while perpetuating the structures that create this dynamic. White male faculty are doing service, but overwhelmingly, caregiving service falls on the shoulders of women and BIPOC faculty—a no-win situation. White faculty who want to engage BIPOC students need access to culturally inclusive faculty development workshops or training. They need support from department heads, administrators, and like-minded peers to meet the unique ethnic and cultural needs of their diverse student population (Jenkins & Alfred, 2018; Livingston 2023).

Cultural Taxation

The experiences of non-White and White faculty when engaging in service are distinctly different. The greatest difference between non-White and White faculty was in their time spent on committees where the recommendations of their work was either ignored or not acted on. All non-White faculty surveyed ($n = 4$) strongly agreed ($M = 6.00$) they had this experience, while White faculty did not have that same experience ($M = 4.50$). Ad hoc committees are often formed to address or solve a problem and are therefore time consuming. They often deal with complex university level issues, which then go unrecognized by the institution.

This pattern of unrecognized service work is relevant to not only the time-burden of service with no reward, but also when 100% ($n = 4$) of this same group of non-White faculty sit on ad hoc committees and just 25% ($n = 1$) engage in administrative service on a regular basis, it directly speaks to the value of privilege in the ability to choose service and the power that comes with that ability to choose (see Table 6.5). BIPOC faculty are in a constant balancing act of considering the opportunity cost of agreeing to additional work (that may not be recognized) with addressing what is necessary to build a successful research agenda or to participate in less taxing service. They feel less supported ($M = 2.50$) and more scrutinized by being held to a different standard ($M = 4.67$) than their White colleagues ($M = 3.56$ and $M = 3.69$, respectively); therefore, the personal and emotional costs can be significant. This supports the findings of King-Jordan and Gil (2021) that support may be found in some groups on campus, but not in the larger university community.

The concept of cultural taxation sheds light on how an individual's identity is exploited by institutions and organizations to access opportunities for institutional advancement and growth. Unfortunately, this often comes at a cost to faculty of color as many are forced to engage in unpaid or invisible services that go unrecognized, ultimately hindering their own career progression and giving space for White colleagues to focus on areas that have more value in the eyes of the university. For example, when respondents were asked if they were invited to join committees because of their expertise in certain academic or administrative areas, White faculty ($M = 3.88$) more strongly agreed they were asked for this reason than non-White faculty

TABLE 6.5 Frequencies of Response to Questions Sometimes or Regular Participation by Type of Service by Race (non-White/White)

	Non-White		White	
	n	%	*n*	%
Ad Hoc	4	100%	12	75.1%
Standing	3	75%	13	81.3%
Governance	3	75%	9	56.3%
Research	3	75%	14	93.0%
Administrative	1	25%	13	81.3%

($M = 3.00$). This finding reveals an inequity that takes valuable time and energy from non-White faculty to service the university rather than their own interests or research agendas. Even with this small sample, these findings also support the work of Guillaume and Apodaca (2022) who found faculty of color are expected to spend time on committees, educating other faculty, staff and students on minority issues, teaching courses that focus on race or diversity, and advising students of color or faculty of color without additional recognition from administration or compensation. Faculty who are invited to join committees that support their interests have the privilege to be more selective in their service while other faculty, specifically those BIPOC faculty, have less choice in the service they are expected to do while also supporting their own interests. This is an instance of cultural taxation, whereby BIPOC faculty labor is exploited for the university's benefit (Cleveland et al., 2018).

Despite BIPOC faculty possessing disciplinary expertise, their perceived expertise is often confined to their personal experiences as BIPOC faculty. Therefore, it is imperative to be critical when examining results that directly compare White faculty experiences with non-White experiences. On its face, White faculty are engaged in more service; however, both male and female faculty of color are often overburdened with committee tasks and responsibilities to maintain diversity in these activities (Gibson, 2019; Mohamed & Beagan, 2019). These disparities are likely greatest when considering work around DEIJ efforts, as faculty of color are more likely to take on committee requests—even if they do not want to—because they know it will then be pushed onto another faculty member of color if they decline (Rideau, 2021). BIPOC faculty members, being experts in their own lived experiences, need to be involved in and wherever possible, lead the DEIJ efforts. However, such work needs to be of equal value when compared to formal research and administrative leadership responsibilities when it comes to tenure and promotion. Moreover, if a BIPOC faculty member participates in DEIJ initiatives, the audience for their work may be limited, thereby limiting their visibility and access to higher leadership positions. The American Association of University Professors recently reported on the need to acknowledge that BIPOC faculty are unofficially expected to contribute more than what is expected to meet tenure requirements in the name of diversity and, thusly, take on a larger share of the service burden both at the department and university levels (Pittman, 2023).

White faculty in leadership from this study were overwhelmingly more engaged in service related to research or their discipline than their non-White colleagues at 93% ($n = 14$) and 75% ($n = 3$), respectively. Still, some administrators often fail to acknowledge their exploitative behavior when they expect more from faculty of color than their White counterparts. It is important to acknowledge that some individuals may view service as a mere "check the box" activity solely for the purpose of achieving a promotion. However, this perspective completely disregards the added responsibilities that women and faculty of color have to bear. The university requires them to fulfill certain service obligations in order to be promoted, and it is unfair to diminish the ongoing commitment and dedication they have to maintain that promotion. It also assumes their expectations of service are unrelated to a culture of belonging, despite evidence and research to the contrary (Mohamed & Beagan, 2019; Rideau, 2021). Being able to check the box suggests that the individual participated in service obligations as a means to an end, rather than as something meaningful, and will likely not continue after receiving tenure or promotion. It is a privilege to do such a thing and still obtain career advancement within the department and academic community.

LIMITATIONS

While this small-sampled pilot study reveals many inequities in the under-studied segment of faculty leadership, there are some limitations to this work which does preclude its generalizability to other institutions of higher education. First, the small sample size prevented examination of intersectionality between race and gender as disaggregation of the data would compromise confidentiality. Additionally, because this was a pilot study with a small sample size, we included an open-ended question asking for feedback about the survey and the overall study, which was not able to be formally analyzed or disseminated but still yielded data relevant to this manuscript. Lastly, committee membership definitions, specifically for administrative work, did not translate well in fully understanding gender differences. For example, administrative committees vary from director-related work, which is service related to a position of power, to coordinating student orientation, which is a caregiving-related service task. Although types of committees were defined for respondents, a more concrete acknowledgment of specific service work (e.g., DEIJ committees, faculty hiring committees, etc.) would have presented additional opportunity to understand inequities in service by gender and race.

Recommendations for Improving the Academy

Many academic settings highlight inclusivity initiatives and have mission statements, which suggests they are actively fighting against racism, homophobia, sexism, and more. Concurrently, these same institutions are intentionally or unintentionally perpetuating the exclusive structures of higher education and fail to support BIPOC faculty through recruitment, retention, and research support (Settles et al., 2021). To establish an inclusive and supportive atmosphere for diversity, equity, and belonging, it is essential to hire BIPOC faculty. To address the needs of individuals who want to progress from the lower levels to higher levels of leadership, higher education institutions must address the power dynamics that hinder leadership progression. (Morin, 2018). Additionally, the university and its administrators must make a systemic change by deciding what service responsibilities are more critical for the promotion and tenure of faculty, particularly for those who are people of color. Ideally, all services should be weighed equally.

Women can find support in mentoring relationships (Vaccaro, 2011) and service creates a culture of belonging for BIPOC faculty (Rideau, 2021). Not all iterations of service weigh the same in terms of tenure and promotion determinations (Boyer, 1990; Green, 2008; Miller, 2012), and the power of privilege leaves various groups of people without the supports that are needed in order to feel represented in these spaces and to foster success within the work itself. These additional service obligations can be framed as an opportunity with the appropriate level of support from university administration and recognition in the tenure and promotion process. In order for a culture change to occur, every faculty member should be given the opportunity to learn how to effectively work with BIPOC students and be held accountable for actively engaging in visible and invisible service responsibilities. This change will help alleviate the burden placed on BIPOC faculty to provide this service to institutions (Social Sciences Feminist Network Research Interest Group, 2017).

FURTHER IMPLICATIONS AND CONCLUSION

The importance of highlighting disparities in service is essential to culture change in the academy. One respondent from this study felt, "There are markedly lower standards for DEI people versus White males," which leaves us to acknowledge there are colleagues in faculty leadership positions who minimize the disparities in service. It is common for women, especially those from minoritized backgrounds, to take on demanding service-related responsibilities (King-Jordan & Gil, 2021; Walters et al., 2022). Unfortunately, their efforts often go unacknowledged by their male colleagues, who are not expected to perform the same tasks. Instead, men have the privilege of focusing on research and publishing, which are crucial for tenure and promotion. This research supports the works of Trejo (2020) and Choo and Ferree (2010) who posited meaningful systemic change occurs when all faculty members are engaged in the design and implementation of data-driven DEIJ strategies. Policy changes at the institutional level will codify equitable recognition of service burden in matters of tenure and promotion.

REFERENCES

Agresar, G., Callewaert, J., Skerlos, S., & Millunchick, J. (2022, June 26–29). *WIP developing learning objectives for an "equity-centered" undergraduate engineering program* [Paper presentation]. ASEE Annual Conference & Exposition, Minneapolis, MN. https://peer.asee.org/41777

Babcock, L., Recalde M. P., Vesterlund, L., & Weingart, L. (2017). Gender differences in accepting and receiving requests for tasks with low promotability. *American Economic Review, 107*(3), 714–747. https://doi.org/10.1257/aer.20141734

Bowles, H. R., Thomason, B., & Macias-Alonso, I. (2022). When gender matters in organizational negotiations. *Annual Review of Organizational Psychology and Organizational Behavior, 9,* 199–223. https://doi.org/10.1146/annurev-orgpsych-012420-055523

Boyer, E. L. (1990). *Scholarship reconsidered: Priorities of the professoriate.* Carnegie Foundation for the Advancement of Teaching. https://www.umces.edu/sites/default/files/al/pdfs/BoyerScholarshipReconsidered.pdf

Buchanan, N. T., & Settles, I. H. (2019). Managing (in)visibility and hypervisibility in the workplace. *Journal of Vocational Behavior, 113,* 1–5. https://doi.org/10.1016/j.jvb.2018.11.001

Cetrulo, A., Guarascio, D., & Virgillito, M. E. (2020). The privilege of working from home at the time of social distancing. *Intereconomics, 55,* 142–147. https://www.intereconomics.eu/contents/year/2020/number/3/article/the-privilege-of-working-from-home-at-the-time-of-social-distancing-6222.html

Choo, H. Y., & Ferree, M. M. (2010). Practicing intersectionality in sociological research: A critical analysis of inclusions, interactions, and institutions in the study of inequalities. *Sociological Theory, 28*(2), 129–150. https://doi.org/10.1111/j.1467-9558.2010.01370.x

Cleveland, R., Sailes, J., Gilliam, E., & Watts, J. (2018). A theoretical focus on cultural taxation: Who pays for it in higher education. *Advances in Social Sciences Research Journal, 5*(10), 95–98. https://doi.org/10.14738/assrj.510.5293

Cooke, N. A., & Sánchez, J. O. (2019). Getting it on the record: Faculty of color in library and information science. *Journal of Education for Library and Information Science, 60*(3), 169–181. https://www.jstor.org/stable/26754754

Craig, T., Rozsa, L., & Knowles, H. (2023, February 15). Alarmed by DeSantis, Black leaders protest and prepare for 2024. *The Washington Post.* https://www.washingtonpost.com/nation/2023/02/15/ron-desantis-black-leaders-protest/

Docka-Filipek, D., Draper, C., Snow, J., & Stone, L. B. (2023). 'Professor moms' & 'hidden service' in pandemic times: Students report women faculty more supportive & accommodating amid US COVID crisis onset. *Innovative Higher Education, 48,* 787–811. https://doi.org/10.1007/s10755-023-09652-x

Docka-Filipek, D., & Stone, L. B. (2021). Twice a "housewife": On academic precarity, "hysterical" women, faculty mental health, and service as gendered care work for the "university family" in pandemic times. *Gender, Work & Organization, 28*(6), 2158–2179. https://doi.org/10.1111/gwao.12723

Domingo, C. R., Gerber, N. C., Harris, D., Mamo, L., Pasion, S. G., Rebanal, R. D., & Rosser, S. V. (2022). More service or more advancement: Institutional barriers to academic success for women and women of color faculty at a large public comprehensive minority-serving state university. *Journal of Diversity in Higher Education, 15*(3), 365–379. https://doi.org/10.1037/dhe0000292

Frey Knepp, K. A. (2012). Understanding student and faculty incivility in higher education. *The Journal of Effective Teaching, 12*(1), 33–46. https://files.eric.ed.gov/fulltext/EJ1092106.pdf

Geiger, K. A., & Jordan, C. (2014). The role of societal privilege in the definitions and practices of inclusion. *Equality, Diversity, and Inclusion: An International Journal, 33*(3), 261–274. https://doi.org/10.1108/EDI-12-2013-0115

Gewin, V. (2020). The time tax put on scientists of colour. *Nature, 583*(7816), 479–481. https://doi.org/10.1038/d41586-020-01920-6

Gibson, A. N. (2019). Civility and structural precarity for faculty of color in LIS. *Journal of Education for Library and Information Science, 60*(3), 215–222.

Green, R. (2008). Tenure and promotion decisions: The relative importance of teaching, scholarship, and service. *Journal of Social Work Education, 44*(2), 117–127. https://doi.org/10.5175/JSWE.2008.200700003

Griffin, K. A. (2013). Voices of the "othermothers": Reconsidering Black professors' relationships with Black students as a form of social exchange. *Journal of Negro Education, 82*(2), 169–183. https://doi.org/10.7709/jnegroeducation.82.2.0169

Guarino, C. M., & Borden, V. M. (2017). Faculty service loads and gender: Are women taking care of the academic family? *Research in Higher Education, 58*(6), 672–694. https://www.jstor.org/stable/26451569

Guillaume, R. O., & Apodaca, E. C. (2022). Early career faculty of color and promotion and tenure: The intersection of advancement in the academy and cultural taxation. *Race Ethnicity and Education, 25*(4), 546–63. https://doi.org/10.1080/13613324.2020.1718084

Hanasono, L. K., Broido, E. M., Yacobucci, M. M., Root, K. V., Pena, S., & O'Neil, D. A. (2019). Secret service: Revealing gender biases in the visibility and value of faculty service. *Journal of Diversity in Higher Education, 12*(1), 85–98. https://doi.org/10.1037/dhe0000081

Harper, S. R. (2013). Am I my brother's teacher? Black undergraduates, racial socialization, and peer pedagogies in predominantly White postsecondary contexts. *Review of Research in Education, 37*(1), 183–211. https://www.jstor.org/stable/24641961

Haynes, C. (2023). The susceptibility of teaching to White interests: A theoretical explanation of the influence of racial consciousness on the behaviors of White faculty in the classroom. *Journal of Diversity in Higher Education, 16*(1), 97–108. https://doi.org/10.1037/dhe0000256

Hirschfield, L., & Joseph, T. (2012). We need a woman, we need a Black woman: Gender, race, and identity taxation in the academy. *Gender & Education, 24*(2), 213–227. https://doi.org/10.1080/09540253.2011.606208

Hogan, K. J. (2012). Superserviceable feminism. In M. A. Massé & K. J. Hogan (Eds.), *Over 10 million served: Gendered service in language and literature workplaces* (pp. 55–72). SUNY Press.

Jenkins, C., & Alfred, M. (2018). Understanding the motivation and transformation of White culturally responsive professors. *Journal of Adult and Continuing Education, 24*(1), 81–99. https://doi.org/10.1177/1477971417738793

King-Jordan, T., & Gil, K. (2021). Dismantling privilege and White supremacy in social work education. *Advances in Social Work, 21*(2/3), 374–395. https://doi.org/10.18060/24088

Ladson-Billings, G. (2009). Just what is critical race theory and what's it doing in a nice field like education? In E. Taylor, D. Gillborn, & G. Ladson-Billings (Eds.), *Foundations of critical race theory in education* (pp. 17–36). Routledge.

Laschever, S., & Babcock, L. (2021). *Women don't ask: Negotiation and the gender divide.* Princeton University Press.

Leider, C. M., & Dobb, C. L. (2022). Being "diverse" in the midst of a pandemic and protests: Understanding misalignments between institutional and individual values for women of color academics. *New Horizons, 34*(3), 5–16. https://doi.org/10.1002/nha3.20358

Livingston, P. K. (2023). *Context matters: Culturally inclusive and equitable pedagogies across instructional contexts in undergraduate education* (Publication No. 30486380) [Doctoral dissertation, University of Wisconsin-Madison]. ProQuest Dissertations & Theses Global.

Martinez, M. A., Chang, A., & Welton, A. D. (2017). Assistant professors of color confront the inequitable terrain of academia: A community cultural wealth perspective. *Race Ethnicity and Education, 20*(5), 696–710. https://doi.org/10.1080/13613324.2016.1150826

Miller, T. (2012). The academy as a public works project. *Academe, 98*(6), 34–38. https://www.jstor.org/stable/23414775

Mills, C. W. (1997). *The racial contract.* Cornell University Press.

Misra, J., Lundquist, J. H., Holmes, E., & Agiomavritis, S. (2011). The ivory ceiling of service work. *Academe, 97*(1), 22–26. https://www.jstor.org/stable/25799863

Mohamed, T., & Beagan, B. L. (2019). 'Strange faces' in the academy: Experiences of racialized and Indigenous faculty in Canadian universities. *Race Ethnicity and Education, 22*(3), 338–354. https://doi.org/10.1080/13613324.2018.1511532

Moore, K. K., Cid-Martinez, I., Toney, J., Smith, J. A., Kalb, A. C., Shin, J. H., & Spalter-Roth, R. M. (2018). Who climbs the academic ladder? Race and gender stratification in a world of Whiteness. *The Review of Black Political Economy, 45*(3), 216–244. https://doi.org/10.1177/0034644618813667

Morin, M. F. (2018). *En su propia vos [In her own voice]: Illuminating the community cultural wealth of Latina chief student affairs officers* [Unpublished doctoral dissertation]. University of Maryland-College Park.

O'Meara, K., Kuvaeva, A., Nyunt, G., Waugaman, C., & Jackson, R. (2017). Asked more often: Gender differences in faculty workload in research universities and the work interactions that shape them. *American Educational Research Journal, 54*(6), 1154–1186. https://doi.org/10.3102/0002831217716767

Owen, D. S. (2009). Privileged social identities and diversity leadership in higher education. *The Review of Higher Education, 32*(2), 185–207. https://doi.org/10.1353/rhe.0.0048

Padilla, A. M. (1994). Ethnic minority scholars, research, and mentoring: Current and future issues. *Educational Researcher, 23*(4), 24–27. https://doi.org/10.2307/1176259

Patitu, C. L., & Hinton, K. G. (2003). The experiences of African American women faculty and administrators in higher education: Has anything changed? *New Directions for Student Services, 2003*(104), 79–93. https://doi.org/10.1002/ss.109

Patton, L. D. (2016). Disrupting postsecondary prose. *Urban Education, 51*(3), 315–342. https://doi.org/10.1177/0042085915602542

Pittman, C. T. (2023). *Achieving racial equity in promotion and tenure: What will it take to address the persistent underrepresentation of faculty members of color?* American Association of University Professors. https://www.aaup.org/article/achieving-racial-equity-promotion-and-tenure

Pyke, K. (2015). Faculty gender inequity and the "just say no to service" fairy tale. In K. De Welde, & A. Stepnick (Eds.), *Disrupting the culture of silence* (pp. 83–95). Routledge. https://doi.org/10.4324/9781003444299-6

Rainer, J. P. (2015). Understanding and challenging White privilege in higher education as a means of combating and neutralizing racism. *Multicultural Learning and Teaching, 10*(2), 149–161. https://doi.org/10.1515/mlt-2015-0011

Reddick, R. (2004). *"Ultimately, it's about love": African-American faculty and their mentoring relationships with African-American students* [Unpublished qualifying paper]. Harvard Graduate School of Education.

Rideau, R. (2021). "We're just not acknowledged": An examination of the identity taxation of full-time non-tenure-track women of color faculty members. *Journal of Diversity in Higher Education, 14*(2), 161–173. https://doi.org/10.1037/dhe0000139

Schneider, K., & Radhakrishnan, P. (2018). Three dilemmas for academics: Gender disparities in scholarship, teaching, and service. *Industrial and Organizational Psychology, 11*(3), 428–433. https://doi.org/10.1017/iop.2018.94

Settles, I. H., Buchanan, N. T., & Dotson, K. (2019). Scrutinized but not recognized: (In)visibility and hypervisibility experiences of faculty of color. *Journal of Vocational Behavior, 113*, 62–74. https://doi.org/10.1016/j.jvb.2018.06.003

Settles, I. H., Jones, M. K., Buchanan, N. T., & Dotson, K. (2021). Epistemic exclusion: Scholar(ly) devaluation that marginalizes faculty of color. *Journal of Diversity in Higher Education, 14*(4), 493–507. https://doi.org/10.1037/dhe0000174

Seyranian, V., Atuel, H., & Crano, W. D. (2008). Dimensions of majority and minority groups. *Group Processes & Intergroup Relations, 11*(1), 21–37. https://doi.org/10.1177/1368430207084843

Smith, M. (2010). Gender, whiteness, and "other Others" in the academy. In S. Razack, M. Smith, & S. Thobani (Eds.), *States of race: Critical race feminism for the 21st century* (pp. 37–58). Between the Lines.

Social Sciences Feminist Network Research Interest Group. (2017). The burden of invisible work in academia: Social inequalities and time use in five university departments. *Humboldt Journal of Social Relations, 39*, 228–245. http://www.jstor.org/stable/90007882

Stein, W. J. (1996). The survival of American Indian faculty. In C. Turner, M. Garcia, A. Nora, & L. I. Rendón (Eds.), *Racial and ethnic diversity in higher education* (pp. 101–113). Pearson Custom Publishing.

Sue, D. W. (2003). *Overcoming our racism: The journey to liberation.* Jossey-Bass.

Tippeconnic Fox (Comanche), M. J. (2005). Voices from within: Native American faculty and staff on campus. *New Directions for Student Services, 2005*(109), 49–59. https://doi.org/10.1002/ss.153

Trejo, J. A. (2020). The burden of service for faculty of color to achieve diversity and inclusion: The minority tax. *Molecular Biology of the Cell, 31*(25), 2752–2754. https://doi.org/10.1091/mbc.E20-08-0567

Turner, C. S. V., Myers, S. L., Jr., & Creswell, J. W. (1999). Exploring underrepresentation: The case of faculty of color in the Midwest. *The Journal of Higher Education, 70*(1), 27–59. https://doi.org/10.1080/00221546.1999.11780753

Vaccaro, A. (2011). Divisions among us: Women administrators, faculty, and staff on the complicated realities of support and sisterhood. *NASPA Journal About Women in Higher Education, 4*(1), 26–49. https://doi.org/10.2202/1940-7890.1063

Walters, C., Mehl, G. G., Piraino, P., Jansen, J. D., & Kriger, S. (2022). The impact of the pandemic-enforced lockdown on the scholarly productivity of women academics in South Africa. *Research Policy, 51*(1). https://doi.org/10.1016/j.respol.2021.104403

Wilder, C. S. (2013). *Ebony and ivy: Race, slavery, and the troubled history of America's universities.* Bloomsbury.

Wilson, J. L., & Tugas, F. (2022). Institutions can say they encourage staff DEI professional development... But the individual chooses to embrace it. *Planning for Higher Education, 51*(1), 1–8. https://www.scup.org/resource/journal-institutions-can-say-they-encourage-staff-dei-professional-development/

Yoder, J. D. (2002). 2001 division 35 presidential address: Context matters: Understanding tokenism processes and their impact on women's work. *Psychology of Women Quarterly, 26*(1), 1–8. https://doi.org/10.1111/1471-6402.00038

CHAPTER 7

TOWNS AND GOWNS

A Study in Crisis Leadership

S. Gavin Weiser
Illinois State University

Linsay DeMartino
Arizona State University

Paige Buschman
Illinois State University

ABSTRACT

Educational institutions across PreK–12 and higher education claim to be entry points for policies of greater community partnerships and commitments to justice, equity, diversity, and inclusion (JEDI). In the United States educational institutions were forced into emergency, remote measures to navigate the COVID-19 crisis testing their commitments to both their communities and JEDI. This project attempts to document and craft nuanced understandings of the experiences of educational administrators under extreme crisis to ascertain what might be learned for educational leaders and institutions to better respond to crises in the future. Using phenomenological methods

Justice, Equity, Diversity, and Inclusion in Education, pages 141–160
Copyright © 2024 by Information Age Publishing
www.infoagepub.com
All rights of reproduction in any form reserved.

and photovoice these narratives were collected from educational leaders. The focus of this chapter is on the distinct differences in the ways that higher education and K–12 school districts engaged with their community during the beginning of the pandemic. Our results indicate the use of vastly different manners of engagement which are caused by and contribute to the decline of democratization in higher education, including the reliance on mimetic isomorphism, the lack of civic engagement, and the continued ascendency of the neoliberal institution.

The onset of the COVID-19 pandemic caused a major shift in the function of society in the United States, prompting a vast conversation about mutual aid and community support. In the beginning, the U.S. federal government was of little help in mitigating the pandemic's spread and impact, forcing both state and local leadership, including K–12 schools and institutions of higher education (IHE), to navigate the crisis. While many communities had well-developed disaster plans and were accustomed to utilizing aid networks in response to natural disasters, COVID-19 prompted these communities to rethink their systems and adapt their practices; this lack of preparedness sometimes exacerbated the crisis itself. Many of the tangible actions taken by universities happened nearly a year after the onset of the pandemic (when this study began). For example, the University of California at San Diego required weekly COVID-19 testing as students and employees returned to campus in early 2021 and even installed vending machines to distribute the tests (NBC 7 San Diego, 2021). Personnel could scan a barcode, complete their nasal swabs, and drop off completed tests to receive results through a mobile application. In contrast, the University of Florida began with a huge expansion of face-to-face classes in spring 2021 (Kumar, 2021). The faculty were excluded from this planning and found themselves under heightened surveillance as upper administration encouraged students to report faculty members who did not show up for in-person instruction. D'Andra Mull, vice president for Student Affairs, sent a welcome email to students reiterating COVID-19 safety protocols and testing requirements and directed them to use a mobile application to report on "inconsistencies with course delivery for your face-to-face or online courses, such as not being provided the opportunity to meet in person for your face-to-face class" (Flaherty, 2021, para. 8). The faculty, many of whom were denied accommodations to teach remotely, were outraged and questioned this divisive administrative action (Flaherty, 2021; Kumar, 2021). These contrasts were addressed in a report from the U.S. Centers for Disease Control and Prevention; in the 21-day periods before and after classes started, counties with large colleges or universities with remote instruction experienced a 17.9% decrease in COVID-19 incidence compared to a 56% increase in incidence in university counties with in-person instruction, suggesting that "effective mitigation activities at colleges and universities with in-person instruction could minimize on-campus COVID-19 transmission and reduce county-level incidence" (Leidner et al., 2021). Given these disparities in response to the pandemic, we argue that increased collaboration among institutions coupled with greater community engagement could minimize the impact of future crises.

The U.S. institutions of higher education have long been cornerstones for community and civic engagement. However, despite this commitment, IHEs were slow to respond to the community on issues related to COVID-19 in contrast to their K–12 peers.

THE DEMOCRATIC INSTITUTION

Jacoby (2014) detailed the history of civic engagement in higher education, concluding, "American higher education has always included among its mission the preparation of effective citizens" (p. 10). Over the years, the focus of these efforts shifted from preparing the individual to participate in civic society, such as voting or individually getting involved in electoral politics, to promoting student and faculty engagement in the community to solve worldly problems and educating students for important jobs created by emerging global issues (Jacoby, 2014).

Lagemann and Lewis (2012) argued that the first shift in IHE civic engagement occurred after the Civil War with the emergence of scientific research that was thought to have been at odds with civics. They also noted that academic professionalization and the freedom of faculty to act as relatively autonomous agents also gave rise to the degradation of civicism. In 1946, President Truman's Commission on Higher Education explored the potential "social role" of higher education noting that "all too often the benefits of education have been sought and used for personal and private profit to the neglect of public and social service" (Zook, 1947, p. 9). Lagemann and Lewis (2012) attributed this to the changing economic landscape but also argued that some of the decline in civic engagement related directly to issues with American democracy.

The concept of civic engagement remains popular; however, the lack of centrality in the modern IHE curriculum is notable and concerning despite the lip-service paid to preparing students to engage in their democratic reality and serve the public good (Lagemann & Lewis, 2012; Saavedra et al., 2022; Saltmarsh, 2005). These institutions end up preparing workers rather than an engaged citizenry (Attick, 2017; Giroux, 2005). Lagemann and Lewis (2012) also noted how "the nuts and bolts of civic education are a staple of K–12 schooling" but "despite that, many college students would have trouble passing the U.S. Naturalization Exam" (p. 11). The authors pointed out, "To teach civic responsibilities, institutions must practice civic responsibilities" (p. 13). In other words, IHEs should see themselves as spaces that, without reservation, promote social change (Weiser, 2023) and innovation so that students may be the beneficiaries of the necessary knowledge and skill to fully participate in engagement themselves.

Civic and Community Engagement

Civic engagement has evolved and what it looks like on any given college campus varies greatly and is dependent on several factors, including the state where the IHE is situated, the size of the institution, the campus and surrounding community, the prioritization of civic engagement work, and the amount of funding for this work. Saltmarsh et al. (2009) compiled a list of civic engagement activities one might see on a college campus: "Community-based learning, service learning, action research, public and community service, deliberative dialogues, community building, and public deliberation, among others" (p. 50). However, scholarship has tended to focus on the benefits of civic engagement for the student rather than for the community.

Collegiate leadership prioritizes student development. IHEs do not prioritize the health of their community and build positive partnerships with the community to promote engagement goals. Scholars have made a point to address this issue by writing about best practices for campus–community partnerships but creating positive partnerships does not inherently acknowledge the philosophical issue at hand: IHE missions are particularly self-centered, a claim we agree with, and the data from our project largely illustrate this as well.

Saltmarsh et al. (2009) noted that there is "near universal agreement" from service-learning practitioners in higher education that "this nation faces significant societal challenges, and higher education must play a role in responding to them," and that "the civic engagement movement has not realized its full potential" (p. 3). They outlined five reasons why this is so, including the lack of public support for the civic engagement agenda, the failure of higher education professionals to agree on the language and direction of the civic engagement movement, the issue of avoiding politics in civic engagement, and the conflict between academic epistemology and the civic engagement agenda (Saltmarsh et al., 2009). Others have explored how the practice of civic engagement in the classroom setting strengthens later orientations to community engagement and also weakens a proclivity to notions of social dominance (Saavedra et al., 2022). Despite researchers acknowledging the importance of civic and community engagement for students, Kliewer (2013) suggested that IHEs effectively "fail" to advance social issues (p. 77); rather, their alignment with neoliberal ideology disrupts that cause. In brief, neoliberalism has turned educators into *homo economicus* who train workers instead of thinkers Attick, 2017). As such, deep engagement with social issues is often at odds with the preparation of workers rather than thinkers. While these issues are largely outside of the scope of this paper, they give context to why higher education may struggle with the coordination of civic engagement on their campuses: It is both a logistical and philosophical challenge. In contemporary, pandemic times, the decline of both democratization and civic engagement in higher education is further threatened by mimetic isomorphism and neoliberalism, which we speak to and explore in the findings section of this chapter.

THE DECLINING DEMOCRATIZATION OF INSTITUTIONS OF HIGHER EDUCATION

Over the last several decades we have seen a significant drop in engagement grounded in the democratic ideal within the landscape of higher education (Attick, 2017; Giroux, 1985; Saunders & Blanco Ramirez, 2017). Instead of preparing engaged citizens, IHEs have begun to prepare workers to fulfill the needs of the workforce in isolation of their engagement with critical thought. Attick (2017) described the transition of the human experience from that of homo sapiens to that of homo economicus. Rather than education for learning and the love of learning, neoliberalism has crept in and radically transformed the practice of education with a different set of ideals, namely individualism, accountability, governmentality, and the free marketization of education and educational spaces. Education as the practice of freedom (hooks, 1994) has been replaced by education as a training space for industry. This has major implications on all levels of education from the teacher-proofing of curriculum in PK–12 spaces (Giroux, 1985) to a prioritization of revenue generation in higher education (Saunders & Blanco Ramirez, 2017). Together these ensure a radical shift in educational practice that focuses not on liberation and mutual good but instead on the commodification of people in homo economicus with a focus on consumption.

The movement away from critical thinking and civic engagement into workforce preparation demonstrates a marked shift in the purpose of education. We argue that this shows up within this project through the understanding of education as a business, namely using business framing for educational practices in times of great peril illustrated through the use of frameworks such as mimetic isomorphism and academic capitalism in IHE decision-making processes rather than a student-centered approach, which is often noted as a primary orientation (Wright, 2011). In a subsequent section on our findings and lessons, we briefly juxtapose the use of

Mimetic Isomorphism

business-oriented language, policies, and practices between both K–12 and IHE professionals, where K–12 administrators were more centered on the wellness of the community rather than the business-as-usual approach of mimetic isomorphism and academic capitalism in the higher education landscape during the onset of COVID-19.

Mimetic Isomorphism

Mimetic isomorphism is a term from business literature that speaks to how organizations imitate similar organizations. This imitation creates organizations that are largely similar to one another. Mimetic isomorphism is when one organization tries to replicate another institution that they perceive as successful in an attempt to replicate the other's success. Mimetic isomorphism results from "standard responses to uncertainty" (DiMaggio & Powell, 1983, p. 150). Yang and Hyland (2012) specifically spoke to how organizations engage in mimetic isomorphism "in order to remain competitive or to reduce the risk of unexpected outcomes" (p. 1076). Moreover, mimetic isomorphism is one form of isomorphism that organizations may engage in, but the formation is directly correlated to an attempt to survive crisis and uncertainty.

IHEs have faced uncertainty over the past several decades with more and more funding reductions from state and federal governments. As many of us who lived through the spring of 2020 can attest to, there is no higher amount of uncertainty than a global pandemic. While economic downturns may be common drivers for prospective students to return to school (and are often even seen as drivers for community college enrollment), these factors cannot account for a global pandemic. Romano and Palmer (2015) explored the topic of disruptive change to higher education, particularly in regard to community college financing, drawing attention to "big challenges of any kind that are not easily anticipated, that are not localized, and that causes [*sic*] discontinuity and upheaval in an industry" (p. 166). As such, Romano and Palmer (2015) rejected the notion of further investigating the impact of large-scale disruptions, such as pandemics and environmental disasters.

Moreover, most literature on the economic realities of education in a recession does not account for the impact of global pandemics as this would lead scholars too far astray (Barr & Turner, 2013; Breneman, 2009; Callan, 2002; Douglass, 2010). This is not to discredit the work of Romano and Palmer but to highlight how little globalized pandemics were considered in educational literature as related to educational economics. As such, a global pandemic certainly counts as a moment of uncertainty, further exacerbating the realities of institutions of higher education engaging in mimetic isomorphism. Further, while economic downturns do often lead to an "upsurge in community college enrollments" they also deal with "a downturn in state fiscal support at precisely the time more funding is needed" (Romano & Palmer, 2016, p. 53). This connects to notions of academic capitalism as the continual decline of state and federal funding for higher education has led educational leaders to try and make up the difference.

Academic Capitalism and Critical University Studies

Institutions of higher education are impacted by larger cultural, social, and institutional forces. However, as the importance of public schools, colleges, and universities grows, their support and funding, particularly in higher education, are downsized. According to Samuels (2017), "This trend forces us to ask how we can educate people in an unequal society and what role universities play in reinforcing the ideological myths that naturalize and rationalize the political and economic status quo" (p. 2). Overarching defunding of education coupled with the deprofessionalization of educators are two legacies of public schooling and higher education programming.

Colleges and universities have long suffered from decreased public funding. To make up for a loss of state support, turning away from their public missions, these institutions sought outside funding from private organizations (Samuels, 2017). With this shift to profit and the existence of academic capitalism (Slaughter & Leslie, 1997; Slaughter & Rhoades, 2004), these mechanisms begin to coalesce under critical university studies (CUS), a framework we use here to understand the radical shift in educational practice and purpose. In most cases, this manifests as the uneasiness of changes grounded in neoliberal and fundamentalist free market ideologies (Giroux, 2005; Moorish, 2020).

> Thus, due in part to the ideology of neoliberalism, the reduction of public funding for higher education was coupled with a more general retreat from welfare state policies and a turn to the free market as the supposed solution to all social and economic problems. (Samuels, 2017, p. 2)

As a result, the emphasis on the neoliberal agenda in higher education shifted the focus to efficiency and accountability.

Having adopted the tenets of neoliberalism, to be more ambitious in a market-driven economy, IHEs became more competitive to draw in institutionally-based funding through increased student enrollment and a hyper-emphasis on marketing. Further, this emphasis on competition was purposively designed to sow insecurity through the various ranks of the university—and these actions have largely been successful (Moorish, 2020, p. 237). Accordingly, some of the key features of the neoliberal academy are (a) audit culture and performance management, where we see an upswing in surveillance, benchmarking, "quality" audits, and new workload models; (b) new academic identity formation with entrepreneurship (masked as "industry standards"), branding, and directives; and, lastly, (c) deprofessionalization of personnel and an attack on academic freedom through conformity efforts and hostility towards risk-taking (Moorish, 2020). These key features of the neoliberal academy result in transitioning the culture of audit and high stakes testing out of the primary and secondary level into the post-secondary level, thus changing focus from preparing active and engaged citizens into homo economicus (Attick, 2017).

In sum, the neoliberal academy is synonymous with the marketized academy and driven by the idea of students as consumers (Moorish, 2020). As a critique of these mechanisms, "CUS encourages university inhabitants to look askance at these structures, and to query why they endure, how they came to take their current form, and whom they serve" (Khoo et al., 2021, pp. 2–3). Furthermore, because of increased anxieties due to the impact of the COVID-19 pandemic on colleges and universities (Khoo et al., 2021; Witze, 2020), an understanding of CUS is important to critique the neoliberal motivations, decision-making, and emergency protocols set by the academic capitalistic institutions of higher education during this time.

METHODOLOGY

Beginning in March 2020, the pandemic drastically impacted the daily lived realities of American educators. Even though the pandemic began to make headway in the United States earlier in the year (World Health Organization, 2023), it was in March when the impact began to be felt in education. At this time, we began a project to explore the experiences of IHE and K–12 administrators during the pandemic. Other, earlier studies on higher education leaders during and after times of crisis—such as the 1999 collapse of the student-run bonfire at Texas A&M University—impacted and influenced our study (Treadwell, 2017; Treadwell et al., 2020). Whereas these influential projects aimed to work in reflection of the tragedy, we understood that we could attempt to capture some of the experiences of surviving as an educational leader in the moment of an emergency such as the COVID-19 pandemic. Thus, this study began with phenomenological interviews, via Zoom online video-conferencing technology, to better understand the experiences of these leaders during these unprecedented times. After completion of this first interview, all participants were invited into the second round of the study, which consisted of a modified version of photovoice (Castleden et al., 2008; Wang & Burris, 1997). Photovoice is a method that encourages participant agency in the form of pictures. All who engaged in round two were instructed to share with our team images that typify their experiences during the pandemic with an emphasis on their role as educational leaders. The shared images were sometimes images they themselves took, but occasionally they shared other images taken from the internet such as memes, or headlines from newspapers. Of the original 15 participants, all but two were willing to share images with us. The breakdown of participants can be found in Table 7.1.

The use of images provides not only an additional layer of data from which to understand these experiences but also provides visual proof of these experiences beyond the narratives collected through interviews and focus groups. In our visual society, not engaging in visual-oriented research is folly (Holm, 2008). Moreover, engaging in the visual nature of data representation is to look "for ways to utilize visual arts in studying the human experience in more complex ways" (Holm et al., 2017, p. 311). Photovoice, as an arts-based research method, is useful as a tool to "enlarge human understanding" (Barone & Eisner, 2011, p. 8) as well as to subvert normative thinking and challenge oppressive ideologies (Leavy, 2017). As such, in the study of educational administrators, who often represent the institution, it is a queer choice (Weiser et al., 2023). However, we argue that despite being agents of the institution, educational leaders are not always of the institution. As such, this is a strong method to better understand the experiences of the photographing

TABLE 7.1	Interview Participants	
Pseudonym	K–12 or Post-Secondary Administration	Photos
Alima	Higher Education Administration	no
Annamae	Higher Education Administration	yes
Bowie	K–12	yes
Cassia	K–12	yes
David	Higher Education Administration	yes
Frank	K–12	yes
Idele	Higher Education Administration	yes
Kelly	K–12	no
Laura	K–12	yes
Lisa	Higher Education Administration	yes
Phyllis	K–12	yes
Richard	K–12	yes
Sam	Higher Education Administration	yes
Suzie	Higher Education Administration	yes
Zach	K–12	yes

participants (round two) and to spark conversations with them, so we all have a more nuanced understanding of their experiences, in their own words and images (Call-Cummings & Martinez, 2016). Moreover, arts-based research and photovoice have been used in higher education to explore the burn-out experiences of administrators (Lynch & Glass, 2020) as well as to better understand their experiences (Latz et al., 2016).

Using both visual data and the narratives, as well as our reflective notes collected during the interviews offered an abundance of data from which to better understand these experiences. In coding visual data, one must be overly cautious to not reduce images to words (Saldaña, 2015). These codes for the visual data serve merely to accompany these images and not to take their place. As such, within this article, you will find images presented alongside the accompanying narrative. This is to both bolster the narrative and also ensure that these images are not taken out of context (Call-Cummings & Martinez, 2016). Finally, through thematic analysis based on several coding rounds, we present findings alongside our analysis. As such, through several rounds of coding, we arrived at several themes. We will focus on just two: mimetic isomorphism and community engagement. We close with some thoughts and reflections about how the focus on the business end of education removes the idea of education as the practice of freedom (hooks, 1994) and has major implications on equity and inclusion within higher education.

FINDINGS AND LESSONS LEARNED

This paper is one part of a larger study that takes into account the experiences of higher education and K–12 leaders and their actions and inactions during the immediate onset of the COVID-19 pandemic. Moreover, it must be noted that while the world was working through a viral pandemic, the United States was also continuing to contend with the racial pandemic that was once again brought to the forefront of individuals' minds with the murder of George Floyd by Minneapolis police. Additionally, only 2 days later, Tallahassee police murdered Tony McDade, a Black transman. Further, the media and police continued to misgender Tony, even after murdering his body. As such, these battling pandemics set the context of educational leaders' experiences during this project

Mimetic Isomorphism

Perhaps unsurprisingly, several of our higher education participants spoke about waiting to see what other institutions would do before their institutions would act, reflecting a larger trend of engaging in mimetic isomorphism. Accordingly, many of them spoke about waiting in a type of limbo, or even paying closer attention to not only what other local institutions were going to do, but what their peer and aspirant institutions were doing across the country. Moreover, a few brought up other institutions with whose actions they agreed even while their own university had not yet acted.

Alima, one of the first higher education leaders with whom we spoke, explained that she felt that her institution, which was located in New York City, an early hotspot for the pandemic, was looking to "our peer institutions and seeing how they're reacting to things and then also waiting on guidelines from the state of New York" as the state had its own set of guidelines. This finding is related to the rise of mimetic isomorphism we observed during the COVID-19 pandemic. Similarly, connected to both the marketization of higher education and the neoliberal agenda of new academic identity formation, Suzie noted that her institution, a for-profit school, was looking to industry standards more so than other universities as "our students are going into those industries." Noting that her school is different from other institutions of higher education, she explained that they used industry-specific signage to communicate new policies and expectations for students, faculty, and staff upon returning to working in situ.

Moreover, David remarked that the show of pride that his school had for graduating students (Figure 7.1) was "the only school at the time [at his university] who had done something for our graduates, something physical

Figure 7.1 Honoring graduates higher education.

at least." He went on to remark that while other schools and colleges within the university had done videos or the like, this was the first physical representation of pride for graduating students the university had implemented. As a major institution with evidence of a neoliberal agenda,[1] this finding is quite surprising as the marketization of their institution is in part reliant on increasing student enrollment through student-friendly draws such as elaborate graduation ceremonies. In addition, this was a major point of departure between higher education and K–12, wherein virtually all of the K–12 administrators spoke about the importance of celebrating their graduates within their community. For instance, as illustrated in Figure 7.2, the district that Frank came from hosted a parade for their graduates. Similarly, many school districts also gave out yard signs or participated in parades to honor their graduates. Eventually, some universities engaged in similar practices or hosted virtual graduation ceremonies to support their students and their achievements. Perhaps the most visually interesting point of contrast between David and Frank's images is the presence of the community

Figure 7.2 Honoring graduates P–12.

and the people. Universities largely shunned students from campus and—as universities do not draw exclusively from the geo-contained region in contrast to K–12 school districts—their students may have been across the nation from where they once studied and lived.

Community Engagement

Although this chapter focuses on the experiences of higher education leaders and their community engagement, the larger educational context matters. So, despite focusing here on higher education, K–12 experiences were also ever present in both our data collection and analysis. As such, one thing that stood out to us was the distinct difference in the ways that IHEs and K–12 school districts engaged with their community at the beginning of the pandemic. As illustrated above, even when engaging in mimetic isomorphism, IHEs still often lacked the community engagement that K–12 fostered. They lacked engagement beyond the gown and into the town, and when IHE community engagement did occur, it was often driven by individuals, rather than the institution. For example, Annamae worked at a school in the deep south where mask mandates were not yet in place, and adoption of masks, as well as materials to create them, were scarce. As part of her engagement with a local service and leadership organization, she took up the call from this organization to sew masks for the local community and hand them out on campus (Figure 7.3).

Figure 7.3 Annamae on campus giving out masks.

At this time, when masks were rare, Annamae created these masks for her community. The response was overwhelmingly positive, and she "got so many messages you know a few people even when they came to get the mask, kept profusely thanking me"; some wanted to stay and talk as she was the "only human" they had seen in person in "2 or 3 weeks." Annamae's act of engagement was not lost on behalf of her institution. The institution highlighted her act of service in the "business school newsletter about the masks and how she had given them out to some of the students," but stopped short of officially working to support her efforts (financially or otherwise) or expanding upon them.

Sam is a student affairs staff member at an urban university in northeastern United States. She shared that the university announced, at a recent town hall, that it was going to reduce the capacity of courses by 25%. Despite this town hall announcement, the communication with the external community has been lacking; Sam believed "they could do a little bit more." This is particularly important, as the city where Sam is located is very expensive to live in, and as such, Sam, similar to many of the students, relied upon public transportation to commute into the city. Her story correlates with Saltmarsh et al. (2009), where higher education must play a more pivotal role in responding to societal crises but often fails due to a lack of agreement on their role in civic engagement and contrasting priorities. Here institutions were slow to react for several reasons, including an unclear role in promoting civic and community engagement.

In addition, Sam's school, like many across the country, was dealing with furloughs. Furloughs have an impact, not only on the individual who is furloughed, but on the greater community as well. As a student affairs staff member, she felt that she was more informed than other staff, but that the university had not done a "blanket update to students or the larger community which is kind of frustrating" and that the only thing the university had been transparent about was when they postponed commencement. In Sam's case, their institution failed to provide sufficient information to the internal and greater community because of the deprofessionalization of their personnel and failure to prioritize civic engagement with the surrounding community. On the other hand, Suzie provided a different leadership perspective on the notion of furloughs. She stated that her institution's administration stated that the president's salary is the "first thing to turn off" in the event of an economic downturn. Because her university is a "very big employer in [city name where the school is located] it's also in our school's interest to keep us working and paying so we can continue to give back to the community." These disparate approaches were rooted not only in the economic realities of the institution itself but also in recognition of the role the institution had within the respective community.

COMMUNITY ENGAGED SCHOLARSHIP

IHEs have made moves in the last decade to do more in regards to civic and community engagement. For instance, in 2006, the Carnegie Classification of Institutions of Higher Education began listing IHEs with a commitment to community engagement. Now there are over 350 different institutions of higher education that have met their threshold to earn the Elective Classification for the Community Engagement (Carnegie Classification of Institutions of Higher Education, 2023). They define community engagement as an intentional collaboration between IHEs and their larger community that results in a "mutually beneficial exchange of knowledge and resources in a context of partnership and reciprocity" (Carnegie Classification of Institutions of Higher Education, 2023, para. 1). Notably, these engagements also result in the sharing of knowledge and resources to better serve both parties and to "prepare educated, engaged citizens; strengthen democratic values and civic responsibility; address critical societal issues; and contribute to the public good" (Carnegie Classification of Institutions of Higher Education, 2023, para. 1).

We agree that community-engaged scholarship should contribute to the public good and that research should be in partnership, working with community partners rather than on them. The IHEs illustrated within this chapter are still in a fledgling stage of engagement with community engagement; in times of crisis they defer back to a more insular model of leadership, leaving their communities to fend for themselves. This is perhaps the rationale that institutions of higher education are less habituated to the communities in which they are located than their K–12 peers, which draw their student bodies from the geo-located region of their districts. Despite this, there are still connections between the town and gown, and institutions need to do better to engage purposefully with their colleagues beyond the ivory tower. While this project only focused on seven different American IHEs, none of them were, at the time of data collection, engaging with the community in their COVID-19 response. Most damning, however, is that of the eight K–12 institutions that were part of this project, all of those leaders talked about how they were engaging with the community in which they are situated. Many of these K–12 leaders shared how this made things harder at times, but ultimately it engendered trust and transparency.

FUTURE DIRECTIONS FOR INSTITUTIONS OF HIGHER EDUCATION

The COVID-19 pandemic has forced IHEs to confront long-standing challenges in higher education, such as an over-reliance on skyrocketing tuition costs and perceptions of elitism and internal institutional hierarchies (Witze, 2020). IHEs will never be the same, nor should they be (Weiser & DeMartino, 2022). The over-reliance on bureaucratic formations of leadership, which reflects a business-oriented construction of leadership, needs to be re-examined. The post-bureaucratic type of leadership suggests alternative leadership structures should be considered (Heckscher, 2011; Weiser & DeMartino, 2021). This post-bureaucratic style of leadership would enable more flexibility in decision-making, empowering all members of the organization and crafting more nimble responses to serve our communities.

Moreover, engaging in mutual aid (Spade, 2020) efforts, alongside and with a community rather than acting for a community—as illustrated by Annamae's work—will make for a more robust, authentic, and human response to leadership. Drawing from the work of Dean Spade (2020), we understand that mutual aid is that radical act of both caring for one another and the community, while simultaneously trying to change the world. These radical acts of mutual aid cannot be accomplished under a bureaucratic style of leadership where decisions are made from the top down and acts of mutual aid are always either squashed or coopted. To truly engage in the radical act of mutual aid, we must challenge outdated and hegemonic structures of leadership.

In alignment with Moorish (2020), we recommend that "universities must observe the safeguards enshrined in law, and they must become more democratic and open to scrutiny from the members of the academic community who constitute them" (p. 247). The reliance on mimetic isomorphism, academic capitalism, and neoliberal ideals deters the democratization of education. Any increase in college and university-level bureaucracy acts as a daunting gatekeeper to more robust civic engagement with the greater school community. The town/gown divide significantly exasperates this discontinuity. In closing, we call for movement beyond a mere bridge between town and gown to its ultimate destruction by working toward increased engagement while carefully treading the line of the neoliberal influence on knowledge-seeking.

NOTE

1. This institution is a major sports school; one can buy athletic-branded merchandise at major retailers across the nation.

AUTHOR NOTES

S. Gavin Weiser https://orcid.org/0000-0003-1181-255X
Linsay DeMartino https://orcid.org/0000-0001-7674-0847

Paige Buschman, https://orcid.org/0009-0000-3048-5131
We have no known conflicts of interest.

Correspondence concerning this chapter should be addressed to S. Gavin Weiser, Illinois State University, Campus Box 5900 Normal, IL 61790-590. Email: smweis1@ilstu.edu

REFERENCES

Attick, D. (2017). Homo economicus at school: Neoliberal education and teacher as economic being. *Educational Studies, 53*(1), 37–48. https://doi.org/10.1080/00131946.2016.1258362

Barone, T., & Eisner, E. W. (2011). *Arts based research* (1st ed.). SAGE.

Barr, A., & Turner, S. E. (2013). Expanding enrollments and contracting state budgets: The effect of the great recession on higher education. *The ANNALS of the American Academy of Political and Social Science, 650*(1), 168–193. https://doi.org/10.1177/0002716213500035

Breneman, D. (2009). US higher education and the current recession. *International Higher Education*, (55). https://doi.org/10.6017/ihe.2009.55.8431

Callan, P. M. (2002). *Coping with recession: Public policy, economic downturns and higher education.* National Center for Public Policy and Higher Education; Pew Charitable Trusts; Ford Foundation. https://eric.ed.gov/?id=ED462896

Call-Cummings, M., & Martinez, S. (2016). Consciousness-raising or unintentionally oppressive? *The Qualitative Report, 21*(5), 798–810. https://doi.org/10.46743/2160-3715/2016.2293

Carnegie Classification of Institutions of Higher Education. (2023). *The elective classification for community engagement.* American Council on Education. https://carnegieclassifications.acenet.edu/elective-classifications/community-engagement/

Castleden, H., Garvin, T., & First Nation, H. (2008). Modifying photovoice for community-based participatory Indigenous research. *Social Science & Medicine, 66*(6), 1393–1405. https://doi.org/10.1016/j.socscimed.2007.11.030

DiMaggio, P. J., & Powell, W. W. (1983). The iron cage revisited: Institutional isomorphism and collective rationality in organizational fields. *American Sociological Review, 48*(2), 147–160. https://doi.org/10.2307/2095101

Douglass, J. A. (2010). *Higher education budgets and the global recession: Tracking varied national responses and their consequences* (Research & Occasional Paper Series: CSHE.4.10). Center for Studies in Higher Education. https://eric.ed.gov/?id=ED511965

Flaherty, C. (2021, January 20). Snitch switch. *Inside Higher Ed.* https://www.insidehighered.com/news/2021/01/21/u-florida-asks-students-report-professors-who-arent-teaching-person

Giroux, H. A. (1985). Teachers as transformative intellectuals. *Social Education, 49*(5), 376–379.

Giroux, H. A. (2005). The terror of neoliberalism: Rethinking the significance of cultural politics. *College Literature, 32*(1), 1–19. https://doi.org/10.1353/lit.2005.0006

Heckscher, C. (2011). Defining the post-bureaucratic type. In M. Godwyn & J. H. Gittell (Eds.), *Sociology of organizations: Structures and relationships* (pp. 98–106). Pine Forge Press.

Holm, G. (2008). Visual research methods: Where are we and where are we going? In S. N. Hesse-Biber & P. Leavy (Eds.), *Handbook of emergent methods* (1st ed., pp. 325–342). The Guilford Press.

Holm, G., Sahlström, F., & Zilliacus, H. (2017). Arts-based visual research. In P. Leavy (Ed.), *Handbook of arts-based research* (1st ed., pp. 311–335). The Guilford Press.

hooks, b. (1994). *Teaching to transgress: Education as the practice of freedom.* Routledge.

Jacoby, B. (2014). *Service-learning essentials: Questions, answers, and lessons learned.* Wiley.

Khoo, T., Burford, J., Henderson, E., Liu, H., & Nicolazzo, Z. (2021). Not getting over it: The impact of Sara Ahmed's work within critical university studies. *Journal of Intercultural Studies, 42*(1), 84–98. https://doi.org/10.1080/07256868.2020.1859209

Kliewer, B. (2013). Why the civic engagement movement cannot achieve democratic and justice aims. *Michigan Journal of Community Service Learning, 19*(2), 72–79. https://files.eric.ed.gov/fulltext/EJ1013498.pdf

Kumar, D. (2021, February 6). At University of Florida, a rise in face-to-face classes prompts pushback. *Tampa Bay Times.* https://www.tampabay.com/news/education/2021/02/06/at-university-of-florida-a-rise-in-face-to-face-classes-prompts-pushback/

Lagemann, E., & Lewis, H. (2012). Renewing civic education. Time to restore American higher education's lost mission. *Harvard Magazine, 3*, 42–45.

Latz, A. O., Phelps-Ward, R., Royer, D., & Peters, T. (2016). Photovoice as methodology, pedagogy, and partnership-building tool: A graduate and community college student collaboration. *Journal of Public Scholarship in Higher Education, 6*, 124–142. https://eric.ed.gov/?id=EJ1123809

Leavy, P. (Ed.). (2017). *Handbook of arts-based research* (1st ed.). The Guilford Press.

Leidner, A. J., Barry, V., Bowen, V., Silver, R., Musial, T., Kang, G., Ritchey, M., Fletcher, K., Barrios, L., & Pevzner, E. (2021). Opening of large institutions of higher education and county-level COVID-19 incidence—United States, July 6–September 17, 2020. *Morbidity and Mortality Weekly Report, 70*, 14–19. https://doi.org/10.15585/mmwr.mm7001a4

Lynch, R. J., & Glass, C. R. (2020). The cost of caring: An arts-based phenomenological analysis of secondary traumatic stress in college student affairs. *The Review of Higher Education, 43*(4), 1041–1068. https://doi.org/10.1353/rhe.2020.0030

Moorish, L. (2020). Academic freedom and the disciplinary regime in the neoliberal university. In S. Dawes & M. Lenormand (Eds.), *Neoliberalism in context* (pp. 235–253). Palgrave. https://doi.org/10.1007/978-3-030-26017-0_13

NBC 7 San Diego. (2021, January 5). *Vending machines distribute COVID-19 tests to returning UC San Diego students.* https://www.nbcsandiego.com/news/local/vending

-machines-distribute-covid-19-tests-to-returning-uc-san-diego-students/
2487271/

Romano, R. M., & Palmer, J. C. (2015). *Financing community colleges: Where we are, where we're going.* Rowman & Littlefield.

Romano, R. M., & Palmer, J. C. (2016). The community college and the business cycle. *Change: The Magazine of Higher Learning, 48*(5), 52–57. https://doi.org/10.1080/00091383.2016.1227676

Saavedra, J. A., Ruiz, L., & Alcalá, L. (2022). Critical service-learning supports social justice and civic engagement orientations in college students. *Michigan Journal of Community Service Learning, 28*(1). https://doi.org/10.3998/mjcsl.292

Saldaña, J. (2015). *The coding manual for qualitative researchers* (3rd ed.). SAGE.

Saltmarsh, J. (2005). The civic promise of service learning. *Liberal Education, 91*(2), 50–55. https://eric.ed.gov/?id=EJ697354

Saltmarsh, J., Hartley, M., & Clayton, P. (2009). *Democratic engagement white paper.* New England Resource Center for Higher Education. https://repository.upenn.edu/entities/publication/18eae8e1-9819-4c6f-a419-b25cee4cdf2d

Samuels, R. (2017). Introduction: Teaching critical university studies. *Radical Teacher, 108*(1), 1–4. https://doi.org/10.5195/rt.2017.382

Saunders, D. B., & Blanco Ramirez, G. (2017). Resisting the neoliberalization of higher education: A challenge to commonsensical understandings of commodities and consumption. *Cultural Studies↔Critical Methodologies, 17*(3), 189–196. https://doi.org/10.1177/1532708616669529

Slaughter, S., & Leslie, L. L. (1997). *Academic capitalism: Politics, policies, and the entrepreneurial university.* JHU Press.

Slaughter, S., & Rhoades, G. (2004). *Academic capitalism and the new economy: Markets, state, and higher education.* JHU Press.

Spade, D. (2020). *Mutual aid: Building solidarity during this crisis (and the next).* Verso.

Treadwell, K. L. (2017). Learning from tragedy: Student affairs leadership following college campus disasters. *Journal of Student Affairs Research and Practice, 54*(1), 42–54. https://doi.org/10.1080/19496591.2016.1206019

Treadwell, K. L., Lane, F. C., & Paterson, B. G. (2020). Reflections from crisis: A phenomenological study of the Texas A&M bonfire collapse. *Journal of Student Affairs Research and Practice, 57*(2), 119–131. https://doi.org/10.1080/19496591.2019.1614939

Wang, C., & Burris, M. A. (1997). Photovoice: Concept, methodology, and use for participatory needs assessment. *Health Education & Behavior, 24*(3), 369–387. https://doi.org/10.1177/109019819702400309

Weiser, G., & DeMartino, L. (2022). "We're not going back to what was before, and we don't know what the future will look like either": Exploring the voices and images of educational administrators in crisis. *Transformative Dialogues: Teaching and Learning Journal, 15*(2), Article 2. https://doi.org/10.26209/td2022vol15iss21633

Weiser, S. G. (2023). Activism as leadership: Supporting progressive activists within our work. *Journal of Campus Activities Practice and Scholarship, 5*(2), 23–37. https://doi.org/10.52499/2023013

Weiser, S. G., & DeMartino, L. (2021). Who leads the leaders? K–12 and higher education leadership under duress. *Curriculum in Context, 46*(2), 15–21. https:// ir.library.illinoisstate.edu/cgi/viewcontent.cgi?article=1020&context=fped

Weiser, S. G., DeMartino, L., & Stasicky, A. (2023). Like a pig in mud: Rejecting the manicured boundaries of the patriarchy. *Journal of School Leadership, 33*(2), 214–236. https://doi.org/10.1177/10526846221149218

Witze, A. (2020). Universities will never be the same after the coronavirus crisis. *Nature, 582*(7811), 162–164. https://doi.org/10.1038/d41586-020-01518-y

World Health Organization. (2023). *Timeline: WHO's COVID-19 response.* https:// www.who.int/emergencies/diseases/novel-coronavirus-2019/interactive -timeline#event-16

Wright, G. B. (2011). Student-centered learning in higher education. *International Journal of Teaching and Learning in Higher Education, 23*(1), 92–97. https://eric .ed.gov/?id=EJ938583

Yang, M., & Hyland, M. (2012). Re-examining mimetic isomorphism: Similarity in mergers and acquisitions in the financial service industry. *Management Decision, 50*(6), 1076–1095. https://doi.org/10.1108/00251741211238346

Zook, G. F. (1947). The president's commission on higher education. *Bulletin of the American Association of University Professors (1915–1955), 33*(1), 10–28. https://doi .org/10.2307/40221180

SECTION IV

RIGHTFUL PRESENCE

CHAPTER 8

DISABILITY AS DIVERSITY IN HIGHER EDUCATION SPACES

Rebecca B. Smith Hill
University of South Carolina

Chelsea VanHorn Stinnett
University of Massachusetts–Boston

ABSTRACT

Conversations, initiatives, and programming aimed at enhancing diversity, equity, and inclusion (DEI) of marginalized groups in higher education have come to the fore in the past decade. This chapter puts forth the idea that disability is a form of human diversity, and as such, should be included in the DEI strategic planning for colleges and universities. As a historically marginalized group in higher education spaces, disabled students should not only be included, but feel a sense of belonging on college campuses which can lead to their success as college students. We argue for a reframing of the narrative surrounding disability in higher education. Here we provide an overview of disability history in higher education and details of the current landscape of higher education for people with disability, including the growing number

---

Justice, Equity, Diversity, and Inclusion in Education, pages 163–186
Copyright © 2024 by Information Age Publishing
www.infoagepub.com
All rights of reproduction in any form reserved.

of college students with intellectual disability. Particularly, we demonstrate through a review of the relevant research, how the inclusion of students with intellectual disability through inclusive postsecondary education (IPSE) programs benefits the entire higher educational system and community. We also offer an example for how to include all students with disability in research aimed at improving their experiences in higher education. Overall, this chapter aims to examine disability not as a form of impairment, but as a category of identity and diversity, worthy of rightful presence (Calabrese Barton & Tan, 2020) and recognition in postsecondary education spaces.

The current movement to address issues of diversity, equity, and inclusion (DEI) in higher education settings in the United States is long overdue. With roots in the American Civil Rights movement of the 1960s, current DEI initiatives aim to move beyond mere tolerance and acceptance of diverse and marginalized groups into all spaces to demanding equity in access and recognition of inherent value in the inclusion of these groups (Beavers, 2018). Institutions of higher education (IHE) have been charged with doing their part to make their spaces welcoming and accessible for students from a variety of historically marginalized and diverse backgrounds. In the past decade, actions by the Obama administration through the U.S. Department of Education encouraged many IHEs to voluntarily pursue enhanced diversity in postsecondary education. This included efforts to expand college opportunity for historically underserved students (Office of Planning, Development, and Policy Development, 2016). Many IHEs have adopted unique programs and/or missions to promote enhanced campus diversity. The first requirement in support of DEI efforts by the Council for Higher Education Accreditation took effect in 2022. However, many diversity movements and initiatives leave out disability as a political and cultural category of marginalized students, focusing more acutely on racial and ethnic minorities (Aquino, 2016; Higbee et al., 2007).

Disability is part of the human condition; a "form of human variation" (Asch, 2001, p. 297), as much as any other diversity category. When disability is included as a dimension of diversity—alongside race, ethnicity, gender, sexuality, and others—this reinforces the idea that there is no "normal," and society's ableist othering of people with disability can be effectively addressed (Davis, 2011; Leake & Stodden, 2014; Scheef et al., 2020). Unfortunately, the current approach to programming and accommodations among IHEs perpetuates disability as an individualized, medical condition and does not recognize those who identify as disabled as a valued social group (Shallish, 2017).

While efforts to integrate and diversify IHEs in regards to minority and diversity status (such as race and gender) is admirable and an ongoing need, we argue that an equal and more forthright focus on inclusion of individuals with disability is also necessary. One in four adults in the United

States identify as having a disability (Okoro et al., 2018); therefore the likelihood of intersectionality across marginalized groups is high. In Anderson's (2006) call for the academy to recognize the embodied experience of disability, he posits that "disability is not just another speciality with concerns loosely related to other minorities. The experience of disability is relevant to all marginalized groups—*for all groups have people with disabilities in them*" (p. 367, emphasis in original). Given the fact that this position is over 17 years old at the time of this writing, our calls for equity in higher education for students with disability is not new but still needed. When targeted efforts are made to include students with disability, groups at all intersections of oppression and marginalization benefit.

Through this chapter we aim to provide an overview of disability history in higher education and address the exclusion of disability as a social category from the diversity narrative. We will also intentionally explore inclusive postsecondary education (IPSE) programs for students with intellectual disability as a growing phenomenon within higher education. There is evidence that the inclusion of people with intellectual disability benefits the entire educational system and community. We propose disability as not a form of impairment, but rather as a category of identity and diversity, worthy of rightful presence (Calabrese Barton & Tan, 2020) and recognition in postsecondary education. The phrase "worthy of rightful presence" intimates that equitable access, including a sense of authentic belonging, should underlie the inclusion of students with disability in IHEs.

HISTORY OF DISABILITY IN HIGHER EDUCATION

Historically, young adults with disability in the United States have often been unable to access postsecondary institutions (Snyder & Dillow, 2015). When Section 504 of the Rehabilitation Act was passed in 1973, it barred all organizations receiving federal funding, including many IHEs, from discrimination against "otherwise qualified handicapped individuals" (Mattlin, 2022). Prior to this monumental legislation, IHEs routinely discriminated against people with disability and had no legal mandate to provide accommodations for their inclusion. The Americans With Disabilities Act (1990), which gives legal rights to inclusion for people with disabilities in areas of employment, transportation, public accommodations, communications, and others, is a mere thirty-three years old at the time of this publication.

In addition to the relative nascence of the disability rights movement and subsequent legal protections related to opportunity and access, the central role of ableism on higher education campuses has yet to be adequately addressed (Bornstein & Manaseri, 2018; Dolmage, 2017). It is historically evident that disability is frequently viewed as a lesser identity within a postsecondary diversity setting (Aquino, 2016; Kim & Aquino, 2017; Linton, 1998), or left out of the diversity discussion altogether (Scheef et al., 2020; Shallish, 2017). Because the world of higher education has so stolidly held onto the academic gatekeeping associated with admitting students with disability, Aquino (2016) has aptly called equity for students with disability "the last frontier" of higher education inclusion (p. 325).

Strauss and Sales (2010) posit that IHEs should be catalysts for social change, economic development, and the generation of inquiry and knowledge. Yet, when these institutions have historically been created and perpetuated to serve only students without disability, the changes, developments, and knowledge generated are not necessarily advantageous to those with disability. It is not enough to solely provide individual services by way of accommodations in an attempt to equitably serve disabled students. The very rhetoric of "accommodating disability" admits to the dominance and privilege of those who are not disabled (Dolmage, 2017). Entire systems, environments, and mindsets must be changed, shifted, and upheaved in order for students with disability to be effectively included (Dolmage, 2017; Higbee et al., 2007; Strauss & Sales, 2010).

The Omission of Disability From the Diversity Narrative

The increasing call for inclusion of folks from all backgrounds, minority groups, and marginalized populations in higher education brings to light the glaring omission of the largest marginalized group of all: students with disability. At the most foundational level, colleges and universities advertise and recruit the students they wish to see in their spaces through their mission and diversity statements. Scheef and colleagues (2020) recently conducted a review of 300 mission statements and diversity materials of 4-year college and university websites. The researchers sought to understand the extent to which disability was included in these statements and documents as a facet of diversity. They found that while 153 of the 300 (51%) randomly selected IHEs mentioned diversity in their mission statement, only 14 (4.6%) of those specified disability explicitly (Scheef et al., 2020). This troubling exclusion reinforces the notion that disability is an unwelcome population in IHEs, or at the very least, reifies the historically accepted and ableist norm of students with disability as an unrecognized or unacknowledged community of learners.

Leake and Stodden (2014) reviewed the articles appearing in five journals devoted exclusively to higher education from 2006 to 2012. Of the 906 articles examined, only 11 (or 1.2%) focused on students with disability. With the advent of the inclusion of students with intellectual disability on college campuses via IPSE programs in the past two decades (which we will address in more detail later in the chapter), the need to recognize and welcome folks with disability in IHEs is more salient than ever.

In response to Lennard Davis' question in the title of a 2011 *Chronicle of Higher Education* article—"Why Is Disability Missing From the Discourse of Diversity?"—Lauren Shallish (2017) posited that this is due to the fact that IHEs lack an understanding of people with disability as a social group. While social groups are shaped based on a collective experience of norm-based difference, those with disability have historically been viewed as suffering from individualized medical-related issues. This framing places disability as an individual problem rather than a societal one to be recognized as a form of human variation. When disability is viewed as a deficit, framed using the medical model, it removes the construct from the diversity dialogue and deems it a problem to be solved as opposed to a social or political identity. Colleges and universities can technically be in compliance with the ADA, providing the most basic civil rights by way of individualized accommodations for students with disability, but continue to devalue those with disability as a valid social group if they do not recognize the inherent ableism in common institutional barriers such as the medicalized process for qualifying for accommodations and the ableist perception that related services provide an unfair advantage (Shallish, 2017; Williams & Ceci, 1999).

THE CURRENT LANDSCAPE OF DISABILITY IN HIGHER EDUCATION

Because higher education continues to be a goal for so many Americans, campuses should reflect society in all its rich diversity, including people with disability (Hill et al., 2020). Approximately 19% of students enrolled in postsecondary education programs have identified themselves as an individual with a disability (Digest of Education Statistics, 2021). However, while the number of disabled students attending IHEs has rapidly grown (Kauffman et al., 2023), the number of disabled students graduating from these institutions has not grown at nearly the same rate (Griful-Freixenet et al., 2017; Woolf & de Bie, 2022). Sixteen percent of U.S. citizens 25 and older with a disability have a bachelor's degree or higher, compared to 35% for those with no disability (The Economics Daily, 2015). While there are a myriad of likely explanations for these trends, higher education professionals must examine this phenomenon in order to fully understand and rectify this seemingly inaccessible environment for students with disabilities. The bare minimum of legally mandated entry into an institution does not necessarily correlate to equitable access for students with disability.

In addition to a disparity in rates of college completion, there is much research revealing barriers to disability disclosure, accommodation-seeking, and sense of belonging for students with disability in higher education. In their systematic review of barriers and facilitators of disability disclosure and accommodations in postsecondary settings, Lindsay and colleagues (2013) found barriers such as a lack of programming to support transition from secondary to postsecondary settings, financial and transportation barriers, as well as physical inaccessibility and attitudinal barriers such as discrimination and lack of awareness of disability. A secondary analysis of national transition-related data reflected that fewer than 10% of students with disability have obvious or "visual" disabilities with the great majority having hidden or invisible disabilities (Newman et al., 2011). This fact is significant to the discussion of disability as diversity on college campuses as the infrequency of visibility may give the false impression that disability is rare among students at IHEs (Leake & Stodden, 2014).

Students with disability have been recognized and legally given access on college campuses since the 1970s with the provision of services offered by disability resource or support offices, yet the concept of a fully-inclusive and accessible campus has eluded most IHEs (Dolmage, 2017; Shaewitz & Crandall, 2020). Despite the significant growth of students with disability in higher education, these students continue to have lower rates of graduation and experience low rates of persistence (Wynants & Dennis, 2017). Only through recognition and understanding of students with disability and their experiences on college campuses can we have the necessary information to construct evidence-based practices to establish a sense of belonging for students with disability in higher education (Kim & Aquino, 2017).

Ableism on College Campuses

Ableism is defined as stereotyping, prejudice, discrimination, and social oppression toward people with disability (Bogart & Dunn, 2019). Dolmage (2017) argued in his book *Academic Ableism* that this societally ingrained belief system that positions people with disability as having less value than non-disabled people is rampant in higher education. He has intimated that disability has essentially been constructed as the antithesis of higher education, positioned as a problem to be solved in a space that inherently values ability. Inquiry on disability and higher education reveals that many hold the ableist view that services provided to people with disability provide an unfair advantage (Shallish, 2017; Williams & Ceci, 1999). This position of difference that stems from a normative presentation of ability is an enormous barrier in higher education spaces despite the legislation providing for access (Shallish, 2017).

Existing research points time and again to higher education faculty as a primary barrier to inclusion on a college campus (Evans et al., 2017). Faculty

Disability as Diversity in Higher Education Spaces • **169**

members' lack of experience working with people with disability coupled with their lack of awareness of legal requirements regarding necessary accommodations has caused resistance to understanding and providing what is needed for student success (Love et al., 2015; Redpath et al., 2013). A recent study anchored in a critical disability studies framework looked at the experiences of college students with disability in navigating expectations of them in postsecondary education settings (Woolf & de Bie, 2022). The existing research literature highlights self-advocacy as a vital skill that students with disability need in order to be successful in higher education; however, much of this literature claims students with disability have "skills-deficit" in this area, effectively adopting a deficit-focused approach to successful inclusion (Woolf & de Bie, 2022, para. 1). Fleming and colleagues (2017) pointed out that blaming students for lack of skills fails to acknowledge the role and responsibility of university faculty and staff in creating barriers to effective inclusion, an inherently ableist orientation to the problem at hand. As we enter a new era of DEI, this fact should be addressed using a social justice model of disability and changes to enhance inclusion going forward should always center the voices of those affected by the inequities.

Until environments are created to include disability, from the outset, then students will not be able to claim disability without fear of discrimination. People with disability should be the agents of negotiations regarding making the environment accessible and inclusive (Dolmage, 2017). The opportunity to attend IHEs born of legal mandates is not enough to ensure inclusion for students with disability. Because those with disability must request services and accommodations, they continue to be marginalized and "othered" within IHE settings (Griffen & Tevis, 2017).

Reframing the Disability Narrative

As one redress for this historically ingrained ableism, Scheef and colleagues (2020) called for IHE personnel to become familiar with different models of disability, such as the social model (Shakespeare, 2013), the social relational model (Reindal, 2008), or the social justice model (Riddle, 2020) as opposed to the traditional medical model. The medical model of disability takes a deficit-focused lens, focusing on an impairment or difference within a person's body. The medical model takes a normative view of disability, meaning anyone who is not able-bodied is abnormal. Reframing the concept of disability as one of access and rightful presence (Calabrese Barton & Tan, 2020), is essential to effectively addressing higher education's ableism. When the lens is focused on access rather than difference or limitations, disability is promoted as a form of diversity as opposed to a deficit (O'Neil Green et al., 2017; Scheef et al., 2020).

Davis (2011) argued that because disability is often understood through a medical model lens, it is often considered abnormal and "outside the healthy, energetic bodies routinely depicted in celebrations of diversity" (para. 11). In IHE contexts, the focus on disability as a medical impairment or abnormality is reinforced by the necessity of students to provide medical documentation in order to receive necessary accommodations for accessibility (Scheef et al., 2020; Shallish, 2017). Requesting accommodations to the academic curriculum or campus environment is the most common form of IHE compliance with the ADA and Section 504 of the Rehabilitation Act. Accommodations are adjustments to the tasks, environment, or to the way things are usually done that enable individuals with disabilities to have an equal opportunity to participate academically (Gould et al., 2019). While all publicly funded IHEs must legally provide accommodations, research has shown that there are several barriers to registering with disability resource offices on university campuses and subsequently requesting and receiving meaningful accommodations towards an equitable education (Lindsay et al., 2018; Woolf & de Bie, 2022). The fact that environments and curricula must be changed or differentiated in order to accommodate students with disabilities suggests that the environments were informed by dominant pedagogies, design, and narratives and not set up for them in the first place (Dolmage, 2017).

A better approach is for higher education leaders and professionals to inquire and then listen to students with disabilities about their experiences. Researchers on college campuses can do this through participatory action methods ([PAR], described later in the chapter). Disability service professionals can encourage and support students with disabilities and believe them when they advocate for their needs (Vaccaro et al., 2015). Campuses can employ Universal Design (UD), which refers to the design of products, environments, and systems that are accessible, usable, and inclusive for people with diverse abilities, ensuring equal participation and enjoyment. The concept originated in the field of architecture and has since expanded to various disciplines, including education. One widely recognized definition of UD comes from the Center for Universal Design at North Carolina State University: "Universal design is the design of products and environments to be usable by all people, to the greatest extent possible, without the need for adaptation or specialized design" (Connell et al., 1997, p. 2). This definition emphasizes the goal of creating inclusive designs that accommodate a wide range of individuals, regardless of their age, size, ability, or other characteristics. It emphasizes the importance of designing for diversity from the outset, rather than retrofitting or making adaptations later.

Within the concept of UD is Universal Design for Learning (UDL), which applies these same principles to learning materials. University faculty can utilize UDL in an attempt to make their courses accessible from inception,

Disability as Diversity in Higher Education Spaces • **171**

but then practice humility and empathy when working with students in need of accommodations. This reframing is further necessitated by the growing number of students with disabilities enrolling in higher education, including the increasing numbers of students with intellectual disability enrolling in colleges and universities across the country in record numbers.

INCLUSIVE POSTSECONDARY EDUCATION PROGRAMS

A grim future awaits young adults with intellectual disability after high school. They experience low rates of employment and independent living compared to their peers without intellectual disability (Newman et al., 2011). A college education can offer these students training and credentials that will lead to career attainment and advancement. Parents and their students with intellectual disability have long believed that college is the next, natural step toward a professional career, but access is often limited.

The concept of IPSE programs for students with intellectual disability is not new. In fact, some IHEs across the country have been meeting the needs of students with intellectual disability for more than 2 decades. They have modified college coursework, seeking ways to discover and pursue their career field of interest. In recent years, key legislation, the availability of federal funding, and the development of two national centers to support the emergence of high-quality IPSE programs all have led to an increase in the number of college students with intellectual disability. In 2008, the passage of the Higher Education Opportunity Act permitted students with intellectual disability access to federal financial aid if they attended a comprehensive transition and postsecondary program. In 2010, $10 million in federal funding was awarded to model demonstration programs charged with creating and expanding access to IPSE for students with intellectual disability via the Transition and Post-Secondary Programs for Students With Intellectual Disability or TPSID program funding. Additionally, the national coordinating center, Think College, was awarded federal funding to support the development of these model programs. Since 2010, over 126 programs have been funded in 34 states. In 2010 there were close to 100 IPSE programs, and we have since witnessed substantial growth as there are currently 317 college programs for students with intellectual disability across the country, serving approximately 8,000 students (Grigal et al., 2022).

Inclusive Postsecondary Education as a Benefit for All

Students with intellectual disability who also have a postsecondary education earn higher wages and utilize 31% less in government services than those who do not access higher education (Cimera et al., 2018), and they have a decreased reliance upon social security benefits (Sannicandro et al., 2018). Furthermore, these individuals are twice as likely to be employed (Sannicandro et al., 2018) and they report higher levels of overall health and active friendships (Butler et al., 2016). As a result of attending IPSE programs, these students display more adaptive skills and require less support over time (Prohn et al., 2018).

IPSE for students with intellectual disability is essentially the embodiment of a typical IHE diversity, equity, and inclusion statement. The work being accomplished in this niche field is informing how we best support all students as we implement UD to ensure that all campus members have access to the full breadth of campus life. This reaches far beyond academic access to residential living, campus membership, and credentialing. UD that accounts for students with intellectual disability can improve how all students experience a sense of belonging on an accessible campus.

Perceptions of Emerging Professionals: Peer Mentors

IPSE programs have provided a way for emerging professionals to perfect their craft while in training. Many IPSE programs subscribe to peer mentoring models, where other undergraduate or graduate students support students with intellectual disability. For many peer mentors, this experience can shape their opinion of the capabilities of people with disability and affect their own professional development. In a systematic review aimed at identifying peer mentor perspectives after working in IPSE, Carter and McCabe (2021) examined the perspectives of approximately 2,670 peers on their involvement with their institution's IPSE program. They found that peers had multiple motivators to get involved with the IPSE programs and that the positive impact of their experience included professional evolution, perceptions of disability, social relationships, personal growth, academic impact, and remuneration or course credit/payment for services. The authors concluded that peers from 12 studies believed that their campus as whole benefitted from the IPSE program being part of their institution (Carter & McCabe, 2021).

As further illustration, Plotner et al. (2023) conducted a study on the effects of participating in an IPSE program on special education teacher candidates. In their mixed-methods study, the authors found that current teachers who graduated from a college/university with an IPSE program, who in turn worked for the program, attributed this experience to their positive professional development. Specifically, these young professionals credited the way they viewed disability and framed their expectations for students with intellectual disability to their experience with the IPSE program (Plotner et al., 2023). As a rule, working with students with disability in a pre-service capacity allows peers to develop skills and confidence in working with all co-workers, where 21% of the workforce is people with disabilities (Bureau of Labor Statistics, 2023).

Athamanah and colleagues (2020) also explored the experiences and perceptions of college peer mentors who work with students with intellectual disability. The study involved interviews with eight peer mentors who worked in a program designed to support students with intellectual disability at a large public university. The findings suggested that the peer mentors had positive experiences and felt that they were making a meaningful impact on students' lives. The authors suggested that this was a positive and impactful experience for the peer mentors and may have contributed to a more inclusive and supportive campus culture. Additionally, they suggested that the program may have raised awareness and understanding of the needs and experiences of individuals with intellectual disability among the broader campus community (Athamanah et al., 2020).

Perceptions of Campus Community Members: Faculty

College has historically not been a space where students with intellectual disability are considered when developing coursework. For this reason, there may be an assumption from faculty members that students with intellectual disability are unable to successfully complete course assignments and engage meaningfully in the classroom environment with their peers without intellectual disability. In fact, while the attitudes of including students with intellectual disability on campus are socially generally positive, attitudes towards academic inclusion are less positive and may vary by discipline (Carothers et al., 2021). The attitudes of faculty members are varied and complex. Some faculty members may feel positively about the inclusion of students with disabilities and may see it as an opportunity to promote diversity and inclusion in higher education. McCabe et al. (2022) examined the viewpoints of faculty members regarding the inclusion of college students with intellectual disability in higher education; they focused on understanding the reasons behind faculty members' interest in inclusion as well as the perceived benefits and challenges associated with inclusive practices.

Faculty members expressed a genuine interest in including college students with intellectual disability in their classes. They viewed inclusion as an opportunity to enhance diversity, promote social justice, and foster a more inclusive learning environment. Faculty members highlighted the positive impacts on the learning experiences of all students, such as increased empathy, critical thinking, and a broader understanding of human differences. They also noted the positive effects on the personal growth and development of the students with intellectual disability themselves. Similar to previous studies, the authors called attention to some associated challenges; faculty members expressed concerns about the availability of necessary support and resources, potential disruptions to the learning environment, and the need for appropriate training and professional development to effectively teach and support students with intellectual disability (McCabe et al., 2022).

However, faculty at the postsecondary level also report feeling unsure of how to incorporate students with intellectual disability into their courses (Gibbons et al., 2015; Grigal et al., 2013; Love et al., 2019). Almutairi and colleagues (2021) explored the attitudes of faculty members and administrators on this topic. The authors conducted a survey of 150 faculty members and administrators at a university in Saudi Arabia; they found that while faculty members and administrators generally had positive attitudes towards the inclusion of students with intellectual disability in postsecondary education, they still held some concerns and reservations. Faculty members and administrators identified their own lack of training and support as a significant barrier to inclusion, with many feeling that they lacked the knowledge and resources necessary to effectively support these students. Additionally, some participants expressed concerns about the potential impact of inclusion on academic standards and the overall quality of education.

Despite these concerns, the majority of faculty members and administrators expressed a willingness to support the inclusion of students with intellectual disability in postsecondary education. Overall, the authors emphasized the importance of addressing the attitudes of faculty members and administrators towards inclusion and suggested that targeted training and support programs may be needed to address the concerns and reservations of faculty members and administrators towards greater inclusion.

Barriers to Successful Inclusion of Students With Intellectual Disability in College

While there are many benefits to hosting an IPSE program for various campus stakeholders, there are some barriers. Lee and Taylor (2022) acknowledged that accessing IPSE can be challenging for many students with intellectual disability due to several barriers. One of the primary barriers identified is a lack of awareness and understanding of the benefits of postsecondary education for students with intellectual disability among educators, service providers, and families. Many people may assume that these students are not capable of pursuing higher education. Another barrier is limited funding and resources; programs that support students with intellectual disability in college may be underfunded or lack the necessary

Disability as Diversity in Higher Education Spaces • **175**

resources to provide comprehensive services and supports. This can result in these students facing challenges in areas such as housing, transportation, and academic accommodations, which in turn could contribute to hesitation among administrators and faculty members about inclusion of (Lee & Taylor, 2022).

Additional barriers identified by Taylor et al. (2021) include confusion over the status of students auditing coursework, as many students in IPSE programs often do. Faculty members expressed confusion over whether to assign students a letter grade or what their expectations should be for classroom participation, given their audit status. They also reported apprehension over whether to require students to take tests, exams, or complete projects the same as their peers in the course. Others felt they received limited information about the student and their support needs from the IPSE program. Many faculty members expressed feeling inadequate or nervous to meet students' needs given their lack of preparation in teaching students with disability (Taylor et al., 2021).

In an attempt to provide some solutions to more effectively include students with intellectual disability in their classrooms, faculty members in Taylor et al. (2021) provided valuable suggestions to overcome some of these common barriers. These suggestions included providing on-going support to faculty on best practices for teaching and assessing students with intellectual disability. Others called for more alignment between IPSE programs and existing IHE processes, including how students are registered and graded, how accommodations are provided, and removing barriers for students to access the courses that will contribute to their employment goals and outcomes (Taylor et al., 2021).

UNIVERSAL DESIGN AS FACILITATOR OF INCLUSION OF STUDENTS WITH INTELLECTUAL DISABILITY

Despite thorough documentation of the benefits of IPSE and including students with varied disabilities, there is still a need for robust training and implementation of UD to ensure that students with disabilities can access college life. UD promotes inclusive education by creating learning environments that are accessible and beneficial to all students, regardless of their abilities or disability. It aims to remove barriers and provide equal opportunities for learning and participation. College classrooms are diverse, with students coming from various backgrounds, experiences, and abilities. UDL recognizes this diversity and provides flexibility in teaching methods and materials to accommodate different learning styles and needs. It allows students to engage with the content in ways that work best for them. By adopting UDL principles, college settings can enhance learning outcomes

TABLE 8.1 Guiding Questions for Content Display From Love et al., 2019

Considerations	Guiding Questions
1. Content presentation	• Does my presentation only include essential information? • Do I provide multiple representations (e.g., text, pictures, video) of my essential information? • Is the text in my presentation presented in an informal or conversational way?
2. Aiding content processing	• Does my presentation highlight key information (e.g., highlighted, provided in a different font, provided in an excerpt) in a clear way? • Are items that correspond to each other (e.g., text and clarifying pictures/videos) displayed near each other? • Does my presentation cover or provide necessary background information?
3. Providing digital copies to students	• Is my presentation in a format I can upload to my course learning management system? • Does my presentation provide accessibility options (e.g., narration, readable font, text-to-speech options, closed captioning for videos)? • Can students self-pace the presentation? • Can students customize the presentation (e.g., change colors, fonts, take notes in/on the presentation) on their own?

for all students. The accessibility and flexibility provided by UDL strategies enable students to better understand and engage with the course content, leading to improved academic performance and a deeper understanding of the subject matter. The employment of UD and UDL ensures that all students have equal opportunities to participate fully in educational activities, contribute their perspectives, and benefit from the college experience. For students with intellectual disability, UDL can facilitate access to college life, including coursework (Love et al., 2019). UDL strategies can enhance students' access to the curriculum, increase their engagement, and foster their independence and self-advocacy skills, while also supporting their academic growth and overall success (Love et al., 2019).

Love and colleagues (2019) provided strategies and considerations for implementing UDL in courses that include college students with intellectual disability (see Table 8.1).

THIS WORK IN ACTION: DISABILITY JUSTICE THROUGH PARTICIPATORY ACTION RESEARCH

In this section we aim to integrate our call to re-write the disability narrative in higher education with our discussion of the importance of including students with intellectual disability on college campuses through a description of our experience utilizing PAR with college students. In order to realize inclusive education ideals, which center around honoring all forms of human diversity as beneficial and recognizing and supporting every person's capacity for learning (Beneke et al., 2020; Love & Beneke, 2021), there is a need for a fundamental change in higher education, and this includes how we as academics conduct research.

In order to inform these new justice-minded higher education spaces, people with disability and their experiences must be centered. Research that purports to enhance IHE experiences for students with disability must include those students in the research process, not as subjects but as co-researchers. McTaggart (1994) stated that PAR is simultaneously concerned with changing individuals, the culture of the group, as well as the institutions and societies to which they belong. PAR was created as a tool to work with marginalized communities and to allow for co-creation of knowledge, centering the participants as experts in their own lives (Tuhiwai Smith, 2021).

Through coursework that we created and explored with students enrolled in two separate courses in our IHE, we carried out two separate but tangential photovoice projects in fall 2022. Photovoice as a method has three main goals: (a) to have people record and reflect their community's strengths and concerns, (b) to encourage people to talk about important community issues through large and small discussion of photographs, and (c) to share findings with the community and reach the people who can make change (Wang & Burris, 1997). The methodology is underpinned by Friere's (1970) critical consciousness, Haraway's (1988) feminist standpoint theory, and documentary photography (Milne & Muir, 2020). These frameworks come together to center the participants' experiences as true and believed. Photovoice participants are assumed to be experts in their own situation (Wang et al., 1996) and are called upon to "tell *their* story rather than *the* story" (Sutton-Brown, 2014, p. 171, emphasis in original). And their story is important for making our community and larger society more equitable.

We embedded photovoice projects into coursework related to higher education access, self-determination, and agency for students with disability in college. All students enrolled in *Equity in Action: Disability and Accessibility in Higher Education* identified the accessibility needs on our campus through the eyes of undergraduate students with and without disability as they lived out these experiences in real time. Students enrolled in the other course, *Agency in College*, used photos of their own experiences in college as students with intellectual or developmental disability to express their understanding and development of self-determination and agency.

We used a critical constructivist framework, which recognizes that our realities are created by our individual experiences within the society and environment in which we live (Bentley, 2003). The goal of each study was to empower students to become co-researchers and share their own knowledge and lived experiences in regards to campus accessibility with the larger community. The photos culminated in an on-campus museum exhibit titled *Experiences in Equity and Agency: Disability in Higher Education*. All student co-researchers had control over which of their photos were shared and their voices were highlighted through the accompanying narrative with each photo on display.

RECOMMENDATIONS FOR HIGHER EDUCATION SPACES

We propose a transformation of higher education to a place that welcomes and celebrates disability as a form of diversity. However, some key changes are necessary. What follows are our recommendations for ensuring people with disability, including those with intellectual disability, are included, valued, and welcomed at colleges and universities and thus properly represented in DEI efforts moving forward.

Change the Narrative Around Disability

"When disability is seen as something 'suffered' by a very few, and otherwise invisible and non present, then disability can never change the culture of higher education..." (Dolmage, 2017, p. 93). We must move away from the medical model of understanding disability and towards disability justice. Disability justice was defined by Berne and colleagues (2018) as a movement towards a world where all bodies and minds are accepted and celebrated. A first step in this is for IHEs to acknowledge and then tackle ableism head-on. Norms must be re-established in order to make a campus barrier-free and welcoming, a place where disability is recognized as a form of human variation just as all other forms of diversity (Leake & Stodden, 2014). Disability must be seen as a form of diversity, not a deficit, and this reframing must be embraced by all members of the higher education community.

Include People With Disabilities as Co-researchers and Partners in This Change

Policy-makers and arbiters of the theoretical, conceptual, and physical changes on campuses must include disability voices and knowledge. The disability rights movement-coined mantra, "nothing about us without us" must be acknowledged and adhered to in order for the changes to be meaningful. PAR methods are well-suited to engaging historically marginalized groups in research and subsequent social change for good. As well, we must include intersectionality as a lens when conducting research (Esposito & Evans-Winters, 2021).

Embrace Universal Design

UD and UDL should be employed to ensure accessible spaces, coursework, and ideas. Traditional and historical higher education spaces were not designed to include people with disabilities. An intentional re-design of spaces, curriculum, and pedagogy is the way forward in ensuring access. This process starts with engaging disabled students and campus members in evaluating spaces and processes that are not accessible and could be improved. For faculty, there are likely several opportunities, for example, some offer support through their Center for Teaching Excellence or other affiliates of the Professional and Organizational Development Network in Higher Education (podnetwork.org), to learn more about best practices in implementing UD.

Enhance Training for IHE Faculty and Staff to Better Include People With Disabilities

Faculty members have been identified as one of the main barriers to students with disability feeling accepted and valued in higher education (Lombardi & Lalor, 2017; Love et al., 2015; Wynants & Dennis, 2017). Historically, faculty and staff have not been legally required to train for inclusion of students from diverse or marginalized backgrounds into IHE spaces. We put forth that faculty and staff training in UDL and the tenets of inclusive pedagogy could go a long way toward enhancing accessibility. O'Shea and colleagues (2016) pointed out that while the rhetoric around inclusion has been embraced by higher education, it is not apparent that the pedagogical principles behind social inclusion have been put into practice. Inclusive pedagogies include specific student-centered approaches to teaching that attend to the varied backgrounds, learning styles, and abilities of all learners. Additionally, an emphasis on accessibility from the outset should supplant a reliance upon accommodations later; the more accessible an environment, process, or course is from its inception, the less need there will be for accommodations (O'Neil Green et al., 2017).

Include Disability in Diversity Statements

Intentional wording in DEI statements is a necessity to communicate that people with disabilities are welcome in higher education. Parallel to the long history of exclusion for other marginalized communities, those with disability have not historically had legal access until recently nor been welcomed in IHEs. This practice cannot be changed until the very words meant to connote diversification and inclusion of marginalized groups include people with disability.

After a long history of marginalization and exclusion from educational opportunities, people with disabilities now have legal access to postsecondary education options. While this is a first step in the right direction, it is our position that much is left to be done to make those spaces welcoming and inclusive for this community of learners. While access and inclusion are pieces of this, an understanding of the rightful presence (Calabrese & Tan, 2020) of people with disability in higher education spaces is the next step to ensure equity in higher education spaces.

REFERENCES

Almutairi, A., Kawai, N., & Alharbi, A. (2021). Faculty members' and administrators' attitudes on integrating students with intellectual disability into postsecondary education. *Exceptionality, 29*(1), 29–40. https://doi.org/10.1080/093628 35.2020.1727330

Americans with Disabilities Act of 1990, 42 U.S.C. § 12101 *et seq.* (1990). https://www.ada.gov/law-and-regs/ada/

Anderson, R. C. (2006). Teaching (with) disability: Pedagogies of lived experience. *The Review of Education, Pedagogy, and Cultural Studies, 28*(3–4), 367–379. https://doi.org/10.1080/10714410600873258

Aquino, K. C. (2016). A new theoretical approach to postsecondary student disability: Disability-diversity (dis)connect model. *Journal of Postsecondary Education and Disability, 29*(4), 317–330. https://files.eric.ed.gov/fulltext/EJ1133815.pdf

Asch, A. (2001). Disability, bioethics, and human rights. In G. L. Albrecht, K. D. Seelman, & M. Bury (Eds.), *Handbook of disability studies* (pp. 297–326). SAGE. https://doi.org/10.4135/9781412976251.n12

Athamanah, L. S., Fisher, M. H., Sung, C., & Han, J. E. (2020). The experiences and perceptions of college peer mentors interacting with students with intellectual and developmental disabilities. *Research and Practice for Persons with Severe Disabilities, 45*(4), 271–287. https://doi.org/10.1177/1540796920953826

Beavers, D. (2018). *Diversity, equity, and inclusion framework: Reclaiming diversity, equity, and inclusion for racial justice.* The Greenlining Institute. https://greenlining.org/wp-content/uploads/2018/05/Racial-Equity-Framework.pdf

Beneke, M. R., Newton, J. R., Vinh, M., Blanchard, S. B., & Kemp, P. (2020, April 11). *Practicing inclusion, doing justice: Disability, identity, and belonging in early childhood.* Zero to Three. https://www.zerotothree.org/resource/journal/practicing-inclusion-doing-justice-disability-identity-and-belonging-in-early-childhood/

Bentley, M. L. (2003, October 29–November 2). *Introducing critical constructivism* [Paper presentation]. The Annual Meeting of the American Educational Studies Association, Mexico City, Mexico. http://web.utk.edu/~mbentle1/Crit_Constrc_AESA_03.pdf

Berne, P., Morales, A. L., Langstaff, D., & Invalid, S. (2018). Ten principles of disability justice. *Women's Studies Quarterly, 46*(1–2), 227–230. https://doi.org/10.1353/wsq.2018.0003

Bogart, K. R., & Dunn, D. S. (2019). Ableism special issue introduction. *Journal of Social Issues, 75*(3), 650–664. https://doi.org/10.1111/josi.12354

Bornstein, J., & Manaseri, H. (2018). Disability studies and educational leadership preparation: The moral imperative. *Review of Disability Studies, 14*(3). https://www.rdsjournal.org/index.php/journal/article/view/818

Bureau of Labor Statistics. (2023, February 23). *Persons with a disability: Labor force characteristics–2022.* U.S. Department of Labor. https://www.bls.gov/news.release/pdf/disabl.pdf

Butler, L. N., Sheppard-Jones, K., Whaley, B., Harrison, B., & Osness, M. (2016). Does participation in higher education make a difference in life outcomes for students with intellectual disability? *Journal of Vocational Rehabilitation, 44*(3), 295–298. https://doi.org/10.3233/jvr-160804

Calabrese Barton, A., & Tan, E. (2020). Beyond equity as inclusion: A framework of "rightful presence" for guiding justice-oriented studies in teaching and learning. *Educational Researcher, 49*(6), 433–440. https://doi.org/10.3102/0013189x20927363

Carothers, D., Aydin, H., & Halpern, C. (2021). Campus attitudes toward academic and social inclusion of students with intellectual disability. *Journal of Curriculum Studies Research, 3*(2), 122–147. https://doi.org/10.46303/jcsr.2021.2

Carter, E. W., & McCabe, L. E. (2021). Peer perspectives within the inclusive postsecondary education movement: A systematic review. *Behavior Modification, 45*(2), 215–250. https://doi.org/10.1177/0145445520979789

Cimera, R. E., Thoma, C. A., Whittenburg, H. N., & Ruhl, A. N. (2018). Is getting a postsecondary education a good investment for supported employees with intellectual disability and taxpayers? *Inclusion, 6*(2), 97–109. https://doi.org/10.1352/2326-6988-6.2.97

Connell, B. R., Jones, M., Mace, R., Mueller, J., Mullick, A., Ostroff, E., Sanford, J., Steinfeld, E., Story, M., & Vanderheiden, G. (1997). *The principles of universal design* (Version 2.0). NC State University, College of Design, Center for Universal Design. https://design.ncsu.edu/wp-content/uploads/2022/11/principles-of-universal-design.pdf

Davis, L. J. (2011, September 25). Why is disability missing from the discourse on diversity? *The Chronicle of Higher Education.* https://www.chronicle.com/article/why-is-disability-missing-from-the-discourse-on-diversity/?sra=true&cid=gen_sign_in

Digest of Education Statistics. (2021). *Table 311.10. Number and percentage distribution of students enrolled in postsecondary institutions, by level, disability status, and selected student characteristics: 2015–16* [Data table]. U.S. Department of Education, Institute of Education Sciences, National Center for Education Statistics. https://nces.ed.gov/programs/digest/d20/tables/dt20_311.10.asp

Dolmage, J. T. (2017). *Academic ableism: Disability and higher education.* University of Michigan Press. https://doi.org/10.3998/mpub.9708722

Esposito, J., & Evans-Winters, V. (2021). *Introduction to intersectional qualitative research.* SAGE.

Evans, N. J., Broido, E. M., Brown, K. R., & Wilke, A. K. (2017). *Disability in higher education: A social justice approach.* Jossey-Bass.

Fleming, A. R., Oertle, K. M., Plotner, A. J. (2017). Student voices: Recommendations for improving postsecondary experiences of students with disabilities. *Journal of Postsecondary Education and Disability, 30*(4), 309–326. https://files.eric.ed.gov/fulltext/EJ1172798.pdf

Friere, P. (1970). *Pedagogy of the oppressed.* Herder & Herder.

Gibbons, M. M., Cihak, D. F., Mynatt, B., & Wilhoit, B. E. (2015). Faculty and student attitudes toward postsecondary education for students with intellectual disabilities and autism. *Journal of Postsecondary Education and Disability, 28*(2), 149–162. https://eric.ed.gov/?id=EJ1074661

Gould, R., Harris, S. P., & Mullin, C. (2019). *Higher education and the ADA: An ADA knowledge translation center research brief.* ADA National Network. https://adata.org/research_brief/higher-education-and-ada

Griffen, J., & Tevis, T. (2017). Tools for moving the institutional iceberg: Policies and practices for students with disabilities. In E. Kim & K. C. Aquino (Eds.), *Disability as diversity in higher education* (pp. 153–168). Routledge. https://doi.org/10.4324/9781315644004-11

Griful-Freixenet, J., Struyven, K., Verstichele, M., & Andries, C. (2017). Higher education students with disabilities speaking out: Perceived barriers and opportunities of the universal design for learning framework. *Disability & Society, 32*(10), 1627–1649. https://doi.org/10.1080/09687599.2017.1365695

Grigal, M., Hart, D., & Weir, C. (2013). Postsecondary education for people with intellectual disability: Current issues and critical challenges. *Inclusion, 1*(1), 50–63. https://doi.org/10.1352/2326-6988-1.1.050

Grigal, M., Papay, C., Weir, C., Hart, D., & McClellan, M. (2022). Characteristics of higher education programs enrolling students with intellectual disability in the United States. *Inclusion, 10*(1), 35–52. https://doi.org/10.1352/2326-6988-10.1.35

Haraway, D. (1988). Situated knowledges: The science question in feminism and the privilege of partial perspective. *Feminist Studies, 14*(3), 575–599. https://doi.org/10.2307/3178066

Higbee, J. L., Siaka, K., & Bruch, P. L. (2007). Student perceptions of their multicultural learning environment: A closer look. In J. L. Higbee, D. B. Lundell, & I. M. Duranczyk (Eds.), *Diversity and the postsecondary experience* (pp. 3–23). The Center for Research on Developmental Education and Urban Literacy. https://files.eric.ed.gov/fulltext/ED499036.pdf#page=9

Disability as Diversity in Higher Education Spaces • **183**

Hill, E., Shaewitz, D., & Queener, J. (2020). *Higher education's next great challenge: Ensuring full inclusion for students with disabilities.* Institute for Educational Leadership. https://files.eric.ed.gov/fulltext/ED615532.pdf

Kauffman, J. M., Anastasiou, D., Felder, M., Lopes, J., Hallenbeck, B. A., Hornby, G., Ahrbeck, B. (2023). Trends and issues involving disabilities in higher education. *Trends in Higher Education, 2*(1), 1–15. https://doi.org/10.3390/higheredu2010001

Kim, E., & Aquino, K. C. (Eds.). (2017). *Disability as diversity in higher education: Policies and practices to enhance student success.* Routledge. https://doi.org/10.4324/9781315644004

Leake, D. W., & Stodden, R. A. (2014). Higher education and disability: Past and future of underrepresented populations. *Journal of Postsecondary Education and Disability, 27*(4), 399–408. https://eric.ed.gov/?id=EJ1059990

Lee, C. E., & Taylor, J. L. (2022). A review of the benefits and barriers to postsecondary education for students with intellectual and developmental disabilities. *The Journal of Special Education, 55*(4), 234–245. https://doi.org/10.1177/00224669211013354

Lindsay, S., Cagliostro, E., & Carafa, G. (2018). A systematic review of barriers and facilitators of disability disclosure and accommodations for youth in post-secondary education. *International Journal of Disability, Development, and Education, 65*(5), 526–556. https://doi.org/10.1080/1034912X.2018.1430352

Lindsay, S., McDougall, C., & Sanford, R. (2013). Disclosure, accommodations, and self-care at work among adolescents with disabilities. *Disability and Rehabilitation, 35*(26), 2227–2236. https://doi.org/10.3109/09638288.2013.775356

Linton, S. (1998). *Claiming disability; Knowledge and identity.* New York University Press.

Lombardi, A. R., & Lalor, A. R. (2017). Faculty and administrator knowledge and attitudes regarding disability. In E. Kim & K. C. Aquino (Eds.), *Disability as diversity in higher education* (pp. 108–121). Routledge. https://doi.org/10.4324/9781315644004-8

Love, H. R., & Beneke, M. R. (2021). Pursuing justice-driven inclusive education: Disability critical race theory (DisCrit) in early childhood. *Topics in Early Childhood Special Education, 41*(1), 31–44. https://doi.org/10.1177/0271121421990833

Love, M. L., Baker, J. N., & Devine, S. (2019). Universal design for learning: Supporting college inclusion for students with intellectual disabilities. *Career Development and Transition for Exceptional Individuals, 42*(2), 122–127. https://doi.org/10.1177/2165143417722518

Love, T. S., Kreiser, N., Camargo, E., Grubbs, M. E., Kim, E. J., Burge, P. L., & Culver, S. M. (2015). STEM faculty experiences with students with disabilities at a land grant institution. *Journal of Education and Training Studies, 3*(1), 27–38. https://doi.org/10.11114/jets.v3i1.573

Mattlin, B. (2022). *Disability pride: Dispatches from a post-ADA world.* Beacon Hill Press.

McCabe, L. E., Hall, C. G., Carter, E. W., Lee, E. B., & Bethune-Dix, L. K. (2022). Faculty perspectives on the appeal and impact of including college students with intellectual disability. *Inclusion, 10*(1), 71–86. https://doi.org/10.1352/2326-6988-10.1.71

McTaggart, R. (1994). Participatory action research: Issues in theory and practice. *Educational Action Research, 2*(3), 313–337. https://doi.org/10.1080/0965079940020302

Milne, E.-J., & Muir, R. (2020). Photovoice: A critical introduction. In L. Pauwels, & D. Mannay (Eds.), *The SAGE Handbook of Visual Research Methods* (pp. 282–296). SAGE. https://doi.org/10.4135/9781526417015.n17

Newman, L., Wagner, M., Knokey, A.-M., Marder, C., Nagle, K., Shaver, D., & Wei, X. (2011). *The post-high school outcomes of young adults with disabilities up to 8 years after high school: A report from the National Longitudinal Transition Study-2* (NLTS2; NCSER 2011–3005). National Center for Special Education Research. https://eric.ed.gov/?id=ED524044

Office of Planning, Development, and Policy Development. (2016, November). *Advancing diversity and inclusion in higher education: Key data highlights focusing on race and ethnicity and promising practices.* U.S. Department of Education, Office of the Under Secretary. https://www2.ed.gov/rschstat/research/pubs/advancing-diversity-inclusion.pdf

Okoro, C. A., Hollis, N. D., Cyrus, A. C., & Griffin-Blake, S. (2018, August 17). Prevalence of disabilities and healthcare access by disability status and type among adults—United States 2016. *Morbidity and Mortality Weekly Report, 67*(32), 882–887. http://doi.org/10.15585/mmwr.mm6732a3

O'Neil Green, D., Willis, H., Green, M. D., & Beckman, S. (2017). Access ryerson: Promoting disability as diversity. In E. Kim & K. C. Aquino (Eds.), *Disability as diversity in higher education* (pp. 200–215). Routledge. https://doi.org/10.4324/9781315644004-14

O'Shea, S. , Lysaght, P., Roberts, J., & Harwood, V. (2016). Shifting the blame in higher education—Social inclusion and deficit discourses. *Higher Education Research and Development, 35*(2), 322–336. https://doi.org/10.1080/07294360.2015.1087388

Plotner, A. J., Marshall, K., & Smith-Hill, R. B. (2023). Special education teachers' pre-service experience with inclusive postsecondary education programs: Impact on professional practices and dispositions for secondary transition professionals. *Teacher Education and Special Education, 46*(2), 89–107. https://doi.org/10.1177/08884064221091580

Prohn, S. M., Kelley, K. R., & Westling, D. L. (2018). Students with intellectual disability going to college: What are the outcomes? A pilot study. *Journal of Vocational Rehabilitation, 48*(1), 127–132. https://doi.org/10.3233/JVR-170920

Redpath, J., Kearney, P., Nicholl, P., Mulvenna, M., Wallace, J., & Martin, S. (2013). A qualitative study of the lived experiences of disabled post-transition students in higher education institutions in Northern Ireland. *Studies in Higher Education, 38*(9), 1334–1350. https://doi.org/10.1080/03075079.2011.622746

Reindal, S. M. (2008). A social relational model of disability: A theoretical framework for special needs education? *European Journal of Special Needs Education, 23*(2), 135–146. https://doi.org/10.1080/08856250801947812

Riddle, C. A. (2020). We do not need a 'stronger' social model of disability. *Disability & Society, 35*(9), 1509–1513. https://doi.org/10.1080/09687599.2020.1809349

Sannicandro, T., Parish, S. L., Fournier, S., Mitra, M., & Paiewonsky, M. (2018). Employment, income, and SSI effects of postsecondary education for people with intellectual disability. *American Journal on Intellectual and Developmental Disabilities, 123*(5), 412–425. https://doi.org/10.1352/1944-7558-123.5.412

Scheef, A., Caniglia, C., & Barrio, B. L. (2020). Disability as diversity: Perspectives of institutions of higher education in the U.S. *Journal of Postsecondary Education and Disability, 33*(1), 49–61. https://eric.ed.gov/?id=EJ1273652

Shaewitz, D., & Crandall, J. R. (2020, October 19). Higher education's challenge: Disability inclusion on campus. *Higher Education Today.* https://www.higheredtoday.org/2020/10/19/higher-educations-challenge-disability-inclusion-campus/

Shakespeare, T. (2013). The social model of disability. In L. J. Davis (Ed.), *The disability studies reader* (4th ed., pp. 214–221). Routledge. https://doi.org/10.4324/9780203077887-25

Shallish, L. (2017). A different diversity? Challenging the exclusion of disability studies from higher education research and practice. In E. Kim & K. C. Aquino (Eds.), *Disability as diversity in higher education* (pp. 19–30). Routledge. https://doi.org/10.4324/9781315644004-2

Snyder, T. D., & Dillow, S. A. (2015, May). *Digest of education statistics 2013* (NCES 2015-011). U.S. Department of Education, Institute of Education Sciences, National Center for Education Statistics. https://nces.ed.gov/pubs2015/2015011.pdf

Strauss, A. L., & Sales, A. (2010). Bridging the gap between disability studies and disability services in higher education: A model center on disability. *Journal of Postsecondary Education and Disability, 23*(1), 79–84. https://files.eric.ed.gov/fulltext/EJ888647.pdf

Sutton-Brown, C. A. (2014). Photovoice: A methodological guide. *Photography and Culture, 7*(2), 169–185. https://doi.org/10.2752/175145214X13999922103165

Taylor, A., Domin, D., Papay, C., & Grigal, M. (2021). "More dynamic, more engaged": Faculty perspectives on instructing students with intellectual disability in inclusive courses. *Journal of Inclusive Postsecondary Education, 3*(1). https://doi.org/10.13021/jipe.2021.2924

The Economics Daily. (2015, July 15). *People with a disability less likely to have completed a bachelor's degree.* U.S Department of Labor, Bureau of Labor Statistics. https://www.bls.gov/opub/ted/2015/people-with-a-disability-less-likely-to-have-completed-a-bachelors-degree.htm

Tuhiwai Smith, L. (2021). Decolonizing methodologies: Research and indigenous peoples (1st ed.). Zed Books. https://doi.org/10.5040/9781350225282

Vaccaro, A., Kimball, E. W., Wells, R. S., & Ostiguy, B. J. (2015). Researching students with disabilities: The importance of critical perspectives. *New Directions for Institutional Research, 163,* 25–41. https://doi.org/10.1002/ir.20084

Wang, C., & Burris, M. A. (1997). Photovoice: Concept, methodology, and use for participatory needs assessment. *Health Education & Behavior, 24*(3), 369–387. https://journals.sagepub.com/doi/pdf/10.1177/109019819702400309

Wang, C., Burris, M. A., & Ping, X. Y. (1996). Chinese village women and visual anthropologists: A participatory approach to reaching policymakers. *Social Science & Medicine 42*(10), 1391–1400. https://doi.org/10.1016/0277-9536(95)00287-1

Williams, W. M., & Ceci, S. J. (1999, August 6). Accommodating learning disabilities can bestow unfair advantages. *Chronicle of Higher Education*, B4–5.

Woolf, E., & de Bie, A. (2022). Politicizing self-advocacy: Disabled students navigating ableist expectations in postsecondary education. *Disability Studies Quarterly, 42*(1). https://doi.org/10.18061/dsq.v42i1.8062

Wynants, S. A., & Dennis, J. M. (2017). Embracing diversity and accessibility: A mixed methods study of the impact of an online disability awareness program. *Journal of Postsecondary Education and Disability, 30*(1), 33–48. https://eric.ed.gov/?id=EJ1144611

CHAPTER 9

A TEACHER'S SUCCESSFUL EFFORTS TO SUPPORT DIVERSITY AND EQUITY

Despite Contextual Obstacles

Mariana Alvayero Ricklefs
Northern Illinois University

ABSTRACT

In this chapter, I report on a single-case study of a teacher who successfully supported diversity and equity in her classroom despite institutional obstacles. My purpose is two-fold: (a) to examine linguistically responsive teaching (LRT) practices employed by the teacher to support English learner (EL) students' diverse backgrounds and enhance their learning and (b) to explore how the teacher promoted EL students' rightful presence in the school community. My data sources include classroom observations, interviews, and documents. My data analysis encompasses open and focused coding with the identification of theme and subtheme patterns. The findings demonstrate that the teacher utilized various LRT practices focused on key vocabulary, semantic complexity of text, and linguistic scaffolding. My findings also re-

Justice, Equity, Diversity, and Inclusion in Education, pages 187–210
Copyright © 2024 by Information Age Publishing
www.infoagepub.com
All rights of reproduction in any form reserved.

188 ▪ M. A. RICKLEFS

veal that the teacher promoted ELs' rightful presence via a collective disruption of power and authority. Together, the teacher and students interrupted normative knowledge and power relationalities in their classroom learning. This chapter provides examples of the teacher's pedagogical practices that supported diversity and equity in an antagonistic school context that created obstacles for the teaching and learning of EL students.

In this chapter, I examine the instructional practices that a teacher of English learners (EL)—whom I will refer to subsequently as Mrs. Smith (a pseudonym)—successfully employed to support the education of a group of ELs amid contextual obstacles. Obstacles to the education of minoritized students in the micro-level context of the classroom are often embedded in school, district, community, and societal macro-level contexts (Ricklefs, 2019, 2020, 2021, 2022, 2023).

As a qualitative case study of an EL teacher, this research took place at a public elementary school in the Midwestern United States. The school was located in a suburban and predominantly White community. However, over a third of the student body was composed of Hispanic EL children who were bused to the school from two low-income neighborhoods.

Given that the focal participant (Mrs. Smith) is an EL teacher, I utilize the theoretical perspective of linguistically responsive teaching ([LRT], Lucas & Villegas, 2011, 2013; Lucas et al., 2008; Villegas et al., 2018) to examine how she supported the learning of ELs—children who speak primary language(s) distinct from English in their homes (e.g., Arabic, Mandarin, Spanish) and are learning English as an additional language in American schools. The literature shows that it takes about 7 years for ELs to learn English at a level of academic or school success when appropriate instruction is provided (Echevarría et al., 2017; Thomas & Collier, 2012). Thus, teachers need to provide appropriate instruction to make the curriculum of the content areas accessible to ELs. LRT includes knowledge, skills, and practices that serve to differentiate instruction for ELs as well (Tomlinson, 2017).

I also use the frame of *rightful presence* (Calabrese Barton & Tan, 2019, 2020; Squire & Darling, 2013) to explore how Mrs. Smith promoted such presence for and with her EL students. The framework of rightful presence is understood through three tenets, which can be paraphrased as political struggle through disciplinary learning, making (in)justice visible, and collective disruption of power and authority modes. My case study of Mrs. Smith provides relevant information and examples about what educators can do to support EL students' diversity, equity, and access to social justice in schools. This is significant for teachers—such as Mrs. Smith—who do not have racial/ethnic, cultural, or linguistic minority backgrounds but teach diverse EL students daily. In this chapter, I also uncover tensions and possibilities for rightful presence and "translat[e] this complex idea into concrete pedagogical and schooling practices" (Calabrese Barton & Tan, 2020, p. 438). Therefore, I investigated the following research questions:

RQ1: *Which linguistically responsive teaching practices did Mrs. Smith employ to support EL students' diverse backgrounds and enhance their learning?*

RQ2: *How did Mrs. Smith promote EL students' rightful presence in the school?*

LINGUISTICALLY RESPONSIVE TEACHING AND RIGHTFUL PRESENCE

The theoretical perspectives of LRT and rightful presence form the framework of this case study. LRT includes knowledge, skills, and practices that serve to make content responsive to ELs, which can be addressed in three major areas: learning about ELs, identifying language demands, and providing linguistic scaffolding (Lucas & Villegas, 2011, 2013; Lucas et al., 2008; Villegas et al., 2018). In the sections that follow, I focus on the second and third areas.

One important aspect of LRT is identifying language demands. Learning and using English in content areas poses various challenges for ELs, for example, the language demands of particular classroom tasks, such as key vocabulary, semantic complexity of texts, and specific purposes and situated uses of language. Identifying language demands allows teachers to anticipate when explicit instruction is needed and when to adapt instruction (Lucas et al., 2008; Villegas et al., 2018).

Another relevant aspect of LRT is providing linguistic scaffolding, which refers to specific instructional adaptations to make content understandable for ELs. It includes offering direct instruction regarding syntax in comprehensible ways. Linguistic scaffolding also includes teachers' modified speech rate, as well as their use of different visual aids, realia, multimedia resources, and various participation structures in the classroom (Lucas et al., 2008; Villegas et al., 2018). It also encompasses providing differentiated instruction for ELs (Tomlinson, 2017).

The theoretical perspective of rightful presence (Calabrese Barton & Tan, 2019, 2020; Squire & Darling, 2013) also informs my research study. The frame of rightful presence is understood through three tenets, paraphrased as political struggle through disciplinary learning, making (in)justice visible, and collective disruption of power/authority modes. The collective disruption of power and authority refers to interrupting normative knowledge and power relationalities in classroom learning. First, this demands changing what counts as knowledge and what it means to know and do, for example, within disciplinary learning, such as literacy in the EL classroom. Second, this tenet also relates to shifting social hierarchies, for instance, between the teacher and EL students in my study, so that both are capable sharers of knowledge. Finally, it calls for collective work in the classroom toward social justice. Together, educators and EL students, for example, can engage in what Calabrese Barton and Tan (2020) describe as a "collective and iterative endeavor shared between the more powerful and the historically less powerful" (p. 437), which fosters social transformation. As they went on to affirm, this requires "reconfiguring the discourses and practices of who, and what, legitimately belong in the disciplines and society" (p. 437).

METHODOLOGY

In this chapter, I report on a qualitative case study. There are several types of qualitative case study research designs depending on their characteristics, disciplinary orientation, and purpose (Hancock et al., 2021; Yin, 2018). Specifically, I employed a single-case holistic, descriptive, and critical design. I considered the single case—the EL teacher, Mrs. Smith—in both holistic (in-depth, various facets) and critical (challenging/confirming/extending theory) ways. This design is also descriptive because it illustrates the key features of a social phenomenon within its context (Hancock et al., 2021; Yin, 2018): classroom instruction that supports diversity, equity, and social justice. This research design was appropriate for my investigation because it matched the focus of my study—Mrs. Smith's teaching practices that supported EL students' diversity and equity in the classroom.

The EL Teacher

At the time of my case study, Mrs. Smith was a woman in her 50s who had approximately 30 years of teaching experience, particularly with EL students. She identified herself as a White female and a native English speaker who also knew some Spanish, Latin, and German. She described herself as growing up in a middle-class family with strong educational and ethical values. She was originally from Arizona but had lived in the American Midwest for most of her teaching career.

It is important to note that my case study was part of a larger ethnographic project in which several community stakeholders were involved—including Mrs. Smith. She was invited to participate because of her teaching credentials and vast experience, and because she was the only EL teacher at the school.

The School and Community

At the school where Mrs. Smith worked with ELs, there had been constant and abrupt changes in the program and teaching practices with ELs, which occurred during 10 years of disagreement and conflict among different school personnel and community stakeholders (see Ricklefs, 2022, for a comprehensive examination of this situation).[1] Ironically, the rights and needs of the students for whom a language program had been created in the school district were overlooked because of the students' being moved between two schools in the same district, without parental consent, repeatedly excluding them from appropriate education. First, the ELs were excluded from the multicultural program at one school, because some school board and community city council members did not consider them as "really" multicultural. Later, these ELs were moved to a school that warranted Title I funds but did not have administrative and teacher support for them. This is the school where Mrs. Smith had come to work, at the time of my study.

A major issue was that ELs were not considered to belong in the community because of their socioeconomic, cultural, and linguistically diverse backgrounds. The community was predominantly middle class and White. Accordingly, to a large degree, the school administrators, stakeholders, and students aligned with the demographics of the community.

The conflict among different community stakeholders brought to the foreground the myth that, for minority students, simply attending the community school guarantees equal opportunity. This myth "ignores the fact that it is actually the lack of quality education . . . that underserved populations around the globe encounter in school that contributes to reproducing grave social disparity" (Valdiviezo & Nieto, 2015, p. 102). Indeed, the decisions of district leaders, school board members, and the city council revealed underlying, and probably unaware, biases toward ELs and other minority students (Ricklefs, 2022).

In this hostile environment, power struggles and apparent differences in social status among community members influenced the school culture as well. Mrs. Smith felt rejected and relegated to a less powerful social status because she often spoke out about school and community issues to try to find solutions that would benefit her students. Despite her specialized training and many years of teaching experience with ELs, she felt ignored and undervalued. She reported feeling like a "teacher of convenience . . . [when] the school would get an extra FTE [full-time equivalent]" and was not viewed as a "real teacher" because she taught ELs, not students in general education classrooms (Ricklefs, 2022, p. 19).

Data Sources

I utilized different types of data to ensure a comprehensive qualitative research dataset (Hancock et al., 2021). The data included information obtained from classroom observations, interviews, and documents. I observed

Mrs. Smith teaching in her classroom during the English reading block (approximately 90 minutes each) once a week throughout the semester. I took detailed field notes and diagrammed seating arrangements to complement my classroom observations. Additionally, I interviewed Mrs. Smith using initial and final semi-structured interview protocols. I also wrote comments in a research journal to reflect on several informal conversations I had with Mrs. Smith regarding her teaching and the school context. Finally, I collected and examined relevant documents, such as the English curriculum in the school, EL students' work samples completed during the classes I observed, and copies of instructional resources (e.g., graphic organizers, worksheets, stories, visual aids) that Mrs. Smith used in the classes I observed.

Data Analysis

I analyzed the data from my study in two coding cycles. The first cycle included open or initial coding. Initial coding was useful because it allowed me to "remain open to all possible theoretical directions suggested by [my] interpretation of data" (Saldaña, 2021, p. 148). I remained alert to possibilities of codes while sorting data from transcripts and notes from classroom observations, documents, and transcripts from my interviews with Mrs. Smith. I refrained from imposing my ideas, nor did I force my expectations onto the data. During the first cycle, Saldaña (2021) recommended "to fracture or split the data into individually coded segments" (p. 302). I fractured the data by breaking them down into discrete parts, which I marked with numbers in superscript format. See examples in Table 9.1, in the Data column. Next, I assigned representative labels to these meaningful units of information (e.g., picture, needs, story). See examples in Table 9.1, in the column Initial Codes.

In my second cycle, I used focused coding to categorize the codes that I had generated in the first analytical cycle. Focused coding was pertinent because it permitted me to search "for the most frequent or significant codes to develop the most salient categories in the data corpus" (Saldaña, 2021, p. 303). During the second cycle, I began with a fine-tuned analysis of the initial codes comparing and contrasting them against the data from observations, documents, and interviews. Hence, this was an iterative and methodical process. Next, I proceeded to organize and cluster together into categories similar or semantically related codes (e.g., visual aids, background knowledge, figurative language). See examples in Table 9.2, in the column Categories of Codes.

After forming categories, I evaluated these clusters by re-reading the codes and data. I reorganized some categories and deleted others. Then, I continued the iterative analytic process to see if there were major patterns of

A Teacher's Successful Efforts to Support Diversity and Equity ▪ **193**

TABLE 9.1 Example of First Coding Cycle

Source	Data	Initial Codes
Observation: Transcript of video recording complemented with notes	Mrs. Smith: "A boat like this"[1] Mrs. Smith: "So, Sally is the boat, her apron she holds up[2] like a sail, and she's got a leg in the water[4] like a rudder[5] . . . Ha-ha! Pretty crazy lady, huh?"[6] Notes: The teacher lifts her sweater[3] up with her right hand and moves her left leg on the floor.[7] The students chuckle.[8]	1. Picture 2. Hand gesture 3. Object 4. Posture 5. Vocabulary: "rudder" 6. Humor 7. Body movement 8. Humor
Interview: Transcript of audio recording	Mrs. Smith: "they are high-performing students[9] . . . So, they could function fully[10] in a regular classroom,[11] but I still see the needs of EL students[12] as somewhat different from those of native English speakers.[13] One [need] is still vocabulary development."[14]	9. ELs "high performing" 10. ELs "function fully" 11. "Regular classroom" 12. ELs have "needs" 13. "Different" needs 14. "Vocabulary development"
Document: Excerpt from the textbook's chapter	"A tall tale[15] starts out like a regular story,[16] but it tends to stretch the facts a little.[17] Well, actually, it stretches the facts a lot. [18] Where was the first tall tale told? Probably around a campfire. Out on the frontier[19] of the 1800s,[20] American settlers[21] liked to exaggerate.[22] They created heroes[23] and heroines[24] who were larger than life,[25] capable of amazing deeds.[26] In a big land with wild weather[27] and wild animals,[28] the stories had to be just as big[29] and just as wild."[30]	15. Vocabulary: "tall tale" 16. "A regular story" 17. "Stretch the facts a little" 18. "Stretches the facts a lot" 19. Vocabulary/History: "the frontier" 20. U.S. history "the 1800s" 21. Vocabulary/History: "American settlers" 22. Hyperbolize: "Exaggerate" 23. Vocabulary: "Heroes" 24. Vocabulary: "Heroines" 25. Hyperbole: "larger than life" 26. Vocabulary: "Amazing deeds" 27. Uncertainty/Metaphor: "wild weather" 28. Danger: "wild animals" 29. Bravery/Simile: "just as . . . as . . ." 30. Encouragement/Simile: "just as . . . as . . ."

ideas or "themes" (Saldaña, 2021, p. 369). As Saldaña (2021) recommended, I carefully linked categories of codes as a heuristic to combine them semantically and systematically into themes and subthemes. I employed gerunds in sentences (e.g., identifying linguistic demands is essential to

194 ▪ M. A. RICKLEFS

TABLE 9.2 Example of Second Coding Cycle	
Categories of Codes	**Tentative Themes and Subthemes**
Category 1: Visual Aids	Theme: Addressing linguistic demands is essential to teach effectively ELs
Code 1. Picture Code 3. Object	
Category 2: Body Language	• Subtheme: Providing linguistic scaffolding
Code 2: Hand gesture Code 4: Posture Code 7: Body movement	• Subtheme: Using non-verbal means
Category 3: Comfortable Classroom	Theme: Creating a responsive classroom is important when working with ELs
Code 6: Humor Code 8: Humor	
Category 4: Positive Views of ELs	• Subtheme: Creating a fun and engaging classroom
Code 9: ELs "high performing" Code 10: ELs "function fully" Code 11: "Regular classroom"	• Subtheme: Considering ELs as capable students
Category 5: Educational Needs	• Subtheme: Responding to particular educational needs
Code 12: ELs have "needs" Code 13: "Different" needs Code 14: "Vocabulary development"	
Category 6: Vocabulary	Theme: Addressing linguistic demands is essential to teach effectively ELs
Code 5: Vocabulary: "rudder" Code 14: "Vocabulary development" Code 15: Vocabulary: "tall tale" Code 19: Vocabulary/History: "the frontier" Code 21: Vocabulary/History: "American settlers" Code 23: Vocabulary: "Heroes" Code 24: Vocabulary: "Heroines" Code 26: Vocabulary: "Amazing deeds"	• Subtheme: Teaching key vocabulary
Category 7: Background Knowledge	Theme: Addressing linguistic demands is essential to teach effectively ELs
Code 16: "A regular story" Code 19: Vocabulary/History: "the frontier" Code 20: US history: "the 1800s" Code 21: Vocabulary/History: "American settlers" Code 28: Danger: "wild animals"	• Subtheme: Activating prior knowledge • Subtheme: Building background knowledge
Category 8: Figurative Language	Theme: Addressing linguistic demands is essential to teach effectively ELs
Code 17: "Stretch the facts a little" Code 18: "Stretches the facts a lot" Code 22: Hyperbolize: "Exaggerate" Code 25: Hyperbole: "larger than life" Code 27: Uncertainty/Metaphor: "wild weather" Code 29: Bravery/Simile: "just as…as" Code 30: Encouragement/Simile: "just as…as…"	• Subtheme: Teaching the semantic complexity of texts • Subtheme: Teaching types of figurative language

effectively teach ELs) to gather and represent these patterns. The use of gerunds (e.g., identifying, creating, building) enabled me to connote action in the thematic patterns, which was suitable for investigating teaching *practices* which were at the core of my research questions. See examples in Table 9.2, in the column of Tentative Themes and Subthemes. Lastly, I confirmed the trustworthiness of data analysis through member checks with Mrs. Smith.

FINDINGS

Regarding my first research question ("Which linguistically responsive teaching (LRT) practices did Mrs. Smith employ to support EL students' diverse backgrounds and enhance their learning?"), my findings revealed that Mrs. Smith utilized various practices for identifying language demands (e.g., teaching key vocabulary and the semantic complexity of texts) and for providing linguistic scaffolding. She explicitly and directly employed LRT practices to facilitate comprehension of the English language arts curriculum and materials provided by the school district. In the following sections, I discuss examples of Mrs. Smith's instructional practices that aligned with LRT.

LRT Practices

Teaching Key Vocabulary

During the classes I observed, vocabulary teaching was a common practice. This is an important LRT practice when identifying language demands for ELs in the content areas. Language demands may have a major impact on ELs' comprehension and learning, and Mrs. Smith was aware of this issue. She considered that EL students, even if they were high performing, had vocabulary needs different from those of native English speakers. During an interview, she affirmed:

> These [EL] students had sixes [the highest score in the standardized test of English proficiency used in the school for ELs] primarily, and they are high-performing students.... So, they supposedly could function fully in a regular classroom, but I still see the needs of EL students as somewhat different from those of native English speakers. One [need] is still vocabulary development.

Mrs. Smith explained new words in the readings from the English Language Arts textbook. This type of contextualized teaching aligns with LRT. She did not teach a list of isolated words devoid of context, nor did she

196 ▪ M. A. RICKLEFS

merely provide a quick preview of key vocabulary before reading the stories in the textbook. As an illustration, after an EL student read a paragraph from a story, Mrs. Smith explained that "one of the words was 'forage' for berries, and that means to go hunt for them. Animals forage for food in the forest. They go hunt and look around for that." She defined the term "forage" using simple words and examples that the students could understand. Thus, she facilitated their understanding of the text by creating comprehensible input, which aligned with the LRT pedagogical framework.

On another day, Mrs. Smith used pictures and gestures to teach new vocabulary from the reading. After Manuel,[2] an EL student, read a paragraph from a story about tall tales, Mrs. Smith explained what the term "rudder" meant. Alicia, another EL student, made an interesting comment that demonstrated understanding. Here is an excerpt of the conversation between the teacher and her EL students.

> **Manuel:** (Reading out loud) "Sally is so very special," said the schoolmarm. "She lives to whip across the Salt River, using her apron for a sail and her left leg for a rudder!"
> **Mrs. Smith:** Uh-huh, and do you understand that?
> **Manuel:** No, I don't.
> **Mrs. Smith:** The "rudder"... let's see if I have that (she goes to her desk and gets a card with a picture of a boat with a rudder). When there is a boat, a boat like this (she shows students the picture), a boat like this in the water couldn't tip over. So, there's a rudder underneath it, and it usually looks like that (pointing to the boat and its rudder in the picture).
> **Students:** Ohhh!
> **Mrs. Smith:** To keep the boat from falling over and to make the boat go in the right direction. So, Sally is the boat. Her apron, uh, she holds up like a sail, and she's got a leg in the water to keep it from falling over and just let the wind blow her across the water (with her right hand, the teacher lifts her sweater up in the air like a sail and moves her left leg on the floor like a rudder. The students chuckle.)
> **Mrs. Smith:** Ha-ha! Pretty crazy lady, huh?
> (The students chuckle a bit)
> **Manuel:** Yes.
> **Alicia:** It's making an exaggeration... it's a tall tale!
> **Mrs. Smith:** Uh-huh.

In this example, Mrs. Smith taught new vocabulary to make language and content comprehensible to her EL students. She explained the term "rudder" in context and used simple words to paraphrase the reading. She

A Teacher's Successful Efforts to Support Diversity and Equity • **197**

also used visual aids (a picture of a boat) and gestures (her hand waving her sweater in the air and moving her foot on the floor) to demonstrate what the protagonist in the story did.[3] The students' comments suggested that they understood the tall tale story ("Ohhh!"; "It's making an exaggeration"). Mrs. Smith's practice aligned with linguistically responsive teaching because once she realized that the students did not understand all the words in the textbook, she proceeded immediately to explain key vocabulary in the context of the reading. She quickly identified the language demands that this particular reading posed to EL students. Identifying language demands is an important component of LRT, and the use of gestures and body language in her explanation also aligns with LRT.

At the end of class, Mrs. Smith's students often thanked her for helping them understand the textbook. In conversations with me, they also expressed admiration for her and considered her a very good instructor. They sometimes noted how different her teaching was from the other teachers they had, who mostly handed out worksheets for them to complete without making sure they understood the vocabulary or content. This example of Mrs. Smith's typical instruction also demonstrates her use of linguistic scaffolding in the form of visual aids. Linguistic scaffolding is another LRT practice that I will address later in this chapter.

Teaching the Semantic Complexity of Texts

Mrs. Smith made language and content comprehensible to her EL students by teaching them the semantic complexity of texts, particularly when the meaning was unstated or unclear. In figurative language, the meaning is unstated and must be inferred by the reader, which can be complex when the reader's background knowledge is missing. Figurative language is influenced by cultural and historical contexts common to American native English speakers, but not to EL students who have different sociocultural backgrounds. The LRT practice of directly explaining similes and metaphors as they are used in the context of readings is paramount for facilitating EL students' comprehension, and Mrs. Smith often utilized this LRT practice in her teaching. For instance, when the EL students participated in shared reading, she led a short discussion about the figurative language used in their English language arts textbook. On one occasion, Alicia, an EL student in the classroom, read a paragraph of a story about Davy Crocket, and the teacher explained how figurative language was used in the story. Here is an excerpt of the conversation:

> **Alicia:** (Reading out loud) "One early spring day, when the leaves of the white oaks were about as big as a mouse's ear, Davy Crocket set out alone through the forest to do some bear hunting."

Mrs. Smith: I like that description, where the leaves of the oaks were about as big as a mouse's ear, or small like a mouse's ear. That tells us that it was early, early in the springtime, doesn't it? Before the leaves got really big! So, there is a hint as to what time of the year it was (the students and teacher chuckle a bit).

The teacher explained how a simile was employed in the story to describe the season. She used simple words familiar to the students to indicate that it was "early in the springtime." She also directly explained the simile, wherein the leaves were "as big as a mouse's ear," meaning that they were "small like a mouse's ear" and "before the leaves got really big!" The conversation continued:

Alicia: (Reading out loud) "Davy slept so hard, he didn't wake up until near sundown. And when he did, he discovered that some way or another in all that sleeping, his head had gotten stuck in the crotch of the tree, and he couldn't get it out."

Mrs. Smith: Ok, (reading in the book) "the crotch of the tree" is where the tree goes up, and then the big branches go this way and this way (she uses her arms and hands to point to her left and right sides). So the crotch of the tree is like that fork or that "Y" (she says the letter) in a tree. Do you understand my directions here with my hands? (She moves her hands to her sides.) So the tree goes up and then splits (she moves her hands to the sides again). It looks like maybe he was sitting down on the ground and put his head down between those branches, and it kind of got stuck there. Do you see the picture on page 121? Look here.

Students: (Nodding) Yeah, yeah.

Here, Mrs. Smith elucidated again how figurative language was used in the text. She directly explained the metaphor (the crotch of the tree) to describe the shape of the tree. Her explanation helped make sense of why Davy's head could have gotten stuck in this tree while he fell asleep. She used simple words and gestures to explain the metaphor and directed their attention to the illustration of the tree included at the end of the long story. Her explanation of the use of figurative language in the reading made it more comprehensible for EL students.

As we can see, Mrs. Smith facilitated EL students' understanding by using LRT practices while identifying and addressing the language demands of the English textbook. She noticed that a simile, and then a metaphor, in

A Teacher's Successful Efforts to Support Diversity and Equity • **199**

the story interfered with the students' reading comprehension and quickly proceeded to explain these forms of figurative language. Additionally, by using her gestures and the tree picture, she provided extra-linguistic support as a medium (other than the language of the text) through which her EL students could access the content of the textbook and the English curriculum of the school.

Providing Linguistic Scaffolding

Mrs. Smith employed the LRT practice of linguistic scaffolding when the EL students struggled with grammar and reading comprehension, which encompasses explicit instruction in contextualized ways. That is, she used various examples and visuals to facilitate understanding. Her linguistic scaffolding resembled contextualized mini-lessons on English grammar.

Mrs. Smith believed that this type of teaching would help her EL students to better understand, learn the language, and be more fluent speakers of English. In fact, during an interview, she said, "I still see the needs of EL students as somewhat different from those of native English speakers. One is still grammar construction and more: spelling, word formation, and word order." She considered that her instruction should meet the educational needs of her EL students, and those needs related to the learning of different features of English grammar. Her grammar instruction included roots and affixes, homophones, appositives, spelling, punctuation, syllabication, verbs, direct objects, clipped words, and genre. For instance, in an observed class, her grammar instruction focused on root words and prefixes. She explained to Manuel how to make derivative words, as he was struggling with reading, thereby providing linguistic scaffolding. Here is an excerpt illustrating this type of instruction:

Mrs. Smith: Manuel, what happened here?

Manuel: The words! I don't get it. I don't get it (he points to the page).

Mrs. Smith: (She looks at the page in the textbook) Oh, words from the root?

Manuel: Yeah ... I don't get it. I don't understand it.

Mrs. Smith: Ok, let's do it this way. Suppose I have ... (the teacher goes to the whiteboard) What would be a good word we can use to do that? Let's think of one that is a regular verb. Let's use work (the teacher writes words on the whiteboard in a column: work, working, worked). Do you know that word? (She points to the word "work" written on the whiteboard). Do you know this word? (She points to "working"). Do you know this word? (She points to "worked"). (Manuel nods yes to each word).

Do you know this word? (She points to the word "re-worked").

(Manuel shakes his head).

Reworked? Do you know what "re" means?

Manuel: Again?

Mrs. Smith: Again.

So . . . ?

Manuel: Ahhhh!

Mrs. Smith: So, what does it mean?

Manuel: Work again!

Mrs. Smith: Yes. Now, let's try . . . what's this word? (She writes "re-write" on the whiteboard)

Manuel: Write again.

Mrs. Smith: Write again. You got it!

Mrs. Smith helped Manuel understand how to make a new word by adding a prefix to a word root. Manuel did not understand what he was supposed to do in that particular exercise in the workbook. Instead of just giving him the correct answer, or ignoring his need, the teacher used a simple example to help him understand derivative words and how to build new words by adding the prefix "re-." She provided linguistic scaffolding by explicitly teaching word formation or structural analysis in a comprehensible manner and by using the content of the story. She also engaged in a contextualized mini-lesson on the prefix "re-" to directly address the syntactic difficulty that had interfered with Manuel's reading comprehension of the text at hand.

Mrs. Smith's practice of linguistic scaffolding also encompassed other elements of English grammar, such as punctuation. A typical example is when she and her students read a story that included some quotes, and she pointed to the use of quotation marks. Diego read aloud from the English Language Arts textbook. Here is an excerpt of the conversation:

Mrs. Smith: Diego, would you continue, please?

Diego: Ok (reading). "She is a good ol' . . . ol . . . friend of mine . . ." (he struggles).

Mrs. Smith: "Good ol'," meaning good **old** (emphasis added) friend of mine.

Diego: Ok, "a good old friend of mine"

Mrs. Smith: Remember, in quotation marks, they say what the people said. It doesn't mean that it is grammatically right, but it's what came out of people's mouths. "Oh, yeah! She's a good ol' friend of mine!" and not "Oh, she is a good **old** friend of mine."

Mrs. Smith used this brief, teachable moment to remind students about the role of quotation marks. She pointed out that even if an expression inside quotation marks is not grammatically correct, we have to say it as if it were uttered by the person ("She is a good ol' friend of mine"). At the same time, she helped the EL student with vocabulary and pronunciation. Diego did not know what "ol'" meant or how to pronounce it. She pronounced this word contraction as "old," emphasizing what she considered the right form (grammatically correct) as opposed to "ol'." Mrs. Smith used the short window of time as an opportunity to teach different aspects of the English language and grammar, which is illustrative of the LRT practice of linguistic scaffolding.

Rightful Presence Practices for the Collective Disruption of Power and Authority

Regarding my second research question (How does Mrs. Smith promote EL students' rightful presence in the school?), my findings revealed that Mrs. Smith and her EL students engaged in collective disruption of power or authority. Their rightful presence practices (Calabrese Barton & Tan, 2019, 2020; Squire & Darling, 2013) included changing what counted as knowledge and what it meant to know and act within disciplinary learning, such as literacy for EL students. In the context of the school at which Mrs. Smith taught, the only type of literacy deemed acceptable for EL students was English. However, Mrs. Smith accepted other types of literacy, as she invited and supported the use of EL students' native or home languages. She also allowed cross-linguistic transfer to facilitate their reading comprehension and learning. By doing so, she and her students interrupted normative language knowledge (only English), and the students assumed an agentic role in the social hierarchy of the school.

Indeed, Mrs. Smith considered that transferring from the home language to English, and vice versa, would enhance EL students' learning. During an interview, she talked about what her EL students needed to learn to "function fully in a classroom." She explained,

> They need a lot of ties from English to Spanish. This is how it is in Spanish. This is how it is in English. Look at how your Spanish can help you learn English. Look at how English can help you learn Spanish. You know, those kinds of things.

On another occasion, Mrs. Smith talked about the use of cognates, which are words in different languages that share a similar spelling or pronunciation and have similar meanings. She explained, "I know there's a lot more

202 ▪ M. A. RICKLEFS

that could be brought in [teaching ELs] that I don't know about...like cognates, I think. Luckily, I had Latin, so I know when English words have a Latin root, and I know there's usually a cognate in Spanish."

In the following sections, I provide typical examples of Mrs. Smith's instructional practices that supported her EL students' diverse linguistic backgrounds. This, in turn, disrupted the school's expectations for mono-lingual English literacy and instead affirmed minoritized students' partic-ular ways of knowing (e.g., native language, bilingualism, biliteracy). For instance, one day, she directly asked the EL students what the Spanish cog-nate was for some English terms, and what the equivalent Spanish word was for "synonyms." This discussion arose as a teachable moment during a reading from the English language arts workbook. Here is an excerpt of the conversation between Mrs. Smith, and four of her EL students—Manuel, Lorena, Alicia, and Patricia:

> **Mrs. Smith:** (Reading the instructions in the workbook) "Write a word from the list that is related in meaning," Ok? So, we are looking for words that are...what's that word that means words are alike in what they mean?
>
> **Manuel:** Homophones?
>
> **Lorena:** Compound?
>
> **Mrs. Smith:** No, it starts with sssss (The teacher makes the "s" letter sound)
>
> **Manuel:** Synonyms!
>
> **Students:** Oh, yeah.
>
> **Mrs. Smith:** Synonyms are words that mean the same, not just sound the same, but mean the same.
>
> **Manuel:** Like synonym and cinnamon? (He smiles).
>
> **Lorena:** Cinnamon?
>
> **Mrs. Smith:** (She laughs a bit and Manuel smiles) No, I don't think so, but the word is the same in Spanish, is it not?...Sinomios or something like that?
>
> **Alicia:** Sinónimos (She says the word in Spanish).
>
> **Mrs. Smith:** (She nods yes) Yes, it's very similar.
>
> **Alicia:** Yeah.

By asking questions, Mrs. Smith helped her EL students recall the term "synonyms" and its Spanish cognate "sinónimos," in the context of the in-structions in the English language arts workbook. This incident evidenced her belief in the importance of cross-linguistic transfer—here in the use of Spanish-English cognates—for reading comprehension and affirming these children's ways of knowing and linguistic repertoires. Additionally, by positioning the students at the center of the discussion, Mrs. Smith allowed

A Teacher's Successful Efforts to Support Diversity and Equity • 203

them to assume agentic roles in the classroom. They too had the power to initiate learning.

Another example of teaching using cross-linguistic transfer was when Mrs. Smith asked her EL students what the equivalent Spanish word was for "Native Americans" while they were reading together a story in the English language arts textbook. She was providing context for this term, and she again prompted the students to use their knowledge of Spanish—their home language—and equivalents to English words, to facilitate their reading comprehension. Here is an excerpt of the classroom conversation between her and four EL pupils—Manuel, Patricia, Alicia, and Lorena:

> **Manuel:** They used to call them Indians because they . . . I don't know.
> **Patricia:** I think they used to call them Indians because they thought they came from India.
> **Alicia:** Yes, India!
> **Mrs. Smith:** Right, because when the explorers came, Christopher Columbus thought he had landed in India. That's where he was going. He thought he could leave Europe, go past the Atlantic, and be in India. He didn't know North America was there.
> **Alicia:** So, he just called them Indians?
> **Mrs. Smith:** When he landed on those islands down there near the Gulf of Mexico, he thought he was in India, and they have dark skin and black hair like people from India, so he thought he had found India and the name kind of stuck. Later, they were called Native Americans or . . . how do we call them in Spanish?
> **Alicia:** Uh, indios? (She says the word "Indians" in Spanish)
> **Lorena:** Noooo, Nativos Americanos?
> **Mrs. Smith:** Yes, or indigenous people? Is that right?
> **Students:** Ohhhh! Yes, indígenas. (They say the word "indigenous," which can be a noun or an adjective in Spanish)
> **Mrs. Smith:** Uh-huh, that's the word. That's the cognate. You did have that, right? Aztec, Maya, uh, Toltec? I believe. I'm not sure. I'm not very good about my Mexican history. You know more than I do (the teacher and students smile).

In this example, Mrs. Smith prompted the use of EL students' home language and cross-linguistic transfer to make the reading comprehensible to them. While reading a story in the English language arts textbook about Native Americans, she led a short discussion about this term and availed of another teachable moment. After providing a brief historical context, she directly asked the EL students what the cognates or equivalent words were in Spanish ("How do we call them in Spanish?"), and the children gave different answers ("Indios," "Nativos Americanos"). She continued eliciting cross-linguistic transfer by asking the EL students for another equivalent term in Spanish ("or indigenous people"). The students then provided the corresponding cognate ("indígenas").

As I have illustrated, Mrs. Smith prompted the use of her ELs' primary language and cross-linguistic transfer, in the form of cognates, to make the English texts comprehensible. By employing this teaching practice, she valued her EL students' Spanish as a resource for learning, even in her English classroom. This teaching practice supported EL students' rightful presence (Calabrese Barton & Tan, 2019, 2020; Squire & Darling, 2013) in the classroom and at school. Collectively, Mrs. Smith and her students disrupted the English-dominant monolingual practices for the teaching and learning of EL students, and thus disrupted language power and teaching authority. The students became more than passive recipients of knowledge; they became effective agents of their own language processing and learning.

DISCUSSION

The two-fold purpose of my single-case qualitative research study was to examine LRT employed by Mrs. Smith to support EL students' diverse backgrounds and enhance their learning, and to explore how she promoted EL students' rightful presence in the school community. My findings demonstrated that Mrs. Smith utilized various LRT practices for identifying the language demands of key vocabulary, the semantic complexity of texts, and provided linguistic scaffolding. These practices aligned with Common Core State Standards (https://corestandards.org/) and English Language Development standards—used to determine goals for and level of language proficiency of ELs at the school.

Vocabulary learning is critical for EL students because it is strongly related to reading comprehension and academic achievement (August & Shanahan, 2006; Stahl & Nagy, 2006). Even common words that native speakers know or use on a daily basis are foreign to many EL students (Beck et al., 2002; Echevarría et al., 2017). The LRT practice of teaching key vocabulary is also relevant to ELs' learning of content-area vocabulary and the English language simultaneously (Lucas & Villegas, 2013; Lucas et al., 2008; Villegas et al., 2018).

Additionally, Mrs. Smith employed the LRT practice of teaching semantic complexity embedded in the context of the English language arts (ELA) readings in the textbook. This is important because complex language structures, such as figurative language and idiomatic expressions, tend to be difficult for EL students to comprehend (Blok et al., 2020; Echevarría et al., 2017; Lucas et al., 2008). Even when translated into the EL students' native language, figurative language does not convey a literal meaning. Mrs. Smith was aware of these issues, and thus consistently taught English semantic complexity by generating comprehensible input—making the message understandable for EL students without altering the essence of the text (Krashen, 1985; Krashen & Mason, 2020). She enabled comprehensible input with direct instruction of figurative language. She also used straightforward equivalent words, body language, and pictures to enable her EL students to understand the simile and metaphors found in the ELA textbook. In alignment with LRT practices, she employed a variety of means to make the readings responsive to her EL students.

Moreover, Mrs. Smith deployed the LRT practice of linguistic scaffolding during her reading block with EL students. This practice allowed her "to keep the cognitive demands of instruction high by providing students some type of language support to help them access that content" (Villegas et al., 2018, p. 148). All students, especially EL students, need language support in the form of different types of scaffolding to facilitate their reading comprehension. Scaffolding (Bruner, 1983) is often associated with Vygotsky's (1978) theory of the Zone of Proximal Development, and basically entails providing instructional support to assist students to learn new information and perform related tasks (Blok et al., 2020). Thus, linguistic scaffolding assists EL students to learn specific aspects of the English language that are new to them, or that they do not know how to interpret in the context of new readings.

Linguistic scaffolding includes explicit instruction of syntax, such as word formation (e.g., roots and affixes; Stahl & Nagy, 2009), in comprehensible and contextualized ways (Blok et al., 2020; Villegas et al., 2018). Mrs. Smith also employed linguistic scaffolding by modifying her speech, gesturing, using facial expressions, providing examples and elaborating, showing pictures and visual aids, or teaching impromptu mini-lessons, all in the context of readings from the ELA textbook.

Furthermore, my findings revealed that Mrs. Smith engaged together with the EL students, in the practice of collective disruption of power and authority, which aligned with the instructional approach of rightful presence (Calabrese Barton & Tan, 2019, 2020; Squire & Darling, 2013). This practice included changing what counts as knowledge (e.g., in what language concepts were expressed), and what it meant to know and act (e.g., with language) within disciplinary learning, such as literacy for EL students. Mrs. Smith's instructional practices (e.g., cross-linguistic transfer) supported the EL students' diverse linguistic repertoires. This, in turn, disrupted the school's expectations for literacy and instead affirmed these minority students' diverse ways of knowing (e.g., their language backgrounds) and what counts as worthy knowledge and literacy (e.g., bilingualism, biliteracy).

The literacy expected of the EL students, based on the school and community context (see Ricklefs, 2022 for a thorough explanation), was exclusively English literacy. Such an approach supported a monoglossic ideology of language (García, 2009; García et al., 2018) because English was considered the only desired language for learning at the school. A monoglossic English ideology devalues dialects (i.e., African American Vernacular English, Labov, 1972/2009; Ladson-Billings, 2022; Leonardo, 2009; Smitherman, 2000) and the home/native languages of EL students and their families (García, 2009; García et al., 2018; Ricklefs, 2022, 2023; Rosa & Flores, 2017; Urciuoli, 2013), considering linguistic diversity a liability and an obstacle for learning standardized English in schools. However, Mrs. Smith invited and supported the use of EL students' background knowledge, even during her English reading block, to facilitate the students' comprehension and enhance their learning.

My findings are pertinent because mainstream discourse and customary teaching practices (Ricklefs, 2019, 2020, 2021) position minority children, including EL students, as "missing" culturally, academically, historically—and linguistically (I would add)—in schools (Calabrese Barton & Tan, 2020, p. 433). Contrary to the teacher-centered discourse and instruction predominant in many traditional schools (Ricklefs, 2021, 2022) that replicate unjust "modes of power," in Mrs. Smith's classroom such modes of power appeared to be "challenged, disrupted, and . . . restructured" (Calabrese Barton & Tan, 2020, p. 433).

Certainly, the rightful presence of the collective disruption of power and authority relates to the transformation of social hierarchies between teachers and students. In this case, Mrs. Smith and her EL students jointly disrupted the school's traditional teacher-centered classroom and transformed it into a student-centered one. She became a facilitator of instructional conversations (Goldenberg, 1992) or academic conversations (Zwiers & Crawford, 2011) around text—the stories found in the ELA textbook (Blok et al., 2020; Echevarría et al., 2017; García et al., 2018)—which supported the students in assuming agentic roles in their own learning. Thus, by emphasizing student involvement, the teacher promoted a more balanced social hierarchy in the classroom,[4] which promoted diversity and equity as well.

CONCLUDING REMARKS

Educational research on diversity, equity, and social justice has more often addressed culturally relevant instruction than LRT. Certainly, culture occupies a central role in the way educators interact with, and teach, ELs and other diverse students. Culture is also closely linked to language in complex ways. However, in this chapter, I chose to focus on LRT because I wanted to underscore language-related issues for the teaching and learning of minoritized students, which are overlooked in some equity research (Lucas et al., 2008).

Mrs. Smith's instruction in my case study exemplified the LRT practices (Lucas et al., 2008; Lucas & Villegas, 2011, 2013; Villegas et al., 2018) of identifying linguistic demands, teaching key vocabulary, addressing semantic complexity, and using linguistic scaffolding. These best practices, or high-quality practices, became even more striking given two important facts. First, Mrs. Smith did not share the same diverse backgrounds as her students. Second, she adjusted the school's English curriculum and expectations to meet the needs and strengthen the abilities of her students.

Mrs. Smith's instruction also represents rightful presence pedagogical practices (Calabrese Barton & Tan, 2019, 2020; Squire & Darling, 2013) for collective disruption of authority. She and her students changed the monolingual authority of the English teaching and learning approach that pervaded the school. She elicited cross-linguistic transfer for learning and reinforced the ELs' use of their native/home language. Thus, bilingualism was supported by her teaching. Additionally, her instruction illustrated rightful presence by positioning her students at the center of the classroom as capable knowledge sharers. She shifted the social hierarchy of the teacher-centered instruction characteristic of their school.

More research regarding how educators can ensure the rightful presence of and equitable education for minority children in American schools will further enrich our understanding of equitable education for ELs. ELs deserve teaching practices that acknowledge their diversity and respond to their needs and sociocultural contexts. As Calabrese Barton and Tan (2020) asserted,

> Equity as inclusion... [questions] who has access to high-quality learning opportunities... [and] involves the extension of rights to disciplinary learning to *all* students, with special attention paid to ensuring that minoritized students gain access to such rights. Rights extended include access to pedagogies, tools, and materials that can be differentiated to learners' needs and sociocultural contexts. (p. 434)

NOTES

1. Ricklefs (2022) focused on the school and community context, among other issues. In this chapter I centered on Mrs. Smith's teaching practices to illustrate quality instruction for ELs.
2. All proper nouns are pseudonyms.
3. The children were able to understand the concept of a tall tale from Mrs. Smith's explanation, even though she confused the role of a keel on a sailboat with the role of a rudder.

4. Interestingly, given the focus on student engagement and involvement, the rightful presence practices of Mrs. Smith in my research study overlapped with some instances of LRT.

REFERENCES

August, D., & Shanahan, T. (2006). *Developing biliteracy in second-language learners: A report of the National Literacy Panel on language-minority children and youth.* Erlbaum.

Beck, I. L., McKeown, M. G., & Kucan, L. (2002). *Bringing words to life: Robust vocabulary instruction.* Guilford Press.

Blok, S., Lockwood, R. B., & Frendo, E. (2020). *The 6 principles for exemplary teaching of English learners: Academic and other specific purposes.* TESOL.

Bruner, J. S., & Watson, R. (1983). *Child's talk: Learning to use language.* Norton.

Calabrese Barton, A., & Tan, E. (2019). Designing for rightful presence in STEM: The role of making present practices. *Journal of the Learning Sciences, 28*(4–5), 616–658. https://doi.org/10.1080/10508406.2019.1591411

Calabrese Barton, A., & Tan, E. (2020). Beyond equity as inclusion: A framework of "rightful presence" for guiding justice-oriented studies in teaching and learning. *Educational Researcher, 49*(6), 433–440. https://doi.org/10.3102/0013189X20927363

Echevarría, J., Vogt, M. E., & Short, D. (2017). *Making content comprehensible for English Learners. The SIOP model* (5th ed.). Pearson.

García, O. (2009). *Bilingual education in the 21st century: A global perspective.* Wiley-Blackwell.

García, O., Kleifgen, J. A., & Cummins, J. (2018). *Educating emergent bilinguals: Policies, programs, and practices for English Language Learners* (2nd ed.). Teachers College Press.

Goldenberg, C. (1992). Instructional conversations: Promoting comprehension through discussion. *The Reading Teacher, 46*(4), 316–326. https://www.jstor.org/stable/20201075

Hancock, D. R., Algozzine, B., & Lim, J. H. (2021). *Doing case study research: A practical guide for beginning researchers* (4th ed.). Teachers College Press.

Krashen, S. D. (1985). *The input hypothesis: Issues and implications.* Longman.

Krashen, S., & Mason, B. (2020). The optimal input hypothesis: Not all comprehensible input is of equal value. *CATESOL Newsletter, 53*(5), 1–2. https://www.catesol.org/v_newsletters/article_151329715.htm

Labov, W. (2009). *Language in the inner city: Studies in the Black English vernacular.* University of Pennsylvania Press. (Originally published in 1972)

Ladson-Billings, G. (2022). *The dream-keepers: Successful teachers of African American children* (3rd ed.). Jossey-Bass.

Leonardo, Z. (2009). *Race, Whiteness, and education.* Routledge.

Lucas, T., & Villegas, A. M. (2011). A framework for preparing linguistically responsive teachers. In T. Lucas (Ed.), *Teacher preparation for linguistically diverse classrooms: A resource for teacher educators,* (pp. 55–72). Routledge.

Lucas, T., & Villegas, A. M. (2013). Preparing linguistically responsive teachers: Laying the foundation in preservice teacher education. *Theory Into Practice*, *52*(2), 98–109. https://doi.org/10.1080/00405841.2013.770327

Lucas, T., Villegas, A. M., & Freedson-Gonzales, M. (2008). Linguistically responsive teacher education: Preparing classroom teachers to teach English language learners. *Journal of Teacher Education*, *59*(4), 361–373. https://doi.org/10.1177/0022487108322110

Ricklefs, M. A. (2019). Teachers' conceptualizations and expectations of culturally and linguistically diverse young students. *The International Journal of Diversity in Education*, *19*(2), 33–44. https://doi.org/10.18848/2327-0020/CGP/v19i02/33-44

Ricklefs, M. A. (2020). Young English learners re-construct their literacy identity. *The International Journal of Learner Diversity and Identities*, *27*(1), 15–31. https://doi.org/10.18848/2327-0128/CGP/v27i01/15-31

Ricklefs, M. A. (2021). Functions of language use and raciolinguistic ideologies in students' interactions. *Bilingual Research Journal*, *44*(1), 90–107. https://doi.org/10.1080/15235882.2021.1897048

Ricklefs, M. A. (2022). "Politics at its finest!": Language management and ideologies affecting the education of minoritized students. *SN Social Sciences*, *2*(61), 1–25. https://doi.org/10.1007/s43545-022-00359-y

Ricklefs, M. A. (2023). Variables influencing ESL teacher candidates' language ideologies. *Language and Education*, *37*(2), 229–243. https://doi.org/10.1080/09500782.2021.1936546

Rosa, J., & Flores, N. (2017). Unsettling race and language: Toward a raciolinguistic perspective. *Language in Society*, *46*(5), 621–647. https://doi.org/10.1017/S0047404517000562

Saldaña, J. (2021). *The coding manual for qualitative researchers* (4th ed.). SAGE.

Smitherman, G. (2000). *Talkin that talk: Language, culture, and education in African America*. Routledge.

Squire, V., & Darling, J. (2013). The "minor" politics of rightful presence: Justice and relationality in *City of Sanctuary*. *International Political Sociology*, *7*(1), 59–74. https://doi.org/10.1111/ips.12009

Stahl, S. A., & Nagy, W. E. (2009). *Teaching word meanings*. Routledge.

Thomas, W. P., & Collier, V. P. (2012). *Dual language education for a transformed world*. Fuente Press.

Tomlinson, C. A. (2017). *How to differentiate instruction in academically diverse classrooms* (3rd ed.). ASCD.

Urciuoli, B. (2013). *Exposing prejudice: Puerto Rican experiences of language, race, and class*. Waveland Press.

Valdiviezo, L. A., & Nieto, S. (2015). Culture in bilingual and multilingual education: Conflict, struggle, and power. In W. E. Wright, S. Boun, & O. García (Eds.), *The handbook of bilingual and multilingual education*, (pp. 92–108). Wiley-Blackwell. https://doi.org/10.1002/9781118533406

Villegas, A. M., SaizdeLaMora, K., Martin, A. D., & Mills, T. (2018). Preparing future mainstream teachers to teach English language learners: A review of the empirical literature. *The Educational Forum*, *82*(2), 138–155. https://doi.org/10.1080/00131725.2018.1420850

Vygotsky, L. S. (1978). *Mind in society: The development of higher psychological processes.* Harvard University Press.

Yin, R. (2018). *Case study research and applications: Design and methods* (6th ed.). SAGE.

Zwiers, J., & Crawford, M. (2011). *Academic conversations: Classroom talk that fosters critical thinking and content understandings.* Stenhouse.

CHAPTER 10

UNDERSTANDING TEACHER PERCEPTIONS OF LGBTQ+ REPRESENTATION THROUGH PORTRAITURE

S. Luke Anderson
Tennessee Technological University

ABSTRACT

Tennessee is currently in the middle of the national conversation regarding LGBTQ+ representation in education and society. This means state educators interested in matters of social justice are increasingly under scrutiny from the government, school districts, and parents. In exploring the intersection of schools and diversity/inclusion matters, more specifically understanding teacher perceptions of LGBTQ+ representation in schools, I interviewed high school English Language Arts teachers from Middle Tennessee. Utilizing interpretivism, queer theory, and portraiture methodology, four response categories were identified in answering research questions. The resulting analysis formed the basis for three participant portraits which provided insight into multiple factors concerning teachers considering the LGBTQ+ community in their classrooms. These factors included the pos-

Justice, Equity, Diversity, and Inclusion in Education, pages 211–234
Copyright © 2024 by Information Age Publishing
www.infoagepub.com
All rights of reproduction in any form reserved.

sible negative consequences of discussing controversial topics, especially in conservative southern schools; a lack of teacher training or knowledge on LGBTQ+ subjects; the normalization of queer discussions or topics in school through representation in curricula; and celebrating or understanding diversity in classrooms and curricula.

"That was great tbh [to be honest]. I really went the whole lesson thinking, 'Don't call on me, I will cry,' [because] that poetry was powerful" (personal communication). I received this recently from one of my high school English language arts (ELA) students. We had just finished analyzing spoken word poetry by nonbinary and transgender artists during a unit on how poets comment on gender. In the subsequent discussion, I learned my class had never encountered these ideas in a classroom setting, making them a bit hesitant and cautious at first. A wide range of opinions and reactions were shared, but everyone did so in a respectful manner.

I could never have known when I planned this lesson the previous summer that mere days before that lesson, the student from the email would come out to me as nonbinary and ask me to start using their preferred name. I could see the emotion on their faces as we listened to the poems and talked through them as a class, and so, contrary to my normal habit of ensuring all voices in the room are heard at least once per class, I spared them having to speak. Later, I slipped them a post-it to check in and ensure they were handling everything alright. The above email was part of their response.

I share this story because if I hadn't considered the possibility of having LGBTQ+ students when I was planning my curriculum, this would have never happened. This student and all my students, whether part of the queer community or not, would have gone another year without any form of LGBTQ+ representation in school. At what cost? And why do more teachers not plan inclusive lessons? This chapter describes research helping answer these and other important questions that arise when considering queer representation in school curricula, specifically from a teacher perspective. This topic is particularly important for educators, like the ones in this study, who are in more conservative areas of the country where LGBTQ+ issues can be considered controversial or taboo in classrooms, especially considering the heightened and increasingly prevalent political debate on the subject. The findings of this study, presented through three portraits punctuating the chapter and discussed in depth at the end, point out the need for more teacher access to inclusive curricula and more training on handling LGBTQ+ matters in a classroom context.

PORTRAIT ONE: VIVIAN WARD

It could have been a chilly experience sitting in an expansive classroom with unusually high ceilings and no students while the air conditioner blasted on a brisk Fall Break day, but Vivian Ward's warmth and energy radiated throughout the room. She was clearly in love with her job, something palpable immediately any time she talked about teaching. "I love it, love the kids, love my co-workers. We all get along really well and work as a family unit, so I really love that," she said, clasping her hands to her heart. She had a kind and self-effacing presence that instantly conveyed a genuine compassion and concern for others over herself. Ward often talked about her students like they were her own children. She even told a story about how she would let a student who had an unsafe and unstable home life sleep on a palate behind her desk during class because it was the only place the student could relax and feel safe.

Ward attributed this kind of care and compassion to both her small-town Bible Belt upbringing and her leaving that same area for her education and early career before returning. Leaving was particularly important to her: "I think that just opened me to being more open to different concepts . . . seeing from a different perspective than some." She regularly mentioned the "cookie-cutter" way of thinking prevalent in the rural community where she teaches English, which can hinder teachers who have the few diverse students present in her school. "They have compassion for their kids, but I don't know that they completely understand the different aspects of where their kids come from."

LGBTQ+ students made up one small segment of the diversity present in her school. It was clear that Ward was often uncomfortable with how to speak about this segment of students, oscillating between calling them students who were "struggling" or "battling" before realizing the unstated implications of those adjectives, using outdated terms like "sex change" for transitioning students, and fumbling through the letters LGBT before saying she was sure she left something out unintentionally. This was quite a shift from the effusive and effortless demeanor she had when discussing her teaching job in general.

Perhaps this discomfort came from the lack of exposure she had to discussing these topics in a school setting, saying she had never had formal training of any kind on LGBTQ+ topics, texts, or lessons. "I would really want more training on how to deal with the [LGBTQ+] population. Yes, we can show compassion, but do we really know what they're struggling with?" Ward regularly mentioned feeling ill-equipped for the social-emotional aspects of dealing with queer students, clearly concerned with providing the appropriate kinds of support for them while under her care. She said she had tried to do a little reading on the subject on her own, but she honestly has not done her own "due diligence" when it came to preparing for queer students or topics. Ward's teacher training programs did not specifically prepare her for the subject matter either, and she said she had only ever read one book in college that had queer characters and never any before that. This left her feeling at a bit of a loss: "A lot of it is that we just don't know. You're uncomfortable with things that you don't understand."

This discomfort did not mean that Ward thought LGBTQ+ representation was unimportant; she wished the teaching staff could expose students to more queer authors, inventors, and artists. In this way, it would "normalize" the queer experience, showing them "it's possible to live a normal, productive life in whatever you are." She hoped that her assigned reading materials would help these students know they were not alone, even if they are in the minority in her rural area. However, her community could make teaching LGBTQ+ topics in class challenging: "I don't think this particular area would ever allow for that to be a part of the curriculum or to normalize." This fear of controversy is the primary reason that most LGBTQ+-sympathetic teachers like her would still avoid the subject.

It was clear that Ward felt torn about the tension that existed between meeting the needs of all her students and not wanting to upset parents or administrators. "A lot of times we brush over these topics because it's uncomfortable and we don't want that blow-back. We don't want the parents to say anything." And so, as Ward said, most teachers she knew chose to avoid "hot topics" that could garner "blow-back" or criticism, especially because of the conservative religious ideology of her area. "People will get up in arms about pushing ideas on their kids, even though that's not what we're doing," she said, later adding, "They would feel we were pushing ideologies, whether it be politics or religion or whatever on these kids, even though . . . it's just exposure to things outside of what their norm is."

In the end, however, Ward seemed more interested in knowing about the social-emotional needs of her students over incorporating queer themes and authors into her lessons. Perhaps this was due to her compassionate nature that wanted to nurture and protect all her students as if they were her own children. Perhaps it was due to remembering the struggles of her close childhood friend from the same rural area who was forced to hide his sexuality due to the predominant heteronormative culture in their high school. Or, perhaps it was because she understood how challenging, or maybe even impossible, it would be to include queer representation in the curricula in her area, and so learning more about LGBTQ+ students in general would be a more realistic starting point. "I think that the training is gonna be key. So, if I could recommend, suggest, any of that would be to find some way to train on the emotional aspects and the development [of queer students]."

REVIEW OF RELEVANT LITERATURE

Ward's experiences in the first portrait, as well as the others presented later in the chapter, are best contextualized alongside experiences and research found in other academic work on the same subject. For the purposes of this study, the review of relevant literature focused on studies including teacher attempts at implementing LGBTQ+-inclusive curricula in secondary ELA classrooms or the need for such attempts being made. Three categories of study emerged from the review: student experience, educator attempts at representation, and teacher preparation.

Regarding student experience, LGBTQ+ representation or lack thereof directly impacted students' finding their own voice and becoming a thriving adult (Cayari, 2019) or challenging deeply-ingrained patterns of heteronormativity (Schey & Blackburn, 2019). In addition, teachers and schools creating a supportive school environment, one that included LGBTQ+-inclusive curriculum, proved vital for students' academic, mental, physical, and emotional well-being (Adams, 2018; Lott, 2017). For example, students self-identifying with the queer community were less likely to experience psychological distress or other negative health outcomes in schools where they felt supported (Adams, 2018). Additionally, there were positive academic benefits of an LGBTQ+-inclusive curriculum demonstrated through increased ACT scores (Lott, 2017), which is particularly helpful in the current educational climate so heavily focused on standardized tests. Despite these benefits, many schools were not increasing these types of supportive or inclusive policies, which included the presence of a Gay–Straight Alliance, banning harassment, professional development on LGBTQ-related topics for faculty, and having identified "safe spaces" for queer students in the school (Demissie et al., 2018, p. 557).

Though many schools were not increasing supportive policies, the literature included some examples of teachers creating supportive environments in their individual classrooms; however, many teachers were left to their own devices due to the lack of materials or training available for handling these topics (Kavanagh, 2016). Most educators felt forced to focus on state-mandated curriculum and high-stakes testing instead of diverse representation (Leichtman, 2018; McCoy, 2016). The teachers who were implementing LGBTQ+-inclusive curricula found navigating the delicate balance between being openly supportive and not violating student privacy especially challenging (Kavanagh, 2016; Schey, 2019). These teachers also found that high school students have a natural tendency toward discussing matters of sexuality, but few educators felt comfortable or prepared enough to facilitate such discussions in a classroom setting (White & Ali-Khan, 2020).

216 ▪ S. L. ANDERSON

This lack of preparation might be due to the lack of social-emotional learning, inclusion, or diversity training in teacher preparation programs, particularly at the university level, which often left preservice teachers without an understanding of the serious implications their curricular decisions have for their students (Caughlan et al., 2017; McCoy, 2016; Staley & Leonardi, 2016). Some researchers even said teacher preparation programs for English language arts have been "complicit" in the silencing of gender and sexuality diversity discussions in their university programming (Staley & Leonardi, 2016, p. 210). Besides intentional omission, the growing prevalence of alternative teacher certification programs created to address nationwide teacher shortages (Caughlan et al., 2017) might bear some of the blame for the lack of teacher training on diversity and inclusion matters because they offer a truncated version of an educational degree that leaves little time for new and emerging methods of addressing specific student demographics. A third potential reason for the lack of teacher training in ELA programs is that students often take broad survey courses covering "literature, composition, language, and linguistics" all together in one course (Caughlan et al., 2017, p. 278), leaving little time for addressing the importance of diversity or inclusion in curriculum or the practical issues of handling sexuality through literature, writing, or class discussion.

In addition to the broad categories of student experience, educator attempts at representation, and teacher preparation, the review of literature revealed an obvious lack of research in certain parts of the United States. This dearth was particularly obvious in the South, as most LGBTQ+-themed studies have taken place in "metropolitan areas of the industrial North or the far West, particularly California" (Sears, 1991, p. 11). Thus, a study of teacher perceptions of LGBTQ+ representation in contemporary Tennessee curricula and classrooms is needed, especially considering research from this study included rural areas in the South where little similar work has been conducted.

THE TENNESSEE RESEARCH SETTING

Even though studies make a case for the importance of representation (Adams, 2018; Lott, 2017), this topic is handled very differently in various parts of the country. Tennessee, for example, is a state with a primarily conservative approach when it comes to public policy, which means a complicated history regarding LGBTQ+ issues. This is especially true when it comes to schools, and many recent examples can be cited. Conservative state lawmakers, such as Representative Martin Daniel, made a public outcry when the University of Tennessee at Knoxville was "straying" into LGBTQ+ issues with their pushes for diversity and inclusion in 2016

(Brown, 2016, p. 3). More recently, Tennessee legislators made headlines for banning transgender participants from playing girls' school sports despite none of the bill's supporters being able to cite a specific instance of this problem in Tennessee schools (Kruesi, 2021). These are just two of many such examples from the state.

Even more germane to this study are the laws regarding teaching policies and curricula. While not currently part of the neighboring block of southern states with *No Promo Homo* laws that specifically ban teachers from any positive references to the LGBTQ+ community in their classrooms (GLSEN, 2023), Tennessee state lawmakers have attempted such legislation multiple times, such as the *Don't Say Gay* bill (SB 234) introduced in 2013 (Marra, 2013). Recently, similar legislation was back on the docket. Introduced by Representative Bruce Griffey in February of 2021 and debated through legislative sessions lasting through 2022, House Bill 0800 would have instituted a law that read:

> Prohibits the State Textbook and Instructional Materials Commission (Commission) from recommending, the State Board of Education (SBE) from approving, and local education agencies (LEAs) and public charter schools from adopting or using textbooks and instructional materials that promote, normalize, support, or address lesbian, gay, bi-sexual, or transgender (LGBT) issues or lifestyles. (Tennessee General Assembly, 2022)

While that law has yet to pass, Senator Paul Rose and Representative Debra Moody introduced legislation in February 2021 placing a parental notification burden on teachers wanting to cover LGBTQ+ topics and allowing parents to opt their children out of such lessons (Tennessee General Assembly, 2021); this bill was signed into law in May of 2021. Considering the aggressively anti-LGBTQ+ stance that many state lawmakers continue taking year after year, queer representation in Tennessee school classrooms is understandably limited. It would be fruitless for teachers to spend their time or resources developing and implementing such programming only to be banned shortly thereafter.

In addition, many resources that teachers might use when teaching about queer issues are currently blocked by school internet filtering systems. Storts-Brinks (2010) provided one example that came from her lawsuit in Knox County, Tennessee, where a school filtering system provided by Education Networks of America (ENA) blocked websites such as that of Gay, Lesbian, and Straight Education Network (GLSEN), which is backed by the National Education Association (p. 23). According to Chen (2022), this is still a problem happening across the country. These are just a few of the issues that educators face in Tennessee, which means investigating queer representation in Tennessee classrooms makes for an intriguing study about how such matters are handled.

218 ▪ S. L. ANDERSON

It is challenging, though, conducting research in places where there is a conservative political climate that consistently brings forth legislation potentially outlawing LGBTQ+ representation efforts in schools; this places researchers undertaking such a study, and teachers participating, at risk. However, considering the LGBTQ+ students who lack representation through their curricula and yet pursue an education in an environment when they are regularly ignored or harassed, this was a risk worth taking to learn more.

RESEARCH DESIGN AND METHODS STATEMENT

After realizing the need (based on the literature review) for a specific study in more rural southern parts of the United States, I identified the best way to research the topic in that location. Since the goal of the study was understanding teacher perceptions of LGBTQ+ representation, the use of an interpretivist, queer theory approach was most fitting. Data were collected from teacher interviews, followed by analysis through portraiture methodology to discover key emerging themes.

Theoretical and Methodological Framework

First, the study was grounded in the interpretivist stance of theorists such as Max Weber, Wilhelm Dilthey, Wilhelm Windelband, and Heinrich Rickert, who suggested that interpretivism "looks for culturally derived and historically situated interpretations of the social life-world" (Crotty, 1998, p. 67); this was critical due to the social, political, and religious aspects that factor into the topic of this study. Interpretivism was also a relevant choice because it "entails an *ontology* in which social reality is regarded as the product of processes by which social actors together negotiate the meanings for actions and situations" (Blaikie, 1993, p. 96). In wanting to understand teacher perceptions of LGBTQ+ representation in ELA curricula, the teacher participants served as the "social actors" in this case helping me "negotiate" my understanding of this phenomenon. This idea was echoed by Sipe and Constable (1996), who said, "In the interpretivist paradigm, there is an ongoing, reciprocal influence between the researcher and the researched, and the researched are not subjects, but rather valued 'others,' whose perspectives and worldview the researcher attempts to discover" (p. 154). In interpretivist fashion, the teacher participants' input and insight shaped the findings of this study.

In addition to interpretivism, queer theory was also central to the study. Queer theory researchers have been studying the impact of how we distinguish between sex, sexual identity, gender, and gender identity, in addition to the implications of heterosexuality becoming the "natural and default sexuality" in most schools (Kedley & Spiering, 2017, p. 54). This sends a very clear message to queer students about being outside of the "norm" compared with their peers. Other queer theorists have commented on this phenomenon and how to handle it, noting that curriculum is "largely heterosexualised" in general, and so queer theory "seeks to disrupt underlying heteronormativity by stripping away the illusion that the curriculum is neutral and non-sexualised" (Wilmot & Naidoo, 2014, p. 325). While most students and teachers fail to realize this, most curricula carry a very particular message about sexuality that should be faced and addressed. Hedgespeth (2020) commented on this when saying, "What we choose to teach (or exclude) in the classroom makes a clear statement about what we think is important, whose voices matter, and whose voices do not" (p. 109). An unstated message is sent to any group left out that they matter less than those who are represented, or who are represented more fully, in curricula. This applies to all underrepresented groups, but particularly to LGBTQ+ youth, who are often the last group to be included in curricula. According to Blackburn and Buckley (2005), "Even when they provide for the physical safety and espouse respect for diversity, few secondary schools advocate studying literature that addresses sexual diversity" (p. 202). While meeting the basic needs of students is essential for their educational attainment, actual representation in instruction meets students' need for esteem, respect, and belonging, which many queer students are lacking. Wilmot and Naidoo (2014) agreed, also noting that there is a "prevalence of heteronormativity, low coverage of LGBT sexualities and the association of LGBT with negative contexts in textbooks" (p. 236) in schools across the world. This indicates not only a lack of queer representation, but also the representation that is present is often negative in nature.

Purpose Statement, Participant Descriptions, and Research Questions

Utilizing a queer theory, interpretivist lens for the portraiture study, I interviewed high school English language arts teachers from Middle Tennessee schools to ascertain their understanding of LGBTQ+ representation in their teaching and curricula. My desire was understanding this issue on a local level first, and then thinking about how that relates to the larger landscape.

For this study, participants were recruited through networking with local educational professionals. They were from three different schools in Middle Tennessee, primarily from rural schools. All three participants came from schools in the 500–1,000 student range that were made up predominantly by White students. Two of the teachers were educators between 5

220 • S. L. ANDERSON

TABLE 10.1 Participant Demographics

Participant Pseudonym	Vivian Ward	Edward James	Lane Coleman
Gender Presentation	Female	Male	Male
Race	White	White	White
Self-Identifies With LGBTQ+ Community	No	Yes	No
Education Experience	10–15 years	5–10 years	5–10 years
School Role(s)	Teacher	Teacher/Interventionist	Teacher/Administrator
School Size	500–1000 students	500–1000 students	500–1000 students
Rural School	Yes	No	Yes
Minority Enrollment	Less than 10%	Less than 10%	Less than 10%
Location	Middle Tennessee	Middle Tennessee	Middle Tennessee

Note: Demographic information provided is based on self-reported numbers from the 2021–2022 school year. In this study, rural is defined as either a school of less than 600 students or a town of less than 2,500 people.

and 10 years, while one was an educator between 10 and 15 years. All three taught English Language Arts, but one of them had moved into administration after teaching. One of the three teachers self-identified as part of the LGBTQ+ community. Their individual demographics can be found in Table 10.1. The participants are identified by their pseudonyms: Vivian Ward, Edward James, and Lane Coleman.

When conducting the interviews and research, the following questions guided this study:

- What are teachers' perspectives on the issue of LGBTQ+ representation in curricula?
- In what ways have teachers been informed about or prepared to teach LGBTQ+ subject matters or texts?

PORTRAIT TWO: EDWARD JAMES

Edward James's home was a blend of slightly aged charm and unique personality. After passing through the freshly vacuumed formal living room in the front of the house, he settled into a clearly more lived-in family room. It included a brown sectional sofa, broken in by years of wear, and a large square coffee table cluttered with papers, mail, and the leftovers from a lively gathering the night before. The difference between the living room and family room felt indicative of many dichotomies present in James.

For starters, James identified as part of the queer community himself, although he didn't like labels; he oscillated between referring to himself as a "gay," "queer," and "bi" at various times. Despite this, he thought it was important that his students understood his identification with the LGBTQ+ community: "I wear a rainbow bracelet. I'm not trying to hide anything." This was because he never saw that kind of representation when he was in school. "I think I may have had one teacher who was openly gay in my entire K–12 experience." He admitted to growing up with a negative impression of the queer community because of the lack of representation: "Openly gay people were like outcasts of society. They couldn't hold jobs... I never saw them." Due to this, James thought it was important to show himself an example of a "semi-successful man" who is a "queer person [with] a functional life." However, he admitted to not always being as open with younger students since having nuanced conversations with them was not always possible. Still, James felt being generally open was important.

There were a few reasons why positive queer representation was so meaningful to James beyond the impact it would have made in his own life. For one, he had seen many negative reactions to queer students, both from their peers and teachers. At the worst, he said LGBTQ+ students were often "criminalized" or the target of homophobic jokes or religious condemnation; at the least, they were told, "Just don't be gay around me" or "Don't rub it in my face." He attributed this to the lack of normalization of the queer community through representation in schools, whether that means having visible queer adult role models, reading about or discussing queer characters or texts in classrooms, or being able to talk about matters of diverse sexuality openly in schools. This was especially relevant considering the recent legislation across the United States blocking such discussions, particularly a few making it more difficult to happen here in Tennessee. One reason James felt so passionate about queer inclusion was that he had seen it work first-hand when a curricular text he taught openly discussed a queer artist: "Having it in the curriculum gave it the power of being normal... The kids saw it printed there... It's another thing when they're reading it. This has authority, this has power."

Unfortunately, according to James, many teachers were unwilling to celebrate this kind of diversity in a classroom setting, often saying that school was not the place for those topics or that they were afraid of the potential consequences of discussing "controversial" topics like the LGBTQ+ community. One contributing factor could be the increasingly tense political climate around the subject. Or it might be due to the lack of teacher training on handling such topics that James mentioned was common, which could make some teachers uncomfortable or reticent to explore them. Or perhaps it is just a difference in mindset from those teachers who were willing to wade into "real conversations" that might be more disruptive or challenging, such as the kind James embraced. "One of the things that I prize is putting difficult material in front of kids, difficult [or] controversial." Part of the reason he embraced difficult material is because students are already discovering and discussing their own sexuality, with or without a safe space in the classroom for such topics.

Despite such a commitment to challenging conversations, when James reflected on his own teaching career, he wondered if he had done enough to create space for LGBTQ+ representation in his classrooms. He remembered staying silent at a district meeting when they were discussing whether to include a unit with a queer-themed text because he felt too overwhelmed to speak out. He admitted to having more of a "covert" approach generally in his own classroom, like when he would slip in tidbits about an author, they were reading being queer. "Maybe I've been a little quiet on that front," he concluded upon further reflection, but then added, "If I can have a totally normal conversation with my students about...a person's sexuality, or...how the social perception of their sexuality might have influenced them as a person...that makes it become more normal." And, ultimately, representation leading to normalization was his goal. Despite not teaching much about the LGBTQ+ community directly, James's openness about his own place in the queer community and the safe space that he created for students to feel comfortable about themselves in his classroom were just as critical to this process of normalization.

DATA ANALYSIS AND PRESENTATION: PORTRAITURE

As can be seen through Ward's and James's portraits, portraiture is an effective way to analyze and convey qualitative research findings. Portraiture is best defined by Lawrence-Lightfoot and Davis, the authors of *The Art and Science of Portraiture* (1997), which is the seminal text for the methodology. In their opening chapter, they define portraiture as a "method of inquiry and documentation" that seeks to "combine systematic, empirical description with aesthetic expression, blending art and science, humanistic sensibilities with scientific rigor" (p. 3). This blending of more traditional scientific inquiry with artistic expression is one of the hallmarks of the method, which was also discussed by Bruhn and Jimenez (2020): "In portraiture, rigorous scientific empiricism is complemented by careful attention to the aesthetics of communication for the purposes of deepening perception and expanding common frames of reference" so that the audience might "see and think about the world in new ways" (p. 49). It is the presentation of the data through more artistic or literary formats that allows portraiture this unique ability to direct the audience to such new ways of thinking.

Lawrence-Lightfoot and Davis (1997) said that throughout the data collection process, portraits are "shaped through dialogue between the portraitist and the subject, each one participating in the drawing of the image" (p. 3) through their unique contributions, which include the direct words of the participant alongside the observations and reflections of the researcher recorded in field notes, memos, or journals (Hart, 2018). Then, the researcher analyzes the data for emerging themes that form the basis of the final stage of the method.

At this juncture, the scientific rigor meets the aesthetic artistry because out of this careful analysis of the data emerges a portrait. The final product of portraiture is an "aesthetic whole" (Lawrence-Lightfoot & Davis, 1997, p. 243) that weaves together the key elements and themes of the research process into a narrative depiction. These written portraits are meant to "capture the richness, complexity, and dimensionality of human experience in social and cultural context, conveying the perspectives of the people who are negotiating those experiences" (Lawrence-Lightfoot & Davis, 1997, p. 3). A portraitist's ability to contextualize is a critical component of situating participant experiences properly and conveying them accurately.

In addition to contextualization, there are other significant aspects of portraiture worth noting that differentiates it from other methods. A few of these include its ability to acknowledge the complexity of the subject, focus on the goodness of the subject, and highlight the story's aesthetic qualities (Bruhn & Jimenez, 2020). First, understanding the complex relationships involved affords portraiture a uniquely nuanced voice in research because it combines the voices of the researcher with the researched; this gives it the ability "not only to inform, but also to inspire and provoke" (Kakli, 2011, p. 180). Also, a focus on goodness is a critical component of portraiture. As Kakli (2011) stated, the methodology is "explicit in its focus on documenting the goodness of the phenomena under study, not failure or pathology" (p. 180). In presenting a complex, contextualized, and nuanced picture, the researcher chooses to highlight the positive and give benefit of the doubt when there is room for interpretation.

Another aspect of this complexity in the interweaving of the researcher's voice along with those of the participants is the addition of elements of researcher's background that relate to the study (Lawrence-Lightfoot & Davis, 1997). This aspect is significant because it acknowledges the positionality of the researcher and the influences that are likely to impact their own interpretations of the data. This characteristic makes portraiture "nimble" enough to allow researchers to explore complex modern issues in a way that combines what we can "prove, identify, and measure" with what we "believe, imagine, and feel" (Taylor, 2017, p. 55). This flexibility gives it

224 ▪ S. L. ANDERSON

an ongoing relevance to make significant social commentary alongside its presentation of rigorously captured scientific data.

All these characteristics make portraiture more accessible to the general public than typical scholarship. This is by design, as Lawrence-Lightfoot and Davis (1997) referenced a kind of scholarship that is for all people, not just the academic elite. Portraiture aiming for a "broader audience than merely the 'academy'" (Hart, 2018, p. 43) is aided by its literary style of the data presentation, which can be more engaging and easier to digest than typical academic reporting, especially with more personal topics like human sexuality.

While there are many helpful facets of portraiture, there are some critiques of the methodology. The most significant criticism of the methodology is that the close relationship formed between the researcher and participants disrupts what should be a "clear, distant, and formal" relationship; to "blur the boundaries or reduce the distance would be to distort the researcher's objectivity and threaten the rigor and validity of the research" (Lawrence-Lightfoot & Davis, 1997, p. 137). However, proponents of portraiture would rebut that those closer relationships with participants allow for better and more in-depth data and a "more responsible ethical stance" (p. 137).

Tidying Up and Open Coding

In the early stages of data analysis, portraiture is like other forms of qualitative methodology in its search for "emerging themes" (Lawrence-Lightfoot & Davis, 1997, p. 188), which is often referred to as coding. For this study, I followed steps similar to inductive analysis by coding the transcripts of all three interviews. I first completed the "tidying up" process with the data, a term that comes from Romagnano (1991, as cited in LeCompte & Preissle, 1993), which includes the idea of arranging all the collected data into an easily usable and appropriate format prior to analysis (p. 235), including gathered information about the current political and educational environment in Tennessee since that was continuing to evolve and change in significant ways throughout my study.

The next step taken after tidying up the data was an open coding process (Dey, 1999) that included finding *in vivo* codes, which are "catchy terms" that draw attention to a particular concept, as stated directly by a participant (Strauss & Corbin, 1990, p. 115). One example of this was Ward's repeated use of the term "blow-back" (Ward, 10/11/21). The variation of open coding I utilized was line-by-line analysis, which Strauss and Corbin (1990) emphasized is critical early in a study for rapid category generation. In addition to the coding, I was also memoing, which included both reflexive thinking that I was drawing from beginning analysis (Charmaz, 2002) and initial responses to the interviews through journaling. This would relate to what Lawrence-Lightfoot and Davis (1997) termed an "Impressionistic Record" in portraiture meant as a "ruminative, thoughtful piece that identifies emerging hypotheses, suggests interpretations, describes shifts in perspective, points to puzzles and dilemmas... that need attention, and develops a plan of action" (p. 188). For example, part of my exit notes taken immediately following the interview with Edward James read, "He rarely made eye contact with me when he was talking, even though I mostly made direct eye contact with him. He... was mainly talking toward the wall" (Anderson, 10/7/21). These kinds of details were especially helpful when later constructing the portrait.

Emergent Themes

After the open coding process was completed, I grouped codes into categories based on the "selective or focused coding" of Charmaz (2002, pp. 684–686). After thinking through the initial categories I produced, I whittled them down to the four most recurring or interesting to emerge from the transcripts, allowing for a more focused number of categories that still represented the heart of the data. This completed the step of identifying the emergent themes discussed by Lawrence-Lightfoot and Davis (1997), which would become the main concepts used in creating the portraits.

Creating the Portraits

Once the emergent themes had been identified, I started crafting a narrative that would depict the primary findings from all three participants. This meant starting with a detailed description of the setting and context, for which I utilized my field notes to ensure "thick description... necessary to convey the nuance" (Taylor, 2017, p. 56) of the topic and participant's contributions. In deciding what to include, I strove for equal weight between the personal participant stories and the phenomena I was studying, ensuring I considered the principles of goodness, keeping a "generous, holistic lens," and an appropriate balance between the participants' voices and a restrained version of my own researcher voice (Kakli, 2011, p. 180). In considering the appropriate amount of my own voice in the portrait, I remembered Hart's (2018) assertion that a portraitist must "richly and thickly describe... a personal place from which she or he will paint the portrait" (p. 42). This meant creating space for my own positionality and perspective in the portrait. As a queer educator myself, I felt that overtly shaping the narrative into something that would be intentionally beneficial for the LGBTQ+ community was important to avoid for the trustworthiness of the study; at the same time, allowing my experiences as both an educator and a queer person to inform my own understanding and presentation of the topic was a part of my expertise in conducting the study. Finally, I kept in mind the goal of creating "an authentic narrative that illuminates the meaning that the participant ascribes to a phenomenon, event, or situation" (Barth et al., 2019, p. 1229).

PORTRAIT THREE: LANE COLEMAN

Lane Coleman's office was an appropriate reflection of Lane Coleman the man. Papers crowded a desk overwhelmed with the endless work of an administrator. Mostly bare, neutral-colored walls belied a straightforward and business-like attitude. Standard-issue furniture filled the space: an L-shaped desk, two chairs for receiving visitors, a workstation for shelving and storage. However, upon closer inspection, there was also warmth and personality, whether found through family photos on the shelves or evidence of an affinity for a local sports team. Still, this was a very different working environment from his former classroom. He had transitioned from English teacher to administrator after one of his superiors saw administrative potential in him before he saw it in himself.

Amid the piles of administrative work, something grabbed his attention: a stink bug. These are persistent pests in this part of Tennessee. Coleman, with his smooth and quiet southern speech, laughed off the uninvited visitor, but kept a close eye on it. This is a familiar tactic used toward visitors in such a close-knit, insular community. Most residents of his town grew up there, or at least married into it, but he was quick to add with a grin, "Not to say that it's a community that's not welcoming of others."

Still, Coleman saw himself differently than many of the people he grew up alongside, partially because he went away for college. "I think [it] has to do with education, being educated. Not that you're somehow better if you've got four degrees on the wall, but being exposed to different viewpoints, being around different people." This made Coleman understand the impact of diverse representation: "I just think going and being exposed to all different kinds of people helped me to kinda become more accepting of different kinds and see why it was important to have that representation."

Despite the lack of diversity in his community or school, there had always been an LGBTQ+ presence, even when he was a teacher. "I always had at least one or two students of color or students who I knew were part of the LGBTQ community...They might not be very open about it, but I knew." His background, being exposed to more diversity than many other teachers around him, made him sensitive to the experiences of these students, especially in comparison to his own experiences as a student. "I read all the time when I was a kid, that's why I became an English teacher, and I love reading," he said before adding pensively, "I read books where the characters looked like me and thought like me...we have so many students that they're reading things that they're not represented in."

When expanding on the issue of the lack of representation Coleman saw as a teacher, he identified a few central causes. While outdated curricula and lack of teacher autonomy can play roles, for him, it started with a lack of awareness of the LGBTQ+ community and the importance of representation in curricula. "I think that increasing an awareness about LGBTQ representation will lead to more representation and better representation." He gave a recent example of the concept. He had been watching a television show with an LGBTQ+ character and reflected on how much more media representation of the queer community there is now than when he was a kid; this led to the normalization of the queer community for him and others, one of the effects of representation, but he admitted in reference to his community, "Some places more than others, it's a little more slow to be represented."

In addition to the lack of awareness, Coleman cited the lack of training for teachers on LGBTQ+ issues or lessons as another reason for little representation. The only research or information he had been given on the topic as an educator related to youth suicide rates or bullying due to sexual orientation. When personally faced with having transgender students for the first time, he took it upon himself to seek out a professional development session online, finding out more information to address his self-admitted ignorance on the topic. He found the session helpful and thought that a professional development over the unique needs and challenges of LGBTQ+ students, if presented the right way, would be "effective and beneficial" for the teachers in his building. "There would be teachers in this building who would rail against it, but there would also be...a majority who would welcome that." This acknowledgment that while many would embrace the opportunity to learn more, there would be some adamant resistance led him to expanding on the final obstacle to more queer representation in curricula and classroom teaching: controversy.

Especially in his rural area, any class discussion or text dealing with the LGBTQ+ was usually avoided because teachers didn't want to "ruffle people's feathers" on a topic that could "very easily get people mad" who tended to "express those concerns loudly." In a smaller area, word spreads quickly about what happens at schools, and a teacher discussing anything that could be deemed politically or religiously controversial could have both social and vocational consequences in such a conservative area. Fear of parent complaints or job security concerns, especially when combined with the previously mentioned lack of training on the subject, prevented most teachers from broaching the subject. Those that did allow conversations about queer topics usually did so in a more covert manner by avoiding overtly queer texts or authors, instead opting to teach lessons that could lend themselves to discussion of queer topics if the class so chose.

> Coleman had clearly thought a lot about this topic, both formerly as a teacher and now as an administrator. His tactic was moving the needle toward inclusion slowly by asking questions such as "Why is it important to read texts that are written by different types of people and not just a bunch of old White men?" And, ultimately, he hoped students and teachers at his school could have the same diverse exposure he was given that made him a more inclusive thinker.

FINDINGS

As can be seen in Coleman's portrait, as well as the others, when trying to understand teacher perceptions about LGBTQ+ representation in classrooms, the participant interviews were helpful in developing four emergent themes of responses: *controversy, diversity, normalization/representation*, and *teacher issues/perceptions*. These represent a combination of the overarching themes from all three individual interview transcripts.

Four Emergent Themes

The first theme to emerge from the data was controversy. This included 19 total codes from the three transcripts. While all three participants spoke at length about how dealing with LGBTQ+ subjects in schools, especially as part of a curricula, could be controversial, they diverged in their attitudes on how they personally handled the situation. Ward, for instance, repeatedly talked about wanting to avoid the "blow-back" that would come from people who would "get up in arms about pushing ideas on the kids" (Ward, 10/11/21). Coleman agreed, saying he was regularly cautious about discussing any topic that could "ruffle people's feathers" (Coleman, 10/12/21) because when something can relate to a religious or political issue, then parents tend to "express those concerns loudly." James often mentioned the importance of having real conversations with students about potentially challenging topics like the LGBTQ+ community, but he did acknowledge that many teachers were hesitant or feared controversy. He juxtaposed his own disruptive "anti-institutional tendencies" (James, 10/7/21) with other teachers or administrators who came from a more religious or conservative background not wanting to discuss such matters. On the other hand, Coleman brought up that being associated with controversy could threaten a teacher's job security or ability to advance, which is another reason teachers are hesitant to teach LGBTQ+ lessons.

The second emerging theme was diversity, which included 19 total codes from the three transcripts. All three teachers noted that some teachers celebrated various forms of diversity, such as transgender students or students from different racial or ethnic backgrounds, while many other teachers did not. Both Coleman and Ward differentiated themselves from the two small-town, insular communities from which they came, saying that because they had lived or studied in more diverse communities elsewhere and then came back, they felt like they had a broader perspective; this also meant they perceived LGBTQ+ students and topics in a more tolerant light than many others who worked in their schools or districts. James taught at schools with similar demographics, but he said he was surprised to find many educators who were "equitably minded, more intentional in their classrooms... helping their students feel welcome... embracing diversity and celebrating diversity" (James, 10/7/21). Interestingly, all three participants first associated questions about diversity with race, and then sometimes would move on to other types of diversity like sexual orientation.

The third theme was normalization/representation, which included 10 total codes; while there were a smaller number of total codes for this theme, there was a higher frequency of occurrence than other codes. The normalization of queer characters, themes, and texts through representation in schools, as well as the LGBTQ+ community being open and visible as a part of that normalization, was extremely important to James. This theme was discussed throughout his interview at various points, with James saying, "Having [queer representation] in the curriculum gave it the power of being normal... The kids saw it printed there... when they are reading it... [it] has authority, [it] has power" (James, 10/7/21). While Ward agreed that it was important to normalize queer authors and texts, she added, "I don't think this particular area would ever allow for that to be a part of the curriculum [or] normalize" (Ward, 10/11/21). James also talked about being open about self-identifying with the queer community as another form of normalizing LGBTQ+ topics in school.

Along with the normalization of the queer community in school settings, there was also a discussion of how representation fit into the equation. Coleman saw a lack of awareness as a core problem, but that increasing awareness about the importance of representation would make an impact: "I think that as people start to understand why that's important... the quality and the amount of representation will increase" (Coleman, 10/12/21). James went so far as to question himself on whether he had done enough to represent the queer community with whom he self-identified because he thought representation was "incredibly important for students" (James, 10/7/21). Coleman added that sometimes a more covert approach to representation, like selecting texts that will start conversations, was more

230 ▪ S. L. ANDERSON

effective than overtly choosing queer-themed texts or lessons that could cause backlash.

The final theme was teaching issues/perceptions, with 22 total codes between the three transcripts. This included participant discussions of either experiencing positive teacher collaboration or lacking it, as well as experiencing teacher control over lesson planning or lacking that control due to tight administrative restrictions. They also talked about having many outdated or poor teacher resources that lacked diverse representation. Ward mentioned how parent complaints could cause curricular changes by the district. James, however, had an optimistic attitude about the overall direction of LGBTQ+ representation in schools despite any challenges he had experienced as a teacher.

One challenge all three teachers agreed on was the lack of teacher training or experience with queer lessons or texts. All three had little or no specific training on how to approach the subject with students, and two out of three had never explicitly taught a lesson regarding an LGBTQ+-centered text, subject, or character. The only teacher who had ever experienced a professional development since starting his career on LGBTQ+ topics sought it out for himself to better understand a trans student he was working with at the time. Despite these challenges, Coleman said that he thought many teachers in his building, although not all, would welcome a professional development session on issues facing the queer community; however, he stopped short of saying that they would welcome training on the inclusion of queer topics or texts in classroom lessons.

In total, these four categories help create a framework for the perceptions of the three participants, in addition to providing a framework for analysis moving forward. They spoke to the impact of the local community in Tennessee on teachers' willingness to speak about LGBTQ+ topics in their classrooms. They discussed teacher perceptions of diversity and understanding the queer community specifically. And they talked about the hesitance of teachers due to lack of control, lack of training, or fear of repercussions when tackling potentially controversial issues.

DISCUSSION AND CONCLUSIONS

In revisiting the research questions after completing data analysis, a few conclusions emerged. With respect to the first research question about teachers' perspectives regarding LGBTQ+ representation in curricula, these teachers were generally hesitant to include LGBTQ+ authors or texts primarily due to their fear of controversy or their lack of curricular control. Teachers understood the potential consequences of tackling politically or religiously controversial subjects, which included backlash from parents, pressure from school administrators, or even job security issues. In addition, many schools required a set curriculum that didn't leave room for supplemental teaching, and the set curriculum did not include much diverse representation of any kind, especially for the LGBTQ+ community.

All three educators understood the need for queer representation, as well as the normalization of LGBTQ+ topics in schools. They mentioned celebrating diversity and supporting students who were exploring their sexuality or gender identity. Even though all three worked in schools they considered conservative, they were committed to supporting these students in the ways they felt were possible for them, even if it meant being more covert through creating opportunities for conversations about queer topics rather than directly teaching queer texts, characters, or authors. This proves that even in rural schools in conservative southern states such as Tennessee there are teachers who are making attempts at creating representative spaces, even if in small and covert ways.

In addition, the queer-identifying teacher felt that despite the lack of substantial LGBTQ+ representation in his curriculum, his being an open and visible part of the community helped with normalization and was, in and of itself, an alternative form of representation. This brings up an interesting topic for further study in considering what types of representation are significant for students from the LGBTQ+ community. If teachers are hesitant or banned from teaching on queer subject or authors in more conservative communities, can having openly queer teachers help with normalization and representation in these schools?

Regarding the second research question about teacher preparedness for LGBTQ+ lessons or subject matters, it was clear that all three participants felt unprepared. This was due to the lack of teacher preparation on the topic that took place during their formal teacher training combined with the lack of ongoing professional development on the topic. Two of three participants had never formally taught a lesson on the subject; the one teacher who had taught on the subject self-identified as part of the queer community, which made him more personally invested in the subject matter. All three teachers touched on their personal desire for current training about the topic and the need they saw for this in their schools.

Offering this kind of training is an obvious starting point moving forward. However, the current political, religious, and social climate surrounding American schools and LGBTQ+ education is becoming increasingly hostile, so offering this type of training is tricky, especially in Tennessee. Perhaps it must start with providing administrators and school boards with data about the percentage of their student population who are likely to self-identify with the LGBTQ+ community along with the challenges this community faces. Then, they might understand the need for the representation of this group in their curricula.

232 ▪ S. L. ANDERSON

Or maybe an easier starting point is just trying to educate teachers about the LGBTQ+ community in general before pushing for more inclusive curricula (Anderson, 2023). If these three teachers, all of whom considered themselves more progressive and sympathetic than most teachers around them, generally felt uninformed and unprepared for discussing LGBTQ+ topics with students, then the general teacher population would most likely feel even more uniformed and unprepared. Considering the research on the importance of representation, this widespread ignorance on the topic will mean negative consequences for students. However, the encouraging part of this study was the willingness of all three to participate in more training and education on LGBTQ+ issues and lessons, as well as their belief that many other teachers would feel the same way.

REFERENCES

Adams, S. E. (2018). *School support protects LGB and heterosexual students from sexual orientation victimization: A latent moderated structural equation model* (Publication no. 10929235) [Doctoral dissertation, University of California, Santa Barbara]. ProQuest Dissertations and Theses Global.

Anderson, S. L. (2023). Think piece: A starting place for LGBTQ+ professional development in conservative school districts. *Practice, 5*(1), 48–52. https://doi.org/10.1080/25783858.2023.2179894

Barth, A. L., Rheineck, J. E., & Merino, C. (2019). Exploring counselors' personal guiding theories: A qualitative study using portraiture. *The Qualitative Report, 24*(6), 1227–1241.

Blackburn, M. V., & Buckley, J. (2005). Teaching queer-inclusive English language arts. *Journal of Adolescent & Adult Literacy, 49*(3), 202–212. https://doi.org/10.1598/JAAL.49.3.4

Blaikie, N. (1993). *Approaches to social enquiry.* Polity Press.

Brown, S. (2016, February 17). Under fire from lawmakers, a flagship tries to explain why diversity matters. *Chronicles of Higher Education, 62*(24), A14. https://www.chronicle.com/article/under-fire-from-lawmakers-a-flagship-tries-to-explain-why-diversity-matters/

Bruhn, S., & Jimenez, R. L. (2020). Portraiture as a method of inquiry in educational research. *Harvard Educational Review, 90*(1), 49–53.

Caughlan, S., Pasternak, D. L., Hallman, H. L., Renzi, L., Rush, L. S., & Frisby, M. (2017). How English language arts teachers are prepared for twenty-first-century classrooms: Results of a national study. *English Education, 49*(3), 265–297. https://library.ncte.org/journals/EE/issues/v49-3

Cayari, C. (2019). Musical theater as performative autoethnography: A critique of LGBTQIA+ representation in school curricula. *International Journal of Education & the Arts, 20*(10), 1–22. https://doi.org/10.26209/ijea20n10

Charmaz, K. (2002). Qualitative interviewing and grounded theory analysis. In J. Gubrium & J. A. Holstein (Eds.), *Handbook of interview research* (pp. 675–694). SAGE.

Chen, G. (2022, May 20). Does your public school ban LGBT websites? Sue with ACLU. *Public School Review.* https://www.publicschoolreview.com/blog/does-your-public-school-ban-lgbt-websites-sue-with-the-aclu

Crotty, M. (1998). *The foundations of social research: Meaning and perspective in the research process.* SAGE.

Demissie, Z., Rasberry, C. N., Steiner, R. J., Brener, N., & McManus, T. (2018). Trends in secondary schools' practices to support lesbian, gay, bisexual, transgender, and questioning students, 2008–2014. *American Journal of Public Health, 108*(4), 557–564. http://doi.org/10.2105/ajph.2017.304296

Dey, I. (1999). *Grounding grounded theory: Guidelines for qualitative inquiry.* Academic Press.

GLSEN. (2023). *Policy Maps.* https://www.glsen.org/policy-maps

Hart, K. E. (2018). Understanding school in rural Cambodia: Portraits of elementary teachers. *International Electronic Journal of Elementary Education, 11*(1), 41–48. http://doi.org/10.26822/iejee.2018143959

Hedgespeth, S. R. (2020). Responding to the lack of representation in the ELA canon. *English Journal, 109*(5), 108–110. https://www.proquest.com/docview/2415031727/fulltext/13E24CC456F54EBBPQ/1?accountid=28932

Kakli, Z. (2011). Doing the work: A portrait of an African American mother as an education activist. *The Urban Review, 43*(2), 175–195. https://doi.org/10.1007/s11256-009-0147-9

Kavanagh, S. S. (2016). The promise of anonymity: An investigation on the practices of ELA teachers facilitating discourse about LGBTQ topics. *Teachers College Record, 118*(12), 1–36. http://doi.org/10.1177/016146811611801208

Kedley, K. E., & Spiering, J. (2017). Using LGBTQ graphic novels to dispel myths about gender and sexuality in ELA classrooms. *English Journal, 107*(1), 54–60. https://rdw.rowan.edu/cgi/viewcontent.cgi?article=1017&context=education_facpub

Kruesi, K. (2021, March 22). Tennessee bill to ban transgender athletes heads to governor. *U.S. News.* https://www.usnews.com/news/politics/articles/2021-03-22/tennessee-bill-to-ban-transgender-athletes-heads-to-governor

Lawrence-Lightfoot, S., & Davis, J. H. (1997). *The art and science of portraiture.* Jossey-Bass.

LeCompte, M. D., & Preissle, J. (1993). Analysis and interpretation of qualitative data. In M. D. LeCompte, J. Preissle, & R. Tesch (Eds.), *Ethnography and qualitative design in educational research* (2nd ed., pp. 234–278). Academic Press.

Leichtman, A. (2018). *Creating spaces for culturally responsive pedagogy amid standards driven curriculum in secondary school English/Language Arts classes* (Publication no. 10844946) [Doctoral dissertation, Florida Atlantic University]. ProQuest Dissertations and Theses Global.

Lott, S. (2017). *Curricula as complements: Inclusive content-based literature and the goals of common core in secondary students' English achievement* (Publication no. 10690823) [Doctoral dissertation, University of South Carolina]. ProQuest Dissertations and Theses Global.

Marra, A. (2013, February 1). *GLSEN condemns reintroduction of Tennessee's "Don't Say Gay."* GLSEN. https://www.glsen.org/news/glsen-condemns-reintroduction-tennessees-dont-say-gay

McCoy, M. K. (2016). *Examining high school teachers' experiences with social and emotional learning: An interpretative phenomenological analysis* (Publication no. 10193655) [Doctoral dissertation, Northeastern University]. ProQuest Dissertations and Theses Global.

Schey, R. (2019). Youths' choices to read optional queer texts in a high school ELA classroom: Navigating visibility through literacy sponsorship. *English Education, 52*(1), 38–69.

Schey, R., & Blackburn, M. (2019). Queer ruptures of normative literacy practices: Toward visualizing, hypothesizing, and empathizing. *Research in the Teaching of English, 54*(1), 58–80. https://library.ncte.org/journals/rte/issues/v54-1/30241

Sears, J. T. (1991). *Growing up gay in the South: Race, gender, and journeys of the spirit.* Routledge.

Sipe, L., & Constable, S. (1996). A chart of four contemporary research paradigms: Metaphors for the modes of inquiry. *Taboo: The Journal of Culture and Education, 1*(Spring), 153–163. https://bpb-us-w2.wpmucdn.com/sites.gsu.edu/dist/7/3504/files/2016/12/Sipe-and-Constable-1996-A-chart-of-four-contemporary-research-paradigms-Meaphors-for-the-modes-of-inquiry-1ma0vf7.pdf

Staley, S., & Leonardi, B. (2016). Leaning in to discomfort: Preparing literacy teachers for gender and sexual diversity. *Research in the Teaching of English, 51*(2), 209–229. https://library.ncte.org/journals/rte/issues/v51-2/28875

Storts-Brinks, K. (2010). Censorship online: One school librarian's journey to provide access to LGBT resources. *Knowledge Quest, 39*(1), 22–28. https://go.gale.com/ps/i.do?id=GALE%7CA239272680&sid=googleScholar&v=2.1&it=r&linkaccess=abs&issn=10949046&p=AONE&sw=w&userGroupName=nysl_oweb

Strauss, A., & Corbin, J. (1990). Open coding. In A. Strauss & J. Corbin (Eds.), *Basics of qualitative research: Grounded theory procedures and techniques* (2nd ed., pp. 101–121). SAGE.

Taylor, A. J. (2017). Putting race on the table: How teachers make sense of the role of race in their practice. *Harvard Educational Review, 87*(1), 50–73, 157. http://doi.org/10.17763/1943-5045-87.1.50

Tennessee General Assembly. (2021, May 3). *SB 1229 by Rose.* https://wapp.capitol.tn.gov/apps/BillInfo/default.aspx?BillNumber=SB1229&GA=112

Tennessee General Assembly. (2022, March 17). *HB 0800 by Griffey.* https://wapp.capitol.tn.gov/apps/BillInfo/Default.aspx?BillNumber=HB0800&GA=112

White, J. W., & Ali-Khan, C. (2020). Sex and sexuality in the English language arts classroom. *English Education, 52*(4), 282–309. https://library.ncte.org/journals/EE/issues/v52-4/30766

Wilmot, M., & Naidoo, D. (2014). 'Keeping things straight': The representations of sexualities in life orientation textbooks. *Sex Education, 14*(3), 323–337. https://doi.org/10.1080/14681811.2014.896252

SECTION V

SOCIAL EMOTIONAL LEARNING

CHAPTER 11

CULTIVATING COLLABORATION AND CENTERING COMMUNITY

Making Youth Matter: A School–University–Community-Based Partnership

Celeste L. Hawkins
Eastern Michigan University

ABSTRACT

Community partnerships are a critical pillar to the education of new professionals and the ongoing development of socially just societies. In Fall 2015, a collaborative partnership was launched between Eastern Michigan University's (EMU) School of Social Work and Ypsilanti Community Schools (YCS) titled the Making Youth Matter Mentoring (MYM) program. As part of a broader effort underway to address the variegated needs of students in YCS, MYM was developed to support students' academic, social, and emotional development as an intervention to mitigate risk factors associated with

Justice, Equity, Diversity, and Inclusion in Education, pages 237–258
Copyright © 2024 by Information Age Publishing
www.infoagepub.com
All rights of reproduction in any form reserved.

youth being funneled through the school-to-prison pipeline. MYM utilized a strengths-based perspective by focusing on engaging student voice, engaging caregivers as contributors to success, connecting youth with resources outside of school, and engaging in activities that enrich student experiences. MYM was designed to complement existing school supports for young people and to promote positive outcomes and strengthen school success. Collaborative partnerships that center equity and communities provide an opportunity to proactively address pressing and emerging challenges in K–12 schools.

The history of education in the United States is intertwined with inequities that intersect with race/ethnicity, class, gender, and disability. Disparities in education have plagued the United States for decades with few reform efforts that have resulted in positive, sustainable change for non-dominant groups who experience marginalization and feelings of "otherness" in schools. Despite attempts to respond to the needs of an increasingly diverse population of students attending public schools today, policies and practices have fallen short of addressing the needs of those students who are most vulnerable to exclusion and marginalization. Shifting the focus from the individual to the educational system reframes the discourse from "getting the child 'ready' for school" to how do we get the "school 'ready' to serve increasingly diverse children?" (Swadener 1995, p. 18).

Research consistently demonstrates that many low-income and minority students continue to be excluded from educational, social, and cultural opportunities, thus diminishing their chances of realizing their full potential (Fine, 1991; Lipman, 1998; Noguera, 2009; Oakes, 1985). The exclusion is evidenced in a deficit-based discourse and lower teacher expectations for children of color, and thus higher disciplinary rates, inadequate and under-resourced schools in vulnerable and oppressed communities, which leads to disparities in academic achievement (Gorski, 2013; Gutiérrez et al., 2002; Oakes, 1985; Skiba et al., 2014). Despite numerous studies highlighting the ways current policies and practices disproportionately push students of color from the classroom to the courtroom, patterns of inequity continue.

The disproportionate rate of disciplinary measures employed with students of color and students with disabilities in K–12 schools has increased markedly over the years (American Psychological Association Zero Tolerance Task Force, 2008; Bradshaw et al., 2010; Graham, 2016; Skiba et al., 2002; Skiba et al., 2014; Wang et al., 2020) leading to factors which place these students at an increased risk of entering what has been termed the *school-to-prison pipeline*. The phrase school-to-prison pipeline describes the way challenged educational systems channel young people, particularly youth living in minoritized communities, toward a future damaged by crime and incarceration. Studies continue to highlight how the school-to-prison pipeline undermines the well-being of caregivers and excludes students from meaningful participation in their schools and communities

(Gage et al., 2018; Krezmien et al., 2014; Noguera, 2009). This chapter calls for partnerships with schools and communities around programs and interventions to interrupt this pipeline and cultivate opportunities that foster equitable outcomes among all K–12 students.

BACKGROUND

In September of 2015, a first-of-its-kind collaborative partnership, titled Making Youth Matter (MYM), between Ypsilanti Community Schools (YCS) and Eastern Michigan University's (EMU) School of Social Work, was formed to promote positive school outcomes. The mission of MYM is to support the academic, social, and emotional development of youth who are facing challenges in school through community and school-based mentoring. The MYM model focuses on the importance of engaging the youth voice, engaging their caregivers and teachers as contributors to their success, engaging with resources outside of school, and engaging in activities in and out of the classroom to enrich student experiences. This is a systems-level response designed to effect change and enhance supports to youth in YCS by integrating evidence-based school and community-based mentoring approaches (Herrera et al., 2007; Noltemeyer et al., 2019). The MYM model provides intensive one-on-one support to students and promotes increased access and exposure to resources in school and beyond. This chapter focuses on the groundbreaking MYM mentoring program as an innovative approach to interrupting the school-to-prison pipeline and the integral role social workers play in supporting students who are facing challenges or need additional support in K–12 schools.

MYM has garnered full support from YCS and EMU stakeholders including administrators, teachers, youth, and caregivers. MYM serves to complement and expand the scope of Multi-Tiered Systems of Supports (MTSS) and Positive Behavior Intervention and Supports (PBIS)—specifically the Intense Student Support services—aimed at impacting educational, social, emotional, and behavioral outcomes. The goal is to expand the scope of interventions, rather than duplicate the existing services of the MTSS and PBIS frameworks. Currently YCS is supporting students through a variety of Tier 2 and Tier 3 interventions, including one-on-one student supports and student groups. MYM builds on this foundation by engaging in activities that focus primarily on Tier 1 interventions, including but not limited to the following: in-school and after-school programming, one-on-one mentoring, and workshops (self-esteem and confidence building, soft skills, executive functioning skills) for students; parent workshops addressing a variety of topics (school success and connectedness, grief/loss, trauma, and mental health); and teacher/staff training workshops (trauma, mental

240 ▪ C. L. HAWKINS

health, school connectedness, and behavioral supports). Over the past 7 years, MYM has engaged 91 EMU social work interns, at the undergraduate and graduate level, for a total of 24,186 hours in supportive work with over 616 students in the YCS district. This huge investment directly supports students, families, district staff, and the community.

The sections that follow provide an overview of the community settings for YCS and EMU. Next, the school-to-prison pipeline is situated in the context of disproportionality along the lines of race, class, and disability. This is followed by a brief literature review with strategies for disrupting the school-to-prison pipeline; MYM is one such intervention and is the focus of this work. Finally, the chapter closes with current opportunities and a conclusion.

THE COMMUNITY SETTING: YPSILANTI COMMUNITY SCHOOLS AND EASTERN MICHIGAN UNIVERSITY

The city of Ypsilanti is situated on the Huron River and began as a French trading post in the early 1800s on a former Potawatomi village. Ypsilanti Community Schools traces its history all the way back to 1840 when, according to an Ypsilanti Gleanings historical archive article, Francis Griffin established a public school in the session house of the Presbyterian Church (Disbrow, 1979). Since then, the district has seen tremendous growth and change, but the teachers' and administrators' mission to provide a first-class education to Ypsilanti's youth has remained constant. YCS is a district that fundamentally believes all scholars have the capacity to excel. YCS operates with a sense of urgency and cultivates change in ways completely different from districts that simply operate to teach children to read or write or do math or to think critically. This level of urgency means nurturing the children, caring for them, adapting the school system to meet their needs equitably, taking students from where they are and having high expectations and high supports to help them reach their goals, and putting programs in place that go beyond mere consequences and punishments to skillfully guide students to the fulfillment of their highest aspirations. YCS serves a diverse student body. According to the *U.S. News and World Report* (2023), 53.5% are Black, 22.9% are White, 3.6% are Asian or Pacific Islander, 9.6% are Hispanic/Latino, 0.2% American Indian or Alaska native, and 0.1% are Native Hawaiian or other Pacific Islander, and 10% of students are two or more races. Additionally, 47% are female and 52% are male.

YCS is located within one mile of EMU's campus. EMU has been an integral partner in the Ypsilanti community since it was first founded in 1849 as Michigan State Normal School to educate students to become teachers in the state of Michigan. The university's mission states,

EMU enriches lives in a supportive, intellectually dynamic and diverse community. Our dedicated faculty balance teaching and research to prepare students with relevant skills and real-world awareness. We are an institution of opportunity where students learn in and beyond the classroom to benefit the local and global communities. (Eastern Michigan University, 2023)

With these two outstanding state institutions and bounds of potential located right next to each other in the heart of Ypsilanti, mutually beneficial collaborations seem almost inevitable. The focus centers on shared outcomes of the institutions that serve within this community. MYM provides a unique opportunity for EMU to support YCS students, caregivers, and educators and positions EMU as a leader in the area of school–university–community partnerships.

THE CONCERN: RACE, CLASS, EXCLUSIONARY PRACTICES AND THE SCHOOL TO PRISON PIPELINE

The Transformed Civil Rights Data Collection reported that "African-American students represent 18% of students in the CRDC sample, but 35% of students suspended once, 46% of those suspended more than once, and 39% of students expelled" (Office for Civil Rights, 2012, p. 2). Disparate discipline and exclusionary practices along the lines of race and class impact student outcomes. Poverty in minoritized communities is compounded by the fact that students today are attending schools that are more segregated than they have been in years, particularly in urban areas where both White flight and a scarcity of resources are common, largely due to desegregation policies established during the era of civil rights legislation (Crenshaw, 1996 Irvine, 2010; Taeuber, 1990).

The rich cultural assets among children living in minoritized communities (Kozol, 1991; Lipman, 2004; Maeroff, 1998; Noguera, 2003) combined with both overt and subtle racism in the classroom results in a discourse that "invidiously highlights the social construction of difference" and otherness (Katz, 1989, p. 5) often stigmatizes children in schools (Swadener, 1995). Institutionalized racism, classism, and segregation are social justice issues that continue to pervade public education and communities. These issues will persist until these issues are addressed through critical interrogation and an examination and removal of the barriers that exist. K–12 public schools often operate with middle-class norms and values, which easily shift the blame away from the school system to the students who seem to lack the means to succeed in school. Instead of systematically addressing the structural inequities facing public education, the blame is often shifted to the individual, the family, and the community. Without a robust structural and systemic critique, the source of educational failure is problematized as an individual, family, or cultural pathology. In our everyday interactions we may intentionally or unknowingly exclude and place limitations on others through our actions and beliefs about what students can or cannot achieve, resulting in limitations being placed on the life chances and opportunities of certain groups. Labeling and categorizing students further contribute to marginalizing experiences and disproportionality in schools. Consequently, those students become targets for policies and practices that push them out of schools and into detention centers and jails (Fisher, 2007; Winn, 2010).

Found in the literature on the sociology of education, reproduction theory explores the ways in which social inequalities structured by race and class are reproduced and maintained through school practices (Apple, 1990; Weis & Fine, 2001). Lipman (2004) echoed these arguments as she aptly appraised how student access and opportunities to learn are often differentiated by race, ethnicity, disability, and class. This research built on reproduction theory by suggesting that social class is not the only dimension reproduced in schools. As Weis (1990) noted, the reproduction of the existing social order is not simply the reproduction of wealth but also of "power and privilege" (p. 3). Moreover, Erickson (1987) wrote, "Domination and alienation of the oppressed does not simply happen by the anonymous workings of social structural forces. People do it" (p. 353). Inequitable practices exacerbate the marginalization of non-dominant groups; this leads to disruptions in students' education and future life trajectories (Apple, 1990; Delpit, 1995; Kozol, 1991; Noguera, 2003). Framing his theory of human capabilities, Sen (2000) argued that limited access to supports and opportunities diminishes the ability of individuals to exercise their full capabilities and to live the life they desire. Sen further pointed out how "capability deprivation" leads to long-lasting social exclusion, resulting in "capability failures" (p. 5). While income may determine the type of life one is able to lead, thereby creating greater access to opportunities and well-being, the non-material impacts of poverty, such as isolation and exclusion, are often far more devastating. MYM considers all of these factors and tailors programming to proactively support students and cultivate successful outcomes.

One of the most significant challenges facing schools across the United States is the provision of equitable and appropriate discipline to students in the school setting. This means addressing their academic, mental health, and behavioral concerns while maintaining a safe and supportive environment. Race and class factors may exacerbate inequities. According to a *U.S. News & World Report* article by Camera published in 2021, efforts to maintain safety through harsh disciplinary measures must also take into account the negative exclusionary consequences for students, especially for students of color, which may derail future outcomes and last into adulthood (see also Skiba & Noam, 2002; Skiba et al., 2014). Research illustrates

Cultivating Collaboration and Centering Community · **243**

that students who are assigned to stricter middle schools are 3.2 percentage points more likely to have been arrested, *[and]* 2.5 percentage points more likely to have been incarcerated as adults. They were also 1.7 percentage points more likely to drop out of high school and 2.4 percentage points less likely to attend a four-year college (Camera, 2021).

The federal Gun-Free Schools Act of 1993 marked a radical shift in educational policies in the United States. Zero tolerance policies were created to enforce mandatory expulsion for weapon and drug violations, which eventually broadened to more minor offenses and ushered in an era of unprecedented educational exclusion from schools for millions of American children over the next 2 decades (Baiyee et al., 2013; Hawkins, 2014). The widespread increase in zero tolerance policies as a means of controlling youth has been named a public assault on American children (Polakow, 2000). Noguera (2009) critiqued such measures of social control as ineffective and forcefully argued that little has been done to engage the voices of youth about their attitudes on violence and the impact of exclusionary discipline policies on their school lives. Zero tolerance policies and practices in schools are implicated in creating what many have termed the school-to-prison pipeline (Advancement Project and Harvard Civil Rights Project, 2000; NAACP Legal Defense and Educational Fund, n.d.). The school-to-prison pipeline crisis has garnered national attention with the White House Office of the Press Secretary (2016) urging school districts across the nation to *Rethink Discipline* and examine how their policies may be adversely impacting students. Despite the prevalence of efforts to raise awareness on the debilitating impact of the school-to-prison pipeline and its connection to educational outcomes, there are few targeted interventions, approaches, and practices that impact the lived experiences and success of students in schools and beyond. Hence, the aim of this chapter is not just to shed light on the disparities impacting education but also to counter and disrupt the dominant deficit-based discourse and the misleading assumptions that attempt to frame the experiences of African American students as a monolithic group.

Although racial disparities in student discipline rates have been well-documented for years, we continue to grapple today with a discipline gap in schools and consequent academic disparities. Black students comprise only 17% of the nation's student population but they represent 40% of the students suspended and were 2.6 times more likely to be suspended than a White student (Fancher, 2009; Office for Civil Rights, 2012). The disproportionate application of such harsh disciplinary measures to African American students has limited their capacity to participate fully in their own education due to lost instructional time which contributes, in turn, to lower achievement and adverse outcomes. Lipman (1998) argued 25 years ago that "the overwhelming failure of schools to develop the talents and

244 • C. L. HAWKINS

potentials of students of color is a national crisis" (p. 2). Racial inequalities, poverty, disproportionate representation in special education and exclusionary disciplinary policies are all significant factors that drastically impact academic achievement among African American students and result in low standardized test scores, low graduation rates, and high drop-out rates. The persistent and pervasive educational challenges facing our society have not produced adequate and wide-spread resolutions, which pose a constant threat and danger to the future of African American students, communities, and our nation.

THE INTERVENTION: THE MAKING YOUTH MATTER MENTORING PROGRAM

The literature on the school-to-prison pipeline and youth mentoring substantiates that MYM is a useful intervention in addressing the risk factors associated with academic challenges, chronic absenteeism, and behavioral concerns. MYM focuses on positively impacting academic achievement, increasing attendance, and mitigating the impact of exclusionary practices and policies. The incorporation of both school and community-based mentoring aspects aligns with the literature on recommended approaches for intervening in the school-to-prison pipeline (Epstein, 2001; Shippen et al., 2012).

The Washtenaw Intermediate School District (WISD) more broadly and YCS specifically, have taken several steps to provide support for youth who are facing challenges. YCS youth—similar to many students across the nation—are not exempt from the impact of harsh zero-tolerance policies. Youth from minoritized communities continue to be disproportionately represented in higher rates of discipline along the lines of race, gender, and disability. Over the past several years, YCS has taken steps to address this disturbing trend. YCS was charged with the task of revising their student code of conduct and examining systems to ensure discipline is applied fairly and consistently across the district. YCS and the WISD have also adopted important initiatives: culturally responsive pedagogical practices, restorative practices, and using an equity-centered approach across the district and throughout the county. Restorative practices are being implemented widely as an alternative to harsh discipline, which allows students to repair the harm caused, take responsibility for their actions, and learn from their mistakes. Equity-centered approaches focus on aligning supports and resources with the unique challenges and needs of students in their respective K–12 districts. These approaches are rooted in the belief that in order to have a healthy school climate, a respectful and collaborative school culture, and a successful academic environment, relationships

Cultivating Collaboration and Centering Community • **245**

between educators and students must be culturally responsive, deep, meaningful, valuable, and respectful.

In alignment with district goals and priorities, MYM provides on-going support and intervention to students, caregivers, and teachers throughout the academic year. The important role local school districts play in uniting communities is vital to the viability and success in K–12 schools. In addition to preparing youth for their future, a strong school district serves as a point of pride, hope, and progress within the community. Through MYM, YCS students are provided with additional supports that lead to positive outcomes. K–12 schools and universities benefit from collaborative partnerships that focus on balanced solutions, embracing diverse perspectives, and engaging in actions that align with district goals and objectives by using a systematic approach to support the academic, social and emotional needs of students.

Central to the success of MYM are three elements: making all decisions by centering equity; helping youth develop a sense of agency through voice and choice; and empowering youth to advocate for their educational, social, and emotional needs to increase their capacity to effectively communicate and work collaboratively with peers and adults. The MYM program model strives to develop leadership skills among youth and encourages youth to develop positive decision-making skills, strengthen their relationships with peers and adults, and promote a strong sense of identity and confidence so they can more effectively identify their capacities, advocate for their educational needs, problem-solve and interact positively in and out of school.

THE UNIVERSITY–SCHOOL PARTNERSHIP

As a collaborative partnership, the MYM mentoring program reflects the unique needs, strengths, and challenges of the Ypsilanti community, YCS, EMU, and their location in Washtenaw County, Michigan. YCS serves a community with unique, systemic, social issues that often strain the school resources. YCS makes every effort to focus its resources on connecting programs and services aligned to the district's vision. MYM is an approach that complements and magnifies the impact of existing approaches that support students in YCS and aligns with the district's vision. The services currently being provided by MYM allow supporters to collaborate on aligned efforts to address the educational disparities for student success. Access and exposure to valuable services both in and out of school give students the opportunity to experience a wider range of services to support their academic, social, emotional growth and development.

MYM supports the mission of the EMU School of Social Work to prepare students to work with underserved individuals, caregivers, and communities. MYM was developed based on the practicum instruction model

246 ▪ C. L. HAWKINS

to create quality learning experiences and strengthen the relationship and commitment to the community. This model of practicum instruction provides a forum for the development and testing of practice competencies aimed at providing preventative and supportive services for caregivers and children. Faculty supervised units provide an environment that fosters:

- practical internship experience training for future practitioners in family and children's services;
- provision of services by the student unit which complement and support agency efforts;
- collaborative planning and development of agency components appropriate for both classroom and agency staff utilization; and
- development of innovative models of practice and service components which can be integrated into existing agency programs.

Undergraduate students in the MYM mentoring program work one-on-one with elementary, middle, and high school students who have historically presented with challenges including factors that may place them at an increased risk of experiencing academic challenges, limited social and emotional supports, chronic absenteeism, mental health concerns, and issues related to familial and housing instability. Undergraduate and graduate students engage in school-wide support, serve as advocates, engage in research, and provide case management services to the caregivers of those youth participating in the programs. Graduate students work directly with caregivers to remove barriers, promote communication, and bridge the gap between home and school.

Research supports the utilization of internship cohorts in social work education as they not only benefit students and universities, but also create mechanisms for addressing community needs and concerns. The internship practicum model provides complementary, yet distinct learning opportunities at the undergraduate and graduate levels. The practicum experience not only provides EMU students with the opportunity to conceptualize, articulate, and apply social work skills in a school and community setting but also allows social work faculty to utilize an innovative teaching approach that integrates practice, policy, theory, and research, allowing us to meet our accrediting body competency standards at the university level.

MYM recognizes the importance of building relationships with the community and key stakeholders in an effort to create systematic and sustainable change to positively impact the lives of youth. MYM also seeks to raise community awareness about social justice issues by highlighting the importance of educational equity, belonging, representation, and inclusion. Research underscores the importance of working with students while also engaging teachers and caregivers in efforts designed to interrupt the school-to-prison pipeline (Barbarin, 2010; Noltemeyer et al., 2019; Osher et al., 2012).

The MYM mentoring program has proven to be beneficial to YCS, EMU, and the larger community. EMU undergraduate and graduate students work directly with students and caregivers while also providing the staff with a trauma-informed lens, which has positively affected the climate and culture within the school buildings. The EMU faculty who oversee the program and are engaged in the community are a critical piece of the success of MYM. Collaborative partnerships between universities and K–12 schools also enhance the access and exposure of students to post-secondary opportunities; thus students may begin to see college as a viable option. However, MYM remains committed to supporting students and addressing social justice issues regardless of what route students choose to take after graduation.

This next section of the chapter focuses on the integral role social workers play in schools; mentoring; community engagement; evaluation and research; school and community impact; university impact, current opportunities and conclusion.

SOCIAL WORKERS IN SCHOOLS

Social Workers are integral to the task of advocacy as it relates to the issues impacting the educational experiences for many vulnerable, underserved youth in schools. Advocacy is a powerful strategy in challenging social injustices. Social workers are poised to advance the interests of social justice and support empowerment for those populations who are disadvantaged, face discrimination, or are disempowered, particularly in schools where issues of bias, discrimination and inequity are especially problematic for poor children and children of color (Hawkins et al., 2001). Social workers play a vital role in supporting students and caregivers by strengthening public education and influencing policy and practice issues in schools to address issues of equity, access, and exposure. Social workers in practice operate from a strengths-based perspective in order to empower and improve the well-being of those who are impacted by exclusionary practices in society or schools. The role of social workers in the education system is important as social workers are tasked with being an advocate for the child and his or her family. In many instances, social workers are vessels of knowledge who carry in-depth histories and provide tremendous insight about the lives of youth and caregivers they serve. Social workers by virtue of their role as advocates establish relationships built on trust and mutual respect and are often able to uncover layers related to a child or family's struggle, which often times impact students in school. Social workers can assist in removing roadblocks facing students in education and their perspectives should be solicited and

248 • C. L. HAWKINS

integrated in how to best serve students in school. Social workers can serve a critical role as a support and advocate in the face of adversity—they become the voice of those who have been silenced, the spark for those who cannot find their fight, and the light for those traveling through a dark tunnel. MYM utilizes the strengths, knowledge, and skills of EMU undergraduate and graduate social work students who serve as mentors to students and provide supports to caregivers and teachers in the YCS district.

MENTORING

There are several reasons why mentoring is a core aspect of MYM. Mentoring offers additional support to youth in the education system who would benefit from another caring and consistent adult in their lives (Thomson & Zand, 2010). The literature suggests that mentoring leads to improvements in peer relationships, life skills, emotional development, motivation, conduct, and self-worth (Du Bois et al., 2011; Rhodes et al., 2000; Rhodes et al., 1999; Rhodes et al., 2005; Taylor et al., 1999). Studies have tied mentoring to improved school outcomes including attendance, grades, and achievement (Du Bois et al., 2011; Zimmerman et al., 2002). MYM is grounded in an understanding that academic achievement is directly associated with engagement, a sense of belonging, and connectedness in schools, which all lead to positive youth outcomes. MYM provides intensive mentoring and support to youth and is focused on reducing barriers to academic success. Under the supervision of EMU faculty who hold both clinical and macro social work licenses, undergraduate and graduate student interns who serve as mentors work closely with students and teachers not only to identify areas of need but also to develop strategies that promote academic success. The one-on-one mentoring provided to students is focused on three key areas: improving academic achievement, reducing truancy rates, and addressing social-emotional and behavioral challenges. EMU students work with YCS students to develop goals based on their individual needs; they assist in classrooms and, in addition, study tables are organized for YCS students who come to the EMU library after school to study and complete homework assignments. YCS students are also able to access EMU's campus facilities, participate in tailored college visits, and are exposed to various community activities. We work closely with the youth in our program to help them develop skills in interacting positively with peers and adults, preparing and applying for jobs, college, and pursuing extracurricular activities in order to stay connected and engaged with the community. Building on the social work education received at EMU, mentors participate in on-going specialized training, workshops, plus individual and group supervision to support their work. EMU students bring a strong knowledge and skill-base related

Cultivating Collaboration and Centering Community ▪ **249**

to social work practice with individuals, caregivers, and communities. This unique program model provides EMU students with various inter-disciplinary learning, training, and service opportunities by affording opportunities to collaborate with fellow students, YCS staff/administrators, and EMU faculty. Mentoring not only promotes academic success but also provides opportunities to engage youth voice and promote leadership.

Undergraduate and graduate student interns engage in school-wide support, serve as advocates, engage in research with faculty supervisors, and provide case management services to the caregivers of those youth participating in the program. MYM recognizes that support must happen at all levels in the district, so the program has incorporated interventions to support students at the elementary, middle, and high school through the implementation of literacy programs, self-esteem workshops, academic enrichment, soft-skills development, and access and exposure to college and career opportunities, which support YCS district priorities and goals.

Community Engagement

The growing needs of students struggling with mental health challenges and behavioral issues has been identified as a concern among educational leaders, mental health experts, and researchers alike (Flett & Hewitt, 2013; Whitley et al., 2018). Behavioral challenges are multi-dimensional and constitute one of the most complex issues in school settings; therefore, it is important to not only focus on academic identities, but also the social and emotional learning aspects that impact success in school. Students today are facing unprecedented demands that require a more focused comprehensive and integrated approach. The impact of COVID-19 illuminated and exacerbated educational inequities in K–12 schools and the unprecedented levels of trauma led to a rise in mental health needs. For many students and caregivers, the transition to remote learning created opportunities; however, the transition also led to increased levels of exclusion, isolation, limited access to resources, and inequities. As August et al. (2018) stated,

> Schools have significant potential and opportunity to lead prevention efforts for children and youth, and never has there been a better time to harness that opportunity within the current climate of MTSS [Multi-tiered Systems of Support] and emphasis on school mental health. (p. 95)

Research continues to demonstrate the positive impact of a tiered approach on the academic, social/emotional, and behavioral needs of students (Bradshaw et al., 2010; Du Bois et al., 2011; Gage et al., 2018) as well as the positive impact these interventions have on teachers' perceptions of student behavior, teaching conditions, and student achievement (Houchens et al., 2017). As stated by McDaniel et al. (2017), a PBIS framework "provides a proactive system for promoting students' success in schools by employing a multi-tiered continuum of support with evidence-based behavior interventions for all students" (p. 35).

MYM recognizes the importance of building relationships with the community and key stakeholders in an effort to create systematic change and to make a sustainable difference for youth. MYM also seeks to raise community awareness about social justice issues by highlighting the importance of educational equity and inclusion. MYM is designed to interrupt a pipeline that could derail educational outcomes by building connections with students, caregivers, schools, and the community to promote positive youth outcomes. EMU students support these efforts by working with students to remove barriers and promoting communication and engagement between home and school.

EVALUATION AND RESEARCH

Faculty involved with the program engage in numerous scholarly research activities in order to both evaluate the outcomes of the mentoring program and explore the mechanisms by which mentoring may impact the risk factors associated with the school-to-prison pipeline. Ongoing research related to the development, implementation, and expansion of the program also provides important information about how universities can partner with communities and schools to promote positive youth outcomes.

An integral component of this program is to seek input and gather feedback from stakeholders in order to strengthen collaboration and sustainability efforts. Over the past seven years, the infrastructure has been created to complement district initiatives and accomplish the objectives of the program. The purpose of this partnership was not only to respond to the current needs of students in YCS by offering direct mentoring services but to also develop a systematic approach for connecting youth and caregivers to services in the community and bridge the gap between home and school. Over the years the goal has been to expand the scope and broaden the reach in the YCS community and beyond. The goal is to build capacity, leverage resources, and create sustainable programming that will integrate and complement the academic, social, and emotional learning efforts already underway in YCS.

The innovative approach of engaging in university–community partnerships serves the community and addresses pressing social justice issues. MYM continues to raise awareness about social justice issues and the importance of educational equity and inclusion. The program aims to remove

Cultivating Collaboration and Centering Community • **251**

risk factors that impede success in school. Echoing the words of Thapa et al. (2013), this partnership addresses school-wide system change by supporting "students, parents/guardians, and school personnel learning and working together to create ever safer, more supportive and engaging K–12 schools" (p. 357).

We believe the following selected quotes from the perspective of youth, parents, counselors, and teachers involved in our program underscore the importance of our efforts:

> A youth participant, shared, "My mentor is always there for me and helps me in school and in life."

> A parent shared, "The mentor actually spent a lot of time with him. No matter what he was going through—so just being there for him was my main thing...you're putting something into that child's life, even if the parent can't do it at that time. You're helping them."

> One of the school counselors stated, "I see the EMU mentors actually connect with the students, there is a relationship, they know the students care about them...I believe it was very beneficial to our students...The more support we have for our students, the better we are...having students come from a university makes a big difference...we love people who are going to love and support our children."

Teachers whose students were involved in the program stated,

> "All the students looked forward to their meetings with their mentor, they liked the mentors coming to check on them in school, they needed them, it was great, they were like their cheerleader..."; "It was more than a big brother, big sister type thing, the mentors showed they really care and they were consistent..."; "I saw a big improvement with students in the program and I saw how the mentors worked hard in helping my students keep their grades up."

As school districts across the state experience financial struggles, their ability to support a growing number of students facing educational, social, emotional, and mental health challenges is often limited. The need for creative, collaborative solutions is paramount. We must strive to give students the support and services they need, when they need them, and not allow barriers to negatively impact the educational outcomes for students.

UNIVERSITY IMPACT

EMU students benefit from an array of service-learning opportunities and training on methods of engagement, research, and the benefit of inter-disciplinary approaches. This innovative model of mentoring is a promising intervention that addresses factors associated with the school-to-prison pipeline. MYM has generated strong interest from social workers, administrators, and educators at presentations at state and national conferences. The demonstrated success of our collaborative partnership positions the university to explore, examine, and prepare for the expansion of this model. Expansion will provide critical academic, social, and emotional supports to YCS students and caregivers; position EMU and YCS as leaders in the area of university–community partnerships; and create service-learning opportunities for EMU students. The innovation and creativity of MYM creates a unique opportunity for engaging EMU and YCS students through various learning experiences. This program model provides a valuable service to the community through targeted efforts of engaging, supporting, and positively impacting the lives of underserved youth and caregivers and engagement of college students in our community.

CURRENT OPPORTUNITIES

In order to improve and expand services and supports for youth facing challenges include the expansion of school-based programs that support the academic, social, and emotional needs of youth is critical. The literature on the school-to-prison pipeline and youth mentoring provides evidence that MYM will be successful in addressing the risk factors associated with academic challenges, chronic absenteeism, and behavioral concerns.

Our focus on academic achievement, attendance, and exclusionary practices is supported in the research literature (Arcia, 2006; Cholewa et al., 2018; Du Bois et al., 2011). The incorporation of aspects of both school and community mentoring also aligns with the literature on recommended approaches for intervening in the school-to-prison pipeline (Shippen et al., 2012). The research on mentoring effectiveness is used to inform program development, youth engagement, mentor roles and expectations (Du Bois et al., 2011).

CONCLUSION

We know that significant and fundamental changes must be made in the structure of our educational system; the real question is whether or not we have the will to apply the solutions. Over 25 years ago, Hornbeck and Salamon (1991) aptly noted that if we create solutions we will succeed, but if we do not, the consequences potentially could be dire economically and politically for this country. It is critical to bring all students into the fold of full participation in order to work toward making youth matter.

Cultivating Collaboration and Centering Community • **253**

MYM represents the strength of collective action. This approach has the ability to manifest the community's highest collective ideals of equality, justice and inclusion. MYM will continue to build on the collaborative partnership established to support youth in the local school district by employing a targeted response and approach to ensure our most vulnerable communities receive the academic, social, emotional, and mental health support that they need and deserve. MYM will maintain a focus on those factors that impede or impact learning with high levels of support through intensive mentoring. Through this collaborative program model, we will continue to explore and address unmet needs or gaps in education through in-school and out-of-school support. Ongoing investment from EMU will help to create sustainability and institutionalize efforts to support YCS students specifically and the community more broadly.

MYM raises awareness about social justice issues facing our youth, the education system, and leverages resources from the local university to address challenges and concerns to promote positive outcomes. The broader community is impacted when this new generation of youth becomes part of our community's fabric, adding high levels of energy, creativity, and productivity to our society; conversely, if they do not become productive members of our society, all of us have diminished futures. MYM builds community support by sharing the benefits of the project with stakeholders in the community. The importance of engaging youth as leaders, partners, and collaborators by focusing on their strengths will continue to be a key component of this partnership. Faculty involved with the program will continue to engage in numerous scholarly research activities in order to both evaluate the outcomes of MYM and disseminate findings at conferences and community presentations. Research related to the development and implementation of the MYM will also provide important information about how universities can partner with communities and schools to promote positive youth outcomes and community engagement and serve as a model for successful school–university–community partnerships.

REFERENCES

Advancement Project and Harvard Civil Rights Project. (2000). *Opportunities suspended: The devastating consequences of zero tolerance and school discipline policies.* https:// civilrightsproject.ucla.edu/research/k-12-education/school-discipline/ opportunities-suspended-the-devastating-consequences-of-zero-tolerance-and -school-discipline-policies/

American Psychological Association Zero Tolerance Task Force. (2008). Are zero tolerance policies effective in the schools?: An evidentiary review and recommendations. *American Psychologist, 63(9),* 852–862. https://doi.org/10.1037/ 0003-066X.63.9.852

254 ▪ C. L. HAWKINS

Apple, M. (1990). *Ideology and curriculum*. Routledge. https://doi.org/10.4324/978 0203241219

Arcia, E. (2006). Achievement and enrollment status of suspended students: Outcomes in a large, multicultural school district. *Education and Urban Society, 38*(3), 359–369. https://doi.org/10.1177/0013124506286947

August, G. J., Piehler, T. F., & Miller, F. G. (2018). Getting "SMART" about implementing multi-tiered systems of support to promote school mental health. *Journal of School Psychology, 66*, 85–96. https://doi.org/10.1016/j.jsp.2017.10.001

Baiyee, M., Hawkins, C., & Polakow, V. (2013). Children's rights and educational exclusion: The impact of zero tolerance policies in schools. In B. Swadener, L. Lundy, J. Habashi, & N. Blanchet-Cohen (Eds.), *Children's rights and education: International perspectives* (pp. 39–62). Peter Lang Publishing.

Barbarin, O. A. (2010). Halting African American boys' progression from pre-K to prison: What families, schools, and communities can do! *American Journal of Orthopsychiatry, 80*(1), 81–88. https://doi.org/10.1111/j.1939-0025.2010.01009.x

Bradshaw, C. P., Mitchell, M. M., O'Brennan, L. M., & Leaf, P. J., (2010). Multilevel exploration of factors contributing to the overrepresentation of black students in office disciplinary referrals. *Journal of Educational Psychology, 102*(2), 508–520. https://doi.org/10.1037/a0018450

Camera, L. (2021, July 27). Study confirms school-to-prison pipeline. *U.S. News and World Report*. https://www.usnews.com/news/education-news/articles/2021-07-27/study-confirms-school-to-prison-pipeline

Cholewa, B., Hull, M. F., Babcock, C. R., & Smith, A. D. (2018). Predictors and academic outcomes associated with in-school suspension. *School Psychology Quarterly, 33*(2), 191–199. https://doi.org/10.1037/spq0000213

Crenshaw, K. W. (1996). Mapping the margins: Intersectionality, identity, politics, and violence against women. In K. W. Crenshaw, N. Gotanda, G. Pellar, & K. Thomas (Eds.), *Critical race theory: The key writings that formed the movement* (pp. 357–383). New Press.

Delpit, L. (1995). *Other people's children: Cultural conflict in the classroom*. New Press.

Disbrow, D. (1979, April). *The early elementary and secondary school of Ypsilanti*. https://aadl.org/ypsigleanings/13459

Du Bois, D. L., Portillo, N., Rhodes, J. E., Silverthorn, N., & Valentine, J. C. (2011). How effective are mentoring programs for youth? A systematic assessment of the evidence. *Psychological Science in the Public Interest, 12*(2), 57–91. https://doi.org/10.1177/1529100611414806

Eastern Michigan University. (2023). *Strategic plan*. https://www.emich.edu/strategic-plan/mission/index.php

Epstein, J. (2001). *School, family, and community partnerships: Preparing educators and improving schools*. Westview Press.

Erickson, F. (1987). Transformation and school success: The politics and culture of educational achievement. *Anthropology & Education Quarterly, 18*(4), 335–356. https://doi.org/10.1525/aeq.1987.18.4.04x0023w

Fancher, M. (2009). *Reclaiming Michigan's throwaway kids: Students trapped in the school-to-prison pipeline*. American Civil Liberties Union of Michigan. https://web.archive.org/web/20140319203806/http://www.aclumich.org/sites/default/files/file/ACLUSTPP.pdf

Fine, M. (1991). *Framing dropouts: Notes on the politics of an urban public high school*. SUNY Press.

Fisher, J. (2007). *Starting from the child* (3rd ed.). Open University Press.

Flett, G. L., & Hewitt, P. L. (2013). Disguised distress in children and adolescents "flying under the radar." *Canadian Journal of School Psychology, 28*(1), 12–27. https://doi.org/10.1177/0829573512468845

Gage, N. A., Lee, A., Grasley-Boy, N., & George, H. P. (2018). The impact of school-wide positive behavior interventions and supports on school suspensions: A statewide quasi-experimental analysis. *Journal of Positive Behavior Interventions, 20*(4), 217–226. https://doi.org/10.1177/1098300718768204

Gorski, P. C. (2013). *Reaching and teaching students in poverty: Strategies for erasing the opportunity gap*. Teachers College Press.

Graham, S. (2016). Commentary: The role of race/ethnicity in a developmental science of equity and justice. *Child Development, 87*(5), 1493–1504. https://doi .org/10.1111/cdev.12602

Gun-Free Schools Act of 1993. H.R. 987. (1993). https://www.congress.gov/ bill/103rd-congress/house-bill/987

Gutiérrez, K. D., Asato, J., Santos, M., & Gotanda, N. (2002). Backlash pedagogy: Language and culture and the politics of reform. *The Review of Education, Pedagogy, and Cultural Studies, 24*, 335–351. https://doi.org/10.1080/10714410214744

Hawkins, C. L. (2014). *Making youth matter: Exclusion and its impact on the school lives of African-American students* (Publication no. 10194621) [Doctoral dissertation, Eastern Michigan University]. ProQuest.

Hawkins, L., Fook, J., & Ryan, M. (2001). Social workers' use of the language of social justice. *British Journal of Social Work, 31*(1), 1–13. https://doi.org/10.1093/ bjsw/31.1.1

Herrera, C., Grossman, J. B., Kauh, T. J., Feldman, A. F., & McMaken, J. (2007). *Making a difference in schools: The Big Brothers Big Sisters school-based mentoring impact study*. Public/Private Ventures.

Hornbeck, D. W., & Salamon, L. M. (1991). *Human capital and America's future: An economic strategy for the nineties*. Johns Hopkins University Press.

Houchens, G. W., Zhang, J., Davis, K., Niu, C., Chon, K. H., & Miller, S. (2017). The impact of positive behavior interventions and supports on teachers' perceptions of teaching conditions and student achievement. *Journal of Positive Behavior Interventions, 19*(3), 168–179. https://doi.org/10.1177/1098300717696938

Irvine, J. (2010). Culturally relevant pedagogy. *Education digest: Essential readings for quick review, 75*(8), 57–61.

Katz, M. B. (1989). *The undeserving poor: From the war on poverty to the war on welfare*. Pantheon. https://doi.org/10.1086/ahr/99.3.999-a

Kozol, J. (1991). *Savage inequalities: Children in America's schools*. Crown Publishers.

Krezmien, M. P., Leone, P. E., & Wilson, M. G. (2014). Marginalized students, school exclusion, and the school-to-prison pipeline. In W. T. Church II, D. W. Springer, & A. R. Roberts (Eds.), *Juvenile justice sourcebook* (267–288). Oxford University Press.

Lipman, P. (1998). *Race, class, and power in school restructuring*. SUNY Press.

Lipman, P. (2004). *High-stakes education: Inequality, globalization, and urban school reform*. Routledge.

256 ▪ C. L. HAWKINS

Maeroff, G. (1998). Altered destinies: Making life better for school children in need. *Phi Delta Kappan, 79,* 424–432. https://www.thefreelibrary.com/Altered+destinies.-a020518113

McDaniel, S. C., Kim, S., & Guyotte, K. W. (2017). Perceptions of implementing positive behavior interventions and supports in high-need school contexts through the voice of local stakeholders. *The Journal of At-Risk Issues, 20*(2), 35–44. https://files.eric.ed.gov/fulltext/EJ1175692.pdf

NAACP Legal Defense and Educational Fund. (n.d.). *Dismantling the school-to-prison pipeline.* http://naacpldf.org/files/publications//Dismantling_the_School_to_Prison_Pipeline.pdf

Noguera, P. A. (2003). *City schools and the American dream. Reclaiming the promise of public education.* Teacher College Press.

Noguera, P. A. (2009). *The trouble with Black boys: . . . And other reflections on race, equity, and the future of public education.* Jossey-Bass.

Noltemeyer, A., Palmer, K., James, A. G., & Petrasek, M. (Ed.). (2019). Disciplinary and achievement outcomes associated with school-wide positive behavioral interventions and supports implementation level. *School Psychology Review, 48*(1), 81–87. https://doi.org/10.17105/spr-2017-0131.v48-1

Oakes, J. (1985). *Keeping track: How schools structure inequality.* Yale University Press.

Office for Civil Rights. (2012). *The transformed civil rights data collection.* United States Department of Education. https://www2.ed.gov/about/offices/list/ocr/docs/crdc-2012-data-summary.pdf

Office of the Press Secretary. (2016, December 9). *White House Report: The continuing need to rethink discipline.* The White House. https://obamawhitehouse.archives.gov/the-press-office/2016/12/09/white-house-report-continuing-need-rethink-discipline

Osher, D., Coggshall, J., Colombi, G., Woodruff, D., Francois, S., & Osher, T. (2012). Building school and teacher capacity to eliminate the school-to-prison pipeline. *Teacher Education and Special Education, 35*(4), 284–295. https://doi.org/10.1177/0888406412453930

Polakow, V. (Ed.). (2000). *The public assault on American's children: Poverty, violence and juvenile injustice.* Teachers College Press.

Rhodes, J. E., Grossman, J. B., & Resch, N. L. (2000). Agents of change: Pathways through which mentoring relationships influence adolescents' academic adjustment. *Child Development, 71*(6), 1662–1671. https://doi.org/10.1111/1467-8624.00256

Rhodes, J. E., Haight, W. L., & Briggs, E. C. (1999). The influence of mentoring on the peer relationships of foster youth in relative and nonrelative care. *Journal of Research on Adolescence, 9*(2), 185–201. https://doi.org/10.1207/s15327795jra0902_4

Rhodes, J. E., Reddy, R., & Grossman, J. B. (2005). The protective influence of mentoring on adolescents' substance use: Direct and indirect pathways. *Applied Developmental Science, 9*(1), 31–47. https://doi.org/10.1207/s1532480xads0901_4

Sen, A. K. (2000). *Social exclusion: Concept, application and scrutiny.* Social Development Papers (No. 1). Office of Environment and Social Development, Asian Development Bank. http://hdl.handle.net/11540/2339

Shippen, M. E., Patterson, D., Green, K. L., & Smitherman, T. (2012). Community and school practices to reduce delinquent behavior: Intervening on the school-to-prison pipeline. *Teacher Education and Special Education, 35*(4), 296–308. https://doi.org/10.1177/0888406412445930

Skiba, R., & Noam, G. G. (Eds.). (2002). *Zero tolerance: Can suspensions and expulsions keep schools safe?* Jossey-Bass.

Skiba, R. J., Arredondo, M. I., & Williams, N. T. (2014). More than a metaphor: The contribution of exclusionary discipline to a school-to-prison pipeline. *Equity & Excellence in Education, 47*(4), 546–564. https://doi.org/10.1080/10665684.2014.958965

Skiba, R. J., Michael, R. S., Nardo, A. C., & Peterson, R. (2002). The color of discipline: Sources of racial and gender disproportionality in school punishment. *Urban Review, 34*, 317–342. https://doi.org/10.1023/a:1021320817372

Swadener, B. B. (1995). Children and families "at promise": Deconstructing the discourse of risk. In B. B. Swadener, & S. Lubeck (Eds.), *Children and families "at promise": Deconstructing the discourse of risk* (pp.17–49). State University of New York Press.

Taeuber, K. (1990). Desegregation of public school districts: Persistence and change. *Phi Delta Kappan, 72*(1), 18–24.

Taylor, A. S., Losciuto, L., Foz, M., Hilbert, S. M., & Sonkowsky, M. (1999). The mentoring factor. *Child & Youth Services, 20*(1–2), 77–99. https://doi.org/10.1300/j024v20n01_07

Thapa, A., Cohen, J., Guffey, S., & Higgins-D'Alessandro, A. (2013). A review of school climate research. *Review of Educational Research, 83*(3), 357–385. https://doi.org/10.3102/0034654313483907

Thomson, N. R., & Zand, D. H. (2010). Mentee's perceptions of their interpersonal relationships: The role of the mentor-youth bond. *Youth & Society, 41*(3), 434–445. https://doi.org/10.1177/0044118x09334806

U.S. News and World Report. (2023). *Ypsilanti community schools.* https://www.usnews.com/education/k12/michigan/districts/ypsilanti-community-schools-109231

Wang, M.-T., Degol, J. L., Amemiya, J., Parr, A., & Guo, J. (2020). Classroom climate and children's academic and psychological wellbeing: A systematic review and meta-analysis. *Developmental Review, 57*, 100912. https://doi.org/10.1016/j.dr.2020.100912

Weis, L. (1990). *Working class without work: High school students in a deindustrializing economy.* Routledge.

Weis, L., & Fine, M. (2001). Extraordinary conversations in public schools. *International Journal of Qualitative Studies in Education, 14*(4), 497–523. https://doi.org/10.1080/09518390110046355

Whitley, J., Smith, J. D., Vaillancourt, T., & Neufeld, J. (2018). Promoting mental health literacy among educators: A critical aspect of school-based prevention and intervention. In A.W. Leschied, D. H. Saklofske, & G. L. Flett (Eds.), *Handbook of school-based mental health promotion* (pp. 143–165). Springer. https://doi.org/10.1007/978-3-319-89842-1_9

Winn, M. T. (2010). 'Our side of the story': Moving incarcerated youth voices from margin to center. *Race Ethnicity and Education, 13*(3), 313–325. https://doi.org/10.1080/13613324.2010.500838

Zimmerman, M. A., Bingenheimer, J. B., & Notaro, P. C. (2002). Natural mentors and adolescent resiliency: A study with urban youth. *American Journal of Community Psychology, 30*(2), 221–243. https://doi.org/10.1023/a:1014632911622

CHAPTER 12

CULTURALLY RELEVANT SOCIAL AND EMOTIONAL STUDENT SUPPORT IN TITLE I SCHOOLS INCREASING THE OPPORTUNITY FOR STUDENT GROWTH

Marie Byrd
University of South Florida Sarasota-Manatee

ABSTRACT

Culturally relevant social and emotional development for students of diverse backgrounds who attend Title I schools is a necessity to positively affect student academic achievement, personal growth, and educational outcomes. This chapter will explore the need for culturally relevant SEL by providing current data and research-based practices. The lens of a Title 1 reading specialist assigned to two schools in a diverse urban community will serve as the foundation for an in-depth, personalized journey, including two students residing in high-poverty communities while attending Title 1 schools. A con-

---

Justice, Equity, Diversity, and Inclusion in Education, pages 259–276
Copyright © 2024 by Information Age Publishing
www.infoagepub.com
All rights of reproduction in any form reserved.

259

tinuous parallel alignment of research and practice will provide the foundation for culturally relevant social and emotional growth of diverse students attending Title I schools.

Social and emotional learning (SEL) that embodies culturally sustaining and transformative principles has been deemed vital for the academic, social, and emotional development of students of color. SEL may enhance the aims of equal educational opportunities by supporting all students in feeling welcomed and seen at school. Furthermore, an intentional focus on equitable opportunities for students of color attending Title I schools enhances SEL practice by ensuring that it is relevant, accessible, and beneficial for students of color (Ramirez et al., 2021). SEL also has the capacity to advance educational equity and excellence through school–family–community partnerships (Collaborative for Academic, Social, and Emotional Learning, 2023c; Niemi, 2020). Research-based best practices for school leaders, teachers, parents, and community organizations that are detailed in a leveled, strategic format ensure practice-based sustainability. Additionally, ensuring the cultural relevance of SEL safeguards respectful, inclusive learning environments that affirm diverse identities and cultural values.

This chapter will detail the need for culturally relevant SEL in Title I schools with diverse student populations through the lens of a Title I reading specialist assigned to two schools. Gloria Ladson-Billings (1995) defined culturally relevant pedagogy as "a theoretical model that not only addresses student achievement but also helps students to accept and affirm their cultural identity while developing critical perspectives that challenge inequities that schools (and other institutions) perpetuate" (p. 469). The concept of culturally relevant pedagogy has ignited countless studies, and the theory has also assumed a central role in teacher education, inspiring a generation of teachers to enter the classroom with a renewed commitment to affirming students' cultural, racial, and ethnic identities.

Ms. Martin (pseudonym), a school district reading specialist, and her mentoring relationship with two students who attend school in a large, diverse urban school district will periodically be the area of focus. John (pseudonym) and Ava (pseudonym) both attend Title I majority minority elementary schools. John's first language was not English, and Ava's first language was a Black/African American English dialect. Their experiences will be aligned with current best practices and research on the need for culturally relevant social and emotional development of underserved, diverse student populations.

Culturally Relevant Social and Emotional Student Support in Title I Schools • **261**

TWO STORIES

John's Story Part 1

John was in a fifth-grade advanced class in an inner-city Title I school. John's father immigrated from a Caribbean country with John and his younger brother. He and his younger brother lived with their father in a low-income area of a major city. John's father made the journey to the United States with the boys alone, leaving their mother in their native country with her family. During the school year, when the reading specialist met John, his grades were high as he appeared to approach academics effortlessly. However, John's mischievous nature frequently caused him to be sent to the office for his behavior by his White female teacher. He had developed a rapport with the art teacher, a Black/African American male. The assistant principal regularly attempted to engender a mentoring relationship for John with the art teacher by involving him in discussing John's misbehavior. The reading specialist was introduced to John by the art teacher while visiting the school. He explained that John was an excellent student academically but needed guidance regarding his poor decision-making when among peers. The reading specialist immediately established a rapport with John due to his wit and inquisitiveness. One of her projects with the school involved developing student talent for a Black History Month poetry contest. While promoting the event at the school, she would allow John to provide updates and announcements regarding Black History Month and the upcoming poetry contest over the school-wide public address system. Showcasing John's ease and articulation while reading the announcements caused a change in his demeanor and behavior. The positive attention and frequent conversations regarding the transformation of his decision-making and self-control enabled him to permit others to envision him through a different lens.

Ava's Story Part 1

Ava was in the second grade at a Title I magnet school. The school was located near a primarily Black/African American middle-class as well as lower-income residential areas of the community. In an effort to diversify the student population and improve academic achievement, the school district converted the elementary school to a magnet school with a specific academic focus. Many middle-class parents who lived outside the neighborhood preferred sending their children to the magnet program at the community school. Ava was the oldest of three children living with a single mother in the lower-income section of the school community. Her teacher was a White female with many years of experience in the school district. Ava had many friends in the classroom. She continually appeared to be the center of activities and attention. She was an average student with a propensity for taking on leadership roles in the classroom. Ava's mother worked from the afternoon to late evening hours, and Ava was responsible for her younger siblings until her mother returned. Ava was accustomed to the responsibility at home and often continued to enact the role at school. This caused several conflicts among her classmates as they perceived her efforts as being "bossy" rather than assuming leadership roles. The teacher had numerous conversations with Ava to temper her verbal assertiveness. The reading specialist met Ava upon visiting the teacher's classroom. Due to her strong reading and verbal abilities, Ava was selected to be a participant in the Black History Month poetry contest. She thrived as her poem was memorized immediately, and she then pursued assisting others with their poems. However, her very strong personality was not always welcomed by others. The reading specialist focused on Ava's propensity for leadership and began to coach her on becoming mindful of others when embarking on opportunities to assist.

DATA SPEAKS VOLUMES

Public school data from the 2021 academic year detailed a shift in the racial/ethnic composition of U.S. public elementary and secondary school enrollments as compared to a decade earlier (Irwin et al., 2023). Furthermore, students of color tended to concentrate in certain schools. According to the National Center for Education Statistics (NCES) annual report, 61% of Hispanic students, 59% of Black/African American students, and 53% of Pacific Islander students attended schools in 2021 where the combined enrollment of students of color was at least 75% of the total school enrollments (NCES, 2023d). In addition, 42% of American Indian/Alaska Native students, 41% of Asian American students, and 22% of students of more than one race attended schools where the total enrollment of students of color was at least 75% of the total enrollment. In Fall 2021, approximately 33% of all public school students attended schools where students of color comprised at least 75% of the total school enrollments. However, only 6% of White students attended such public schools (NCES, 2023d).

Student demographics for high-poverty/Title I schools in the country also indicate greater diversity. The National School Lunch Program (NSLP) utilizes the free and reduced-price school lunch as a substitute measure for the concentration of low-income students attending public schools. According to the 2023 Condition of Education report, high-poverty/Title I schools

Culturally Relevant Social and Emotional Student Support in Title I Schools • **263**

are defined as schools with more than 75% of students identified as eligible for free and reduced-price meals. In the fall of 2021, approximately 10.5 million students were enrolled in high-poverty/Title 1 schools. The percentage of students who attended such schools was highest for Hispanic students (38%), followed closely by Black/African American students (37%), American Indian/Alaska Native students (30%), and Pacific Islander students (23%). The percentage was lowest for White students (7%), Asian students (13%), and students of two or more races (15%; NCES, 2023c).

In contrast to the reported student demographic data, 80% of public school teachers in the 2020–2021 academic year were White and non-Hispanic (NCES, 2023b). Furthermore, the distribution of public-school teachers by gender was not significantly different in 2020–2021 as compared to 2011–2012, with approximately 75% being female. In addition, in 2020–2021, the percentage of K–12 public school teachers who were White (80%) was significantly higher than the percentage of K–12 public school students who were White (45%; NCES, 2023b; NCES, 2023d). Lastly, the percentage of teachers of other racial/ethnic groups was lower than the proportion of students in those groups; for example, 9% of public-school teachers in 2020–2021 were Hispanic compared with 28% of public school students (NCES, 2023b; NCES, 2023d).

According to the NCES (2023a), the majority of public-school principals are White and female. In 2020–2021, compared to 2011–2012, women comprised a higher percentage of elementary and secondary school principals in public schools (56% in 2021 vs. 52% in 2011) and in private schools (63% vs. 55%; see Table 4). However, the number of public and private school principals with 20 or more years of experience declined in the decade from 2011–2012 to 2020–2021 (NCES 2023a). The racial/ethnic composition of public-school principals in 2020–2021 consisted of 77% White, 10% Black/African American, 9% Hispanic, and 1% or less for two or more races, Asian, American Indian/Alaska Native, and Pacific Islander (NCES, 2023a).

Why is the racial/ethnic data of teachers and administrators in comparison to students of note? Effective teachers may originate from varying racial, ethnic, or cultural backgrounds. However, as indicated by Merry and Agirdag (2022), successful majority-minority schools reveal that their success is due to significantly strong social, psychological, and cultural support, student engagement, specialized support for students with emotional or behavioral problems, among other indicators and cultural or ethnic/racial match between school staff and students (see also Carter &Welner, 2013; Cherng & Halpin, 2016; Gonzalez, 2013; Kraft et al., 2015; Ladson-Billings, 2000; Lee, 2007; Rizga, 2016; Yosso et al., 2022). This postulation centers on the value of culturally relevant social and emotional support and development in student and school success in majority-minority public schools.

Intersectionality of Gender and Race

Of note is that Ava was perceived as bossy by her peers. This perception aligns with research in early elementary school grades. Black girls receive less attention than their male counterparts as they are perceived to be more socially mature and self-reliant as compared to boys (Crenshaw et al., 2015). Lack of attention may lead to "benign neglect" that has the propensity to diminish school attachment in both high- and moderate-achieving Black female students (Crenshaw et al., 2015). Black boys receive more than two out of three suspensions, but Black girls are suspended at higher rates (12%) than most boys and more than girls of any other race including Latinas (4%) and White girls (2%; U.S. Department of Education Office of Civil Rights, 2014). Of the 132 school districts in the southern states, 56% of the girls suspended were Black, and 45% of the girls expelled were Black, averaging the highest percentages among both sexes and all racial/ethnic groups (Smith & Harper, 2015). Additionally, 19% of Black girls with disabilities have experiences with out-of-school suspensions (U.S. Department of Education Office of Civil Rights, 2014). Black girls are also most often subjected to discipline based on the judgment of school personnel, many of whom lack cultural competence and may have limited understanding of ways race and racism affect Black girls' relationships. In a study of 282 adolescent Black girls by Winchester et al. (2022), it was determined that mental health symptoms can be moderated by teachers' intentional messaging of gendered racial pride.

TWO STORIES, CONTINUED

John's Story Part 2

John's teacher was previously selected to teach the advanced fifth-grade class due to her high academic expectations, creativity, and high student test scores. She was also the grade-level chairperson and represented the fifth-grade team in meetings with the administration. Many teachers sought her out for advice and/or ideas for lessons. She was personable and seemingly caring. A majority of the students in her class had parents who were not born in the country. However, John was a challenge in class. His father did not speak English. Therefore, when the teacher called the home, she would need an interpreter. In addition, upon hearing of John's misbehavior, his father would administer harsh punishments that concerned the school staff. As a result, they decided to determine the consequences of his misbehavior within the school. Upon the development of John's positive relationship with the reading specialists, she was also included in determining

Culturally Relevant Social and Emotional Student Support in Title I Schools • **265**

the consequences of the misbehavior. On many occasions, this would include not being allowed to participate in the activities arranged for John by the reading specialist. John's attachment to the reading specialist centered on her ability to listen openly while elevating the expectations for his behavior, which he indicated reminded him of his mother. She also expressed interest in his native culture and listened as he shared details of his previous life in his home country. John taught the reading specialist how to count to 10 in his native language and was quick to share his academic accomplishments from class. It was essential for her to assist him in maintaining a positive mindset rather than mentally lingering on past mistakes. Therefore, she began conversing briefly about his emotional well-being and social concerns. Two or three times each week, the reading specialist was able to set aside SEL time for John. John confided to the reading specialist that she was the only adult who encouraged and supported him. His perspective greatly improved upon competing in the poetry contest and winning a trophy. He also slowly began to make gains (some minimal) in each of the five SEL outcomes. The focus was to encourage him to self-reflect, recognize alternative decisions, and enact those decisions.

Ava's Story Part 2

Ava's teacher was very popular with the parents of students who attended the magnet program due to her flexible classroom setting. She equipped the classroom with centers to allow students to choose the most appropriate activity. However, for Ava, this was an organizational challenge; of utmost importance was her need to be in control, ensuring that the activities were implemented according to the instructions detailed on the instructional cards placed in each center. Very few students wanted to work with Ava and consistently complained to the teacher. Nonetheless, Ava viewed the problem through a different lens as she frequently proclaimed, "But I'm just trying to help!" The teacher often moved Ava to another classroom to temporarily resolve the problem. However, there was no attempt to assist Ava in reflecting on her actions so that she may potentially view the issue through the lens of her classmates. Self-awareness, self-management, responsible decision-making, relationship skills, and social awareness (see "CASEL Wheel" https://casel.org/fundamentals-of-sel/what-is-the-casel-framework/) require a level of critical self-reflection that may contribute to a viable resolution. The teacher chose one strategy that might assist in elevating Ava's SEL by asking her to write down her feelings. However, she failed to continue the process with Ava upon the written self-reflection. In all fairness to the teacher, professional development on SEL competencies was not offered at the school nor at the school district level.

BEYOND ACADEMIC STANDARDS

The Intersectionality of Race and Gender

For Ava, her race and gender uniquely shifted her social, emotional, and non-cognitive experiences as she did not understand why she was deemed as bossy. The study of the intersectionality of race and gender during the enculturation process of Black girls is termed as *gendered racial socialization* (Crenshaw, 1989; Hughes et al., 2006). Gendered racial socialization has been summarized as the process of integrating gender with existing racial socialization theories to allow for the consideration of both race and gender identities simultaneously contributing to Black women's distinct lived experiences (Capodilupo & Kim, 2014). This experiential process has been termed Intersectionality as it re-conceptualizes the classic feminist theory to include the experiences of Black women (Crenshaw et al., 2015). Dweck et al. (2014) suggested that psychological interventions that target these critical processes could change academic outcomes for the better:

> Research indicates that for students from groups that have been negatively stereotyped or historically marginalized, building their sense of social belonging in school benefits their long-term academic achievement. These factors also offer promising levers for raising the achievement of underprivileged children and, ultimately, closing achievement gaps based on race and income. (p. 63)

The Whole Child Approach

The whole child approach transitions the focus of student achievement from narrowly defined academic achievement to one that promotes the long-term development of college or career readiness and the future success of all children (ASCD, 2023). It also strengthens the capacity of adults to create relationship-rich environments that support the learning and social and emotional development of students (Pittman et al., 2020). The approach offers the academic, developmental, social, and emotional support needed for success. Research confirms that a whole-child approach in education will develop and prepare students for the challenges and opportunities of today and tomorrow by addressing students' comprehensive needs through the Whole Child Tenets (ASCD, 2023).

According to Dweck et al. (2014), non-cognitive factors embedded within the whole-child approach are critical for the ongoing academic success of students in school. Those non-cognitive factors, students' self-efficacy beliefs about themselves, their goals in school, and their feelings of social belonging, have been deemed critical for student academic performance

Culturally Relevant Social and Emotional Student Support in Title I Schools • **267**

among marginalized populations (Dweck et al., 2014). Self-efficacy development has been shown to have a positive impact on academic achievement (Bandura, 1997). The factors of the positive influence of self-efficacy beliefs about oneself, goals in school, and feelings of social belonging are also critical. In addition, the development of non-cognitive social and interpersonal skills and competencies enables at-risk youth to navigate social situations, resolve conflicts, advocate for themselves, and cooperate and work effectively with others (Aspen Institute, 2019).

The Role of Culturally Relevant Social and Emotional Development

Student SEL promotes the growth of the whole student/child, including their academic progress. The Collaborative for Academic, Social, and Emotional Learning (CASEL) established SEL as an essential part of preschool through high school education (CASEL, 2023a). CASEL developed the SEL framework based on theory, research, and educational best practices to guide the selection of research-based character and social skills (Payton et al., 2000). The SEL competencies include 17 skills and attitudes organized into four groups: awareness of self and others, positive attitudes and values, responsible decision-making, and social interaction skills. Such programs have been instrumental in ensuring students will develop the necessary social and emotional skills needed to improve overall mental health by learning effective coping strategies for everyday stressors, effectively communicating, and employing many other essential tools (Jones et al., 2015).

CASEL has since re-conceptualized SEL competencies for diverse populations of students. The revised model establishes an SEL framework through an equity lens. CASEL has furthered the equity-centered competencies by guiding school districts in advancing equity and excellence by cultivating adult and student practices that close opportunity gaps and create more inclusive school communities (Collaborative for Academic, Social, and Emotional Learning, 2023c).

Research has established that underserved students of color may progress through school without engagement. These students are less often enrolled in honors courses in high school or accepted into competitive four-year colleges; indeed, they are deemed at risk of dropping out of high school (Center for Education Policy Analysis, n.d.; Valant & Newark, 2017). They may also experience diminished concentration and memory in settings where their social-emotional and character developmental needs are not cultivated. If not addressed, this has the potential to lead to behaviors consistent with those identified as at risk, such as inappropriate behavior in the classroom, difficulty developing meaningful relationships with peers and teachers, and trouble processing information, all of which interfere with their capacity for creativity and development (Center for Education Policy Analysis, n.d.). Preventative SEL interventions are necessary for at-risk students of color to build skill sets, increase resilience to adversity, and learn coping skills (Calhoun et al., 2020). In addition, regular participation in programs focused on the whole child's needs that are inclusive of the academic achievement of low-income students improves behavioral outcomes and reduces school absences (Yamashiro, 2021). SEL-focused interventions in Title I schools may improve students' academic performance, mental health, behavior, classroom climate, and teacher practices for up to three years post-intervention (Brackett et al., 2019).

According to Beyer (2017), certain home environmental factors are deemed harmful to normal SEL development for underserved teenagers of color, including trauma, abuse, neglect, instability, isolation, disability, discrimination, structural inequality, and acculturation:

> These factors are prevalent in the families of many children and demonstrate how an opportunity gap in formative social and emotional experiences, such as inclusion, belonging, and safety, may cause differential rates of skill development for traditionally underserved youth populations. (p. 6)

In addition, the 2019–2020 rate of diagnostic and treatment services provided by public schools did not vary measurably by either race/ethnicity or poverty level (NCES, 2022). The only exception was that the percentage of public schools providing diagnostic services was lower for schools in which 25% or less of their enrollment was students of color (50%) than for schools in which 76% or more of their enrollment was students of color (60%; NCES, 2022).

The Role of Social and Emotional Learning for Students Living in Poverty

SEL has been considered necessary for the development of the whole child for students of color living in poverty and attending low-performing Title I schools. Studies have shown that SEL implementation decreases dropout rates, problematic school and classroom behavioral issues, drug use, teen pregnancy, mental health problems, and criminal behavior for secondary students (Kautz et al., 2014). CASEL (2023b) defines SEL as

> the process through which all young people and adults acquire and apply the knowledge, skills, and attitudes to develop healthy identities, manage emotions and achieve personal and collective goals, feel and show empathy for

Culturally Relevant Social and Emotional Student Support in Title I Schools • **269**

others, establish and maintain supportive relationships, and make responsible and caring decisions. (para. 1)

The organization developed the SEL framework to guide the selection of research-based prevention programs that address health, substance abuse, violence prevention, sexuality, character, and social skills (Payton et al., 2000). CASEL describes SEL as

> an integral part of education and human development. SEL is the process through which all young people and adults acquire and apply the knowledge, skills, and attitudes to develop healthy identities, manage emotions and achieve personal and collective goals, feel and show empathy for others, establish and maintain supportive relationships, and make responsible and caring decisions. (Niemi, 2020, para. 4)

However, in 2020 CASEL developed a more inclusive description of SEL:

> SEL advances educational equity and excellence through authentic school-family-community partnerships to establish learning environments and experiences with trusting and collaborative relationships, rigorous and meaningful curriculum and instruction, and ongoing evaluation. SEL can help address various forms of inequity and empower young people and adults to co-create thriving schools and contribute to safe, healthy, and just communities. (Niemi, 2020, para. 3)

The inclusion of educational equity was also confirmed in the revised CASEL Diagram. CASEL's emphasis on establishing equitable learning environments and coordinating practices across the four critical settings of classrooms, schools, families/caregivers, and communities enables an all-inclusive focus on the whole child in diverse settings. In addition, the varied priorities may be aligned with individual community strengths, needs, and cultures.

SEL and Student Equity

The intentional focus on equity enhances SEL practice by ensuring that SEL is relevant, accessible, and beneficial for all students (Jones et al., 2015). SEL advances educational equity and excellence through authentic school–family–community partnerships to establish learning environments and experiences that feature trusting and collaborative relationships, rigorous and meaningful curriculum and instruction, and ongoing evaluation (Jones et al., 2021). In addition, SEL, which embodies culturally sustaining and transformative principles, has been deemed vital for the academic, social, and emotional development of students of color. The relationship between SEL and educational equity is reciprocal: SEL can advance the aims of educational equity by supporting all students to feel welcome, seen, and competent at school. At the same time, an intentional focus on equity enhances SEL practice by ensuring that SEL is relevant, accessible, and beneficial for all students (Ramirez et al., 2021).

THE AFTERMATH

John's Story

Everything changed for John when the reading specialist left the school due to a district transfer. He no longer had someone with whom he could genuinely express his thoughts and perceptions of his experiences without feeling judged. His behavior spiraled downward as he was once again relegated to the timeouts in other classrooms due to misbehavior. After observing John in the office more frequently, the principal asked him why his behavior regressed. John responded that since the reading specialist left, he did not feel supported at the school and that no one cared about him. His father threatened to put him out of the house if his misbehavior continued. However, towards the end of the school year, John and a fellow student were arrested by the police for starting a fire in an empty building. Upon learning of the arrest, the reading specialist visited him in a juvenile detention center. He expressed remorse for his actions and attributed it to the reading specialist leaving and having no one to believe in him. Eventually, John was convicted of arson and was held at a juvenile detention camp for 6 months. Upon being released, John was convicted of a second illegal activity time within 2 months and sentenced to a second juvenile program, which relied on heavy disciplinary measures. When released, John began dating, which eventually resulted in a son's birth. Without a job, he pursued alternative and illegal pathways to obtain money. While initially successful, he was later convicted as an adult of attempted armed robbery. John was sentenced to 15 years in prison. He was able to complete his high school diploma while incarcerated.

School to Prison Pipeline

In a study by Bacher-Hicks et al. (2021), early discipline concerning school misbehavior causes increases in adult crime, which is labeled as the school-to-prison pipeline. "The school-to-prison pipeline refers to the disturbing national trend in which children are funneled out of public schools

Culturally Relevant Social and Emotional Student Support in Title I Schools • **271**

and into juvenile and criminal justice systems. Supporting this system are several policies and practices" (Dancy, 2014, p. 476). Researchers also contend that the negative impact of strict school disciplinary environments is largest for minorities and males, indicating that suspension policies exacerbate gaps in educational attainment and the path to incarceration (Bacher-Hicks et al., 2021). In addition to school discipline, John also experienced isolation at home as he viewed his father as a fierce disciplinarian rather than as a nurturing and/or caring parent. Studies have shown an association in which physical punishment as a child has negative effects on the child's mental health and increases the likelihood of future delinquency in adolescence and engagement in violent crimes in adulthood (Durrant & Ensom, 2012; Gershoff, 2002; Straus, 1991). John's school-to-prison pathway could have been thwarted if there were alternatives for either in-school or out-of-school mentorship opportunities available to him upon the departure of the reading specialist. John possessed academic ability as he was effortlessly astute in elementary school. Nevertheless, he experienced emotional isolation from his father, social isolation in school due to separation as a means of punishment for behaviors, and cultural isolation from his teacher, who was a white, middle-class female who did not express interest in his cultural heritage. In addition, John's teacher primarily taught through an essentialist lens, as the focus was primarily on preparing students to score well on the annual standardized examinations (Ornstein et al., 2015).

Ava's Story

Ava successfully graduated from high school and enrolled in a two-year state college. Her success was partly due to the foundational mentoring by the reading specialist in elementary school. The reading specialist realized her potential while encouraging her to self-reflect on her actions and how they impact others. The cultural relevance of the mentoring allowed Ava to operate within her cultural reality. Ms. Martin consistently affirmed Ava's culture while encouraging her to reflect on her actions. Eventually, Ava altered her communication with others while still exuding the self-confidence she was known for, along with the culture that she embodied. Later, prior to moving on to middle school, Ava was able to thank Ms. Martin for "seeing the best" in her despite her actions. Ms. Martin was able to continue mentoring Ava through the Big Brothers/Big Sisters program. Her mother's work schedule changed so that Ava could become involved in after-school activities without the need to monitor her younger siblings. Although there were challenges with teachers and conflicts with peers, she completed middle school with the support of Ms. Martin's affirmation of her culture and continued support of her social and emotional growth. In high school, Ava thrived in her English classes, joined two clubs focused on public speaking, and maintained her grades. She graduated with hopes of becoming a teacher.

CONCLUSION

Social and emotional competencies are critical for authentic, culturally relevant teaching and learning in culturally diverse Title I schools (Donahue-Keegan et al., 2019). Ms. Martin was able to align culturally relevant SEL with the lived experiences of both Ava and John. The reinforcement of their cultural expressions served as the foundation for developing trusting relationships. Ms. Martin supported their SEL growth as they navigated conflicts within the school and during out-of-school time. However, upon the departure of Ms. Martin from the school, John's behavior deteriorated as he felt unsupported and misunderstood by teachers and staff. While seeking belonging and acceptance, he began to align himself with others who were engaging in mischief during out-of-school hours, causing an additional barrier in his relationship with his father. While incarcerated, John wrote a letter to Ms. Martin promising to turn his life around once he was released, as he did not wish his son to follow in his path. Conversely, Ava received continued culturally relevant social and emotional support from Ms. Martin throughout her school years, allowing her to succeed and eventually enroll in a post-secondary institution. Her goal was to become a teacher in a school community similar to her own. Countless students, such as John and Ava, seek to be seen, heard, and valued in school. However, culturally relevant SEL relationships are absent from numerous classrooms and curricula of diverse Title I schools. Such connections support the development of the whole child, regardless of race/ethnicity or social class, which may positively affect academic achievement, personal growth, and educational outcomes. Culturally relevant social and emotional development affirms the racial, ethnic, and cultural identities of diverse students (Ladson-Billings, 1995) while empowering them to authentically navigate relationships with others and acknowledge their emotions during social contexts in school, at home, and in the community.

REFERENCES

ASCD. (2023). *The ASCD whole child approach to education.* https://www.ascd.org/whole-child

Aspen Institute. (2019). *From a nation at risk to a nation at hope.* National Commission on Social, Emotional, and Academic Development. https://files.eric.ed.gov/fulltext/ED606337.pdf

Culturally Relevant Social and Emotional Student Support in Title I Schools • **273**

Bacher-Hicks, A., Billings, S., & Deming, D. (2021). Proving the school-to-prison pipeline: Stricter middle schools raise the risk of adult arrest. *Education Next, 21*(4), 52–57. https://www.educationnext.org/proving-school-to-prison-pipeline -stricter-middle-schools-raise-risk-of-adult-arrests/

Bandura, A. (1997). *Self-efficacy: The exercise of control.* W. H. Freeman.

Beyer, L. N. (2017). Social and emotional learning and traditionally underserved populations. *American Youth Policy Forum.* https://www.aypf.org/wp-content/ uploads/2017/10/SEL-Special-Populations_Final.pdf

Brackett, M., Bailey, C., Hoffmann, J., & Simmons, D. (2019). RULER: A theory-driven, systemic approach to social, emotional, and academic learning. *Educational Psychologist, 54*(3), 144–161. https://doi.org/10.1080/00461520.2019 .1614447

Calhoun, B., Williams, J., Greenberg, M., Domitrovich, C., Russell, M. A., & Fishbein, D. H. (2020). Social emotional learning program boosts early social and behavioral skills in low-income urban children. *Frontiers in Psychology, 11.* https://doi.org/10.3389/fpsyg.2020.561196

Capodilupo, C. M., & Kim, S. (2014). Gender and race matter: The importance of considering intersections in Black women's body image. *Journal of Counseling Psychology, 61*(1), 37–49. https://doi.org/10.1037/a0034597

Carter, P. L., & Welner, K. G. (Eds.). (2013). *Closing the opportunity gap: What America must do to give every child an even chance.* Oxford Academic. https://doi .org/10.1093/acprof:oso/9780199982981.001.0001

Center for Education Policy Analysis. (n.d.). *The educational opportunity monitoring project: Racial and ethnic achievement gaps.* Stanford University. https://cepa.stanford .edu/educational-opportunity-monitoring-project/achievement-gaps/race/

Cherng, H. Y. S., & Halpin, P. F. (2016). The importance of minority teachers: Student perceptions of minority versus White teachers. *Educational Researcher, 45*(7), 407–420. https://doi.org/10.3102/0013189x16671718

Collaborative for Academic, Social, and Emotional Learning. (2023a). https://casel .org/

Collaborative for Academic, Social, and Emotional Learning. (2023b). *FAQs: Frequently asked questions about social and emotional learning and about CASEL.* https://casel.org/faq/

Collaborative for Academic, Social, and Emotional Learning. (2023c). *Equity and SEL: SEL can be a lever for advancing educational equity and excellence.* https:// schoolguide.casel.org/what-is-sel/equity-and-sel/

Crenshaw, K. (1989). Demarginalizing the intersection of race and sex: A Black feminist critique of antidiscrimination doctrine, feminist theory and antiracist politics. *University of Chicago Legal Forum, 1*(8), 139–167. https://chicago unbound.uchicago.edu/uclf/vol1989/iss1/8/

Crenshaw, K., Ocen, P., & Nanda, J. (2015). *Black girls matter: Pushed out, overpoliced, and under protected.* Columbia Law School Scholarship Archive. https:// scholarship.law.columbia.edu/faculty_scholarship/3227

Dancy II, T. E. (2014). (Un)Doing hegemony in education: Disrupting school-to-prison pipelines for Black males. *Equity & Excellence in Education, 47*(4), 476–493. https://doi.org/10.1080/10665684.2014.959271

274 ▪ M. BYRD

Donahue-Keegan, D., Villegas-Reimers, E., & Cressey, J. M. (2019). Integrating social-emotional learning and culturally responsive teaching in teacher education preparation programs: The Massachusetts experience so far. *Teacher Education Quarterly, 46*(4), 150–168. https://www.jstor.org/stable/26841580

Durrant, J., & Ensom, R. (2012). Physical punishment of children: Lessons from 20 years of research. *Canadian Medical Association Journal, 184*(12), 1373–1377. https://doi.org/10.1503/cmaj.101314

Dweck, C. S., Walton, M. W., & Cohen, G. L. (2014). *Academic tenacity: Mindsets and skills that promote long-term learning.* Bill & Melinda Gates Foundation. https://ed.stanford.edu/sites/default/files/manual/dweck-walton-cohen-2014.pdf

Gershoff, E. T. (2002). Corporal punishment by parents and associated child behaviors and experiences: A meta-analytic and theoretical review. *Psychology Bulletin, 128*(4), 539–79. https://doi.org/10.1037/0033-2909.128.4.539

Gonzalez, G. G. (2013). *Chicano education in the era of segregation* (No. 7). University of North Texas Press.

Hughes, D., Rodriguez, J., Smith, E. P., Johnson, D. J., Stevenson, H. C., & Spicer, P. (2006). Parents' ethnic-racial socialization practices: A review of research and directions for future study. *Developmental Psychology, 42*(5), 747–70. https://doi.org/10.1037/0012-1649.42.5.747

Irwin, V., Wang, K., Tezil, T., Zhang, J., Filbey, A., Jung, J., Bullock Mann, F., Dilig, R., & Parker, S. (2023). *Report on the condition of education 2023* (NCES 2023–144). U.S. Department of Education, National Center for Education Statistics. https://nces.ed.gov/pubsearch/pubsinfo.asp?pubid=2023144

Jones, D. E., Greenberg, M., & Crowley, M. (2015). Early social-emotional functioning and public health: The relationship between kindergarten social competence and future wellness. *American Journal of Public Health 105*, 2283–2290. https://doi.org/10.2105/AJPH.2015.302630

Jones, S. M., Brush, K. E., Ramirez, T., Mao, Z. X., Marenus, M., Wettje, S., Finney, K., Raisch, N., Podoloff, N., Kahn, J., Barnes, S., Stickle, L., Brion-Meisels, G., McIntyre, J., Cuartas, J., & Bailey, R. (2021). *Navigating SEL from the inside out: Looking inside & across 33 leading SEL programs: A practical resource for schools and OST providers* (Revised and expanded 2nd ed.). The Wallace Foundation. https://www.wallacefoundation.org/knowledge-center/Documents/navigating-social-and-emotional-learning-from-the-inside-out-2ed.pdf

Kautz, T., Heckman, J. J., Diris, R., ter Weel, B., & Borghans, L. (2014). *Fostering and measuring skills: Improving cognitive and non-cognitive skills to promote lifetime success* (Working paper 20749). National Bureau of Economic Research. https://www.nber.org/system/files/working_papers/w20749/w20749.pdf

Kraft, M. A., Papay, J. P., Johnson, S. M., Charner-Laird, M., Ng, M., & Reinhorn, S. (2015). Educating amid uncertainty: The organizational supports teachers need to serve students in high-poverty, urban schools. *Educational Administration Quarterly, 51*(5), 753–790. https://doi.org/10.1177/0013161X15607617

Ladson-Billings, G. (1995). Toward a theory of culturally relevant pedagogy. *American Educational Research Journal, 32*(3), 465–491. https://doi.org/10.3102/00028312032003465

Ladson-Billings, G. (2000). Culturally relevant pedagogy in African-centered schools: Possibilities for progressive educational reform. In D. S. Pollard, &

C. S. Ajirotutu (Eds.), *African-centered schooling in theory and practice* (pp. 187–198). Bergin & Garvey.

Lee, C. C. (2007). *Social justice: A moral imperative for counselors* (ACAPCD-07). American Counseling Association. https://www.counseling.org/resources/library/ACA%20Digests/ACAPCD-07.pdf

Merry, M. S., & Agirdag, O. (2022). Majority-minority educational success sans integration: A comparative-international view. *The Review of Black Political Economy*, *50*(2), 194–221. https://doi.org/10.1177/00346446221120825

National Center for Education Statistics. (2022). *Public schools and limitations in schools' efforts to provide mental health services.* U.S. Department of Education, Institute of Education Sciences. https://nces.ed.gov/programs/coe/indicator/a23

National Center for Education Statistics. (2023a). *Characteristics of public and private school principals.* U.S. Department of Education, Institute of Education Sciences. https://nces.ed.gov/programs/coe/indicator/cls

National Center for Education Statistics. (2023b). *Characteristics of public school teachers.* U.S. Department of Education, Institute of Education Sciences. https://nces.ed.gov/programs/coe/indicator/clr

National Center for Education Statistics. (2023c). *Concentration of public school students eligible for free or reduced-price lunch.* U.S. Department of Education, Institute of Education Sciences. https://nces.ed.gov/programs/coe/indicator/clb

National Center for Education Statistics. (2023d). *Racial/ethnic enrollment in public schools.* U.S. Department of Education, Institute of Education Sciences. https://nces.ed.gov/programs/coe/indicator/cge

Niemi, K. (2020, December 15). *CASEL is updating the most widely recognized definition of social-emotional learning: Here's why.* The 74. https://www.the74million.org/article/niemi-casel-is-updating-the-most-widely-recognized-definition-of-social-emotional-learning-heres-why/

Ornstein, A. C., Pajak, E. F., & Ornstein, S. B. (2015). *Contemporary issues in curriculum* (6th edition). Pearson.

Payton, J. W., Wardlaw, D. M., Graczyk, P. A., Bloodworth, M. R., Tompsett, C. J., & Weissberg, R. P. (2000). Social and emotional learning: A framework for promoting mental health and reducing risk behaviors in children and youth. *Journal of School Health*, *70*(5), 179–185. https://doi.org/10.1111/j.1746-1561.2000.tb06468.x

Pittman, K., Moroney, D. A., Irby, M., & Young, J. (2020). Unusual suspects: The people inside and outside of school who matter in whole school, whole community, whole child efforts. *Journal of School Health*, *90*(12), 1038–1044. https://doi.org/10.1111/josh.12966

Ramirez, T., Brush, K., Raisch, N., Bailey, R., & and Jones, S. M. (2021). Equity in social emotional learning programs: A content analysis of equitable practices in PreK–5 SEL programs. *Frontiers in Education*, *6*. https://doi.org/10.3389/feduc.2021.679467

Rizga, K. (2016, September–October). Black teachers matter. *Mother Jones.* https://www.motherjones.com/politics/2016/09/black-teachers-public-schools-education-system-philadelphia/

Smith, E. J., & Harper, S. R. (2015). *Disproportionate impact of K–12 school suspension and expulsion on Black students in southern states.* University of Pennsylvania,

Center for the Study of Race and Equity in Education. https://race.usc.edu/wp-content/uploads/2020/08/Pub-14-Smith-and-Harper.pdf

Straus, M. A. (1991). Discipline and deviance: Physical punishment of children and violence and other crime in adulthood. *Social Problems, 38*(2), 133–154. https://doi.org/10.1525/sp.1991.38.2.03a00010

U.S. Department of Education Office for Civil Rights. (2014, March 21). *Civil rights data collection: Data snapshot (school discipline).* https://www.ojp.gov/ncjrs/virtual-library/abstracts/civil-rights-data-collection-data-snapshot-school-discipline-issue

Valant, J., & Newark, D. (2017, January 16). *Race, class, and Americans' perspectives of achievement gaps.* Brookings. https://www.brookings.edu/articles/race-class-and-americans-perspectives-of-achievement-gaps/

Winchester, L. B., Jones, S. C. T., Allen, K., Hope, E., & Cryer-Coupet, Q. R. (2022). Let's talk: The impact of gendered racial socialization on Black adolescent girls' mental health. *Cultural Diversity and Ethnic Minority Psychology, 28*(2), 171–181. https://psycnet.apa.org/doi/10.1037/cdp0000484

Yamashiro, N. (2021, April 9). New research brief: The evidence base for afterschool and summer. *Afterschool Snack.* https://afterschoolalliance.org/afterschoolsnack/New-research-brief-The-evidence-base-for-afterschool-and_04-09-2021.cfm

Yosso, T., Smith, W., Solorzano, D., & Hung, M. (2022). A critical race theory test of W. E. B. Du Bois' hypothesis: Do Black students need separate schools? *Race Ethnicity and Education, 25*(3), 370–388. https://doi.org/10.1080/13613324.2021.1984099

ABOUT THE EDITORS

R. Martin Reardon (PhD, Educational Policy Planning and Leadership, The College of William and Mary in Virginia, 2000) is associate professor in the Educational Leadership Department of the College of Education at East Carolina University (ECU), Greenville, NC. His instructional contributions to the Educational Leadership Department focus on teaching academic writing and mixed methods approaches to research in the context of the problem-of-practice-oriented education doctorate program.

Stemming from his then 6 years as chair of the School–University–Community Collaborative Research (SUCCR) special interest group (SIG) of the American Educational Research Association (AERA), Reardon co-edited a book in 2016 with two former leaders of the SUCCR SIG that extended an earlier model of school–university collaboration to incorporate the vital role of the community. Subsequently, beginning in 2017, he embarked on an in-depth exploration of the SUCCR theme as the lead editor in an ongoing series—Current Perspectives on School/University/Community Research. The most recent of the prior eight volumes in the series was titled *School–University–Community Research in a (Post) COVID-19 World* (2023). https://www.infoagepub.com/authors/r-martin-reardon

Reardon is one of four coeditors of a 60-chapter, two-volume current undertaking under the auspices of the British Educational Research Association (BERA) to publish the *BERA-SAGE International Handbook of Research-Informed Education Policy and Practice* with an anticipated publication date of 2024. https://www.bera.ac.uk/news/the-bera-sage-international-handbook-of-research-informed-education-policy-and-practice-call-for-authors

---

Justice, Equity, Diversity, and Inclusion in Education, pages 277–278
Copyright © 2024 by Information Age Publishing
www.infoagepub.com
All rights of reproduction in any form reserved.

278 ▪ About the Editors

Jack Leonard (EdD, Boston University) served the Boston Public Schools as a teacher, administrator, and then principal of an award-winning turn-around high school. After earning his EdD from Boston University in 2002, he joined the faculty at the University of Massachusetts Boston. As an associate professor in the leadership in urban schools program at UMass Boston, he directed the graduate programs and educational administration. Leonard retired from the university in 2017. His research focuses on school leadership, school partnerships, and educational history. In addition to his ongoing work with the Current Perspectives in School/University/Community Research series, he recently published two articles on a new performance assessment for principal licensure.

ABOUT THE CONTRIBUTORS

Michelle Allen has worked in the field of Social Services for over 40 years—both as a program manager with individuals with intellectual and physical disabilities at agencies in Pennsylvania and Delaware. In the community residential setting, her job responsibilities included completing required paperwork, preparing work teams for annual state inspections, advocating for the individuals served, and developing relationships with stakeholders. Michelle has significant experience in interviewing and supervising staff and ensuring that all required job training is completed in a timely manner. She retired from Elwyn, Inc. in Media, PA in 2020. Since then, she continues to work at Seeds of Greatness Early Learning Center working with children.

Ayana Allen-Handy, PhD, is a West Philly-born and raised mother-scholar and educator, is an associate professor of urban education in the Department of Policy, Organization, and Leadership in the School of Education at Drexel University. Dr. Allen-Handy received her Bachelor of Arts with Honors from the University of North Carolina at Chapel Hill; a Master of Education from the University of St. Thomas in Houston, TX; her PhD in urban education from Texas A&M University in College Station, TX; and she completed a Post-Doctoral Fellowship at *The Urban Education Collaborative* at University of North Carolina at Charlotte. Prior to becoming a professor at Drexel, Dr. Allen-Handy was a first-grade teacher, a literacy specialist, and a school counselor in the Houston Independent School District for 11 years. In 2019, she founded and currently serves as the director of *The Jus-*

Justice, Equity, Diversity, and Inclusion in Education, pages 279–288
Copyright © 2024 by Information Age Publishing
www.infoagepub.com
All rights of reproduction in any form reserved.

280 ▪ About the Contributors

tice-Oriented Youth Education Lab (The JoY Lab), a diverse, intergenerational collective of youth and community residents, faculty, undergraduate, and graduate research partners who center JoY through a humanizing, asset-forward, and critical-participatory action research approach in pursuit of educational, racial, and social justice.

S. Luke Anderson, EdS, is a secondary English education instructor and PhD candidate at Tennessee Technological University. He has recently completed an EdS in curriculum and instruction, with his research interests including LGBTQ+ studies, educational policy, and curricular representation. He was formerly a secondary English language arts teacher, with experience at various levels ranging from inclusion courses for exceptional learners through Advanced Placement English courses.

Mary A. Avalos, PhD, is a research professor in the Department of Teaching and Learning at the University of Miami. Her research interests include equity-focused projects in public school and community settings. She also works with teachers in their classrooms to improve literacy teaching and learning for culturally and linguistically diverse students across reading/language arts, science, mathematics, and social studies. Since 2021, she has directed the School of Education and Human Development's Community and Educational Well-Being Research Center and works to develop partnerships with community organizations, local schools and districts. Mary has published her work in practitioner and scholarly journals, including *The Elementary School Journal, The Reading Teacher, Bilingual Research Journal,* and *Reading and Writing Quarterly*.

Cassandra Barragan, MSW, PhD, is an associate professor in the School of Social Work and the director of the aging studies program at Eastern Michigan University. She serves as co-chair of the Age-Friendly University (AFU) Steering Committee and is a member of the university Committee for Action on Intersectionality, AntiRacism, and Equity (CAIARE). Her work includes exploring the importance of social networks in student outcomes, service, and faculty of color, and providing opportunities for social engagement for older adults.

Jahyonna Brown is currently an undergraduate student at Drexel University studying global studies with a concentration in global business and economic development while also minoring in French. Prior to enrolling in Drexel University, Jahyonna worked for 3 years as a research data analyst in the JoYLab and is now a research assistant. She is passionate about the preservation of culture and hopes to give minority communities resources they need through JoYLab!

About the Contributors • 281

Paige Buschman, MS (she/they), currently serves as the program coordinator for the Peace Corps Fellows and Applied Community and Economic Development (ACED) Fellows programs at the Stevenson Center for Community and Economic Development at Illinois State University. Paige recruits and advises students and manages relationships with partner organizations to arrange service-learning, professional practice opportunities for Fellows. During her time in the graduate school at Illinois State University for Educational Administration, she served in AmeriCorps through her graduate assistantship at the Center for Civic Engagement and completed research focused on EDI best practices, Title IX, restorative justice and leadership. Paige received their undergraduate degree in sociology from Illinois Wesleyan University where they completed a research fellowship on the relationship between sexual violence and masculinity on college campuses. Paige has worked in a variety of student service areas and brings a passion for equity, inclusion and community development to her work and research.

Wendy Cavendish, PhD, is a professor in the Department of Teaching and Learning at the University of Miami. Her interdisciplinary research focus includes the examination of the relationship between institutional processes involved in educational and transition decision making for culturally and linguistically diverse youth. Her recent work has focused on student and teacher perspectives of effective supports for facilitating high school graduation for multiply marginalized students. She has published over 60 articles and research and policy reports on these topics.

Linsay DeMartino, PhD (she/her), is an assistant professor in the educational leadership at the Mary Lou Fulton Teachers College at Arizona State University. As a former P–12 educational practitioner in Tucson, Arizona, she served as a special education teacher, inclusion specialist, special education department chair, and as an instructional data and intervention administrative coordinator. Her current research examines transformative practices, collaborative community engagement, and justice in schools. She is particularly interested in administrative practices grounded in just schooling and contextual alternatives rather than "best practices" and educational trends. Relatedly, she teaches coursework on leadership for diverse learners, community relations seminar, and equitable human resources administration.

Karena Alane Escalante, MSEd, is a doctoral candidate from Los Angeles, California. Before attending Drexel University School of Education, she earned her BA in psychology from Grinnell College in Iowa and her MSEd from Johns Hopkins University in Baltimore. After teaching for 5 years in Oahu, Hawai'i, Karena became interested in assessing the various ways in which ELL policies on a federal level impact rural learning communities. Her research interests involve advocating for non-native English students

282 ▪ About the Contributors

and illuminating their cultural relevance at multiple levels of the education system. As a woman of color and first-generation PhD candidate, Karena is passionate about dismantling systems of oppression within academia.

Arania Goldsmith-Carter, BS, is a long time native of West Philly who lived down the bottom and attended Martha Washington Elementary School, Shaw Junior High School in Southwest Philadelphia, and West Philadelphia High School class of 1969 where she is a board member of the Alumni Association. She graduated from WPHS and attended Community College of Philadelphia and received her associates degree in health information technology before receiving her BS in public health at Temple. She has been married for 48 years and has 4 children and 9 grandchildren. Her hobbies include traveling, ice skating, roller skating, bike riding, knitting, dancing, book clubs, and gardening.

Kari Havenaar, MA, has a master's in women's and gender studies from Eastern Michigan University. During her time there, she conducted archival research on the local disability community on campus, tracing its development from 1900 to 1990. Her areas of interest include critical disability studies, intersectionality, and queer studies. She firmly believes that mentoring plays a significant role in building resilient communities and ending the cycle of oppression. Havenaar is dedicated to working with marginalized populations and preventing the perpetuation of oppression.

Celeste Hawkins, PhD, is an associate professor at Eastern Michigan University in the School of Social Work. Dr. Hawkins has a diverse range of experiences working in the areas of juvenile justice, homelessness, literacy, family services, and education. Her areas of focus include marginalized youth, educational equity in K–12 public schools, engaging student voice, culturally responsive pedagogical practices, and interrupting the school-to-prison pipeline. Dr. Hawkins's professional career has been dedicated to working with vulnerable, oppressed, and underserved populations and has been a tireless advocate for children and families, particularly those gripped by poverty and social injustice. In addition to her role as professor at EMU and volunteer service as president for the Ypsilanti Community Schools Board of Education, she further contributes to the community through advocacy and volunteerism in various programs and agencies in Washtenaw County.

Isaiah L. Lassiter, MA, is a Philadelphia native and an alumnus of a Philadelphia Charter school that stood for Excellence, No Excuses! He earned a Bachelor of Science in psychology with a concentration in business from Pennsylvania State University and began a career as a human resources professional. In 2014, Lassiter moved to the Washington, DC, metro area and started his graduate studies. He earned a Master of Arts in industrial and organizational psychology, focusing on talent management and organizational development. Before Drexel University, Lassiter worked in public education for 8 years, managing school hiring and onboarding, climate and culture, pathways, attendance, and enrollment programs. Now at Drexel University, his research interest lies within the intersectionality of arts, business, education, technology, and psychology and how their relationship and integration can improve educational experiences for K–12 educators and learners.

LaMicah Lindsey, MEd, PhD candidate, is an educational researcher intern at FHI360, a global nonprofit headquartered in Durham, NC. Mrs. Lindsey obtained her bachelor's degree in Elementary Education and master's degree in Measurement and Evaluation from the University of South Florida in Tampa, Fl. As a former schoolteacher in a Title I school, she recognized the overwhelming disparities minority students face in the school system. As a result, Mrs. Lindsey began her PhD program in Curriculum and Instruction with a focus in teacher education. Her hope is to educate preservice teachers on systematic racism and whiteness in education and to train preservice teachers on how to be an advocate for marginalized students. Throughout her academic career she has participated in numerous research projects that focus on diversity, equity, and inclusion in higher education. Additionally, she has been highlighted as an emerging scholar by the Association of Teacher Educators. Currently, she is working with the past Association of Teacher Educators Association president to publish her Autoethnography that focuses on her experience as a black teacher educator at a predominantly White institution. Her former roles include being a research assistant, elementary teacher, field supervisor, and adjunct professor.

Dyann C. Logwood, PhD, is an assistant professor of women's and gender studies at Eastern Michigan University and a member of the university Committee for Action on Intersectionality, AntiRacism, and Equity (CAIARE). Currently, she offers undergraduate students the chance to mentor youth at a local middle school as part of her Mentoring Youth in Urban Spaces course. Additionally, her work includes developing Black feminist mentorship curriculum, fostering a sense of belonging, and implementing critical classroom practices. She is also the director of the Mentoring for Success Initiative and chair of the Annual Women of Color Symposium.

Jennifer Murray, PhD (she/her), is an educational leader with 20 years of experience as a teacher, assistant principal and vice-principal. She is a graduate of Boston College, Barry University, Florida State University and most recently Florida International University, with a doctorate in educational leadership and policy. Currently, Dr. Murray is an administrative director in the Office of Educational Equity, Access, and Diversity. Dr. Murray is an advocate for all children and believes that every child has the capability of

284 • About the Contributors

meeting their full potential when caring adults take a stand and put students at the forefront of their decision-making.

Catherine Nettles was born and raised in West Philadelphia. She is currently the recording and corresponding secretary of the WPHS Alumni Association. She has served for over 10 years and is from the class of 1987. When she was a student at West, she was told that "we are our brother's keepers" and that made her want to give back to the students and her community. Catherine is a proud mother of an adult daughter who has been inspired by her mother to give back too. Now her daughter works and resides at Fordham University, NYC. While working with this Drexel group, it has inspired Catherine to continue her education in January, 2024.

Bonnie Poole-Linder, BS, was born and raised in Philadelphia, PA. She was educated by Philadelphia public schools. Upon graduation from WPHS in 1973 she relocated to Fayetteville, NC, her Mom's home, where she visited every summer growing up. In 1974, she enrolled in Fayetteville State University and received her BS in Business Education in 1977. In 1979, she returned to Philadelphia and began a career with the U.S. Postal Service, retiring 32 years later in 2011 as a human resources manager. Bonnie is a proud mom of an adult son and daughter and a very special granddaughter. "With this generation, it just seems like so much is lost with the comradery, so maybe if youth see what we're doing, they'll want to get involved. It's important for youth to see what was so that we can see some of the old things return and avoid continuing some of the things that didn't work" (Bonnie Poole-Linder).

Ronald Ray is a retired housekeeping manager who is currently the president of the West Philadelphia High School Alumni Association. He is an active member of the share program at his church. He is also newly wed. Now he is a community researcher in the JoY Lab. When asked about his work in the JoY lab, Ronald shares that he is passionate about preserving the history of the West Philadelphia Community and staying connected to his heritage.

Rachel Renbarger, PhD, is an educational researcher at FHI360, a global nonprofit headquartered in Durham, NC. Raised in a rural and low-income household, Renbarger obtained her teaching licensure to serve the students from her hometown. Upon recognizing the need for increased support for teachers and schools to ensure all students succeed, she obtained her PhD in educational psychology from Baylor University to study resilience and systemic change. Renbarger served as an intern at the Organization for Economic Co-operation and Development (OECD) for the study on social-emotional skills, as a postdoctoral researcher at Duke University, and as research director of the Accelerating Systemic Change Network. In all po-

About the Contributors • **285**

sitions, she focused on students with marginalized identities—particularly rural, first-generation, low-income, and students of color. This research has been published in a variety of outlets ranging from peer-reviewed scholarship (e.g., journal articles, books) to public-facing dissemination avenues such as blogs and workshops. With her degree in human development and quantitative methods, Renbarger now works to improve research methods in education, prioritizing equity and criticality. Her current work includes serving as co-PI of a National Science Foundation grant reviewing and synthesizing the systemic change in higher education literature and leading the research components of a family and community collaboration grant supported by the Bill & Melinda Gates Foundation. She serves as one of the founding members of the Critical Quantitative Methodologies Special Interest Group within the American Educational Research Association and was appointed to the American Psychological Association's Committee for Socioeconomic Status in 2023.

Mariana Alvayero Ricklefs, PhD, is an assistant professor in the College of Education at Northern Illinois University. She has over 15 years of experience working with bilingual/multilingual learners with different cultural, linguistic, socioeconomic, and dis/ability backgrounds. She has taught in EFL, ESL, and two-way immersion programs. Her research interests include raciolinguistics, language ideologies, teacher education, assessment, biliteracy, and bi/multilingual learners with disabilities. She has published several articles and book chapters and has presented her work in professional conferences at the international, national, and state levels. She is a former Fulbright Scholar.

Liza Rodler, MPP, is a social science research analyst with VPD Government Solutions, supporting the Administration of Children and Families Office of Planning, Research, and Evaluation within the U.S. Department of Health and Human Services. She wrote and conducted the research used throughout this chapter while working as an education research associate at FHI 360. Rodler began her research career in the field of social policy with a focus on economic support programs, early childhood education, child welfare, and career pathways programs. Her work was published in multiple reports that informed federal and state-level programs and policy making. She pursued a graduate degree in public policy from Duke University's Sanford School of Public Policy to further the analytical, technical, and presentation skills that are critical to conducting research that can successfully inform practice. At FHI 360, she worked to understand how education systems could best support marginalized students and families to achieve their goals. Her work included mixed-methods research, program evaluations, and technical assistance for K–12 education programs. Her projects included a qualitative study on family and community collaboration, an

286 ▪ About the Contributors

evaluation of federally funded coaching and enrichment programming for middle and high school youth, and technical assistance to develop data dashboards for schools serving marginalized populations in Minneapolis, MN. In 2023, Rodler co-authored a white paper outlining recent research and policy developments in climate change education.

Rachel Roegman is an associate professor of educational leadership in the Department of Educational Policy, Organization and Leadership at the University of Illinois, Urbana-Champaign. Her work has been influenced by her experiences as a middle school teacher in traditional and alternative schools and her commitments to antiracist, equity-focused practice. Her research examines the development and support of equity-focused school and district leaders, as well as the experiences of transgender and gender non-conforming youth.

Nicole Rummel, PhD, is an assistant superintendent of teaching and learning in a K–12 school district in Illinois. During her career, she has worked as a teacher, assistant principal, principal, and director of instruction. She has an undergraduate degree in elementary education from the University of Maine at Machias and master's and doctorate degrees in educational planning, policy, and leadership from the College of William and Mary. She is passionate about supporting teachers in the classroom and providing equitable opportunities for students.

Risa Sackman, MS, is director of U.S. Education at FHI360, an international nonprofit headquartered in Durham, NC. For 3 decades, Ms. Sackman has helped to create effective solutions and programs to promote the wellbeing of young people in formal and informal education settings. In her current role she oversees a portfolio of projects that improve education equity and outcomes for all students. Recent projects include a research study on how districts are overcoming the challenges that get in the way of systemic family and community collaboration (funded by the Bill and Melinda Gates Foundation); the District Summer Learning initiative, a national project that supports 100 school districts to maximize the potential of summer for learning and enrichment (funded by The Wallace Foundation); a partnership with the Consumer Financial Protection Bureau (CFPB) that produced over 250 evidence-based financial education activities and resources teachers, youth practitioners, and families can use to build young people's financial capability; and programs that promote STEM engagement, digital literacy, school–community partnerships, and college and career readiness. Prior to FHI 360, Risa was an educational consultant, building the capacity of organizations and education leaders to develop evidence-based programs, practices, and materials. She was also a co-founder and EVP of Education at TaskStream (now Watermark), an education writer and cur-

About the Contributors ▪ **287**

riculum developer, a school administrator, and a teacher. Ms. Sackman has published and presented on a wide range of education topics, and holds a bachelor's degree from Amherst College and a master's in education from Bank Street College of Education.

Rebecca Smith Hill, MSW, PhD, is an assistant director for CarolinaLIFE, an inclusive postsecondary education (IPSE) program at the University of South Carolina (USC) in Columbia, SC. In this role she works with campus and community partners to ensure inclusion and typicality of experiences for students with intellectual and developmental disabilities (IDD) enrolled in the IPSE program. Prior to working in higher education, Rebecca spent 9 years as a social worker, working with families experiencing homelessness. She also worked as a middle and high school special education teacher for 9 years. Rebecca's research interests include examining the constructs of self-determination, agency, wellness, sense of belonging, and dignity of risk for emerging adults with disabilities, namely intellectual and developmental disability. Her research reflects an onto-epistemological assumption that a better understanding of these constructs can enhance transition outcomes for adults with IDD; namely, related to quality of life. She is also interested in enhancing cultural competency for preservice teachers and others working with people with disabilities, both in school settings and in the community. Rebecca specializes in qualitative research, including using participatory action and critical frameworks to center the voices of people with disabilities. Rebecca earned her PhD in special education in 2023 and her master's in social work from USC in 2007. Her undergraduate degree is in psychology and education.

Chelsea VanHorn Stinnett, PhD, is the training development and technical assistance coordinator for the Think College Inclusive Higher Education Network at the Institute for Community Inclusion at the University of Massachusetts, Boston. In this role, she supports inclusive postsecondary education (IPSE) program professionals, faculty, parents, students, and other key stakeholders in refining and expanding inclusive higher education for students with intellectual disability. Chelsea has BA and MEd in education from Wright State University in Dayton, OH and a PhD in special education from the University of South Carolina. Chelsea has served in a variety of roles in supporting students with disabilities, from paraprofessional to professor. As a former executive director and faculty member at an IPSE program, she is committed to furthering knowledge and quality of programming at colleges and universities across the country to ensure that all aspects of college life are inclusive of the needs of students with intellectual disability. This is reflected in her scholarship, aimed at exploring the development and evaluation of IPSE programs and understanding how college students with intellectual disability develop agency in a college setting.

288 ▪ About the Contributors

Chelsea has secured over three million dollars in grant funding and has produced over twenty-five publications related to postsecondary education or transitioning to adult life for young adults with intellectual disability.

Kevin Tan, PhD, is an associate professor in the School of Social Work and the College of Education at the University of Illinois Urbana–Champaign. His research focuses on promoting social emotional learning (SEL) among K–12 populations, particularly in advancing the ways SEL fosters positive student outcomes. In recent years, his work pivoted to explore how SEL serves as a lever for diversity, equity, and inclusion. Dr. Tan's research encompasses various topics, including youth risk and protective factors, as well as effective school social work practices. Dr. Tan earned accolades from his campus for his outstanding public engagement activities. Notably, he was awarded the 2021 Gary Lee Shaffer Award for his academic contributions to the field of social work by the national School Social Work Association of America.

S. Gavin Weiser, PhD (they|them), is an associate professor in the Department of Educational Administration and Foundations and coordinator of the College Student Personnel Administration master's program. Gavin also holds affiliations with women, gender, and sexuality studies as well as with Latin American/Latino Studies at Illinois State University. Their research interests involve queer and trans subjectivities within educational spaces, and the ethics of community-engaged qualitative research. Gavin is also interested in the intersections of queer theory and education, and how we can continue to challenge the notions of education to create a more radically inclusive space for learning. Prior to serving as faculty, Gavin worked for several years as a university administrator in the Office of Multicultural Student Affairs at the University of South Carolina focusing on social justice and diversity work.

Printed in the USA
CPSIA information can be obtained
at www.ICGtesting.com
CBHW080919270924
14936CB00001B/6